THE FABER BOOK OF GARDENS

Philip Robinson trained as a gardener after leaving university. He has lived and worked in rural Northumberland for seven years. His first novel, *That We Might Never Meet Again*, was published by Faber in 2005.

The Faber Book of
GARDENS

PHILIP ROBINSON

faber and faber

First published in 2007
by Faber and Faber Ltd
Bloomsbury House
74–77 Great Russell Street
London WC1B 3DA
This paperback edition first published in 2009

Typeset in Minion by Faber and Faber Ltd
Printed in England by CPI Mackays, Chatham ME5 8TD

A CIP record for this book
is available from the British Library

ISBN 978–0571–22421–0

2 4 6 8 10 9 7 5 3 1

To all my friends who have proved staunch this year,
and without whom I would not be.

CONTENTS

ACKNOWLEDGEMENTS

The library of the Literary and Philosophical Society of Newcastle Upon Tyne has been an invaluable aid in researching this book, indeed, it would have been impossible without it. The desk staff have been unfailingly helpful. I am grateful to Rachael for first introducing it to me, and recommend the place wholeheartedly. It will continue to survive only if supported. Details can be found at *www.litandphil.org.uk*

My thanks also to the libraries of the University of Oxford, particularly the Radcliffe Science Library and the peerless Bodleian.

My thanks to all the staff at Faber and Faber who have helped this come to fruition, and especially Walter Donohue, who has been an inspiration throughout.

INTRODUCTION

Gardens are easy to identify, difficult to define. There is a great diversity of form between the Japanese gravel garden and an English Landscape garden, or the pocket handkerchief outside a back-to-back terrace and one of the great botanic gardens such as Oxford or Edinburgh, the purpose of which is scientific, taxonomic, pedagogical, and, finally, decorative. Yet all equally are gardens. Divisions of formality-informality, plants and no plants, the inclusion of water, the necessity of a lawn, existence and non-existence – I am not being flippant, gardens do not have to exist to be gardens; these are all incidental. There are gardens drawn on paper at the planning stage, captured in pictures, evoked in music, described in words.

But all gardens have a boundary. There is a wall or a fence or hedge, a boundary which defines a space, and that space we call 'garden'. The area beyond the fence may, at first glance, be indistinguishable – an uncut lawn stands on one side, a field on the other, but the very fact that the field lies beyond the fence, makes it 'other'. Even open-plan developments with grey boundaries denoted by a casual association of shrubs will have lines drawn on the title deeds, boundaries to be referred to when the property is sold or a dispute arises. More significantly perhaps, there will be profound psychological boundaries in the minds of the owners, as entire and impregnable as the ground is open. Even non-existent gardens have fences: poetic gardens are bound in stanzas, prose gardens in paragraphs and chapters.

Where there is garden, there are gardeners. This is a managed space, a space which serves a purpose or a variety of purposes, which can be as diverse as the garden-forms. There are temple gardens for meditation; private gardens for relaxation and to make the neighbours jealous; royal gardens to impress and intimidate; public gardens – the municipal parks – for recreation, to provide a 'green lung' for the city, to offer employment, and to pacify the populace; gardens as museums such as those of the National Trust; gardens as big businesses like the Eden Project or The Alnwick Garden.

I have enjoyed exploring the different gardens of the world: I have fenced a selection between these covers. Those I have included have pleased me, or intrigued me, or surprised me, sit nicely next to one another, saddened me, or impressed me. In short, I have chosen them as I choose plants for a garden. As far as possible, I have maintained a linear chronology, although the dates of, for example, folk songs, are indeterminate. By so doing the book itself can be read as a narrative which records changes in civilisation, transport, literary sophistication, the birth of science, the decline of religion in the West, the whims of fashion, the movement of plants around the world. The inclusion of the factual writing provides a context for the abstract allusions to gardens in contemporaneous poetry and prose: gardens are an evolving construct and what the poet visualises when using the word 'garden' must, necessarily, be different in different ages.

I have enjoyed the respite the gardens of the Far East have afforded. There is a stillness about them which induces quietness and reflection, just as a picture by Giotto or Morandi does. A simplicity and peace which is, to an extent, illusory, but beneficial all the same. Even in a garden of raked gravel and stone, stone the most immutable of garden elements, there is change. The light falls differently through the day as the sun advances, throwing shadows between the ridges. There is dew in the morning, and perhaps rain in the afternoon, or a flight of sparrows across the open space, or scent from blossom drifting on the breeze. Which is to say, that even in our most managed of places, the fences we erect are never secure.

At other times it has seemed as if there was only one garden, and its name was Legion. Or, rather, Eden – a self-replicating virus of a garden, each replication containing a degree of mutation which took it away from or back towards the original, or inverted the values, or revealed something perhaps, a thing which was embedded deeply and hidden in that first garden of significance. Ironically, Eden seemed inescapable.

I returned to Eden, or Genesis, at least, to look again at the story in the light of its influence, to try and see how it all began. Stripped of theology, which, after all, is a later systematisation that at times ignores details that are inconvenient, several seem obvious. Here is a story that remembers a time when man is like the animals. Work, so far as it goes, is subsistence. There is no morality. No property. No marriage. Man's relationship with the divinity is immediate, that is, unmediated by either theology or a priesthood, and physically present, 'And they heard the sound of the Lord God walking in the garden in the cool of the day.' The garden, which is a place of life, not a special house of worship. Furthermore, this immediacy survives Adam and Eve's 'transgression' and is broken only by God's choice.

It is clear that God is economical with the truth. These first people, Adam, 'man of soil' and Eve, are still alive to be questioned by God after eating the forbidden fruit, and have not died as predicted. The serpent, the tempter, appears to have told the truth. Eve, having chosen to eat the fruit of the tree of knowledge, has indeed become like God, discerning the difference between good and evil.

As to the fruit itself? Well, that's part of the mystery. The Christian iconography tends towards the apple whilst Zoroastrian favours the pomegranate, which goes to show that, despite everything, we humans tend to base paradise on where we are at the time. To a large extent, the fruit is incidental to the story; it could have been a vegetable, or a fish, or a honeycomb. The fruit is a cipher. Eve looks at the fruit and judges it good, a judgement *independent of the authority of God*. She is becoming human. The choice of the fruit – the first conscious action – is an action, which, presumptuous perhaps, completes a creation that was, until that moment, unfinished. Man becomes truly human, acquiring self-consciousness and rationality, that defining characteristic of humanity that enables him to 'share in the governance of the universe', as Thomas Aquinas has it in his *Summa Theologiae*, only through the self-creating act of woman. The reward, of course, for becoming too closely the image of God, was banishment, and labour – in all its senses.

So what does it mean to have these physical expressions of an ancient idea, these gardens? Or the constant evocations and allusions to Paradise in later literature? Eden is a place of contradictions. There is innocence but it is valueless as it is unconscious of itself. Consciousness has its beginning but is followed swiftly by suffering. Adam and Eve aspire to be like God, the moral terminus of monotheistic theology, and yet are punished for that aspiration. There is equality but no greatness. There is free-association, which ends with the birth of sexuality. There is language but no poetry. Beauty without art. It is the locus of pre-rational, pre-civilised existence; why do we strive to recreate it? To escape the tyranny of responsibility perhaps.

It strikes me that in addition to a boundary and a gardener, there is one further commonality. All gardens are indeed, as Francis Bacon puts it, the 'purest of human pleasures', but the emphasis is on the purest, being the truest, the most revelatory. 'Show me your garden, provided it be your own, and I will tell you what you are like,' wrote Alfred Austin, three centuries later. A garden is a projection into the physical world of the soul of the maker, replete with the weeds, the rotting leaves, and the sweet-smelling flowers. It is walled with beliefs, paved with disappoint-ments, planted with aspirations, not least of which is the hope of creat-ing something that endures beyond us. Every man who plants a tree grasps at immortality. He can but fail – but what glorious failure! To establish a life which, if oak or Douglas fir or yew, will outlast nations.

Some of us hope to be gods in our gardens, others are content to be Adam. Many would like to be Adam after the Fall, rational and civilised, and readmitted by a god who recognises a peer. Or better still, breaking and entering, and finding, after all these years, no room for the divine in this hypothesis.

As I write, I am facing the end of my professional, by which I mean dirty and physical, gardening career. A back injury sustained over two years ago keeps me in pain unless I rest from the necessary twistings and bendings, liftings and crouchings, usually under load, of gardening. It has taken me two years to accept this idea; two years of ignoring it, being dispirited by it, defying it.

The last garden I made was in the first few months of this year. It was a difficult, decidedly brown-field site – the midden and fire-pit of an ex-farm. In addition to the weeds, annual but mostly perennial, I excavated boulders of assorted sizes, roofing slates – enough for two pigsties – orange nylon baler twine, broken glass, batteries, syringes of sheep medicine, bathroom tiles, scorched newspapers – curiously unrotted and readable after twenty years – pottery, the shoes of a seventeen-legged horse and half a bridle, asbestos, fencing wire, concrete blocks, and miscellaneous plastics. As I dug, I wondered what contaminants I could not see – the engine oil, pesticides, and whatever else had been tipped and forgotten. Everything has a cost, and I pitied my clients, paying to clean up the mess bequeathed to them by previous occupants: a mess which had not been immune to inflation just because it was out of sight. Can there be any more polluted places in Britain than its farms?

When I had dug, levelled, and consolidated the site, I began to remake it. Placing boulders back as path boundaries, building rockeries. Trees and shrubs went in, small and full of promise. They have flowered as requested and now are covered with berries of various shapes and shades. They look as if they belong, and the memory of the nettle-infested ruin is difficult to sustain. Next week I am planting the first of the bulbs: *Tulipa tarda* for the spring and, rather late, *Crocus sativus*, saffron, for the autumn. It is a garden designed for change, as all gardens must be: the swift changes through the seasons, the slower change over the years. It is beautiful now but it should be getting 'about right' in four years' time and beyond.

But, while I worked with change, I could not accept it for myself. I am gardener, indivisible. Or so I was. What is left to me are memories of a time spent in beauty, creating beauty; laughter over a pint once work was over; the deep quiet of hard labour. As to the future, well, the measurements have been taken and the first lines drawn. I think I have a colour scheme. I can enjoy the work of others – a perennial pleasure – and there are the gardens of the mind to continue exploring. Gardens of simplicity or surpassing complexity, gardens which, having no substance, are like Eden, and need no work to maintain them. Gardens in which the weeds only grow and the wasps only sting if you want them to, and no long-suffering gardener is sent out by some stunted potting-shed tyrant to rake leaves in the frozen dark. And in a while, perhaps, a small garden of my own. I will lay it out to please my future self, and potter in it peaceably. It will be the perfect somewhere to press my feet into frost and watch the winter stars. A somewhere where it is good to be alone on bright spring mornings or comfortable with friends and a bottle of wine in the cooling air of a summer's evening bathed in golden light. A somewhere which may or may not yet exist.

Netherwitton, September 2006

EDEN TO AD 400

I have already mentioned the vast influence Eden has exerted, both concretely expressed in the form and contents of a garden, and as a compound idea which resonates down the centuries, crossing languages and cultures. Eden is not alone, however. The 'locked garden' of Solomon, metaphor of virginity and fidelity, will reappear many times, not only in Chaucer but in Austen and de Maupassant. The Solomon author shows a sophisticated appreciation of all the senses. Gardens are for fruit growing, and tasting; trees may be beautiful but they are also fragrant; there is water, living water, introducing movement and reflecting light, sounding in the stillness of the enclosure. The garden of Alcinous likewise, but by another root, lays down a pattern of the fruit-filled garden – as appealing to the eye as to the tongue. There is order: this place of reliable, predictable fecundity must indeed have seemed like a gift from the gods, being immune to the predations of animals, the plants subject to human will.

The texts from the Roman era testify to the existence of horticulture as a science. It is, already, observation-based, tested through practice, repeatable. There is a natural world, which will follow a pattern independent of the vagaries of the gods or the influence of the stars, and thus can be known and manipulated. Much of the advice still holds true – the danger of soil-compaction was acknowledged and the condition avoided, although, even today, most people, including many professionals, do not take it into account. Columella has a fascinating method for establishing hedges. It is not practised today as far as I know, although I see no reason why it would not work on principle. A similar method to provide a complete herbaceous border in the form of a seed-impregnated fibre mat has been on the market for a few years now. I have never bought one and I don't know if they work. Pliny provides insight not only into how gardens are perceived in Rome when he is writing, but also how they have evolved since the foundation of the city. The humanity of Virgil shines for me (I am not a bee). His portrait of a poor man's kitchen garden, established in worthless ground and bordered with beautiful, scented flowers, is perfection. Here is a garden where the owner can be like a king; the ground providing riches beyond his means – true wealth being found in good fresh food and the freedom to enjoy it. This is a model that exists already in Ecclesiastes, is implicit in the philosophy of Epicurus and his disciples, is embedded in Seneca's letters. It is, perhaps, the most benign of the themes recorded in this period, and, regrettably, the least emulated in subsequent traditions.

Eden

Then the Lord God formed man of dust from the ground, and breathed into his nostrils the breath of life; and man became a living being. And the Lord God planted a garden in Eden, in the east; and there he put the man whom he had formed. And out of the ground the Lord God made to grow every tree that is pleasant to the sight and good for food, the tree of life also in the midst of the garden, and the tree of the knowledge of good and evil.

A river flowed out of Eden to water the garden, and there it divided and became four rivers. The name of the first is Pishon; it is the one that flows around the whole land of Havilah, where there is gold; and the gold of that land is good; bdellium and onxy stone are there. The name of the second river is Gihon; it is the one which flows around the whole land of Cush. And the name of the third river is Tigris, which flows east of Assyria. And the fourth river is the Euphrates.

The Lord God took the man and put him in the garden of Eden to till it and keep it. And the Lord God commanded the man, saying, 'You may freely eat of every tree of the garden; but of the tree of the knowledge of good and evil you shall not eat, for in the day that you eat of it you shall die.'

Then the Lord God said, 'It is not good that the man should be alone; I will make him a helper fit for him.' So out of the ground the Lord God formed every beast of the field and every bird of the air, and brought them to the man to see what he would call them; and whatever the man called every living creature, that was its name. The man gave names to all cattle, and to the birds of the air, and to every beast of the field; but for the man there was not found a helper fit for him. So the Lord God caused a deep sleep to fall upon the man, and while he slept took one of his ribs and closed up its place with flesh; and the rib which the Lord God had taken from the man he made into a woman and brought her to the man.

Then the man said, 'This at last is bone of my bones and flesh of my flesh: She shall be called Woman, because she was taken out of Man.'

Therefore a man leaves his father and his mother and cleaves to his wife, and they become one flesh. And the man and his wife were both naked, and were not ashamed.

Now the serpent was more subtle than any other wild creature that the Lord God had made. He said to the woman, 'Did God say, "You shall not eat of any tree of the garden"?' And the woman said to the serpent, 'We may eat of the fruit of the trees of the garden; but God said, "You shall not eat of the fruit of the tree which is in the midst of the garden, neither shall you touch it, lest you die."'But the serpent said to the woman, 'You will not die. For God knows that when you eat of it your eyes will be opened, and you will be like God, knowing good and evil.' So when the woman saw that the tree was good for food, and that it was a delight to the eyes, and that the tree was to be desired to make one wise, she took of its fruit and ate; and she also gave some to her husband, and he ate. Then the eyes of both were opened, and they knew that they were naked; and they sewed fig leaves together and made themselves aprons.

And they heard the sound of the Lord God walking in the garden in the cool of the day, and the man and his wife hid themselves from the presence of the Lord God among the trees of the garden. But the Lord God called to the man, and said to him, 'Where are you?' And he said, 'I heard the sound of thee in the garden, and I was afraid, because I was naked; and I hid myself.'

Genesis 2:7–3:10 (RSV)

The Garden of Alcinous

A radiance like that of sun or moon played over the king's high palace. Walls of bronze ran this way and that, from the entrance to the further end, and these were topped with a frieze of cyanus. Golden doors closed the palace in, and silver posts rose above the threshold; the lintel was of silver, the door-handle was of gold. Each side of the door were gold and silver watchdogs, deathless for ever and unageing, which Hephaestus with his wit and cunning had fashioned as guardians for the great house. Inside, to the left and right, from the entrance down to the very end, there were chairs ranged along the wall, and over these hung coverings of cloth on which women had spent their skill, finely spun and closely woven. Here the leaders of the Phaeacians would often sit as they ate and drank, for they always had abundance. Standing upon shapely pedestals were statues of boys made of gold; they had flaming torches in their hands and gave their light, all the evening through, to the banqueters in the hall. Moreover, the king has in his palace as many as fifty serving-women, some at their hand-mills grinding the yellow corn, some weaving their webs or else sitting down to spin their wool – their moving hands are like quivering leaves on a tall aspen; soft olive-oil drops off from the closely-woven fabric. Just as the Phaeacian men are the world's ablest in seamanship, so the women are deftest in weaving; to them above others Athene has given keen wits and the skill to make very lovely things.

Outside the courtyard, near the entrance, is a great garden of four acres, with a fence running round, this way and that. Here are planted tall thriving trees – pears, pomegranates, apples with glistening fruit, sweet figs, rich olives. The fruit of all these never fails or flags all the year round, winter or summer; here the west wind is always breathing – some fruits it brings to birth, some to ripeness. Pear upon pear matures to fullness, apple on apple, grape-cluster on grape-cluster, fig on fig. There too the king has his fruitful vineyard planted; behind is a warm and level spot, dried by the sun, where some grapes are being gathered and others trodden; in front there are unripe grapes that have scarcely shed their blossom, and others already faintly darkening. There too, bordering the last row of vines, are trim pots of all kinds of herbs that keep fresh all the year round. Lastly there are two springs of water, and one of these is channelled out over the whole space of garden; the other, facing it, flows under the entrance of the courtyard to issue in front of the lofty palace; and from this the townspeople drew their water.

Such were the god's sumptuous gifts in the demesne of King Alcinous.

Homer, *Odyssey*

A Garden Locked

A garden locked is my sister, my bride, a garden locked, a fountain sealed.

Your shoots are an orchard of pomegranates with all choicest fruits,

henna with nard, nard and saffron, calamus and cinnamon, with all trees of frankincense, myrrh and aloes, with all chief spices – a garden fountain, a well of living water, and flowing streams of Lebanon.

Awake, O north wind, and come, O south wind!

Blow upon my garden, let its fragrance be wafted abroad.

Let my beloved come to his garden, and eat its choicest fruits.

I come to my garden, my sister, my bride,
I gather my myrrh with my spice,
I eat my honeycomb with my honey,
I drink my wine with my milk.

Eat, O friends, and drink: drink deeply, O lovers!

I slept, but my heart was awake.

Song of Solomon 4:12–5:2 (RSV)

Redemption or Destruction

Zion shall be redeemed by justice,
and those in her who repent, by righteousness.

But rebels and sinners shall be destroyed together,
and those who forsake the Lord shall be consumed.
For you shall be ashamed of the oaks in which you delighted;
and you shall blush for the gardens which you have chosen.
For you shall be like an oak whose leaf withers,
and like a garden without water.
And the strong shall become tow,
and his work a spark,
and both of them shall burn together,
with none to quench them.

Isaiah 1:27–31 (RSV)

Planting Asparagus

Method of planting asparagus: Break up thoroughly ground that is moist, or is heavy soil. When it has been broken, lay off beds, so that you may hoe and weed them in both directions without trampling the beds. In laying off the beds, leave a path a half-foot wide between the beds on each side. Plant along a line, dropping two or three seeds together in a hole made with a stick, and cover with the same stick. After planting, cover the beds thickly with manure; plant after the vernal equinox. When the shoots push up, weed often, being careful not to uproot the asparagus with the weeds. The year it is planted, cover the bed with straw through the winter, so that it will not be frostbitten. Then in the early spring uncover, hoe, and weed. The third year after planting burn it over in the early spring; after this do not work it before the shoots appear, so as not to injure the roots by hoeing. In the third or fourth year you may pull asparagus from the roots; for if you break it off, sprouts will start and die off. You may continue pulling until you see it going to seed. The seed ripens in autumn; when you have gathered it, burn over the bed, and when the asparagus begins to grow, hoe, and manure. After eight or nine years, when it is old, dig it up, after having thoroughly worked and manured the ground to which you are able to transplant it, and made small ditches to receive the roots. The interval between the roots of the asparagus should be not less than a foot. In digging, loosen the earth around the roots so that you can dig them easily, and be careful not to break them. Cover them very deep with sheep dung; this is the best for this purpose, as other manure produces weeds.

Marcus Porcius Cato, *On Agriculture*

Propagation

In the third method, which consists in transferring shoots from a tree into the ground, if the shoot is buried in the earth, you must be careful, in the case of some, that the shoot be removed at the proper time – that is, before it shows any sign of budding or blossoming; and that what you transplant from the tree you tear from the stock rather than break off a limb, as the heel of a shoot is steadier, or the wider it is the more easily it puts out roots. They are thrust into the ground at once, before the sap dries out. In the case of olive cuttings, care must be taken that they be from the tender branch, sharpened evenly at both ends. Such cuttings, about a foot in length, are called by some *clavolae*, and by others *taleae*. In the fourth method, which consists in running a shoot from one tree to another, the points to be observed are the nature of the tree, the season, and the method of fastening. You cannot, for instance, graft a pear on an oak, even though you can on an apple. This is a matter of importance to many people who pay considerable attention to soothsayers; for these have a saying that when a tree has been grafted with several varieties, the one that attracts the lightning turns into as many bolts as there are varieties, though the stroke is a single one. No matter how good the pear shoot which you graft on a wild pear, the fruit will not be as well flavoured as if you graft it on a cultivated pear. It is a general rule in grafting, if the shoot and the tree are of the same species, as, for instance, if both are of the apple family, that for the effect on the fruit the grafting should be of such a nature that the shoot is of a better type than the tree on which it is grafted. There is a second method of grafting from tree to tree which has been recently developed, under conditions where the trees stand close to each other. From the tree from which you wish to take the shoot a small branch is run to the tree on which you wish to graft and is inserted in a branch of the latter which has been cut off and split; the part which fits into the branch having first been sharpened on both sides with the knife so that on one side the part which will be exposed to the weather will have bark fitted accurately to bark. Care is taken to have the tip of the grafted shoot point straight up. The next year, after it has taken firm hold, it is cut off the parent stem.

As to the proper season for grafting, this must be especially observed: that some plants which formerly were grafted in spring are now grafted in mid-summer also, such as the fig, which, as the wood is not hard, requires warm weather; it is for this reason that fig groves cannot be planted in cold localities. Moisture is harmful to a fresh graft, for it causes the tender shoot to decay quickly, and hence it is the common view that this tree is best grafted in the dog days. In the case of plants which are not so soft, however, a vessel is fastened above the graft in such a way that water may drip slowly to keep the shoot from drying out before it unites with the tree. The bark of the shoot must be kept uninjured, and the shoot itself be sharpened in such a way as not to bare the pith. To prevent moisture or excessive heat from injuring it on the surface it should be smeared with clay and tied up with bark. For this reason the vine is cut off three days before grafting, so that any excessive moisture in it may run out before it is grafted; or else a cut is made a little lower than the graft, so as to allow casual water to run off. On the other hand, figs, pomegranates, and plants of a drier nature are grafted at once. In other graftings, such as of figs, care must be taken that the shoot contains a bud.

Of these four forms of propagation it is better to use quicksets in the case of some slow-growing plants, as is the practice in fig groves; for the natural seed of the fig is on the inside of the fruit which we eat, in the form of very small grains. As the seedling can scarcely spring from these small grains – for all things which are small and dry grow slowly, while those which are of looser texture are also of more rapid growth, as, for instance, the female grows more rapidly than the male, a rule which holds good also in plants to some extent, the fig, the pomegranate, and the vine being, on account of their feminine softness, of rapid growth, while, on the other hand, the palm, the cypress, and the olive are of slow growth; for in this respect the humid [are quicker] than the dry – it is therefore better to plant in the nursery shoots from the fig tree than grains from the fruit; unless this is impracticable, as when you wish to ship seeds overseas or import them hence. In this case we pass a string through the figs when they are ripe for eating, and after they have dried they are tied in bundles and may be sent where we will; and there they are planted in a nursery and reproduce. It was in this manner that the Chian, Chalcidian, Lydian, African, and other varieties of over-sea figs were imported into Italy.

Varro (Marcus Terentius Varro), *On Agriculture*

The Hanging Gardens

There was also, beside the acropolis, the Hanging Garden, as it is called, which was built, not by Semiramis, but by a later Syrian king to please one of his concubines; for she, they say, being a Persian by race and longing for the meadows of her mountains, asked the king to imitate, through the artifice of a planted garden, the distinctive landscape of Persia. The park extended four plethra on each side, and since the approach to the garden sloped like a hillside and the several parts of the structure rose from one another tier on tier, the appearance of the whole resembled that of a theatre. When the ascending terraces had been built, there had been constructed beneath them galleries which carried the entire weight of the planted garden and rose little by little one above the other along the approach; and the uppermost gallery, which was fifty cubits high, bore the highest surface of the park, which was made level with the circuit wall of the battlements of the city. Furthermore, the walls, which had been constructed at great expense, were twenty-two feet thick, while the passage-way between each two walls was ten feet wide. The roofs of the galleries were covered over with beams of stone sixteen feet long, inclusive of the overlap, and four feet wide. The roof above these beams had first a layer of reeds laid in great quantities of bitumen, over this two courses of baked brick bonded by cement, and as a third layer a covering of lead, to the end that the moisture from the soil might not penetrate beneath. On all this again earth had been piled to a depth sufficient for the roots of the largest trees; and the ground, when levelled off, was thickly planted with trees of every kind that, by their great size or any other charm, could give pleasure to the beholder. And since the galleries, each projecting beyond another, all received the light, they contained many royal lodgings of every description; and there was one gallery which contained openings leading from the topmost surface and machines for supplying the garden with water, the machines raising the water in great abundance from the river, although no one outside could see it being done.

Diodorus of Sicily, *Historical Library*

Gardens for Bees

You must put a stop to this empty and irresponsible play.
It is not hard to stop.
Tear off the wings of their queens: while these wait on the ground,
No bee will dare to leave his base or take off for a flight.
Let gardens breathing a scent of yellow flowers allure them:
Let the god of gardens, who watches for birds and robbers, keep them
Safe with his hook of willow.
The bee-keeper for his part should fetch down thyme and pine
From the hills above, and plant them broadly around the bees' home:
His hands should grow work-hardened, bedding the soil with fertile
Shoots, watering them well.
    Indeed, were it not that already my work has made landfall
And I shorten sail and eagerly steer for the harbour mouth,
I'd sing perhaps of rich gardens, their planning and cultivation,
The rose beds of Paestum, that blossom twice in a year,
The way endive rejoices to drink from a rivulet,
The bank all green with celery, the cucumber snaking
Amid the grass and swelling to greatness: I'd not forget
Late-flowering narcissus or gum-arabic's ringlet shoots,
Pale ivy, shore-loving myrtle.
I remember once beneath the battlements of Oebalia,
I saw an old man, a Corycian, who owned a few poor acres
Of land once derelict, useless for arable,
No good for grazing, unfit for the cultivation of vines.

But he laid out a kitchen garden in rows amid the brushwood,
Bordering it with white lilies, verbena, small-seeded poppy.
He was happy there as a king. He could go indoors at night
To a table heaped with dainties he never had to buy.
His the first rose of spring, the earliest apples in autumn:
And when the grim winter still was splitting the rocks with cold
And holding the watercourses with curb of ice, already
That man would be cutting his soft-haired hyacinths, complaining
Of summer's backwardness and the west winds slow to come.
His bees were the first to breed.
Enriching him with huge swarms: he squeezed the frothy honey
Before anyone else from the combs: he had limes and a wealth of pine
    trees:
And all the early blossom, that clothed his trees with promise
Of an apple crop, by autumn had come to maturity.
He had a gift, too, for transplanting in rows the far-grown elm,
The hardwood pear, the blackthorn bearing its weight of sloes,
And the plane that already offered a pleasant shade for drinking.

Virgil (Publius Vergilius Maro), *Georgics*, Book IV (translation by C. Day-Lewis)

Of Hedges

Democritus (of Abdera), in the book which he called Georgic, expresses
the opinion that those people do not act wisely who build strong
defences round their gardens, because neither can an enclosing wall
made of brick last for a long time, since it is usually damaged by rain and
tempests, nor does the expense involved call for the use of stone, which
is too sumptuous for the purpose; indeed a man needs to possess a fortune, if he wishes to enclose a large space of ground. I will, therefore,
myself show you a method whereby, without much trouble, we can make
a garden safe from the incursions of man and cattle.

The most ancient authors preferred a quick-set hedge to a constructed wall, on the grounds that it not only called for less expense but also
lasted for a much longer time, and so they have imparted to us the following method of making a hedge by planting thorn-trees. The area

which you have decided to enclose must, as soon as the ground has been moistened by rain after the autumn equinox, be surrounded by two furrows three feet distant from one another. It is quite enough if the measurement of their depth is two feet, but we shall allow them to remain empty through the winter after having got ready the seed with which they are to be sown. These should be those of the largest thorns, especially brambles and paliurus and what the Greeks call in κυνόσβατον and we call dog's thorn. The seeds of these briers must be picked as ripe as possible and mixed with meal of well-ground bitter-vetch. This mixture, after having been sprinkled with water, is smeared either on old ships' cables or any other kind of rope, and these are then dried and put away in a loft. Then, when mid-winter is passed, after an interval of forty days, about the time the swallow arrives, when the west wind is already rising after February 13th, if any water has stood in the furrows during the winter, it is drawn away, and the loose soil, which had been thrown out in the autumn, is replaced so as to fill half the depth of the furrows. Then the ropes already mentioned are produced from the loft and uncoiled and stretched lengthways along each furrow and covered up in such a manner that the seeds of the thorns, which adhere to the knots on the ropes, may not have too much earth heaped upon them but may be able to sprout. By about the thirtieth day the plants creep forth and, when they begin to grow somewhat, should be trained to grow in the direction of the space lying between the furrows. You will have to place a row of sticks in the middle, over which the thorns from both the furrows may spread, and which provide a kind of support on which they may rest for a time until they grow strong. It is obvious that this thorn-hedge cannot be destroyed unless you care to dig it up by the roots; but there is also no doubt that even if it has been damaged by fire, it only grows up again all the better. This is indeed the method of enclosing a garden which was most approved of by the ancients.

It will be a good plan, if the nature of the ground allows, for a site to be chosen close to the villa, preferably where the soil is rich and it can be irrigated by a stream running into it, or, if there be no flowing water, with water from a well. But that the well may provide the certainty of a continual supply, it should be dug when the sun occupies the last part of Virgo, that is, in the month of September before the autumn equinox; for that is the best time to test the capacity of springs, since the ground is short of rain-water after the long summer drought. But you must take care that the garden is not situated below a threshing-floor, and that the winds during the time of threshing cannot carry chaff and dust into it; for both these things are harmful to vegetables. Next there are two seasons for putting the ground in order and trenching it, since there are also two seasons for sowing vegetables, most of them being sown in the autumn and in the spring. The spring, however, is better in well-watered places, since the mildness of the growing year gives a kindly welcome to the seedlings as they come forth and the drought of summer is quenched by the springs of water. But where the nature of the place does not allow a supply of water to be brought by hand nor to be supplied spontaneously, there is indeed no other resource than the winter rains. Yet even in the driest localities your labour can be safeguarded if the ground is trenched rather deeper than usual, and it is quite enough to dig up a spit of three feet, so that the earth which is thrown up may rise to four feet. But where there is an ample opportunity for irrigation, it will suffice if the fallow ground is turned over with a not very deep double-mattock, that is, with an iron tool measuring less than two feet. But we shall take care that the field which has to be planted in the spring is trenched in the autumn about November 1st; then let us turn over in the month of May the land which we intend to lay out in the autumn, in order that the clods of earth may be broken up by the winter cold or the summer heat, and the roots of the weeds may be killed; and we shall have to manure it not long in advance; but when the time for sowing approaches, the ground will have to be weeded and manured five days beforehand and so carefully dug up a second time that the earth mixes with the dung. The best dung for the purpose is that of asses, because it grows the fewest weeds; next is that of either cattle or sheep, if it has soaked for a year. Human ordure, although it is reckoned to be most excellent, should not necessarily be employed except for bare gravel or very loose sand which has no strength, that is, when more powerful nourishment is required. We shall, therefore, after the autumn let the soil which we have decided to sow in the spring lie, when it has been dug up, so that it may be nipped by the cold and frosts of mid-winter; for by a contrary process like the heat of summer, so the violence of the cold refines the earth and breaks it up after causing it to ferment. Therefore, when mid-winter is past, the time has at last come when the dung is to be spread, and about January 13th the ground, having been dug over again, is divided into beds, which, however, should be so contrived that the hands of those who weed them can easily reach the middle of their breadth, so that those who are going after weeds may not be forced to tread on the seedlings, but rather may make their way along paths and weed first one and then the other half of the bed.

We have now spoken at sufficient length about what has to be done before the season for sowing. Let us now give directions as to what must be cultivated and sown and at what season, and first of all we must speak of the kinds of seed which can be sown at the two seasons, namely autumn and spring. These are the seeds of cabbage, lettuce, artichoke, rocket, cress, coriander, chervil, dill, parsnip, skirret and poppy. For these are sown either about September 1st or better in February before March 1st. In dry or warm districts, however, such as the sea-coasts of Calabria and Apulia, they can be put into the ground about January 13th. On the other hand, the seeds which ought to be sown only in the autumn – provided, however, that we inhabit a district either on the coast or exposed to the sun – are commonly these: garlic, small heads of onion, African garlic and mustard. But let us rather now arrange month by month at what season it is generally fitting that each kind should be put into the ground.

Immediately after January 1st it will be proper to plant pepperwort. In the month of February rue, either as a plant or as a seed, and asparagus, and again the seed of the onion and the leek; likewise, if you want to have the yield in the spring and summer, you will bury in the ground the seeds of radish, turnip and navew. For ordinary garlic and African garlic are the last seeds which can be sown at this season. About March 1st you can transplant the leek in sunny positions, if it has already grown to a good size; and at the end of the month of March you can treat all-heal in the same way, and then about April 1st leeks likewise and elecampane and late plants of rue. Also cucumbers, gourds and capers must be sown that they may come up in good time. The best time to sow beet seed is when the pomegranate blossoms, but heads of leek can still be passably well transplanted about May 15th. After this, when the summer is coming on, nothing ought to be put in the ground except parsley-seed, and this only if you intend to water it; for then it comes on very well during the summer. In August about the time of the feast of Vulcan comes the third sowing time; it is the best time for sowing radish and turnips, also navew, skirrets and alexanders.

So much for the times of sowing.

Columella (Lucius Junius Moderatus Columella), *De Re Rustica*

The Pleasures of the Garden

Having made mention of these productions, it now remains for us to return to the cultivation of the garden, a subject recommended by its own intrinsic merits to our notice: for we find that in remote antiquity, even, there was nothing looked upon with a greater degree of admiration than the gardens of the Hesperides, those of the kings Adonis and Alcinous, and the Hanging Gardens, whether they were the work of Semiramis, or whether of Cyrus, king of Assyria, a subject of which we will have to speak in another work. The kings of Rome cultivated their gardens with their own hands; indeed, it was from his garden that Tarquinius Superbus sent to his son that cruel and sanguinary message of his. In our laws of the Twelve Tables, we find the word 'villa' or 'farm' nowhere mentioned; it is the word 'hortus' that is always used with that signification, while the term 'heredium' we first employed for 'garden'.

There are certain religious impressions, too, that have been attached to this species of property, and we find that it is in the garden and the Forum only that statues of satyrs are consecrated, as a protection against the evil effects of spells and sorcery; although in Plautus, we find the gardens spoken of as being under the tutelage of Venus. At the present day, under the general name of gardens, we have pleasure-grounds situate in the very heart of the City, as well as extensive fields and villas.

Epicurus, that connoisseur in the enjoyments of a life of ease, was the first to lay out a garden at Athens; up to his time it had never been thought of, to dwell in the country in the middle of the town. At Rome, on the other hand, the garden constituted of itself the poor man's field, and it was from the garden that the lower classes procured their daily food

– an aliment how guiltlessly obtained! But still, it is a great deal better, no doubt, to dive into the abysses of the deep, and to seek each kind of oyster at the risk and peril of shipwreck, to go searching for birds beyond the river Phasis even, which, protected as they are by the terrors invented by fable, are only rendered all the more precious thereby – to go searching for others, again, in Numidia, and the very sepulchres of Æthiopia, or else to be battling with wild beasts, and to get eaten one's self while trying to take a prey which another person is to eat! And yet, by Hercules! how little do these productions of the garden cost us in comparison with these! How more than sufficient for every wish and for every want! – were it not, indeed, that here, as in every thing else, turn which way we will, we find the same grounds for our wrath and indignation. We really might be content to allow of fruits being grown of the most exquisite quality, remarkable, some of them for their flavour, some for their size, some, again, for the monstrosities of their growth, morsels all of them forbidden to the poor! We might allow of wines being kept till they are mellowed with age, or enfeebled by being passed through cloth strainers, of men, too, however prolonged their lives, never drinking any but a wine that is still older than themselves! We might allow of luxury devising how best to extract the very aroma, as it were, and marrow only from grain; of people, too, living upon nothing but the choicest productions of the confectioner, and upon pastes fashioned in fantastic shapes: of one kind of bread being prepared for the rich, and another for the multitude; of the yearly produce of the field being classified in a descending scale, till it reaches the humble means of the very lowest classes – but we do not find that these refined distinctions have been extended to the very herbs even, and that riches have contrived to establish points of dissimilarity in articles of food which ordinarily sell for a single copper coin?

In this department even, humble as it is, we are still destined to find certain productions that are denied to the community at large, and the very cabbages pampered to such an enormous extent that the poor man's table is not large enough to hold them. Asparagus*, by Nature, was intended to grow wild, so that each might gather it where he pleased – but, lo and behold! we find it in the highest state of cultivation, and Ravenna produces heads that weigh as much as three pounds even! Alas for the monstrous

---

* The context suggests that artichokes not asparagus are intented (Ed.).

excess of gluttony! It would be surprising indeed, for the beasts of the field to be forbidden the thistle for food, and yet it is a thing forbidden to the lower classes of the community! These refined distinctions, too, are extended to the very water even, and, thanks to the mighty influence of money, there are lines of demarcation drawn in the very elements themselves. Some persons are for drinking ice, others for quaffing snow, and thus is the curse of the mountain steep turned into an appetising stimulus for the palate! Cold is carefully treasured up for the summer heats, and man's invention is racked how best to keep snow freezing in months that are not its own. Some again there are who first boil the water, and then bring it to the temperature of winter – indeed, there is nothing that pleases man in the fashion in which Nature originally made it.

And is it the fact, then, that any herb of the garden is reared only for the rich man's table? It is so – but still let no one of the angered populace think of a fresh secession to Mount Sacer or Mount Aventine; for to a certainty, in the long run, all-powerful money will bring them back to just the same position as they were in when it wrought the severance. For, by Hercules! there was not an impost levied at Rome more grievous than the market-dues, an impost that aroused the indignation of the populace, who repeatedly appealed with loud clamours to all the chief men of the state to be relieved from it. At last they were relieved from this heavy tax upon their wares; and then it was found that there was no tax more lucrative, more readily collected, or less obnoxious to the caprices of chance, than the impost that was levied in exchange for it, in the shape of a property-tax, extended to the poorest classes: for now the very soil itself is their surety that paid the tax will be, their means are patent to the light of day, and the superficial extent of their possessions, whatever the weather may chance to be, always remains the same.

Cato, we find, speaks in high praise of garden cabbages: indeed, it was according to their respective methods of garden cultivation that the agriculturists of early times were appreciated, and it was immediately concluded that it was a sign of a woman being a bad and careless manager of her family, when the kitchen-garden – for this was looked upon as the woman's department more particularly – was negligently cultivated; as in such case her only resource was, of course, the shambles or the herb-market. But cabbages were not held in such high esteem in those days as now: indeed, all dishes were held in disrepute which required something else to help them down, the great object being to economise oil as much as possible; and as to the flesh-market, so much as a wish even to taste its wares was visited with censure and reproach. The chief thing that made them so fond of the garden was the fact that its produce needs no fire and ensures economy in fuel, and that it offers resources which are always ready and at hand. These articles of food, which from their peculiar nature we call 'vinegar-diets', were found to be easy of digestion, by no means apt to blunt and overload the sense, and to create but little craving for bread as an accompaniment. A portion of them which is still used by us for seasonings, attests that our forefathers used only to look at home for their resources, and that no Indian peppers were in request with them, or any of those other condiments which we are in the habit of seeking beyond the seas. In former times the lower classes of Rome, with their mimic gardens in their windows, day after day presented the reflex of the country to the eye, when as yet the multitudes of atrocious burglaries, almost innumerable, had not compelled us to shut out all such sights with bars to the passer by.

Let the garden, then, have its due meed of honour, and let not things, because they are common, enjoy for that the less share of our consideration – and the more so, as we find that from it men of the very highest rank have been content to borrow surnames even; thus in the Valerian family, for instance, the Lactucini have not thought themselves disgraced by taking their name from the lettuce. Perhaps, too, our labours and research may contribute some slight recommendation to this our subject; although, with Virgil, we are ready to admit how difficult it is, by language however elevated, to ennoble a subject that is so humble in itself.

Pliny (Gaius Plinius Secundus), *Natural History*, Book XIX

The Will of Theophrastus

The estate at Stagira belonging to me I give and bequeath to Callinus. The whole of my library I give to Neleus. The garden and the walk and the houses adjoining the garden, all and sundry, I give and bequeath to such of my friends hereinafter named as may wish to study literature and philosophy there in common, since it is not possible for all men to be always in residence, on condition that no one alienates the property or devotes it to his private use, but so that they hold it like a temple in joint possession, and live, as is right and proper, on terms of familiarity and friendship. Let the community consist of Hipparchus, Neleus, Strato, Callinus, Demotimus, Demaratus, Callisthenes, Melantes, Pancreon, Nicippus. Aristotle, the son of Metrodorus and Pythias, shall also have the right to study and associate with them if he so desire. And the oldest of them shall pay every attention to him, in order to ensure for him the utmost proficiency in philosophy. Let me be buried in any spot in the garden which seems most suitable, without unnecessary outlay upon my funeral or upon my monument. And according to previous agreement let the charge of attending, after my decease, to the temple and the monument and the garden and the walk be shared by Pompylus in person, living close by as he does, and exercising the same supervision over all other matters as before; and those who hold the property shall watch over his interests.

Diogenes Laertius, *Lives of Eminent Philosophers*

401–1500

Eleven hundred years of history and a broad sweep of cultures. A new religion is born, Islam, and flowers politically and culturally. With it comes the startling combination of familiar and strange imagery by the Sufi poet Rumi: 'Christ is Spring', beautiful in itself, and embodying a freedom of expression which I fear has been lost in these more 'enlightened' times. Very subtly, the poet evokes elements of the fertility cults of the same milieu of Christianity's conception.

There is the very familiar sentiment of Sa-'Di – that of love in the garden – although the cast-members, both flora and fauna, reflect the local situation. Bulbuls do not sing in Western gardens where nightingales reign, but will sing through the centuries in the East. With time, they learn sadness.

In China and Japan, poets, diplomats, and ladies of the court write with the confidence of a mature literary culture, established and stable societies, and well-formed horticultural traditions. Desire and sensuality, loss and melancholy – all are treated with psychological depth and realism. There is a sophisticated appreciation of the aesthetics of the seasons, autumn in particular. But no matter the subject, there is a clarity of expression and a lightness of touch which makes them most pleasurable to read.

Finally we return to northern and western Europe, and writing imbued with a certain rude energy and a delight in detail, bordering on obsession: every bird, tree, and flower is named and characterised to some extent, then pressed to the service of a variety of themes. The Pearl poet is mourning the death of his daughter; a Scottish king is finding comfort simply in the sight of a garden beyond his prison's walls and is consoled by the song of the birds – a role they play elsewhere.

Despite the variety of forms, the differences in planting, the places of origin and the local significances, these gardens, with one or two exceptions, have several common features. They are, comparatively, small, and in close association with the house or other dwelling, be it palace or prison. Often they are within a courtyard, completely enclosed by the house. The smaller the garden, the greater the significance of the wall around it. A ten-foot wall seen from 1000 yards in an English landscape garden appears small in proportion to the associated features. A wall of the same height around a town garden dominates the space, magnifying the sense of security, separation, seclusion, and intimacy. By extension, those who can see the garden are a privileged few, and those who have the time to rest within it are rarer again.

The idea of rest is an important one. These are not active gardens in the modern sense. Instead, they are gardens for the exercise of the mind. In the Far East, they seem to have found whole worlds of thought in the contemplation of a single flower, or the harmony of fifteen stones bedded in gravel. In the West, the analogy is more with the great structures of the time, the cathedrals. The very form of these buildings is symbolic at many different levels, and the elements from which they are composed are, likewise, all imbued with their own meaning. The building is itself a story. Similarly, the lists of flowers, while interesting as a botanical history, should be regarded as a series of symbols, each of which should prompt associations in the minds of the reader of the poem: the description of the gardens in the Hypnerotomachia Poliphili by Francesco Colonna being a prime example. The more obvious of these, the rose and the lily, endured the longest, but even the humble daisy, the 'day's-eye', seemed the perfect emblem of consciousness. When the time comes, consider again just what it is that Alice is threatening to do in The Garden of Live Flowers!

To the Lady Radegund with Violets

If 'twere the time of lilies,
Or of the crimson rose,
I'd pluck them in the fields for you,
Or my poor garden close:
Small gift for you so rare.

But I can find no lilies,
Green herbs are all I bring.
Yet love makes vetches roses,
And in their shadowing
Hide violets as fair.

For royal is their purple,
And fragrant is their breath,
And to one sweet and royal,
Their fragrance witnesseth
Beauty abiding there.

Venantius Fortunatus

The Merciful

In the Name of God, the Compassionate, the Merciful

It is the Merciful who has taught the Koran.

He created man and taught him articulate speech. The sun and the moon pursue their ordered course. The plants and the trees bow down in adoration.

He raised the heaven on high and set the balance of all things, that you might not transgress that balance. Give just weight and full measure.

He laid the earth for His creatures, with all its fruits and blossom-bearing palm, chaff-covered grain and scented herbs. Which of your Lord's blessings would you deny?

He created man from potter's clay, and the jinn from smokeless fire. Which of your Lord's blessings would you deny?

He has let loose the two oceans: they meet one another. Yet between them stands a barrier which they cannot overrun. Which of your Lord's blessings would you deny?

His are the ships that sail like mountains upon the ocean. Which of your Lord's blessings would you deny?

All that lives on earth is doomed to die. But the face of your Lord will abide for ever, in all its majesty and glory. Which of your Lord's blessings would you deny?

All who dwell in heaven and earth entreat Him. Each day some mighty task engages Him. Which of your Lord's blessings would you deny?

Mankind and jinn, We shall surely find the time to judge you! Which of your Lord's blessings would you deny?

Mankind and jinn, if you have the power to penetrate the confines of heaven and earth, then penetrate them! But this you shall not do except with Our own authority. Which of your Lord's blessings would you deny?

Flames of fire shall be lashed at you, and molten brass. There shall be none to help you. Which of your Lord's blessings would you deny?

When the sky splits asunder, and reddens like a rose or stained leather (which of your Lord's blessings would you deny?), on that day neither man nor jinnee will be asked about his sins. Which of your Lord's blessings would you deny?

The wrongdoers will be known by their looks; they shall be seized by their forelocks and their feet. Which of your Lord's blessings would you deny?

That is the Hell which the sinners deny. They shall wander between fire and water fiercely seething. Which of your Lord's blessings would you deny?

But for those that fear the majesty of their Lord there are two gardens (which of your Lord's blessings would you deny?) planted with shady trees. Which of your Lord's blessings would you deny?

Each is watered by a flowing spring. Which of your Lord's blessings would you deny?

Each bears every kind of fruit in pairs. Which of your Lord's blessings would you deny?

They shall recline on couches lined with thick brocade, and within reach will hang the fruits of both gardens. Which of your Lord's blessings would you deny?

Virgins as fair as corals and rubies. Which of your Lord's blessings would you deny?

And beside these there shall be two other gardens (which of your Lord's blessings would you deny?) of darkest green. Which of your Lord's blessings would you deny?

A gushing fountain shall flow in each. Which of your Lord's blessings would you deny?

Each planted with fruit-trees, the palm and the pomegranate. Which of your Lord's blessings would you deny?

In each there shall be virgins chaste and fair. Which of your Lord's blessings would you deny?

Dark-eyed virgins, sheltered in their tents (which of your Lord's blessings would you deny?), whom neither man nor jinnee will have touched before. Which of your Lord's blessings would you deny?

They shall recline on green cushions and fine carpets. Which of your Lord's blessings would you deny?

Blessed be the name of your Lord, the Lord of majesty and glory!

Koran 55. 1–78

The River-Merchant's Wife: A Letter

You dragged your feet when you went out.
By the gate now, the moss is grown, the different mosses,
Too deep to clear them away!
The leaves fall early this autumn, in wind.
The paired butterflies are already yellow with August
Over the grass in the west garden;
They hurt me. I grow older.
If you are coming down through the narrows of the river Kiang,
Please let me know beforehand,
And I will come out to meet you
As far as Cho-fu-Sa.

Li Po

Plant No Trees

Plant no trees in your garden,
Trees fill the four seasons with sadness.
Sleeping alone, the moon at my southern window,
This autumn seems all autumns past.

Li Ho

Planting Flowers on the Eastern Embankment

I took money and bought flowering trees
And planted them out on the bank to the east of the Keep.
I simply bought whatever had most blooms,
Not caring whether peach, apricot, or plum.
A hundred fruits, all mixed together;
A thousand branches, flowering in due rotation.
Each has its season coming early or late;
But to all alike the fertile soil is kind.
The red flowers hang like a sunset mist;
The white flowers gleam like a fall of snow.
The wandering bees cannot bear to leave them;
The sweet birds also come there to roost.
In front there flows an ever-running stream;
Beneath there is built a little flat terrace.
Sometimes I sweep the flagstones of the terrace;
Sometimes, in the wind, I raise my cup and drink.
The flower-branches screen my head from the sun;
The flower-buds fall down into my lap.
Alone drinking, alone with my singing songs
I do not notice that the moon is level with the steps.
The people of Pa do not care for the flowers;
All the spring no one has come to look.
But their Governor General, alone with his cup of wine
Sits till evening and will not move from the place!

Po Chü-I

On the Day after a Fierce Autumn Wind

On the day after a fierce autumn wind everything moves one deeply. The garden is in a pitiful state with all the bamboo and lattice fence knocked over and lying next to each other on the ground. It is bad enough if the branches of one of the great trees have been broken by the wind; but it is a really painful surprise to find that the tree itself has fallen down and is now lying flat over the bush-clover and the valerians. As one sits in one's room looking out, the wind, as though on purpose, gently blows the leaves one by one through the chinks of the lattice-window, and one finds it hard to believe that this is the same wind which yesterday raged so violently.

On one such morning I caught sight of a woman creeping out from the main hall and emerging a few feet on to the veranda. I could see that she was a natural beauty. Over a dress of dull purple she wore an unlined robe of tawny cloth and a formal robe of some light material. The noise of the wind must have kept her awake during the night and she had just got up after sleeping late. Now she knelt on the veranda and looked into her mirror. With her long hair being blown about and gently puffed up by the wind, she was a truly splendid sight. As she gazed at the scene of desolation in the garden, a girl of about seventeen – not a small girl, but still not big enough to be called grown-up – joined her on the veranda. She wore a night-dress of light violet and over that a faded blue robe of stiff silk, which was badly coming apart at the seams and wet from the rain. Her hair, which was cut evenly at the ends like a miscanthus in a field, reached all the way down to her feet, falling on to the veranda beyond the bottom of her robe. Looking at her from the side, I could make out the scarlet of her trouser-skirt, the only bright touch in her costume.

In the garden a group of maids and young girls were collecting the flowers and plants that the wind had torn up by the roots and were propping up some that were less damaged. Several women were gathered in front of me by the blind, and I enjoyed seeing how envious they looked as they watched the young people outside and wished that they might join them.

Sei Shonagon, *The Pillow Book*

Come Quickly

Come quickly – as soon as
these blossoms open,
they fall.
This world exists
as a sheen of dew on flowers.

Izumi Shikibu

Plum Blossoms

To the tune 'The Honour of a Fisherman'

Already, out of the snow,
You bring news that Spring is here,
Cold plum blossoms, adorning
The glossy jasper branches,
Perfumed faces half showing,
Gracefully fluttering in the middle of the courtyard.
I come, my jade body fresh from the bath,
Newly powdered and rouged.
Even Heaven shares our joy,
Making the bright moon shine splendid on your curving flesh.
Let us celebrate with thick green wine in gold cups.
I will not refuse to get drunk
For this flower cannot be compared to other flowers.

Li Ch'ing-chao

Herbs, Trees and Flowers to Grow in the Garden

The garden should be adorned with roses and lilies, sunflowers, violets, and mandrakes; there you should have parsley and cost, fennel and southernwood, and coriander, sage, savory, hyssop, mint, rue, dittany, celery, pellitory, lettuce, garden cress, and peonies. There should also be planted beds with onions, leeks, garlic, pumpkins and shallots. Cucumbers growing in their curved belly-shape and the stupor-inducing poppy further ennoble the garden, embellished also with daffodils and acanthus.

There should also be pottage herbs if you can get them – beet, dog mercury, orach, sorrel and mallow.

Aniseed and mustard, and white pepper, and wormwood are of some use to the gardener.

The following will also give you a fine garden: medlar, quince, cottana fig, big volema pear, peach, St Regulus's pear, pomegranate, citrus fruit, golden apples, almonds, dates which are the fruit of palms, and figs. Not to mention ginger and peppermint, and cinnamon, liquorice, and zituala, and Syrian flax oozing incense, and myrrh, and aloe, and stacte resin and Styrax officinalis and balsam and galbanum. Nor need I mention cypress and nard, and the drops from cassia. If you take our advice, you will not stint on crocus and saffron. And everyone knows the qualities of wild thyme and fleabane. And everyone recognises how good borage and purslain are to eat. And who doesn't understand that hazelwort, commonly called valerian, gently expels, through the upper opening, digestive upsets? (I refer to the stomach.)

Colewort, on the other hand, and ragwort stir up lust, but the wonderful coldness of plantain offers a remedy for this sickness. Myrtle also is a friend to temperance, which is why it is said to be the usual offering to Venus, as the cockerel is slaughtered for Nycteis the goddess of night, as for the same reason a he-goat is sacrificed to Bacchus and a sow to Ceres.

Those who worry about this kind of work distinguish between sunflowers and our sunflowers which are called pot-marigolds, just as they do between mugwort and our feverfew. All agree, however, that Jupiter's beard and silver-haired woolblade are one and the same.

The iris produces a purple flower, Orris a white one, Flag Iris, a yellow one, but Stinking gladwyn none.

Horehound, hound's tongue, Macedonian rock-parsley and arum, and the three astrological species of ragwort, angelica (also called regina) and coriander are notable plants. But the effects and properties of plants have been thoroughly described by Macer and Dioscorides and many other, so from here we want to pass on to other things.

Alexander Neckam, De Naturis Rerum

The Tree of Paletinus

Valerius tells us, that a man named Paletinus one day burst into tears; and calling his son and neighbours around him, said, 'Alas! alas! I have now growing in my garden a fatal tree on which my first poor wife hung herself, then my second, and after that my third. Have I not therefore cause for wretchedness?' 'Truly,' said one who was called Arrius, 'I marvel that you should weep at such unusual good fortune! Give me, I pray you, two or three sprigs of that gentle tree, which I will divide with my neighbours, and thereby enable every man to indulge his spouse.' Paletinus complied with his friend's request; and ever after found this tree the most productive part of his estate.

from the *Gesta Romanorum*

Christ is Spring

Everyone has eaten and fallen asleep. The house is empty.
We walk out to the garden to let the apple meet the peach,
to carry messages between rose and jasmine.

Spring is Christ,
raising martyred plants from their shrouds.
Their mouths open in gratitude, wanting to be kissed.
The glow of the rose and the tulip means a lamp
is inside. A leaf trembles. I tremble
in the wind-beauty like silk from Turkestan.
The censer fans into flame.

This wind is the Holy Spirit.
The trees are Mary.
Watch how husband and wife play subtle games with their
hands.
Cloudy pearls from Aden are thrown across the lovers,
as is the marriage custom.

The scent of Joseph's shirt comes to Jacob.

A red carnelian of Yemeni laughter is heard
by Muhammad in Mecca.

We talk about this and that. There's no rest
except on these branching moments.

Rumi

Dancing, Singing

The Kashmir Damsel, smiling, loosed the shawl
Draped rich about her hips; set firm the flower
Ablaze in her black hair; salaamed, and swam
Into the Persian measure, waving hands,
And swaying lissom limbs, while Gulbadan
Sang to *Nishastah*, and the beat of feet:

All in a Garden fair I sate, and spied
The Tulips dancing, dancing side by side,
    With scarlet turbans dressed;
All in a Garden green at night I heard
The gladsome voice of night's melodious Bird
    Singing that 'Love is Best!'

The shy white Jasmine drew aside her veil,
Breathing faint fragrance on the loitering gale,
    And nodded, nodded 'Yes!
'Sweetest of all sweet things is Love! and wise!
'Dance, Tulip! Pipe, fond Bird, thy melodies!
    'Wake, Rose of Loveliness!'

'Yet,' sighed the swaying Cypress, 'who can tell
'If Love be wise as sweet? if it be well
    'For Love to dance and sing?
'I see – growing here always – year by year
'The Bulbuls die, and on their grassy bier
    'Rose-petals scattering!'

All in that Garden green the Bulbul trilled:
'Oh, foolish Cypress! thinking Love was killed

'Because he seemed to cease:
'My best-Belov'd hath secrets at her heart,
'Gold seeds of summer-time, new buds to start;
'There will be Roses! peace!'

Then lightlier danced the Tulips than before
To waftings of the perfumed breeze, and more
    Chanted the Nightingale:
The fire-flies in the palms fresh lanterns lit;
Her zone of grace the blushing Rose unknit,
    And blossomed, pure and pale!

Sa'di, *The Book of Love*

The Palace in Khan-balik

Between the inner and the outer walls, of which I have told you, are
stretches of park-land with stately trees. The grass grows here in abundance, because all the paths are paved and built up fully two cubits above
the level of the ground, so that no mud forms on them and no rain-water
collects in puddles, but the moisture trickles over the lawns, enriching
the soil and promoting a lush growth of herbage. In these parks there is
a great variety of game, such as white harts, musk-deer, roebuck, stags,
squirrels, and many other beautiful animals. All the area within the walls
is full of these graceful creatures, except the paths that people walk on.

In the north-western corner of the grounds is a pit of great size and
depth, very neatly made, from which the earth was removed to build the
mound of which I shall speak. The pit is filled with water by a fair-sized
stream so far as to form a sort of pond where the animals come to drink.
The stream flows out through an aqueduct near the mound and fills
another similar pit between the Great Khan's palace and that of Chinghiz
his son, from which the earth was dug for the same purpose. These pits or
ponds contain a great variety of fish. For the Great Khan has had them
stocked with many different species, so that, whenever he feels inclined, he
may have his pick. At the farther end of the pond there is an outlet for the
stream, through which it flows away. It is so contrived that at the entrance
and the outlet there are gratings of iron and copper to stop the fish from
escaping. There are also swans and other water-fowl. It is possible to pass

from one palace to the other by way of a bridge over this stream.

On the northern side of the palace, at the distance of a bow-shot but still within the walls, the Great Khan has had made an earthwork, that is to say a mound fully one hundred paces in height and over a mile in circumference. This mound is covered with a dense growth of trees, all evergreens that never shed their leaves. And I assure you that whenever the Great Khan hears tell of a particularly fine tree he has it pulled up, roots and all and with a quantity of earth, and transported to this mound by elephants. No matter how big the tree may be, he is not deterred from transplanting it. In this way he has assembled here the finest trees in the world. In addition, he has had the mound covered with lapis lazuli, which is intensely green*, so that trees and rock alike are as green as green can be and there is no other colour to be seen. For this reason it is called the Green Mound. On top of this mound, in the middle of the summit, he has a large and handsome palace, and this too is entirely green. And I give you my word that mound and trees and palace form a vision of such beauty that it gladdens the hearts of all beholders. It was for the sake of this entrancing view that the Great Khan had them constructed, as well as for the refreshment and recreation they might afford him.

Marco Polo, *Travels in the Land of Kubilai Khan*

* As lapis lazuli is known to be intensely blue (and indeed in his account of a visit to the Sar-e-Sang lapis lazuli mine in Badakshan, Afghanistan, Marco Polo remarks that a blue pigment is extracted from the stone), this is somewhat puzzling. Perhaps he was misinformed as to the stone Kublai Khan used, or perhaps it was an unusually green form of the stone, which is often flecked with minerals, such as gold-coloured pyrites, that would give it a greenish hue.

A Garden of Fruits and Spices

> But nowhere wold I reste me,
> Till I hadde in all the gardyn be.
>   The gardyn was, by mesuryng,
> Right evene and square in compassing:
> It as long was as it was large.
> Of fruyt hadde every tree his charge,
> But it were any hidous tree,
> Of which ther were two or three.

There were, and that wot I full well,
Of pome-garnettys a full gret dell;
That is a fruyt full well to lyke,
Namely to folk whanne they ben sike.
And trees there were, gret foisoun,
That baren notes in her sesoun,
Such as men notemygges calle,
That swote of savour ben withalle.
And alemandres gret plente,
Fyges, and many a date-tree
There waxen, if men hadde need,
Thorough the gardyn in length and brede.
Ther was eke wexying many a spice,
As clowe-gelofre and lycorice,
Gyngevre and greyn de parys,
Canell and setewale of prys,
And many a spice delitable
To eten whan man rise fro table.
And many homly trees ther were
That peches, coynes, and apples beere.
Meddlers, plowmes, preys, chesteynes,
Cherys, of which many oon fayn is,
Notes, alleys, and bolas,
That for to seen it was solas.
With many high lorer and pyn
Was renged clene all that gardyn,
With cipres and with olyveres,
Of which that nygh no plente here is.
There were elmes grete and stronge,
Maples, assh, ok, asp, planes longe,
Fyn ew, popler, and lyndes faire,
And othere trees full many a payre.
    What shulde I tel you more of it?
There were so many trees yit,
That I shulde al encombred be
Er I rekened every tree.

Geoffrey Chaucer, *The Romance of the Rose*

Love in the Garden

(A Song)
I have a new garden,
And new is begun,
Another such garden
Not known under sun.

In the midst of my garden
Is a pear tree set,
And it will not pears bear
But a pear 'Janet'.

The fairest maid of this town
Prayed me,
To graft her a graft
Of my pear tree.

When I had her grafted,
All at her will,
With joy and with ale,
She did me fill,

And I grafted her
Branch up in her home,
And by that day twenty weeks,
It was quick in her womb.

By that day twelve months
That maid I did meet:
She said it was a pear Robert,
But not a pear Janet!

Anon.

A Garden of Dreams

Pearl, O pleasure for a prince,
Enclosed in gold, so clean and clear,
I own that all the orient's
Fine pearls, though pure, provide no peer
So round, so rich, so wrapped in glints
Of light, so small, so smooth and dear.
In gems that I have judged, no hints
Are seen of her superior.
In a garden green with grass, my cheer
Was lost! It lunged to land. O lot!
A lovelorn, longing look I bear
For that precious pearl without a spot.

In the spot where she once sprang from me,
I've pined and prayed to glean that pure
And welcome one that wondrously
Brought happiness and health. But care,
All raging, racked me wretchedly;
And burning bitterness I bore.
Yet somehow there was sung to me
A sweeter song than chorister
Could ever chant; there came such cheer
In dreams of her, though wrapped in rot!
O earth, you rob a rich and rare
And precious pearl without a spot!

That spot with spices sweet was spread;
For riches there to rot were run.
But blooms of yellow, blue, and red
Still shimmered in the shining sun!
For flower or fruit will not fall dead
If grown against that pearl's grain.
From dying husks new husks are spread;
No wheat would else reach winnow-bin.

From good is every good begun.
So strong a single seed could not
But fructify; so flowers sprung
From precious pearl without a spot.

In that same spot where I had stayed
I gained a garden, gleaming bright,
When August wheat is harvested,
With sickles scythed, and stacked up tight.
Among the shrubs, where she had sped –
Some stood in shade and some in light –
Gillyflower, ginger, and gromwell bred,
And peonies pleased with pure delight.
So sweet it was, all shining bright,
So fresh the fragrance of that plot,
I'm certain that it was the site
Of precious pearl without a spot.

Before that spot I hung my head;
My care had cut me to the core.
From wounds of woe within I bled.
Though reason bid me rage no more,
I suffered still; my sadness spread.
I knew of neither wisdom nor
The consolation Christ had bred.
My saddened soul still showed its sore;
I fell upon that grassy floor
Asleep, my ravaged senses shot,
And dreamed a swooning dream before
My precious pearl without a spot.

Anon., *Pearl*

Thoughts in an English Prison

29

The long dayes and the nyghtis eke
I wold bewaille my fortune in this wise.
For quhich, agane distresse confort to seke,
My custom was on mornis for to ryse
Airly as day: O happy exercise,
By thee come I to ioye out of torment!
But now to purpose of my first entent.

30

Bewailing in my chamber thus alone,
Despaired of all ioye and remedye,
Fortirit of my thought, and wo-begone,
And to the window gan I walk in hye
To se the warld and folk that went forby.
As for the tyme, though I of mirthis fude
Might haue no more, to luke it did me gude.

31

Now was there maid fast by the touris wall
A gardyn fair, and in the corneris set
Ane herber grene with wandis long and small
Railit about; and so with treis set
Was all the place, and hawthorn hegis knet,
That lyf was non walking there forby
That might within scarse ony wight aspye:

32

So thik the bewis and the leues grene
Beschadit all the aleyes that there were.
And myddis euery herber might be sene
The scharp grene suete ienepere,
Growing so fair with branchis here and there,
That (as it semyt to a lyf without)
The bewis spred the herber all about.

33

And on the small grene twistis sat
The lytill suete nightingale, and song
So loud and clere the ympnis consecrate
Of lufis vse, now soft, now loud among,
That all the gardyng and the wallis rong
Right of their song and o the copill next
Of thair suete armony; – and lo the text:

34

Worschippe, ye that loueris bene, this May,
For of your blisse the kalendis ar begonne,
And sing with vs, 'away, winter, away!
Cum somer, cum, the suete sesoun and sonne!'
Awake for schame! that haue your hevynnis wonne,
And amorously lift vp your hedis all:
Thank Lufe that list you to his merci call.

35

Quhen thai this song had song a lytill thrawe,
Thai stent a quhile, and therwith vnaffraid
(As I beheld and kest myn eyne alawe)
From beugh to beugh thay hippit and thai plaid,
And freschly in thair birdis kind arraid
Thair fetheris new, and fret thame in the sonne,
And thankit Lufe that had thair makis wonne.

King James I, *The Kingis Quair*

The Squire of Low Degree

It was a squire of lowe degree
That loved the Kings doughter of Hungré.
The squir was curteous and hend;
Ech man him loved and was his frend.
He served the King, her father dere,
Fully the time of seven yere;

For he was marshall of his hall
And set the lords both great and small.
An hardy man he was and wight,
Both in bataile and in fight.
But ever he was still morning

And no man wiste for what thing;
And all was for the lady,
The Kings doughter of Hungry.
There wiste no wighte in Christenté
Howe well he loved that lady free.
He loved her more than seven yere,
Yet was he of her love never the nere.
He was not riche of gold and fee;
A gentill man forsoth was he.
To no man durst he make his mone,
But sighed sore himselfe alone.

And evermore when he was so,
Into his chambre would he go:
And through the chambre he toke the waye
Into the gardin that was full gaye;
And in the garden, as I wene,
Was an arber faire and grene
And in the arber was a tree,
A fairer in the world might none be.
The tree it was of cypresse,
The first tree that Jesu chose;
The sother-wood and sykamore,
The reed rose and the lyly-floure,
The boxe, the beche, and the larel-tree,
The date, also the damyse,
The filbirdes hanging to the ground,
The figge-tree and the maple round,
And other trees there was mané one,
The piany, the popler, and the plane,
With brode braunches all aboute,

Within the arbar and eke withoute.
On every braunche sate birdes three
Singinge with great melody,
The laverocke and the nightingale,

The ruddocke, the woodwale,
The pee and the popinjaye,
The trustele sange both night and daye,
The marlin and the wrenne also,
The swalowe whippinge to and fro,
The jaye jangled them amonge,
The larke began that merry songe,
The sparrowe spredde her on the spraye,
The mavis songe with notes full gaye,
The nuthake with her notes newe,
The sterlinge set her notes full trewe,
The goldfinche made full merry chere,
Whan she was bente upon a brere,
And many other foules mo,
The osill and the thrushe also;
And they sange with notes clere
In conforting that squiere.

Anon., The Squire of Low Degree

The Second Garden

The second garden enclosure followed immediately after the work just described, then at the end of it another seven stairs began rising towards the centre. On the top step was a variegated hedge whose colours amazed the eye, with towers or pavilions expertly made from orange-trees. Two trunks were planted on either side of the doorway, rose through the wall of the tower past the opening or wings of the door, and extended for three feet above the top of the tower, where they met and joined together as one. Then the thick foliage began, cut like a moderate-sized cypress; and thus it was all round the circle, two paces in height. The hedges between the towers were of various colours and species of tree: between one pair there was juniper, between another, mastic, and then arbutus, privet, rosemary, dogwood, olive and laurel. Their spring greenery was all cut in the same manner, the last replicating the first, making a beautiful specimen of the topiarist's art with not a twig or a dead leaf in sight.

In the middle of the space between the two towers an admirable pine-tree rose up, while box-trees sprang out at intervals from the enclosing wall, exquisitely fashioned in the shape of symmetrical crescent moons. They filled out all the space between the towers, and were cut with singular skill with their openings or mouths upwards. In the middle, between the horns, was a juniper tapering in ten stages and thinning out towards its top, with its pungent leaves as smooth as if it had been turned on a lathe. Its thickest part adjoined the middle of the crescent. One stem rose to a height of one and a half feet beyond the cornice, where there was a well-proportioned ball of box.

Inside this enclosure and between the bordering paths, filling out this whole admirable circuit, were little square gardens of marvellous work, showing arrangements of various edible plants.

The first quadrangle was defined by paths on either side, which caused it to be an irregular square. It had a four-sided lineament of knot-work three palms wide, very neatly made out of bunches of flowers. The outermost band bent round to make a circle at its midpoint; the bands met as they came from the two corners and circled over one another. The resulting loop was knotted round a second band, four feet inside the first one, and the part of the circle that was above went below the other band, so that the two bands wove alternately above and below each other. And this second four-sided band made loops at its corners in which the knots were arranged with the bands going alternately over, then under.

The loops of the first band opened out inside the second square to make a circle that filled it. Next came another square, the same distance from the second as that was from the first, and this also made loops at its corners near the angles of the second band, on the diagonal line, interlacing as they turned over and under each other. Inside this last square there was a lozenge shape, whose corners made tight loops knotted around the middle of the sides of the last square.

In the triangular space between the lozenge and the inside square, on the diagonal lines, was a free circle. Inside the lozenge was an unknotted circle that filled it completely; and in the middle of that circle was an eight-petalled rosette. In the centre of this was set a hollow round alter of yellow Numidian stone with three ox-skulls. Between these, carved in deep relief, hung bunches of leaves and fruits swelling toward the middle, with loose ribbons tied around the heads and securing the bunches. This alter had fine lineaments, both socle and abacus being decorated with a beautiful cyma and other ornaments. Out of it grew a savin in compact cypress-like shape; and the opening of the alter was filled with many chervils.

The horticultural design of the square I have described was expressed with the following arrangement of colours: the first band was densely planted with marjoram, the second with aurotano, the third with ground-pine, and the lozenge with mountain thyme. The circle inside the lozenge was planted with germander; the rosette, with amethystine violets; the circle around the rosette and outside it, densely flowered with white violets; the four circles within the last square, in the triangles made by the lozenge and the enclosed square, with gith or Roman coriander; their interior, with yellow violets; all the background of these triangles, with cyclamen. The loops between the first and second squares were entirely filled with rue; those of the third square, with spring-flowering primula. The first border, between the first and second square, had a design of acanthus leaves pointing in alternate directions, planted with mountain hulwort and edged with maidenhair. In the centre of the circles located on the diagonals stood a ball, raised about a foot and a half and identical in height, diameter and position except in the four circles made by the intersection of the inserted square with the diagonals. In those centres there rose stems of mallow, three cubits high and coloured pink, purple and mauve, many-leaved and five-petalled, with a large crop of flowers. In the first was wormwood, in the second, incense-tree. In the centres of the loops formed when the circle was made by the first, external band were balls of hyssop. The size of this and the other squares was determined by the circular pathways and the straight transverse ones leading to the centre, limited by the green enclosure and the stairs.

Francesco Colonna (attrib.), *Hypnerotomachia Poliphili*

What an age of discovery and expanding worlds! There are the eyewitness accounts of the gardens of the New World – catch them before they vanish – revealing elements of taste, such as pleasant pools and fragrant shrubs, of familiar appeal. In the other direction, there is a renewed interest in the gardens of the ancient Near East; here once more is Alcinous, Babylon, Eden and Epicurus.

There is a growing confidence in the island nation, particularly after the Restoration, and, with the confidence, side-swipes at the Low Countries, France, and Italy. These would get worse before they got better.

It is also an age of visionaries. Thomas More imagines a perfect society in which gardens have an important place, an example echoed by Ebenezer Howard nearly four hundred years later. Francis Bacon is writing essays about all-important things, so of course turns his ferocious attention to gardens. He rejects, in writing at least, the prevailing fashion for knots and topiary and imagines a third of his princely 30-acre garden set aside as wilderness, if such a thing was possible. Wildernesses were not to be the fashion until the end of the century and were still highly formalised, the Wray Wood at Castle Howard (1718, Vanbrugh) being the first, to my knowledge, to stray from the straight path. Sir William Temple thinks 6 acres sufficient for a gentleman but foresees a time when gardens may become 'extravagant'. A mere twenty years later, and the 'State Garden' at Blenheim Palace, just one of a number of elements, is 77 acres.

There are attempts to write scientific horticulture with advice on sowing times and conditions, and soil management – the latter is still a neglected art. *There are experiments with fruit growing, and named varieties become prized. Calendars become popular; Evelyn published one, but it is John Reid's I have chosen. Here, alongside garden management, there is advice on the keeping of bees, and on what produce and drinks should be available in any month of the year. The variety shames most modern gardeners and would challenge many cooks. His guidelines on pest control are depressing and best ignored.*

Twickenham seems now an unlikely horticultural hotbed, but here is Donne's paradise (including serpent) to which he retreats from the city. In the eighteenth century it will locate Pope's (with grotto), and Langley's (formal, with statues). In poetry, flowers are still rich with symbolism, and a garden the perfect metaphor with which to make political statements, ontological observations, and amatory regrets.

Design books are published, complete with diagrams, so that every garden could have its knots. Knots to be filled with flowers, listed with pros and cons, or indeed many another surprising thing, with full installation instructions, all of which were to show off the pattern.

Gardens are becoming conversation pieces and subjects for letters. Evelyn gushes to the Ambassador in the Court of Spain, revealing much about his taste, the plants which were available, and the current methods for transporting large trees. Pepys goes to Whitehall and spends most of his day, or at least that which he cared to record, talking about gardens. Change is coming: walks are growing broader; plain grass is displacing flowers; knots have spread into parterres; urns and statues are creeping in. The burden of meaning is shifting from the living elements to the manufactured objects. And people are strolling.

৵

On Aircastle

The town is surrounded by a thick, high wall, with towers and block-houses at frequent intervals. On three sides of it there's a moat, which contains no water, but is very broad and deep, and obstructed by a thorn-bush entanglement. On the fourth side the river serves as a moat.

The streets are well designed, both for traffic and for protection against the wind. The buildings are far from unimpressive, for they take the form of terraces, facing one another and running the whole length of the street. The fronts of the houses are separated by a twenty-foot carriageway. Behind them is a large garden, also as long as the street itself, and completely enclosed by the backs of other streets. Each house has a front door into the street, and a back door into the garden. In both cases they're double swing-doors, which open at a touch, and close automatically behind you. So anyone can go in and out – for there's no such thing as private property. The houses themselves are allocated by lot, and changed round every ten years.

They're extremely fond of these gardens, in which they grow fruit, including grapes, as well as grass and flowers. They keep them in wonderful condition – in fact, I've never seen anything to beat them for beauty or fertility. The people of Aircastle are keen gardeners not only because they enjoy it, but because there are inter-street competitions for the best-kept garden. Certainly it would be hard to find any feature of the town more calculated to give pleasure and profit to the community – which makes me think that gardening must have been one of the founder's special interests.

By the founder I mean the Utopos himself, who is said to have designed the whole layout of the town right from the start.

Thomas More, *Utopia*

Letter from Mexico

In this city of Yztapalapa live twelve or fifteen thousand inhabitants. It is built by the side of a great salt lake, half of it on the water and the other half on dry land. The chief of this city has some new houses which, although as yet unfinished, are as good as the best in Spain; that is, in respect of size and workmanship both in their masonry and woodwork and their floors, and furnishings for every sort of household task; but they have no reliefs or other rich things which are used in Spain but not found here. They have many upper and lower rooms and cool gardens with many trees and sweet-smelling flowers; likewise there are pools of fresh water, very well made and with steps leading down to the bottom. There is a very large kitchen garden next to the house and overlooking it a gallery with very beautiful corridors and rooms, and in the garden a large reservoir of fresh water, well built with fine stonework, around which runs a well-tiled pavement so wide that four people can walk there abreast. It is four hundred paces square, which is sixteen hundred paces around the edge. Beyond the pavement, toward the wall of the garden, there is a latticework of canes, behind which are all manner of shrubs and scented herbs. Within the pool there are many fish and birds, wild ducks and widgeons, as well as other types of waterfowl; so many that the water is often almost covered with them.

Hernán Cortés, *The Second Letter, Sent to His Sacred Majesty the Emperor*

The Incas' Golden Garden

This Garden was in the Incas time a Garden of Silver and Gold, as they had in the Kings houses, where they had many sorts of Hearbes, Flowers, Plants, Trees, Beasts great and small, wilde, tame, Snakes, Lizards, Snailes, Butterflies, small and great Birds, each set in their place. They had Maiz, Quinva, Pulse, Fruit-trees with the fruit on them all of Gold and Silver, resembling the naturall. They had also in the house heapes of wood, all counterfeit of Gold and Silver, as they had in the house royall: likewise they had great statues of men and women, and children, and many Pirva or Trosses for corne, every day inventing new fashions of greater Majestie, using yearely on the Sunnes chiefe festivities to present him so much Silver and Gold wrought into counterfeit formes. All the Vessell (which was infinite) for the Temples service, Pots, Pans, Tubs, Hogsheads, was of Gold and Silver, even to the Spades, and Pickaxes for the Garden.

Garcilaso de la Vega, *History of Peru*

Mary, Mary, Quite Contrary

Mary, Mary, quite contrary,
How does your garden grow?
With silver bells and cockle shells
And pretty maids all in a row.

Traditional

The March to Mexico

When we arrived near Iztapalapa we beheld the splendour of the other *Caciques* who came out to meet us, the lord of that city whose name was Cuitlahuac, and the lord of Culuacan, both of them close relations of Montezuma. And when we entered the city of Iztapalapa, the sight of the palaces in which they lodged us! They were very spacious and well built, of magnificent stone, cedar wood, and the wood of other sweet-smelling trees, with great rooms and courts, which were a wonderful sight, and all covered with awnings of woven cotton.

When we had taken a good look at all this, we went to the orchard and garden, which was a marvellous place both to see and walk in. I was never tired of noticing the diversity of trees and the various scents given off by each, and the paths choked with roses and other flowers, and the many local fruit-trees and rose-bushes, and the pond of fresh water. Another remarkable thing was that large canoes could come into the garden from the lake, through a channel they had cut, and their crews did not have to disembark. Everything was shining with lime and decorated with different kinds of stonework and paintings which were a marvel to gaze on. Then there were birds of many breeds and varieties which came to the pond. I say again that I stood looking at it, and thought that no land like it would ever be discovered in the whole world, because at that time Peru was neither known nor thought of. But today all that I then saw is overthrown and destroyed; nothing is left standing.

Bernal Díaz del Castillo, *The Conquest of New Spain*

The Commended Times to be Observed in the Bestowing of Seeds and Plants in the Earth, with the Discommodities

The singular D. Niger learnedly uttereth that the more of estimation the seeds and plants are, with travels thereabout bestowed, so much the circumspecter ought every Gardener and husbandman to be; and the more instructions and help the Gardener may attaine, and the greater danger he may therein avoid, the more careful ought he and all others to be.

The daily experience is to the Gardener, as a Schoolmaster to instruct him, how much it availeth and hindreth, that seeds to be sown, plants to be set, yea Cions to be grafted (in this or that time) having herein regard, not to the time especially of the year, as the Sunne altereth the same, but also the Moons increase and wane, yea to the sign she occupieth, and places both above and under the earth.

To the aspects also of the other Planets, whose beams and influence both quicken, comfort, preserve, and maintain or else nip, wither, drie, consume, and destroy by sundry means, the tender seeds, plants, yea and grafts, and these after their property, and vertue natural or accidental.

Herein not to be forgotten, the apt choice and circumspection of the earth, with other matters generally required in the same, for which cause (after the mind of the skilful Astronomers) and prudent experimenters, in either committing seeds to the earth & planting, or other like practise to be used about the seeds, plants and young trees, these rules following are to be understood and kept (which they have left to us for our commodity) in eases of importance, and where the occasion may be imployed.

When the Moon and *Saturne*, are either threescore degrees of the *Zodiack* asunder (which distance in heaven) is named of the skilful, a Sextile aspect, it is then commended to labour the earth, sow, and plant, marked after this manner.

But when these are 126 degrees asunder, which properly is named a Trigon, or trine aspect thus noted Δ for the more part, then is that time better commended for labouring the earth, whether it be for tilling, gardening, sowing, planting, and setting, or cutting of Vines.

When the Moon and *Saturne*, are wel a quarter of the Zodiak distant, which is 90 degrees (named of the skilful a quadrate aspect) thus commonly marked □ then is denied utterly to deal in such matters.

The moon being six signs distant from *Saturne*, so that he occupieth the like degree in *Taurus*, as *Saturne* in *Scorpio*, or the *Moon* otherwise in like degrees of *Gemini* to *Saturne* (right against) in Sagitary, this aspect together is disallowed of the expert Astronomers, and noted after this manner. 8

The Moon possessing her ful light at those times, is alike denied of the skilful; yea the Moon being near to that Section, named of most Astronomers the Dragons taile, is in like manner disallowed for sowing of fine seeds, and setting of dainty plants. Here uttering precepts general as we do now.

But the Moon approached near to that Section, named the Dragons head, the same time for doing the like is very well commended, all things before supposed to be agreeable. But to be brief, and to knit up other observations, answering to the Moons place especially, learn these ensuing.

The Moon increasing and running between the 28 degree of *Taurus*, and the 19 degree of the sign of *Gemini*, sow fine seeds, and plant dainty herbs, your earth afore prepared, and aire answerable.

But the Moon found between the 28 degree of *Gemini*, and the sixt of *Cancer*, (although the increase) yet bestow no dainty seeds in your earth prepared for the purpose.

From the sixt degree of *Cancer*, unto the 19 degree of the same sign (so that the Moon increase) both labour the earth, sow fine seeds, and plant dainty herbs, herein regarding the condition of the aire.

From the 28 degree of the sign *Leo*, unto the 11. degree of *Virgo*, your seeds and plants of value sow and set, the warme aire and Moon aiding thereto.

From the 11 degree of *Virgo*, unto the 24 degree of the same sign, commit seeds to the earth, and set up your dainty plants, so that the wind bloweth not from the North, nor the aire cold.

From the seventh degree of *Libra* unto the nineteenth degree of the same sign (the Moon answering thereto) sow and plant.

From the sixt of *Capricornus*, unto the nineteenth degree of the same sign (both the Moon and the aire aiding thereto) sow your fine seeds and dainty plants set.

From the four and twentieth degree of *Pisces*, unto the seventh degree of *Aries*, the Moon increasing of light, and aire calme, bestow your seeds and plants in the well dressed earth, prepared for the only purpose.

These precepts of the prudent experimenters, wel born away of every careful Gardener, the seeds and plants no doubt, shall prosper and increase the better.

Thomas Hill, *The Gardener's Labyrinth*

The Garden of Adonis

In that same Gardin all the goodly flowres,
Wherewith dame Nature doth her beautify,
And decks the girlonds of her Paramoures,
And fetcht: there is the first seminary
Of all things that are borne to live and dye,
According to their kynds. Long worke it were
Here to account the endlesse progeny
Of all the weeds that bud and blossome there;
But so much as doth need must needs be counted here.

It sited was in fruitfull soyle of old,
And girt in with two walls on either side;
The one of yron, the other of bright gold,
That none might thorough breake, nor over-stride:
And double gates it had which opened wide,
By which in and out men moten pas:
Th' one faire and fresh, the other old and dride
Old Genius the porter of them was,
Old Genius, the which a double nature has.

He letteth in, he letteth out to wend
All that to come into the world desire:
A thousand thousand naked babes attend
About him day and night, which doe require

That he with fleshly weeds would them attire:
Such as him list, such as eternall fate
Ordained hath, he clothes with sinful mire,
And sendeth forth to live in mortall state,
Till they again returne backe by the hinder gate

After that they againe returned beene,
They in that Gardin planted bee agayne,
And grow afresh, as they had never seene
Fleshly corruption, nor mortall payne.
Some thousand yeares so doen they there remayne,
And then of him are clad with other hew,
Or sent into the chaungefull world agayne,
Till thither they retourne were first they grew:
So, like a wheele, arownd they ronne from old to new.

Ne needs there Gardiner to sett or sow,
To plant or prune; for of their owne accord
All things, as they created were, doe grow,
And yet remember well the mighty word
Which first was spoken by th' Almighty Lord,
That bad them to increase and multiply:
Ne doe they need with water of the ford,
Or of the clouds, to moisten their roots dry;
For in themselves eternall moisture they imply.

Infinite shapes of creatures there are bred,
And uncouth formes, which none yet ever knew:
And every sort is in a sundry bed
Sett by it selfe, and ranckt in comely rew;
Some fitt for reasonable sowles t'indew;
Some made for beasts, some made for birds to weare;
And all the fruitfull spawne of fishes hew
In endlesse rancks along enraunged were,
That seemed the Ocean could not containe them there.

Daily they grow, and daily forth are sent
Into the world, it to replenish more;

Yet is the stocke not lessened nor spent,
But still remaines in everlasting store,
As it at first created was of yore:
For in the wide wombe of the world there lyes,
In hatefull darknes and in deepe horrore,
An huge eternall Chaos, which supplyes
The substaunces of natures fruitfull progenyes.

All things from thence doe their first being fetch,
And borrow matter whereof they are made;
Which, whenas forme and feature it does ketch,
Becomes a body, and doth then invade
The state of life out of the grisly shade.
That substaunce is eterne, and bideth so;
Ne when the life decayes and forme does fade,
Doth it consume and into nothing goe,
But changed is, and often altred to and froe.

The substaunce is not chaungd not altered,
But th' only forme and outward fashion;
For every substaunce is conditioned
To change her hew, and sundry formes to don,
Meet for her temper and complexion:
For formes are variable, and decay
By course of kinde and by occasion;
And that faire flowre of beautie fades away,
As doth the lilly fresh before the sunny ray.

Great enemy to it, and to all the rest
That in the Gardin of Adonis springs,
Is wicked Tyme; who with his scyth addrest
Does mow the flowring herbes and goodly things,
And all their glory to the ground downe flings,
Where they do wither, and are fowly mard:
He flyes about, and with his flaggy winges
Beates downe both leaves and buds without regard,
Ne ever pitty may relent his malice hard.

Edmund Spenser, The Faerie Queen

This Garden is a Kingdom

GARDENER [*To first man*]
 Go, bind thou up young dangling apricots
 Which, like unruly children, make their sire
 Stoop with oppression of their prodigal weight.
 Give some supportance to the bending twigs.
 [*To second man*] Go thou, and, like an executioner,
 Cut off the heads of too fast-growing sprays
 That look too lofty in our commonwealth.
 All must be even in our government.
 You thus employed, I will go root away
 The noisome weeds which without profit suck
 The soil's fertility from wholesome flowers.

[FIRST] MAN
 Why should we, in the compass of a pale,
 Keep law and form and due proportion,
 Showing as in a model our firm estate,
 When our sea-wallèd garden, the whole land,
 Is full of weeds, her fairest flowers choked up,
 Her fruit trees all unpruned, her hedges ruined,
 Her knots disordered, and her wholesome herbs
 Swarming with caterpillars?

GARDENER
 Hold thy peace.
 He that hath suffered this disordered spring
 Hath now himself met with the fall of leaf.
 The weeds which his broad spreading leaves did shelter,
 That seemed in eating him to hold him up,
 Are plucked up, root and all, by Bolingbroke –
 I mean the Earl of Wiltshire, Bushy, Green.

[SECOND] MAN
 What, are they dead?

GARDENER

    They are; Bolingbroke
Hath seized the wasteful King. O, what pity is it
That he had not so trimmed and dressed his land
As we this garden! We at time of year
Do wound the bark, the skin of our fruit trees,
Lest, being over-proud in sap and blood,
With too much riches it confound itself.
Had he done so to great and growing men,
They might have lived to bear, and he to taste,
Their fruits of duty. Superfluous branches
We lop away, that bearing boughs may live.
Had he done so, himself had borne the crown,
Which waste of idle hours hath quite thrown down.

[FIRST] MAN

    What, think you then the King shall be deposed?

GARDENER

    Depressed he is already, and desposed
'Tis doubt he will be. Letters came last night
To a dear friend of the good Duke of York's
That tell black tidings.

QUEEN

    O, I am pressed to death for want of speaking!
      She comes forward
Thou, old Adam's likeness, set to dress this garden,
How dares thy harsh rude tongue sound this unpleasing news?
What Eve, what serpent hath suggested thee
To make a second fall of cursed man?
Why dost thou say King Richard is deposed?
Dar'st thou, thou little better thing than earth,
Divine his downfall? Say where, when, and how
Cam'st thou by this ill-tidings? Speak, thou wretch!

GARDENER

>Pardon me, madam. Little joy have I
>To breathe this news, yet what I say is true.
>King Richard he is in the mighty hold
>Of Bolingbroke. Their fortunes both are weighed.
>In your lord's scale is nothing but himself
>And some few vanities that make him light.
>But in the balance of great Bolingbroke,
>Besides himself, are all the English peers,
>And with that odds he weighs King Richard down.
>Post you to London and you will find it so.
>I speak no more than everyone doth know.

QUEEN

>Nimble mischance that art so light of foot,
>Doth not thy embassage belong to me,
>And am I last that knows it? O, thou think'st
>To serve me last, that I may longest keep
>Thy sorrow in my breast. Come, ladies, go
>To meet at London London's king in woe.
>What, was I born to this, that my sad look
>Should grace the triumph of great Bolingbroke?
>Gard'ner, for telling me these news of woe,
>Pray God the plants thou graft'st may never grow.
>*Exit with her Ladies*

GARDENER

>Poor Queen, so that thy state might be no worse
>I would my skill were subject to thy curse.
>Here did she fall a tear. Here in this place
>I'll set a bank of rue, sour herb-of-grace.
>Rue even for ruth here shortly shall be seen
>In the remembrance of a weeping queen.

>>William Shakespeare, *The Tragedy of King Richard the Second*

There is a Garden in Her Face

There is a garden in her face,
Where roses and white lilies grow;
A heav'nly paradise is that place,
Wherein all pleasant fruits do flow.
There cherries grow which none may buy
Till 'cherry-ripe' themselves do cry.

Those cherries fairly do enclose
Of orient pearls a double row,
Which when her lovely laughter shows,
They look like rosebuds filled with snow.
Yet them nor peer nor prince can buy,
Till 'cherry-ripe' themselves do cry.

Her eyes like angels watch them still;
Her brows like bended bows do stand,
Threat'ning with piercing frowns to kill
All that attempt with eye or hand
Those sacred cherries to come nigh,
Till 'cherry-ripe' themselves do cry.

Thomas Campion

Twicknam Garden

Blasted with sighs, and surrounded with tears,
Hither I come to seek the spring,
And at mine eyes, and at mine ears,
Receive such balms, as else cure everything;
But O, self traitor, I do bring
The spider love, which transubstantiates all,
And can convert manna to gall,
And that this place may thoroughly be thought
True paradise, I have the serpent brought.

'Twere wholesomer for me, that winter did
Benight the glory of this place,
And that a grave frost did forbid
These trees to laugh, and mock me to my face;
But that I may not this disgrace
Endure, not yet leave loving, Love, let me
Some senseless piece of this place be;
Make me a mandrake, so I may groan here,
Or a stone fountain weeping out my year.

Hither with crystal vials, lovers come,
And take my tears, which are love's wine,
And try your mistress' tears at home,
For all are false, that taste not just like mine;
Alas, hearts do not in eyes shine,
Nor can you more judge woman's thoughts by tears,
Than by her shadow, what she wears.
O perverse sex, where none is true but she,
Who's therefore true, because her truth kills me.

John Donne

Of the Gardener, and his Wages

Whosoever desireth and endeavoureth to have a Pleasant and Profitable *Orchard*, must (if he be able) provide himself of a Fruiterer, Religious, Honest, Skilful in that Faculty, and therewithal Painful. By Religious, I mean (because many think Religion but a Fashion or Custom to go to Church) maintaining, and cherishing things Religious: as Schools of Learning, Churches, Tythes, Church Goods and Rights, and above all things, God's Word, and the Preachers thereof, so much as he is able, practising Prayers, comfortable Conferences, mutual Instruction to edifie, Alms, and other works of Charity, and all out of a good Conscience.

Honesty in a Gardener, will grace your Garden, and all your house, and help to stay unbridled Serving-men, giving offence to none, nor calling your Name into Question by dishonest acts, nor infecting your Family by evil counsel or example. For there is no Plague so infectious as

Popery and Knavery; he will not purloin your profit, nor hinder your pleasures.

Concerning his Skill, he must not be a Sciolist, to make a shew or take in hand that which he cannot perform, especially in so weighty a thing as an *Orchard*: than the which there can be no humane thing more excellent, either for the pleasure or profit, as shall (God willing) be proved in the Treatise following. And what an hindrance shall it be, not only to the Owner, but to the common good, that the unspeakable benefit of many hundred years shall be lost by the audacious attempt of an unskilful Arborist?

The *Gardener* had not need be an idle or lazy Lubber, forso your *Orchard*, being a matter of such moment, will not prosper, there will ever be something to do. Weeds are always growing, the great Mother of all living Creatures, the Earth, is full of feed in her Bowels, and any stirring gives them heat of the Sun, and being laid near day, they grow: Moles work daily, though not always alike: Winter Herbs at all times will grow (except in extream Frost). In Winter your Trees and Herbs would be lightned of Snow, and your Allies cleansed: drifts of Snow will set Deer, Hares and Conies, and other noisome Beasts, over your Walls and Hedges in your *Orchard*. When Summer cloath your Borders with Green and speckled colours, your *Gardener* must dress his Hedges, and antick works; watch his Bees, and hive them: distill his Roses and other Herbs. Now begin Summer fruits to ripen, and crave your hand to pull them. If he have a Garden (as he must needs) to keep, you must needs allow him good help, to end his labours which are endless; for no one man is sufficient for these things.

Such a *Gardener* as will conscionably, quietly and patiently travel in your *Orchard*, God shall Crown the labours of his hands with joyfulness, and make the Clouds drop fatness upon your Trees; he will provoke your love, and earn his wages and fees belonging to his place. The house being served, fallen fruit, superfluity of Herbs and Flowers, Seed, Graffs, Sets, and besides all other of that Fruit which your bountiful hand shall reward him withal, will much augment his wages, and the profit of your Bees will pay you back again.

If you be not able, nor willing to hire a *Gardener*, keep your profits to your self, but then you must take all the pains; and for that purpose (if you want this faculty) to instruct you, have I undertaken these Labours, and gathered these Rules, but chiefly respecting my Countries good.

William Lawson, *A New Orchard and Garden*

Of Gardens

God Almighty first planted a garden. And indeed it is the purest of human pleasures. It is the greatest refreshment to the spirits of man; without which, buildings and palaces are but gross handiworks; and a man shall ever see, that when ages grow to civility and elegancy, men come to build stately sooner than to garden finely; as if gardening were the greater perfection. I do hold it, in the royal ordering of gardens, there ought to be gardens, for all the months in the year; in which severally things of beauty may be then in season. For December, and January, and the latter part of November, you must take such things as are green all winter: holly; ivy; bays; juniper; cypress-trees; yew; pine-apple-trees; fir-trees; rosemary; lavender; periwinkle; the white, the purple, and the blue; germander; flags; orange-trees; lemon-trees; and myrtles, if they be stoved; and sweet marjoram, warm set. There followeth, for the latter part of January and February, the mezereon-tree, which then blossoms; crocus vernus, both the yellow and the grey; primroses, anemones; the early tulippa; hyacinthus orientalis; chamairis; fritellaria. For March, there come violets, specially the single blue, which are the earliest; the yellow daffodil; the daisy; the almond-tree in blossom; the peach-tree in blossom; the cornelian-tree in blossom; sweet-briar. In April follow the double white violet; the wallflower; the stock-gilliflower; the cowslip; flowerdelices, and lilies of all natures; rosemary-flowers; the tulippa; the double peony; the pale daffodil; the French honeysuckle; the cherry-tree in blossom; the damson and plum-trees in blossom; the white thorn in leaf; the lilac-tree. In May and June come pinks of all sorts, specially the blushpink; roses of all kinds, except the musk, which comes later; honeysuckles; strawberries; bugloss; columbine; the French marigold, flos Africanus; cherry-tree in fruit; ribes; figs in fruit; rasps; vineflowers; lavender in flowers; the sweet satyrian, with the white flower; herba muscaria; lilium convallium; the apple-tree in blossom. In July come gilliflowers of all varieties; musk-roses; the lime-tree in blossom; early pears and plums in fruit; jennetings, codlins. In August come plums of all sorts in fruit; pears; apricocks; berberries; filberds; musk-melons; monks-hoods, of all colours. In September come grapes; apples; poppies of all colours; peaches; melocotones; nectarines; cornelians; wardens; quinces. In October and the beginning of November come services; medlars; bullaces; roses cut or removed to come late; hollyhocks; and such like. These particulars are for the climate of London; but my meaning is perceived, that you may have ver perpetuum, as the place affords.

And because the breath of flowers is far sweeter in the air (where it comes and goes like the warbling of music) than in the hand, therefore nothing is more fit for that delight, than to know what be the flowers and plants that do best perfume the air. Roses, damask and red, are fast flowers of their smells; so that you may walk by a whole row of them, and find nothing of their sweetness; yea though it be in a morning's dew. Bays likewise yield no smell as they grow. Rosemary little; nor sweet marjoram. That which above all others yields the sweetest smell in the air is the violet, specially the white double violet, which comes twice year; about the middle of April, and about Bartholomew-tide. Next to that is the musk-rose. Then the strawberry-leaves dying, which yield a most excellent cordial smell. Then the flower of vines; it is a little dust, like the dust of a bent, which grows upon the cluster in the first coming forth. Then sweet-briar. Then wall-flowers, which are very delightful to be set under a parlour or lower chamber window. Then pinks and gilliflowers, especially the matted pink and clove gillyflower. Then the flowers of the lime-tree. Then the honeysuckles, so they be somewhat afar off. Of beanflowers I speak not, because they are field flowers. But those which perfume the air most delightfully, not passed by as the rest, but being trodden upon and crushed, are three; that is, burnet, wild thyme, and watermint. Therefore you are to set whole alleys of them, to have the pleasure when you walk or tread.

For gardens (speaking of those which are indeed princelike, as we have done of buildings), the contents ought not well to be under thirty acres of ground; and to be divided into three parts; a green in the entrance; a heath or desert in the going forth; and the main garden in the midst; besides alleys on both sides. And I like well that four acres of ground be assigned to the green. The green hath two pleasures: the one, because nothing is more pleasant to the eye than grass kept finely shorn; the other, because it will give you a fair alley in the midst, by which you may go in front upon a stately hedge, which is to enclose the garden. But because the alley will be long, and, in great heat of the year or day, you ought not to buy the shade in the garden, by going in the sun through the green, therefore you are, of either side of the green, to plant a covert alley upon carpenter's work, about twelve foot in height, by which you may go in shade into the garden. As for the making of knots or figures, with divers coloured earths, that they may lie under the windows of the house on that side which the garden stands, they be but toys; you may see as good sights, many times, in tarts. The garden is best to be square, encompassed on all the four sides with a stately arched hedge. The arches to be upon pillars of carpenter's work, of some ten foot high, and six foot broad; and the spaces between of the same dimension with the breadth of the arch. Over the arches let there be an entire hedge of some four foot high, framed also upon carpenter's work; and upon the upper hedge, over every arch, a little turret, with a belly, enough to receive a cage of birds: and over every space between the arches some other little figure, with broad plates of round coloured glass gilt, for the sun to play upon. But this hedge I intend to be raised upon a bank, not steep, but gently slope, of some six foot, set all with flowers. Also I understand, that this square of garden, should not be the whole breadth of the ground, but to leave on either side, ground enough for diversity of side alleys; unto which the two covert alleys of the green, may deliver you. But there must be no alleys with hedges, at either end of this great enclosure; not at the hither end, for letting your prospect upon this fair hedge from the green; nor at the further end, for letting your prospect from the hedge, through the arches upon the heath.

For the ordering of ground, within the great hedge, I leave it to a variety of device; advising nevertheless, that whatsoever form you cast it into, first, it be not too busy, or full of work. Wherein I, for my part, do not like images cut out in juniper or other garden stuff; they be for children. Little low hedges, round, like welts, with some pretty pyramids, I like well; and in some places, fair columns upon frames of carpenter's work. I would also have the alleys, spacious and fair. You may have closer alleys, upon the side grounds, but none in the main garden. I wish also, in the very middle, a fair mount, with three ascents, and alleys, enough for four to walk abreast; which I would have to be perfect circles, without any bulwarks or embossments; and the whole mount to be thirty foot high; and some fine banqueting-house, with some chimneys neatly cast, and without too much glass.

For fountains, they are a great beauty and refreshment; but pools mar all, and make the garden unwholesome, and full of flies and frogs. Fountains I intend to be of two natures: the one that sprinkleth or spouteth water; the other a fair receipt of water, of some thirty or forty foot square, but without fish, or slime, or mud. For the first, the ornaments of images gilt, or of marble, which are in use, do well: but the main matter is so to convey the water, as it never stay, either in the bowls or in the cistern; that the water be never by rest discoloured, green or red or the like; or gather any mossiness or putrefaction. Beside that, it is to be cleansed every day by the hand. Also some steps up to it, and some fine pavement about it, doth well. As for the other kind of fountain, which we may call a bathing pool, it may admit much curiosity and beauty; wherewith we will not trouble ourselves: as, that the bottom be finely paved, and with images; the sides likewise; and withal embellished with coloured glass, and such things of lustre; encompassed also with fine rails of low statuas. But the main point is the same which we mentioned in the former kind of fountain; which is, that the water be in perpetual motion, fed by a water higher than the pool, and delivered into it by fair spouts, and then discharged away under ground, by some equality of bores, that it stay little. And for fine devices, of arching water without spilling, and making it rise in several forms (of feathers, drinking glasses, canopies, and the like), they be pretty things to look on, but nothing to offer health and sweetness.

For the heath, which was the third part of our plot, I wish it to be framed, as much as may be, to a natural wildness. Trees I would have none in it, but some thickets made only of sweet-briar and honeysuckle, and some wild vine amongst; and the ground set with violets, strawberries, and primroses. For these are sweet, and prosper in the shade. And these to be in the heath, here and there, not in any order. I like also little heaps, in the nature of molehills (such as are in wild heaths), to be set, some with wild thyme; some with pinks; some with germander, that gives a good flower to the eye; some with periwinkle; some with violets; some with strawberries; some with cowslips; some with daisies; some with red roses; some with lilium convallium; some with sweet-williams red; some with bear's-foot: and the like low flowers, being withal sweet and sightly. Part of which heaps, are to be with standards of little bushes pricked upon their top, and part without. The standards to be roses; juniper; holly; berberries (but here and there, because of the smell of their blossoms); red currants; gooseberries; rosemary; bays; sweetbriar; and such like. But these standards to be kept with cutting, that they grow not out of course.

For the side grounds, you are to fill them with variety of alleys, private, to give a full shade, some of them, wheresoever the sun be. You are to frame some of them, likewise, for shelter, that when the wind blows sharp you may walk as in a gallery. And those alleys must be likewise hedged at both ends, to keep out the wind; and these closer alleys must be ever finely gravelled, and no grass, because of going wet. In many of these alleys, likewise, you are to set fruit-trees of all sorts; as well upon the walls, as in ranges. And this would be generally observed, that the borders wherein you plant your fruit-trees, be fair and large, and low, and not steep; and set with fine flowers, but thin and sparingly, lest they deceive the trees. At the end of both side grounds, I would have a mount of some pretty height, leaving the wall of the enclosure breast high, to look abroad into the fields.

For the main garden, I do not deny, but there should be some fair alleys ranged on both sides, with fruit-trees; and some pretty tufts of fruit-trees, and arbours with seats, set in some decent order; but these to be by no means set too thick; but to leave the main garden so as be not close, but the air open and free. For as for shade, I would have you rest upon the alleys of the side grounds, there to walk, if you be disposed, in the heat of the year or day; but to make account, that the main garden is for the more temperate parts of the year; and in the heat of summer, for the morning and the evening, or overcast days.

For aviaries, I like them not, except they be of that largeness as they may be turfed, and have living plants and bushes set in them; that the birds may have more scope, and natural nesting, and that no foulness appear in the floor of the aviary. So I have made a platform of a princely garden, partly by precept, partly by drawing, not a model, but some general lines of it; and in this I have spared no cost. But it is nothing for great princes, that for the most part taking advice with workmen, with no less cost set their things together; and sometimes add statuas and such things for state and magnificence, but nothing to the true pleasure of a garden.

Francis Bacon, *Essays*

The Ordering of the Garden of Pleasure

Although many men must be content with any plat of ground, of what forme or quantity forever it bee, more or lesse, for their Garden, because a more large or convenient cannot bee had to their habitation: Yet I persuade my selfe, that Gentlemen of the better sort and quality, will provide such a parcel of ground to bee laid out for their Garden, and in such convenient a manner, as may be fit and answerable to the degree they hold. To prescribe one forme for every man to follow, were too great a presumption and folly: for every man will please his owne fancie, according to the extent he designeth out for that purpose, be it orbicular or round, triangular or three square, quadrangular or foure square, or more long than broad. I will only show you here the severall formes that many men have taken and delighted in, let every man choose which him liketh best, or may most fitly agree to that proportion of ground hee hath set out for that purpose. The orbicular or round forme is held in it owne proper existence to be the most absolute form, containing within its all other formes whatsoever; but few I thinke will choose such a proportion to be joined to their habitation, being not accepted any where I think, but for the generall Garden to the University of Padua. The triangular or three square is such a forme also, as is seldom chosen by any that may make another choice, and as I thinke is only had where another forme cannot be had, necessitie constraining them to be therewith content. The foure square forme is the most usually accepted by all, and doth best agree to any mans dwelling, being (as I said before) behinde the house, all the backe windowes thereof opening into it. Yet if it bee longer than the breadth, or broader than the length, the proportion of walkes, squares, and knots may be soon brought to the square forme, and be so cast, as the beauty thereof may bee no lesse than the foure square proportion, or any better forme, if any be. To forme it therfore with walks, crosse the middle both waies, and round about it also with hedges, with squares, knots and trayles, or any worke within the four square parts, is according as every mans conceit alloweth of it, and they will be at the charge: For there may be therein walkes eyther open or close, eyther publicke or private, a maze or wildernesse, a rocke or mount, with a fountaine in the midst thereof to convey water to every part of the Garden, eyther in pipes under the ground, or brought by hand, and emptied into large Cisternes or great Turkey Jarres, placed in convenient places to serve as an ease to water the nearest parts thereunto. Arbours also being both gracefull and necessary, may be appointed in such convenient places, as the corners, or elsewhere, as may be most fit, to serve both for shadow and rest after walking. And because many are desirous to see the formes of trayles, knots, and other compartiments, and because the open knots are more proper for these Out-landish flowers; I have here caused some to be drawne, to satisfie their desires, not intending to cumber this worke with over mannie, in that it would be almost endlesse, to expresse so many as might bee conceived and set downe, for that every man may invent others farre differing from these, or any other can be set forth. Let every man therefore, if hee like of these, take what may please his mind, or out of these or his own conceit, frame any other to his fancy, or cause others to be done as he liketh best, observing this *decorum*, that according to his ground he do cast out his knots, with convenient roome for allies and walks; for the fairer and larger your allies and walkes be, the more grace your Garden shall have, the lesse harme the herbes and flowers shall receive, by passing by them that grow next unto the allies sides, and the better shall your Weeders cleanse both the beds and the allies.

John Parkinson, *Paradisi In Sole*

The Flower

How fresh, O Lord, how sweet and clean
Are thy returns! ev'n as the flowers in spring;
To which, besides their own demean,
The late-past frosts tributes of pleasure bring.
Grief melts away
Like snow in May,
As if there were no such cold thing.

Who would have thought my shrivel'd heart
Could have recover'd greennesse? It was gone
Quite under ground; as flowers depart
To see their mother-root, when they have blown;
Where they together
All the hard weather,
Dead to the world, keep house unknown.

These are thy wonders, Lord of power,
Killing and quickening, bringing down to hell
And up to heaven in an houre;
Making a chiming of a passing bell.
We say amisse,
This or that is:
Thy word is all, if we could spell.

O that I once past changing were,
Fast in thy Paradise, where no flower can wither!
Many a spring I shoot up fair,
Offring at heav'n, growing and groning thither:
Nor doth my flower
Want a spring-showre,
My sinnes and I joining together.

But while I grow in a straight line,
Still upwards bent, as if heav'n were mine own,
Thy anger comes, and I decline:

What frost to that? what pole is not the zone,
Where all things burn,
When thou dost turn,
And the least frown of thine is shown?

And now in age I bud again,
After so many deaths I live and write;
I once more smell the dew and rain,
And relish versing: O my onely light,
It cannot be
That I am he
On whom thy tempests fell all night.

These are thy wonders, Lord of love,
To make us see we are but flowers that glide:
Which when we once can finde and prove,
Thou hast a garden for us, where to bide.
Who would be more,
Swelling through store,
Forfeit their Paradise by their pride.

George Herbert, *The Temple*

The Garden

How vainly men themselves amaze
To win the Palm, the Oke, or Bayes;
And their uncessant Labours see
Crown'd from some single Herb or Tree.
Whose short and narrow verged Shade
Does prudently their Toyles upbraid;
While all Flow'rs and all Trees do close
To weave the Garlands of repose.

Fair quiet have I found thee here,
And Innocence thy Sister dear!
Mistaken long, I sought you then
In busie Companies of Men.

Your sacred Plants, if here below,
Only among the Plants will grow
Society is all but rude,
To this delicious Solitude.

No white nor red was ever seen
So am'rous as this lovely green.
Fond Lovers, cruel as their Flame,
Cut in these Trees their Mistress name.
Little, Alas, they know, or heed,
How far these Beauties Hers exceed!
Fair Trees! where s'eer your barkes I wound,
No name shall but your own be found.

When we have run our Passions heat,
Love hither makes his best retreat.
The *Gods*, that mortal Beauty chase,
Still in a Tree did end their race.
Apollo hunted *Daphne* so,
Only that She might Laurel grow.
And *Pan* did after *Syrinx* speed,
Not as a Nymph, but for a Reed.

What wond'rous Life in this I lead!
Ripe Apples drop about my head;
The Luscious Clusters of the Vine
Upon my Mouth do crush their Wine;
The Nectaren, and curious Peach,
Into my hands themselves do reach;
Stumbling on Melons, as I pass,
Insnar'd with Flow'rs, I fall on Grass.

Mean while the Mind, from pleasure less,
Withdraws into its happiness:
The Mind, that Ocean where each kind
Does straight its own resemblance find;
Yet it creates, transcending these,
Far other Worlds, and other Seas;

Annihilating all that's made
To a green Thought in a green Shade.

Here at the Fountains sliding foot,
Or at some Fruit-trees mossy root,
Casting the Bodies Vest aside,
My Soul into the boughs does glide:
There like a Bird it sits, and sings,
Then whets, and combs its silver Wings;
And, till prepar'd for longer flight,
Waves in its Plumes the various Light.

Such was that happy Garden-state,
While Man there walk'd without a Mate:
After a place so pure, and sweet,
What other Help could yet be meet!
But 'twas beyond a Mortal's share
To wander solitary there:
Two Paradises 'twere in one
To live in Paradise alone.

Andrew Marvell

Perturbation at Dawn

Day comes . . .

And when she sees the withering of the violet garden
And the saffron garden flowering,
The stars escaping on their black horse
And the dawn on her white horse arriving,
She is afraid.

Against the sighing of her frightened breasts
She puts her hand;
I see what I have never seen,
Five perfect lines on a crystal leaf
Written with coral pens.

Ebn Maatuk

A Contemplation upon Flowers

Brave flowers, that I could gallant it like you
And be as little vaine;
You come abroad, and make a harmeless shew,
And to your beds of earth againe;
You are not proud, you know your birth
For your Embroiderd garments are from Earth:

You doe obey your months, and times, but I
Would have it ever springe,
My fate would know noe winter, never dye
Not thinke of such a thing;
Oh that I could my bed of Earth but view
And Smile, and looke as chearefully as you:

Oh teach me to see death, and not to feare
But rather to take truce;
How often have I seene you at a Beere,
And there looke fresh and spruce;
You fragrant flowers then teach me that my breath
Like yours may sweeten, and perfume my death.

Henry King

On the Gardens of Antiquity

That Vulcan gave arrows unto Apollo and Diana the fourth day after
their nativities, according to Gentile theology, may pass for no blind
apprehension of the creation of the sun and moon, in the work of the
fourth day: when the diffused light contracted into orbs, and shooting
rays of those luminaries. Plainer descriptions there are from Pagan pens,
of the creatures of the fourth day. While the divine philosopher unhap-
pily omitteth the noblest part of the third, and Ovid (whom many conceive to have borrowed his description from Moses), coldly deserting the
remarkable account of the text, in three words describeth this work of

the third day – the vegetable creation, and first ornamental scene of nature, – the primitive food of animals, and first story of physic in dietetical conservation.

For though Physic may plead high, from that medical act of God, in casting so deep a sleep upon our first parent, and Chirurgery find its whole art, in that one passage concerning the rib of Adam; yet is there no rivality with Garden contrivance and Herbery; for if Paradise were planted the third day of the creation, as wiser divinity concludeth, the nativity thereof was too early for horoscopy: gardens were before gardeners, and but some hours after the earth.

Of deeper doubt is its topography and local designation; yet being the primitive garden, and without much controversy seated in the east, it is more than probable the first curiosity, and cultivation of plants, most flourished in those quarters. And since the ark of Noah first touched upon some mountains of Armenia, the planting art arose again in the east, and found its revolution not far from the place of its nativity, about the plains of those regions. And if Zoroaster were either Cham, Chus, or Mizraim, they were early proficients therein, who left, as Pliny delivereth, a work of Agriculture.

However, the account of the pensile or hanging gardens of Babylon, if made by Semiramis, the third or fourth from Nimrod, is of no slender antiquity; which being not framed upon ordinary level of ground, but raised upon pillars, admitting under-passages, we cannot accept as the first Babylonian gardens, – but a more eminent progress and advancement in that art than any that went before it; somewhat answering or hinting the old opinion concerning Paradise itself, with many conceptions elevated above the plan of the earth.

Nebuchodonosor (whom some will have to be the famous Syrian king Diodorus) beautifully repaired that city, and so magnificently built his hanging gardens, that from succeeding writers he had the honour of the first. From whence overlooking Babylon, and all the region about it, he found no circumscription to the eye of his ambition; till over-delighted with the bravery of this Paradise, in his melancholy metamorphosis he found the folly of that delight, and a proper punishment in the contrary habitation – in wild plantations and wanderings of the fields.

The Persian gallants, who destroyed this monarchy, maintained their botanical bravery. Unto whom we owe the name of Paradise, wherewith we meet not in Scripture before the time of Solomon, and conceived originally Persian. The word for that disputed garden expressing, in the Hebrew, no more than a field enclosed, which from the same root is content to derive a garden and a buckler.

Cyrus the Elder, brought up in woods and mountains, when time and power enabled, pursued the dictate of his education, and brought the treasures of the field into rule and circumscription. So nobly beautifying the hanging gardens of Babylon, that he was also thought to be the author thereof.

Ahasuerus (whom many conceive to have been Artaxerxes Longimanus), in the country and city of flowers, and in an open garden, entertained his princes and people, while Vashti more modestly treated the ladies within the palace thereof.

But if, as some opinion, King Ahasuerus were Artaxerxes Memnon, that found a life and reign answerable unto his great memory, our magnified Cyrus was his second brother, who gave the occasion of that memorable work, and almost miraculous retreat of Xenophon. A person of high spirit and honour, naturally a king, though fatally prevented by the harmless chance of post-geniture; not only a lord of gardens, but a manual planter thereof, disposing his trees, like his armies, in regular ordination. So that while old Laertes hath found a name in Homer for pruning hedges, and clearing away thorns and briars; while King Attalus lives for his poisonous plantations of aconites, henbane, hellebore, and plants hardly admitted within the walls of Paradise; while many of the ancients do poorly live in the single names of vegetables; all stories do look upon Cyrus as the splendid and regular planter.

According whereto Xenophon describeth his gallant plantation at Sardis, thus rendered by Strebæus. 'Arbores pari intervallo sitas, rectos ordines, et omnia perpulchrè in Quincuncem directa.' Which we shall take for granted as being accordingly rendered by the most elegant of the Latins, and by no made term, but in use before by Varro. That is, the rows and orders so handsomely disposed, or five trees so set together, that a regular angularity, and thorough prospect, was left on every side. Owing this name not only unto the quintuple number of trees, but the figure declaring that number, which being double at the angle, makes up the letter X, that is, the emphatical decussation, or fundamental figure.

Now though, in some ancient and modern practice, the area, or decussated plot might be a perfect square, answerable to a Tuscan pedestal, and the *quinquernio* or cinque point of a dye, wherein by diagonal lines the intersection was rectangular; accommodable unto plantations of large growing trees, and we must not deny ourselves the advantage of this order; yet shall we chiefly insist upon that of Curtius and Porta, in their brief description hereof. Wherein the *decussis* is made within a longilateral square, with opposite angles, acute and obtuse at the intersection, and so upon progression making a *rhombus* or lozenge figuration, which seemeth very agreeable unto the original figure. Answerable whereunto we observe the decussated characters in many consulary coins, and even in those of Constantine and his sons, which pretend their pattern in the sky; the crucigerous ensign carried this figure, not transversely or rectangularly intersected, but in a decussation, after the form of an Andrean or Burgundian cross, which answereth this description.

Of this quincunial ordination the ancients practised much, discoursed little; and the moderns have nothing enlarged; which he that more nearly considereth, in the form of its square rhombus, and decussation, with the several commodities, mysteries, parallelisms, and resemblances, both in art and nature, shall easily discern the elegancy of this order.

That this was in some ways of practice in divers and distant nations, hints or deliveries there are from no slender antiquity. In the hanging gardens of Babylon, from Abydenus, Eusebius, and others, Curtius describeth this rule of decussation. In the memorable garden of Alcinous, anciently conceived an original fancy from Paradise, mention there is of well-contrived order; for so hath Didymus and Eustachius expounded the emphatical word. Diomedes, describing the rural possessions of his father, gives account in the same language of trees orderly planted. And Ulysses being a boy, was promised by his father forty fig-trees, and fifty rows of vines producing all kinds of grapes.

Sir Thomas Browne, *The Garden of Cyrus*

22 July 1666

Lords Day. Up, and to my chamber and there till noon, mighty busy setting money-matters and others things of mighty moment to rights, to the great content of my mind, I finding that accounts but a little let go can never be put in order by strangers, for I cannot without much difficulty do it myself. After dinner to them again till about 4 a-clock, and then walked to White-hall, where saw nobody almost, but walked up and down with Hugh May, who is a very ingenious man – among other things, discoursing of the present fashion of gardens, to make them plain – that we have the best walks of Gravell in the world – France having none, nor Italy; and our green of our bowling-alleys is better than any they have. So our business here being ayre, this is the best way, only with a little mixture of Statues or pots, which may be handsome, and so filled with another pot of such or such, a flower or greene, as the season of the year will bear. And then for Flowers, they are best seen in a little plat by themselfs; besides, their borders spoil any other garden. And then for fruit, the best way is to have Walls built Circularly, one within another, to the South, on purpose for fruit, and leave the walking-garden only for that use.

Thence walked through the house, where most people mighty hush and, methinks, melancholy, I saw not a smiling face through the whole Court; and in my conscience, they are doubtful of the conduct again of the Generalls – and I pray God they may not make their fears reasonable. Sir Rd Fanshaw is lately dead at Madrid.

Guyland is lately over-throwne wholly in Barbary, by the King of Taffiletta. The Fleete cannot yet get clear of the River; but expect the first wind to be out, and then to be sure they fight.

The Queene and Maids of Honour are at Tunbridge.

Samuel Pepys, *Diary*

Paradise

Beneath him with new wonder now he views
To all delight of human sense exposed
In narrow room nature's whole wealth, yea more,
A heaven on earth, for blissful Paradise
Of God the garden was, by him in the east
Of Eden planted; Eden stretched her line
From Auran eastward to the royal towers
Of great Seleucia, built by Grecian kings,
Or where the sons of Eden long before
Dwelt in Telassar: in this pleasant soil
His far more pleasant garden God ordained;
Out of the fertile ground he caused to grow
All trees of noblest kind for sight, smell, taste;
And all amid them stood the tree of life,
High eminent, blooming ambrosial fruit
Of vegetable gold; and next to life
Our death the tree of knowledge grew fast by
Knowledge of good bought dear by knowing ill.
Southward through Eden went a river large,
Nor changed his course, but through the shaggy hill
Passed underneath ingulfed, for God had thrown
That mountain as his garden mould high raised
Upon the rapid current, which, through veins
Of porous earth with kindly thirst up drawn,
Rose a fresh fountain, and with many a rill
Watered the garden; thence united fell
Down the steep glade, and met the nether flood,
Which from his darksome passage now appears,
And divided into four main streams,
Runs diverse, wandering many a famous realm
And country whereof here needs no account,
But rather to tell how, if art could tell,
How from that sapphire fount the crisped brooks,

Rolling on orient pearl and sands of gold,
With mazy error under pendant shades
Ran nectar, visiting each plant, and fed
Flowers worthy of Paradise which not nice art
In beds and curious knots, but nature boon
Poured forth profuse on hill and dale and plain,
Both where the morning sun first warmly smote
The open field, and where the unpierced shade
Embrowned the noontide bowers: thus was this place,
A happy rural seat of various view;
Groves whose rich trees wept odorous gums and balm,
Others whose fruit burnished with golden rind
Hung amiable, Hesperian fables true,
If true, here only, and of delicious taste:
Betwixt them lawns, or level downs, and flocks
Grazing the tender herb, were interposed,
Or palmy hillock, or the flowery lap
Of some irriguous valley spread her store,
Flowers of all hue, and without thorn the rose:
Another side, umbrageous grots and caves
Of cool recess, o'er which the mantling vine
Lays forth her purple grape, and gently creeps
Luxuriant; mean while murmuring waters fall
Down the slope hills, dispersed, or in a lake,
That to the fringed bank with myrtle crowned,
Her crystal mirror holds, unite their streams.
The birds their choir apply; airs, vernal airs,
Breathing the smell of field and grove, attune
The trembling leaves, while universal Pan
Knit with the Graces and the Hours in dance
Led on the eternal spring.

John Milton, *Paradise Lost*

News from Spain

*To the Earle of Sandwich, Ambassador Extraordinary
in the Court of Spaine, at Madrid.*

My Lord,

I am plainely astonish'd at your bounty to me, and I am in paine for words to expresse the sense I have of this greate obligation.

And as I have been exceedingly affected with the Descriptions, so have I ben greately instructed in the other particulars your lordship mentions, and especialy rejoice that your Excellency has taken care to have the draughts of the Places, Fountaines, & Engines for the Irrigation & refreshing their plantations, which may be of singular use to us in England. And I question not but your Excellency brings with you a collection of Seedes; such especially as we may not have com'only in our Country. By your Lordship's description, the *Encina* should be the *Ilex major aculeate*, a sucker whereoff yet remaines in his Majesties Privie-Gardens at White Hall, next the dore that is opposite to the Tennis Court. I mention it the rather, because it certainly might be propagated with us to good purpose, for the father of this small tree I remember of a goodly stature; so as it yearely produc'd ripe Acorns; though Clusius, when he was in England, believed it to be barren: & happily, it had borne none in his tyme. I have sown both the Acorns of the tree, and the Cork with successe, though I have now but few of them remaining, through the negligence of my Gardiner; for they require care at the first raising, 'till they are accostom'd to the cold, and then no rigour impeaches them. What your Excellency meanes by the *Bama de Joseph*, I do not comprehend; but the *Planta Alois*, which is a monstrous kind of *Sedum*, will like it endure no wett in Winter, but certainly rotts if but a drop or two fall on it, whereas in Summer you cannot give it drink enough. I perceive their culture of choice & tender Plants differs little from ours in England, and as it has ben publish'd by me in my *Calendarium Hortense*, which is now the third time reprinting. Stoves absolutely destroy our Conservatories; but if they could be lin'd with cork, I believe it would better secure them from the cold & moisture of the walls, than either matrasses, or reedes with which we co'monly invest them. I thinke I was the first that ever planted Spanish Cardôns in our country for any culinerie use, as your Excellency has taught the blanching; but I know not whether they serve themselves in Spaine with the purple beards of the Thistle, when it is in flower, for the curdling of Milk, which it performs much better than Reinet, and is far sweeter in the Dairy than that liquor, which is apt to putrifie.

Your Excellency has rightly conjectur'd of the Pome-Grand: I have allways kept it expos'd, and the severest of our Winters dos it no prejudice; they will flower plentifully, but beare no fruit with us, either kept in cases & in the repository, or set in the open ayre; at least very trifling, with the greatest industry of stoves & other artifices.

We have Aspargus growing wild both in Lincolnshire & other places; but your Lordship observes, they are small & bitter, & not comparable to the cultivated.

The red Pepper, I suppose, is what we call Ginny-Peper, of which I have rais'd many plants, whose pods resemble in colour the most oriental & polish'd corall: a very little will set the throat in such a flame, as has ben sometimes deadly, and therefore to be sparingly us'd in sauces.

I hope your Lordship will furnish your selfe with Melon seedes, because they will last good almost 20 years; & so will all the sorts of Garavances, Calaburos, & Gourds (whatever Herrera affirme) which may be for divers œconomical uses.

The Spanish Onion-seede is of all the other the most excellent: and yet I am not certaine, whether that which we have out of Flanders & St. Omers, be all the Spanish seede which we know of. My Lady Clarendon (when living) was wont to furnish me with seede that produc'd me prodigious cropps.

Is it not possible for your Excellency to bring over some of those Quince and Cherry-trees, which your Lordship so celebrates? I suppose they might be secur'd in barrells or pack'd up, as they transport other rarities from far countries. But, my Ld: I detaine your Excellency too long in these repetitions, & forget that I am all this while doing injury to the publiq, by suspending you a moment from matters of a higher orb, the Interest of States, & reconciling of Kingdomes: And I should think so of another, did I not know withal, how universal your comprehensions are, & how qualified to support it. I remain, my Lord,

Your &c. Sayes-Court, 21 Aug. 1668

John Evelyn, *Letters*

Of the Manner of Ordering, and Preparing of Garden-Ground, &c.

There are many *Garden-plats* in *England*, and that either for their cold situation, or the cold or unnatural temper of the Soyl, or such like impediments, and by reason of the ignorance of the *Gardiner* or Owner thereof, it produces little or no Fruit or Tillage answerable to the costs, trouble, or expectation of the *Owners* thereof: Wherefore we shall give you here the best *Rules*, Directions, and Instructions we either know, or have read of in any of our Rustick Authors.

If the Land be of a light and warm nature of its self, whereof your Garden is made, there needs onely common *Horse-dung* or *Cow-dung* to be mixed therewith in the digging or trenching, to enrich it; But if the *Ground* or *Mould* incline to a cold clay, or stiff Ground, then procure some good, light, and fertile *Sand*, or *Mould* of that nature, and mix with your *Dung* in some corner of your *Ground* equally together, and suffer so to lye and rot over the *Winter*, which in the *Spring* will prove an excellent warm Manure to lay to the Roots of your Plants, or to make whole Beds thereof, by mixing it in good quantities with the natural *Soyl*, and if you can procure it with conveniency, the more of *Pigeons-dung*, *Poultry-dung*, or *Sheeps-dung* you mix with it, the lighter and warmer it will be: Also an equal composition or mixture of Dung and Earth is necessary to be laid by, that it may be throughly rotten and turned to *Earth* by the *Spring*, that it may then be fit to renew the earth about your *Hops*, *Artichoaks*, and such like, and also for the planting and sowing therein *Coleflowers*, *Cabbages*, *Onions*, &c.

The best and surest way of sowing *Seeds* to have the most advantage of such *Dung* or *Soyl*, and that they may come up most even, be all buried at one certain depth, is thus: First, rake your Bed even, then throw on a part of your mixture of *Earth* and *Dung*, which also rake very even and level, on which sow your *Seeds*, whether *Onions*, *Leeks*, *Lettice*, or such like, then with a wide *Sieve* sift on the *Earth* mixed with *Dung*, that it may cover the Seeds about a quarter of an inch deep, or little more, and you shall not fail of a fruitful Crop.

If your Garden be obvious to the cold windes, which are very injurious to most sorts of Plants, next unto Trees, Pales, Walls, Hedges, &c. lay your ground after this following manner, that is, Let it be laid up in Ridges a foot or two in height, somewhat upright on the *back* or *North side* thereof, and more shelving or sloping to the *South-ward*, for about three or four foot broad, on which side you may sow any of your Garden Tillage, and these banks lying one behinde the other, will much break the *Windes*, and these shelving sides will much expedite the ripening of *Pease* or other Fruits, by receiving more directly the *Beams* of the *Sun*, and in case the ground be over moist, you may plant the higher; and if over dry, then the lower, so that it seems to remedy all extreams, except heat, which rarely injures.

John Worlidge, The Mystery of Husbandry Discovered

To J. Evelyn, Esq.

I never had any other desire so strong, and so like to covetousness, as that one which I have had always, that I might be master at last of a small house and large garden, with very moderate conveniences joined to them, and there dedicate the remainder of my life only to the culture of them and study of nature,

And there (with no design beyond my wall) whole and entire to lie,

In no unactive ease, and no unglorious poverty.

Or, as Virgil has said, shorter and better for me, that I might there

Studiis florere ignobilis otî:

(though I could wish that he had rather said, 'nobilis otii', when he spoke of his own). But several accidents of my ill fortune have disappointed me hitherto, and do still, of that felicity; for though I have made the first and hardest step to it, by abandoning all ambitions and hopes in this world, and by retiring from the noise of all business and almost company, yet I stick still in the inn of a hired house and garden, among weeds and rubbish; and without that pleasantest work of human industry, the improvement of something which we call (not very properly, but yet we call) our own. I am gone out from Sodom, but I am not yet arrived at my little Zoar. *O let me escape thither (is it not a little one?) and my soul shall live.* I do not look back yet; but I have been forced to stop, and make too many halts. You may wonder, sir (for this seems a little too extravagant and pindarical for prose), what I mean by all this preface; it is to let you know, that though I have missed, like a chemist, my great end, yet I account my affections and endeavours well rewarded by something that I have met with by the bye; which is, that they have procured to me some part in your kindness and esteem; and thereby the honour of having my name so advantageously recommended to posterity, by the epistle you are pleased to prefix to the most useful book that has been written in that kind, and which is to last as long as months and years.

Among many other arts and excellencies, which you enjoy, I am glad to find this favourite of mine the most predominant; that you choose this for your wife, though you have hundreds of other arts for your concubines; though you know them, and beget sons upon them all (to which you are rich enough to allow great legacies), yet the issue of this seems to be designed by you to the main of the estate; you have taken most pleasure in it, and bestowed most charges upon its education: and I doubt not to see that book, which you are pleased to promise to the world, and of which you have given us a large earnest in your calendar, as accomplished, as any thing can be expected from an extraordinary wit, and no ordinary expenses, and a long experience. I know nobody that possesses more private happiness than you do in your garden; and yet no man, who makes his happiness more public, by a free communication of the art and knowledge of it to others. All that I myself am able yet to do, is only to recommend to mankind the search of that felicity, which you instruct them how to find and to enjoy.

Abraham Cowley, Preface to The Garden

Four Haiku

From the heart
of the sweet peony,
a drunken bee.

How I long to see
among dawn flowers,
the face of God.

Insect song – over
winter's garden
moon's hair-thin.

Come, see real
flowers
of this painful world.

Basho

The Gard'ners Kalender

November

Contrive or forecast where, and what you are to sow and plant. Trench and fallow all your vacant grounds. Prepare and mix soils and composts thoroughly; miss not high-way earth, cleanings of streets; make compositions of manures, soils, and lyme.

Lay bair roots of trees that need, and manure such as require it. Plant all fruit-trees, and shrubs that lose the leaf, also prune such. Plant cabbage, sow hasties for early peas in warme grounds, but trust not to them.

Gather the seeds of holly, yew, ash &c., ordering them. Furnish your nurseries with stocks.

Shelter tender evergreen seedlings. House your cabbage, carrots, turneeps: and at any time ere hard frosts house your skirrets, potatoes, parsneeps, &c. Cover asparagus, artichocks, as in the last moneth. Sow bairs-ears, plant tulips, &c. Shut the conservatory. Preserve your choicest flowers. Sweep and cleanse the walks of leaves, &c. Stop your bees close so that you leave breathing vents.

Garden Dishes and Drinks in season are
cabbage, coleflower, onions, leeks, shallot, &c. Blanched sellery, succory, pickled asparagus, purslain, &c. French Parsneeps, skirrets, potatoes, carrots, turneeps, beet-rave, scorzonera, parsley and fennel roots, aples, pears, &c.

Cyder, perry, wine of cherries, rasps, currans, goosberries, liquorish, hony, &c.

December

Trench and prepare grounds. Gather together composts; plant trees in nurseries, and sow their seeds that endure it.

Gather firr seed, holly berries, &c. Take up liquorish. Continue your care in preserving choice carnations, anemonies, and ranunculuses from raines and frosts. And keep the green-house close against the piercing colds. Turne and refresh your fruit in a clear serene day. Sharpen and mend tools. Gather osiers and hassell rods and make baskets in stormy weather. Cover your water pipes with leitter lest the frosts do crak them; feed weak bees.

Garden Dishes and Drinks in Season

Colworts, leeks, &c., housed cabbage, onions, shallot. Several dryed sweet herbes. Housed parsneeps, turneeps, skirrets, carrots, potatoes, beet-rave, scorzonera; parsley and fennel roots. Pickled cucumbers, barberries, artichocks, asparagus, purslain, &c.

Housed aples, pears. Conserved cherries, plumes, peaches, apricocks, &c.

Wine of aples, pears, cherries, liquorish, honey, &c.

January

Prepare the grounds, soils and manures. Fell trees for mechanical uses. Prune firrs, plant hawthorn hedges, and all trees and shrubs that lose the leaf if open weather. Also prune the more hardie and old-planted. Manure the roots of trees that need. Drain excessive moisture; gather graffs ere they sprout, and near the end graff. Begin with the stone fruits. Gather holly berries, firr husks, &c. secure choice plants as yet from cold and wet, and earth up such as the frosts uncovered.

Feed weak bees, also you may remove them.

Garden Dishes and Drinks in Season

Colworts, leeks, &c. Dry sweet herbes, housed cabbage, onions, shallot, parsneeps, skirrets, potatoes, carrots, turneeps, beet-rave, scorzonera, parsley and fennel roots in broth.

Pickled artichocks, beet-raves, &c. Housed aples, pears, and other conserved fruits.

Cyder and other wines as before.

February

Plant any trees or shrubs that lose the leaf, also lay such for increase; see *June*. Likewayes sow all your seeds, kyes, kirnells, nuts, stones; also the seeds of several greens, as holly, yew, philyrea, laurels, &c. Prune firrs, &c.

Continue to destroy vermine.

Graffing is now in season, see the last moneth.

Prune all trees and shrubs except tender greens. Nail and dress them at the wall. Cover the roots of trees layed bair the fore-end of winter, if any be. Plant hawthorn hedges, willows, &c.

Plant liquorish, potatoes, peas, beans, cabbage, sow parsley, beets, spinage, marigold, and other hardie pot-herbes.

Let carnations and such be sheltered flowers get air in mild weather. But keep close the green-house.

Now you may remove bees and feed weak stocks.

Garden Dishes, &c.

Cole, leiks, sweet herbes, onions, shallot, housed cabbage, skirrets, turneeps, parsneeps, potatoes, beet-rave, scorzonera, carrots, besides parsley and fennel roots.

Pickled beet-rave, artichock, cucumber; housed aples, pears, and other conserved fruits with cyder and other wines and drinks, as above.

March

Re-delve, mix, and rake your ground for immediate use. Delve about the roots of all your trees. Yet plant trees and rather greens. Also prune such except resinous. Propagate by laying, circumposition, and especially by cuttings. Sow the seeds of most trees and hardie greens. Cover those trees whose roots lay bair and delve down the manures that lay about your young trees all winter, covering on leitter again topt with earth to prevent drought in summer: this is a material observation and more especially for such as are late planted. Slit the bark of ill-thriving trees. Fell such as grow croked in the nurserie. Graffing is yet in season (but too late for stone fruit), cut off the heads of them inoculated.

Set peas, beans, cabbage, asparagus, liquorish. Sow parsley, beets, endive, succory, bugloss, burrage, sellery, fennel, marigold. Plant shallot, garleeks, potatoes, skirrets. Sow onions, lettice, cresses, parsneep, beet-rave, radish, &c. And on the hot-bed coleflower, and if you please, cucumber, &c.

Slip and set physick herbes, July-flowers, and other fibrous-rooted flowers. Be careful of the tender plants; the piercing colds are now on foot. Turn your fruit in the room but open not yet the windows.

Catch moles, mice, snails, worms, destroy frogs' spawn, &c.

Half open passages for bees, they begin to flit; keep them close night and morning: yet you may remove them.

Garden Dishes, &c.

Both green and housed herbes and roots: also pickled, housed, and conserved fruits, with their wines as in the former months.

APRILE

Plant holly hedges and hawthorn too, if not too foreward. Ply and sheer hedges. Nail and prune wall-trees, &c. Sow and plant firrs, and other greens. Slip and set sage, rosemary, thym, rue, savory, and all fibrous rooted herbes and flowers. Uncover and dress strawberries. Plant artichocks, slip them and delve their plottes. Set cabbages, beans, peas, kidnees. Sow asparagus, parsley, beets, and beet-card. Set garleeks, shallot, potatoes, skirrets, sorral. Sow onions, leeks, lettice, cresses, radish, orach, scorzonera, carvy, fennel, &c. And on the hot-bed, cucumbers, coleflowers, purslain, sweet marjorum, basill, summer savory, tobaco, &c.

Set strawberries, violets, July-flowers, &c. Also sow the seeds of July-flowers, &c. Sow all your annuall flowers and rare plants, some requiring the hot-bed. Lay, beat, and roll gravel and grass. Fall to your mowing and weeding.

Destroy moles, mice, worms, and snails.

Open the doors off your bee-hives, now they hatch.

Garden Dishes, &c.

Onions, leeks, colworts, beets, parsley, and other herbes: spinage, sorral, scorzonera; green asparagus, lettice, and other sallads. Pickled artichocks, beet-rave, barberries, cucumbers.

Housed aples and pears, conserved cherries, plumes, peaches, apricocks, goosberries, currans. Also wines of aples, pears, cherries, liquorish, hony, &c.

MAY

Pull up suckers and haw about the trees. Rub off unnecessary buds. Sheer or clip hedges. Prune tender greens (not the resinous), bring furth the housed ones refreshing and trimming them. Plant all sorts of medicinal herbes. Sow all sweet ones which are tender.

Gather snails, worms, and catch moles.

Sow lettice, cresses, purslain, turneep, radish, peas, &c. Continue weeding and watering.

Near the end watch the bees ready to swarm.

Garden Dishes and Drinks in Season

Coleworts and other herbes, (being eaten with contentement are better than a fatted ox without it), sage (with butter), leeks, parsley, thyme, marjorum, sorrall, spinage, &c. Scorzonera, asparagus, lettice, purslain, and other sallades and pot-herbes.

Pickled artichocks, barberries, beet-rave, cucumbers, housed aples and pears for many uses. Early cherries, strawberries, near the end.

Cyder, metheglin, liquorish ail, &c.

JUNE

Cleanse about the roots of trees, suckers, and weeds; water their covered bulks, especially the new planted.

Fell the long small ill-train'd forrest-trees in the nurserie, within half a foot of the ground. Unbind graffs. Prune all wall and standard trees. Towards the end you may inoculate and also increase by circumposition.

Gather elm seed and sow immediately. Transplant coleflowers, coleworts, beets, leeks, purslain, &c., in moist weather; at least water first the ground if dry.

Sow peas, radish, turneep, lettice, chervil, cresses, &c.

Destroy snails, worms, &c.

Begin to lay carnations or July-flowers; shade, support and prune such as will blow. Water the pots and thirsty-plants. Weeding and mowing is in season, and so is distillation.

Bees now swarm, look diligently to them.

Garden Dishes and Drinks in Season

Cole, beets, parsley, sorrall, and other pot-herbes. Purslain, lettice, and others sallads. Radish, scorzonera, asparagus, green peas and artichocks. Green goosberries. Ripe cherries, rasps, currans, strawberries.

Housed aples and pears.

Cyder, metheglin, &c.

JULY

Fallow ground as soon as the crop comes off. Prune and purge all standard trees. Ply, nail, prune, and dress your wall-trees. Pull up suckers and weeds. Haw and water where needful. Inoculate fruit-trees, shrubs, rare greens, and flower-trees; increase the same by laying. Clip your hedges after rain. Suffer such herbes and flowers to run to seed as you would save, cutting the rest a handful from the ground.

Sow turneep, radish, lettice, onion, cole-flower, cabbage, and cole-worts in the full moon. Near the end sow beets, spinage, &c. You may plant strawberries, violets, camomile. Lay July-flowers. Plant their seedlings. Slip and set hypaticas, bearsears, couslips, helibors, &c. Take up bulbous and tuberous ones that are dry in their stalks (if you mind to change their places) and keep till September, but some should be set immediately.

Supply voids with potted annuals. Lay grass and gravell. Make cherrie and raspberrie wine, &c.

Prevent the bees' later swarms. Kill drons, wasps, &c.

Garden Dishes and Drinks in Season

Beets and many pot-herbes and sweet herbes.

Beet-card, purslain, lettice, endive, &c.

Cabbage, cole-flower, scorzonera, beet-rave, carrot, radish, turneep, peas, beans, and kidnees, artichocks, strawberries, rasps, currans, goosberries, cherries, plumes, summer pears and aples.

Cyder, metheglin, and other wines.

AUGUST

Fallow bordures, beds, nurseries, and the bulks of trees. Yet inoculate. Ply and purge trees. Pull up suckers and weeds. Clip hedges. Gather the stones of black cherrie and morella. Gather mezerion berries. Gather the seeds of most herbes and flowers. Cut your physick herbes. In the beginning sow cabbage (tho' I confess it's too late. See last moneth). Beets and beet-card, spinage, black-radish, chervil, lettice, corn-sallade, endive, scorzonera, carvy, marigold, angelica, scurvy-grass, &c. Take up ripe onions, garleeks, and shallot. Unbind buds inoculated. Cut and string strawberries. Lay July-flowers. Sow columbines, holyhoks, larks-heels, candy tuffs, popies, and such as can endure winter.

Take up your bulbs and plant as in the last. Sift the ground for tulips and gladiolus. Plunge in potted annuals in vacants. Keep down weeds by hawing. Lay grass, beat, roll, and mow well. Make goosberrie and curran wine.

Towards the end take bees, take the lightest first; those that are near heaths may differ a little. Destroy wasps, straiten the passage by putting on hecks to secure from robers.

Garden Dishes and Drinks in Season

Many pot-herbes and sallades, cabbage, cole-flower, beet-card, turneep, radish, carrot, beet-rave, scorzonera, peas, beans, and kidnees, artichocks, cucumbers, aples, pears, plumes, apricocks, greens, goosberries, currans, rasps, strawberries, &c.

Cyder, metheglin, cherrie wine, curran wine, goosberrie wine, raspberrie wine, &c.

September

Fallow, trench, and level ground. Prepare pits and bordures for trees. Gather plane seed, also almond, peach, and white plum stones. Gather ripe fruits. Plant furth cabbage. Remove bulbs and plant them. Refresh, trame, and house your tender greens. Refresh and trim pots and cases with July-flowers and other fine flowers and plants; carrying them to pits, shelter and covert, giving them air.

Towards the end gather saffron.

Make cyder, perry, and other wines.

Straiten the entrance to bee-hives, destroy wasps, &c.

Also, you may now remove bees.

Garden Dishes and Drinks in Season

Varieties of pot-herbes and sallades, cabbage, cole-flower, peas, beans, and kidnees, artichocks, beet-card, beet-rave, scorzonera, carrots, turneeps, radish, cucumbers, aples, pears, apricocks, peaches, nectarines, quince, grapes, barberries, filbeards.

Cyder, liquorish ail, metheglin, and wine of cherries, rasps, goosberries, currans, &c.

October

Gather winter fruits. Trench and fallow grounds (mixing with proper soil) to ly over the winter. Prepare manures, mixing and laying in heaps bottom'd and covered with earth. Plant hawthorn hedges, and all trees that lose their leaves. Also lay their branches. Prune roses. Gather seeds of hassell, hawthorn, plan, ash, beach, oak, aple, pear, &c. Cut strawberries, artichocks, asparagus, covering their beds with manure and ashes. Earth up winter sallades, herbes and flowers, a little. Plant cabbage, tulips, anemonies and other bulbs. Sow the seed of bairs-ears, cowslips, tulips, &c. Beat and roll gravel and grass. Finish your last weeding and mowing. Lay bair leopered tree roots and remove what harms them; also delve and manure wherever it be. Pickle and conserve fruits. Make perry and cyder.

You may safely remove bees.

Garden Dishes and Drinks in Season

Coleworts, leeks, cabbage, coleflowers, onions, shallot, beans. Blanched endive and sellery. Pickled asparagus, purslain, &c.

Scorzonera, beet-rave, carrots, turneeps, parsneeps, potatoes, skirrets, artichocks, cucumbers, aples, pears, plumes, almond, &c.

Cyder, perry, and wine of cherries, currans, goosberries, raspberries, ail of liquorish, metheglin, &c.

John Reid, *The Scots Gard'ner*

The Form of a Garden

When I was at Cosevelt, with that Bishop of Munster, that made so much noise in his time, I observed no other trees but cherries in a great garden he had made. He told me the reason was, because he found no other fruit would ripen well in that climate, or upon that soil; and therefore, instead of being curious in others, he had only been so in the sorts of that, whereof he had so many, as never to be without them from May to the end of September.

As to the size of a garden, which will perhaps, in time, grow extravagant among us, I think from four or five to seven or eight acres is as much as any gentleman need design, and will furnish as much of all that is expected from it, as any nobleman will have occasion to use in his family.

In every garden four things are necessary to be provided for, flowers, fruit, shade, and water; and whoever lays out a garden without all these, must not pretend it in any perfection: it ought to lie to the best parts of the house, or to those of the master's commonest use, so as to be but like one of the rooms out of which you step into another. The part of your garden next to your house (besides the walks that go round it) should be a parterre for flowers, or grass-plots bordered with flowers; or if, according to the newest mode, it be cast all into grass-plots and gravel-walks, the dryness of these should be relieved with fountains, and the plainness of those with statues; otherwise, if large, they have an ill effect upon the eye. However, the part next to the house should be open, and no other fruit but upon the walls. If this take up one half of the garden, the other should be fruit trees, unless some grove for shade lie in the middle. If it take up a third part only, then the next third may be dwarf trees, and the last standard fruit; or else the second part fruit trees, and the third all sorts of winter greens, which provide for all seasons of the year.

I will not enter upon any account of flowers, having only pleased myself with seeing or smelling them, and not troubled myself with the care, which is more the ladies' part than the men's; but the success is wholly in the gardener.

Sir William Temple, *Upon the Gardens of Epicurus*

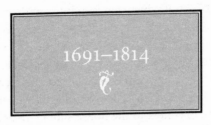

1691–1814

It was perhaps only natural that nature was admitted to the garden gradually – the first instinct being to expand artistry as far from the house as funds would permit. Antoine-Joseph Dezallier D'Argenville considered this virtue of expansion the main reason to bother with building in the country. Gardens should, as a rule, rather than the 'princely' exception (Bacon, 1625), be in the region of 30-40 acres, with half the expense being reserved for the construction of the house, the other for laying out. The second virtue of the country is that it allows for a vista. (A vista serves a vital reconciliatory purpose in these gardens, allowing the large-scale complication of the parterres to be absorbed into a wider landscape, without which they would be oppressive.) The vista he envisages is essential pastoral; mountains, hills, forests, woods, or an inconvenient village are all better excluded by tall planting than allowed to spoil the parterre. This pastoralism puts him closer to Lancelot 'Capability' Brown's idyll than Brown is to the Picturesque movement, which valued the very rugged elements that the others had excluded or ameliorated.

As the main elements of a garden are formal and furnished, a successful designer will have received a liberal education including the classics and geometry, and will have been exposed to the fine arts and their critical discourses.

George London, one of the last of the old formalists, provides technical advice translating Liger on just how to achieve in practice that which D'Argenville has proposed in principle. Switzer and Langley are both concerned to address errors in the placements of statues that they have witnessed, as if the education of gardeners and, indeed, clients could no longer be relied upon.

The piece by Langley fascinates me. His thirty-seven General Directions embody a garden tradition which is about to be broken apart, and which will remain broken until Repton begins to reinstate terraces and parterres, which Brown and his disciples have swept away. The key to the schism lies in Point VII: That all Gardens be grand, beautiful, and natural. The latter two concepts, the beautiful and the natural, become the focus of the competing models and pithy controversies that dominate the last decades of the period. Although the nature of beauty is debated, it is the nature of nature itself, and the true meaning of 'natural' that provokes the conflict. Langley and those before him saw no contradiction in including statues and parterres in 'natural' gardens: human agency is accepted as part of the system. For Pope (before) and Walpole (after), such preference for artifice over the true forms of nature was the vice of the autocrat, the Continental, the vulgar, the French. The enlightened man, 'leaped the garden fence and saw that all nature was a garden', (Walpole of William Kent). What is at stake is not simply some dry aesthetic category, not simply just 'nature', but the true essence of Man, his relation to the world, and by extension, freedom.

It took the perspicacity of Uvedale Price to observe that the supposed freedom of the new informality was fundamentally the same as the old formality re-shaped (and its vision of beauty insipid, to boot). His sometime controversialist Humphry Repton objected that the freedom which the ha-ha, or sunken fence, had enabled was illusory. Its containment was real enough, which is, after all, what should be expected of a garden feature adopted from the handbook of a French Formal Gardener!

One aspect of the period that needs some explanation in this context is the craze for chinoiserie. This, genuinely, was a passion for things in the Chinese style, real or imagined as such, including gardens. It was not universally lauded, as George Mason's remarks attest, but it was a force. Sir William Chambers exploited this fashion to provide a smokescreen for his attack upon the state of gardening in general, and the work of Lancelot Brown, in particular. The very necessity of a smokescreen is significant enough: Sir Uvedale Price and Richard Payne Knight preferred to wait until the man was dead. Chambers' Treatise can be read as a serious manifesto for the 'poetic' garden of the imagination, but its polemic should not be forgotten.

I leave the last word of the period to that arch-observer, Jane Austen, who records the strong and mixed emotions that 'Improvements' provoked.

How to Show the Gardens of Versailles

1 Leaving the Château by the vestibule of the marble courtyard, go onto the terrace. You must stop at the top of the steps to consider the arrangement of the parterres, the pools and the fountains in the Cabinets.

2 Next you must go directly above Latona, and pause to consider Latona, the lizards, the flights of steps, the statues, the Royal Allée, Apollo, the Canal, and then turn round to see the parterres and the Château.

3 Then you must turn left to proceed between the Sphinxes. While walking, you must pause before the Cabinet to consider the tall jet and the sheet of water. Reaching the Sphinxes, pause to see the South Parterre, and then go directly above the Orangery, where you will see the parterre of the orange-trees and the Lake of the Swiss Guards.

4 Turn right, and proceed up between the statues of Apollo in bronze and Antinous; pause at the limit of the terrace where you see Bacchus and Saturn.

5 Go down the flight of steps to the right of the Orangery, and proceed into the garden of the orange-trees. Go straight to the fountain, and there consider the Orangery. Proceed along the allées of large orange-trees, then into the covered orangery, leaving it by the vestibule on the side near the Labyrinth.

6 Enter the Labyrinth. After proceeding down as far as the figures of the fable of the Dog and the Ducks, turn back in order to leave on the side near Bacchus.

7 Go to see the Ballroom. Walk around it, go to the centre, and leave it to reach the bottom of the ascent and steps round Latona.

8 Go straight to the viewpoint below Latona; in passing, look at the small fountain of the Satyr in one of the bosquets. Once at this viewpoint, pause to consider the flights of steps, the vases, the statues, the lizards, Latona and the Château; and on the other side, the Royal Allée, Apollo,

the Canal, the tall jets in the bosquets, Flora, Saturn, and Ceres on the right, Bacchus to the left.

9 Go down by the Girandole which you will see in passing on the way to Saturn. Walk half round Saturn, and go to the Royal Island.

10 Pass onto the causeway, where there are jets of water on both sides; walk round the large pool, and at the far end pause to consider the tall jets, the shells, the basins, the statues and the porticos.

11 Then go as far as the small allée leading to Apollo, and enter the Gallery from the further end. Walk round, and leave by the allée leading to the Colonnade.

12 Enter the Colonnade, go to the centre, and from there walk round to consider the columns, the arches, the bas-reliefs, the vases and the basins. On the way out, stop to see the group by Guidi, then leave on the side next to the Royal Allée.

13 Proceed down to Apollo. Pause there to consider the figures, the vases of the Royal Allée, Latona and the Château, and look also at the Canal. If it is wished to see the Menagery and Trianon on the same day, go there before viewing the rest of the fountains.

14 Enter the small allée which leads to Flora. Go to the Baths of Apollo, and walk round them to consider the statues, cabinets and bas-reliefs.

15 Proceed to Enceladus, walking only half-way round. Having considered this fountain, leave from the lower side.

16 Enter the Council Chamber, then proceed as far as Flora, and walk half-way round.

17 Go to the Mountain. Walk half-way round the small allée which encircles the Mountain before going to the centre of the Star. Once there, walk right round the Mountain.

18 Then pass on to Ceres, in order to reach the Theatre. See the changes, and consider the jets of water in the arcades.

19 Leave at the foot of the steps of the North Parterre, enter the Marais, and walk around it.

20 Enter the Three Fountains from above, proceed downwards; after considering the fountains at each of the three levels, leave along the allée which leads to the Dragon.

21 Walk round the Dragon, and point out the jets of water and the pool of Neptune.

22 Go to the Triumphal Arch, notice the diverse kinds of fountains, jets,

sheets of water, bowls, figures, and the different water-effects.

23 Leave again by the Dragon, and proceed along the Allée of the Children. At the stone that separates the two lower basins, turn to see at one glance all the water-jets of Neptune and the Dragon. Then continue to proceed up the Allée of the Children.

24 Stop below the Sheet of Water and point out the bas-reliefs and the rest of this fountain.

25 Proceed then to the Pyramid, and stop there for a moment. Then return up to the Château by the marble steps between the statues of the Man Sharpening His Knife and the Modest Venus. Turn at the top of the steps to see the North Parterre, the statues, the vases, the Crown Fountains, the Pyramid, and what may be seen of Neptune. Then leave the garden by the same door through which it was entered.

Louis XIV of France (attrib.)

The Church the Garden of Christ

We are a garden walled around,
Chosen and made peculiar ground;
A little spot enclosed by grace
Out of the world's wide wilderness.

Like trees of myrrh and spice we stand,
Planted by God the Father's hand;
And all his springs in Zion flow,
To make the young plantation grow.

Awake, O, heav'nly wind! and come,
Blow on this garden of perfume;
Spirit divine! descend and breathe
A gracious gale on plants beneath.

Make our best spices flow abroad,
To entertain our Saviour God
And faith, and love, and joy appear,
And every grace be active here.

Isaac Watts, Hymns and Spiritual Songs

Of the Disposition and General Distribution of Gardens

To make a complete Disposition and Distribution of a general Plan, Respect must be had to the Situation of the Ground: For the greatest Skill in the right ordering of a Garden is, throughly to understand, and consider the natural Advantages and Defects of the Place; to make use of the one, and to redress the other: Situations differing in every Garden.

The Variety and Diversity of the Composition contributes no less to complete a Garden, than the most discreet and well-contriv'd Distribution; since, in the Opinion of every one, the Gardens that afford the greatest Variety, are the most valuable and magnificent.

'Tis, therefore, the great Business of an Architect, or Designer of Gardens, when he contrives a handsome Plan, with his utmost Art and Œconomy to improve the natural Advantages, and to redress the Imperfections, Shelvings, and Inequalities of the Ground. With these Precautions he should guide and restrain the Impetuosity of his Genius, never swerving from Reason, but constantly submitting, and conforming himself to that which suits best with the natural Situation of the Place.

This is no such easy Task, as some imagine, a fine Garden being no less difficult to contrive and order well, than a good Building; and that which makes a great many Architects, and such as take upon them to give designs of Gardening, often miscarry, is, that most of them form Designs in the Air, no way proper for the Situation of the Place, and at best but stoln, and pick'd here and there from others.

One great Reason why these People have not the Skill necessary to contrive a good Design, is, That this Knowledge coming farther off than they imagine, they are destitute of the Qualifications requisite for this purpose. A Man should know something of Geometry and Architecture, and be able to draw well; he should understand Ornament, and be acquainted with the Properties and Effects of all the Plants made use of in fine Gardens; should design readily; and, with all this, have a right Judgment, and natural good Taste, form'd upon the Contemplation of Things that are excellent, the Censuring of those that are ill, and a consummate Experience in the Art of Gardening.

There are the very meanest Gardeners, who, laying aside the Rake and

Spade, take upon them to give Designs of Gardens, when they understand nothing of the Matter. Unhappy are those that fall into the Hands of such Persons, who put them to a great Expence to plant a sorry Garden; when it costs no more to execute a good Design, than an ill one! The same Trees and Plants are constantly made use of, and produce an ill Effect only through their bad Disposition.

A Man that has Wealth, who would plant a handsome Garden, should do two Things: Make Choice of a Person of very good Ability in the Art of Gardening; and be well advised about the Charge, that the Size of his Building, and the Extent of his Garden, may be answerable to the Expence he would be at. These two Things so essential, that they ought never to be omitted. He should consider, that the larger his Garden is, the more it will cost to make the Ground, to plant, to execute all the Designs, and to keep the same in Order. If there are Fountains, the Basons and Water-works will be larger, the Pipes of greater length, and consequently the Expence will be infinitely more.

It is better, therefore, to be content with a reasonable Spot of Ground, well cultivated, than to be ambitious of having Parks of such Extent, that three Quarters of them are ordinarily neglected. The true Size for a handsome Garden, may take in 30 or 40 Acres, not more. As to the Building, which generally swallows up half the Expence, there is no Necessity that it should be so large and so magnificent, tho' many stand upon it to have Palaces, and to be lodg'd better in the Country than in Town. One may justly say, that a Building in the Country should be proportioned to the Extent of its Garden; for it would be full as disagreeable, to see a magnificent Building in a little Garden, as a small Box in a Garden of vast Extent: These are two Extremes which should be easily avoided, by making the Building correspond with the Garden, and the Garden with the Building. However, it were better of the Two to make shift with a small House, accompanied with a large Garden; by reason a Country-House ought to differ from one in Town, where the Extent of Buildings is more necessary than that of Gardens, on account of being the more usual Place of Dwelling, and of Land bearing a higher Value: The Country we court chiefly, to have our Gardens in it the more vast and magnificent.

These that follow are somewhat near the general Rules one ought to observe in the Disposition and Distribution of Gardens.

There should always be a Descent from the Building to the Garden, of three Steps at least; this renders the Fabrick more dry and wholsome; and from the Head of the Steps you have a general View of the Garden, or of great Part of it, which yields a most agreeable Prospect.

A PARTERRE is the first Thing that should present itself to Sight, and possess the Ground next the Fabrick, whether in Front, or on Sides; as well on Account of the Opening it affords the Building, as for Beauty and Splendour wherewith it constantly entertains the Eye, when seen from every Window of the House. The Sides of a Parterre should be furnished with such Works as may improve and set it off; for this being low, and flat, necessarily requires something raised, as Groves and Palisades are. But, herein, Regard should be had to the Situation of the Place; and it should be observ'd, before you plant, whether the Prospect that way be agreeable; for then the Sides of the Parterre should be kept entirely open, making use of Quarters of Grass, and other flat Works, to make the best of the View, and taking Care not to shut it up with Groves, unless they are planted in Quincunce, or opened with low Hedge-Rows, which hinder not the Eye from piercing through the Trees, and discovering the Beauties of the Prospect on every Side.

If there be no Vista, but, on the contrary, you have a Mountain, Hill, Forest, or Wood, that by their Vicinity deprive you of that Pleasure, or some Village too near adjoining, the Houses of which make no agreeable Sight; you may then edge the Parterre with Palisades and Groves, to hide those ill-favour'd Objects; for by this Means you lose nothing, nor have any thing to regret in Time to come.

Would it not be a great Grievance, to be obliged, some Years after planting, to grub up a Wood, or to cut it down to a certain Height, because 'twas ill placed at first, and takes away the Prospect, which is the most valuable Thing about a Country-Seat?

Antoine-Joseph Dezallier D'Argenville, *The Theory and Practice of Gardening*

A Walk with Sir Roger

We were now arrived at *Spring-Garden*, which is exquisitely pleasant at this time of year. When I considered the Fragrancy of the Walks and Bowers, with the choirs of birds that sung upon the Trees, and the loose Tribe of People that walked under their Shades, I could not but look upon the Place as a kind of *Mahometan* Paradise. Sir Roger told me it put him in mind of a little Coppice by his House in the Country, which his Chaplain used to call an Aviary of Nightingales. *You must understand,* says the Knight, *there is nothing in the World that pleases a Man in Love as your Nightingale. Ah, Mr. Spectator! the many Moon-light Nights that I have walked by my self, and thought on the Widow by the Musick of the Nightingales!* He here fetched a deep Sigh, and was falling into a Fit of musing, when a Masque, who came behind him, gave him a gentle Tap upon the Shoulder, and asked him if he would drink a Bottle of Mead with her? But the Knight, being startled at so unexpected a Familiarity, and displeased to be interrupted in his Thoughts of the Widow, told her, *She was a wanton Baggage,* and bid her go about her business.

We concluded our Walk with a Glass of *Burton*-Ale, and a Slice of Hung-Beef. When we had done eating our selves, the Knight called a Waiter to him, and bid him carry the remainder to the Waterman that had but one Leg. I perceived the Fellow stared upon him at the oddness of the Message, and was going to be saucy; upon which I ratified the Knight's Commands with a Peremptory Look.

As we were going out of the Garden, my old Friend, thinking himself obliged, as a Member of the *Quorum*, to animadvert upon the Morals of the Place, told the Mistress of the House, who sat at the Bar, That he should be a better Customer to her Garden, if there were more Nightingales, and fewer Strumpets.

Joseph Addison, *The Spectator*, No.383

The Guardian, no.173*

TUESDAY, 29 SEPTEMBER 1713

– Nec sera comantem
Narcissum, aut flexi tacuissem Vimen Acanthi,
Pallentesque Haederas, & amantes littoral myrtos.

Virgil

ON GARDENS

I lately took a particular friend of mine to my house in the country, not without some apprehension that it could afford little entertainment to a man of his polite taste, particularly in architecture and gardening, who had been so long conversant with all that is beautiful and great in either. But it was a pleasant surprise to me, to hear him often declare, he had found in my little retirement that beauty that he always thought wanting in the most celebrated seats, or if you will villas, of the nation. This he described to me in those verses with which Martial begins one of his epigrams:

> Baiana nostri villa, Basse, Faustini,
> Non otiosis ordinate myrtetis,
> Viduaque platano, tonsilique buxeto,
> Ingrata lati spatial detinet campi,
> Sed rure vero, barbaroque laetatur.

There is certainly something in the amiable simplicity of unadorned nature, that spreads over the mind a more noble sort of tranquillity, and a loftier sensation of pleasure, than can be raised from the nicer scenes of art.

This was the taste of the ancients in their gardens, as we may discover from the descriptions that are extant of them. The two most celebrated wits of the world have each of them left us a particular picture of a garden; wherein those great masters, being wholly unconfined, and painting at pleasure, may be thought to have given a full idea of what they

The Guardian was an eighteenth-century periodical that included among its contributors many literary figures; sadly it only ran from March 1713 to October 1713. Ed.

esteemed most excellent in this way. These (one may observe) consist entirely of the useful part of horticulture, fruit trees, herbs, water, etc. The pieces I am speaking of are Virgil's account of the garden of the old Corycian, and Homer's of that of Alcinous. The first of these is already known to the English reader, by the excellent versions of Mr Dryden and Mr Addison. The other having never been attempted in our language with any elegance, and being the most beautiful plan of this sort that can be imagined, I shall here present the reader with a translation of it.

The Gardens of Alcinous, from Homer's Odyss. 7[*]

Close to the gates a spacious garden lies,
From storms defended and inclement skies:
Four acres was th' allotted space of ground,
Fenced with a green enclosure all around.
Tall thriving trees confessed the fruitful mold;
The reddening apple ripens here to gold,
Here the blue fig with luscious juice o'erflows,
With deeper red the full pomegranate glows,
The branch here bends beneath the weighty pair,
And verdant olives flourish round the year.
The balmy spirit of the western gale,
Eternal breathes on fruits untaught to fail:
Each dropping pear a following pear supplies,
On apples apples, figs on figs arise:
The same mild season gives the blooms to blow,
The buds to harden, and the fruits to grow.
  Here ordered vines in equal ranks appear
With all th'united labours of the year,
Some to unload the fertile branches run,
Some dry the blackening clusters in the sun,
Others to tread the liquid harvest join,
The groaning presses foam with floods of wine.
Here are the vines in early flower descried,

[*] Ref. Homer, *The Garden of Alcinous*, page 4–5

Here grapes discoloured on the sunny side,
And there in Autumn's richest purple dyed.
  Beds of all various herbs, forever green,
In beauteous order terminate the scene.
  Two plenteous fountains the whole prospect crowned;
This through the gardens leads its streams around,
Visits each plant, and waters all the ground:
While that in pipes beneath the palace flows,
And thence its current on the town bestows;
To various use their various streams they bring,
The people one, and one supplies the king.

Sir William Temple has remarked, that this description contains all the justest rules and provisions which can go toward composing the best gardens. Its extent was four acres, which, in those times of simplicity, was looked upon as a large one, even for a prince. It was enclosed all round for defence; and for conveniency joined close to the gates of the palace.

He mentions next the trees, which were standards, and suffered to grow to their full height. The fine description of the fruits that never failed, and the eternal zephyrs, is only a more noble and poetical way of expressing the continual succession of one fruit after another throughout the year.

The *vineyard* seems to have been a plantation distinct from the *garden*; as also the *beds of greens* mentioned afterwards at the extremity of the enclosure, in the nature and usual place of our *kitchen gardens*.

The two fountains are disposed very remarkably. They rose within the enclosure, and were brought by conduits or ducts, one of them to water all parts of the gardens, and the other underneath the palace into the town, for the service of the public.

How contrary to this simplicity is the modern practice of gardening; we seem to make it our study to recede from nature, not only in the various tonsure of greens into the most regular and formal shapes, but even in monstrous attempts beyond the reach of the art itself. We run into sculpture, and are yet better pleased to have our trees in the most awkward figures of men and animals, than in the most regular of their own.

Hinc & nexilibus videas e frondibus hortos,

Implexos late muros, & Moenia circum
Porrigere, & latas e ramis surgere turres;
Deflexam & Myrtum in Puppes, atque aerea rostra:
In buxisque undare fretum, atque e rore rudentes.
Parte aliá frondere suis tentoria Castris;
Scutaque spiculaque & jaculantia citria Vallos.

I believe it is no wrong observation that persons of genius, and those who are most capable of art, are always most fond of nature, as such are chiefly sensible, that all art consists in the imitation and study of nature. On the contrary, people of the common level of understanding are principally delighted with the little niceties and fantastical operations of art, and constantly think that *finest* which is the least natural. A citizen is no sooner proprietor of a couple of yews, but he entertains thoughts of erecting them into giants, like those of Guildhall. I know an eminent cook, who beautified his country seat with a coronation dinner of greens, where you see the Champion flourishing on horseback at one end of the table, and the Queen in perpetual youth at the other.

For the benefit of all my loving countrymen of this curious taste, I shall here publish a catalogue of greens to be disposed of by an eminent town-gardener, who has lately applied to me upon his head. He represents, that for the advancement of a politer sort of ornament in the villas and gardens adjacent to this great city, and in order to distinguish those places from the mere barbarous countries of gross nature, the world stands much in need of a virtuoso gardener who has a turn to sculpture, and is thereby capable of improving upon the ancients of his profession in the imagery of evergreens. My correspondent is arrived to such perfection, that he cuts family pieces of men, women or children. Any ladies that please may have their own effigies in myrtle, or their husbands in hornbeam. He is a puritan wag, and never fails, when he shows his garden, to repeat that passage in the Psalms, *Thy wife shall be as the fruitful vine, and thy children as olive branches round thy table.* I shall proceed to his catalogue, as he sent it for my recommendation.

Adam and Eve in yew; Adam a little shattered by the fall of the tree of knowledge in the Great Storm; Eve and the serpent very flourishing. The Tower of Babel, not yet finished.

St George in bow; his arm scarce long enough, but will be in a condition to stick the dragon by next April.

A green dragon of the same, with a tail of ground ivy for the present.

N.B. *These two not to be sold separately.*

Edward the Black Prince in cypress.

A Lauristine bear in blossom, with a juniper hunter in berries.

A pair of giants, *stunted*, to be sold cheap.

A Queen Elizabeth in phylyraea, a little inclining to the green sickness, but of full growth.

Another Queen Elizabeth in myrtle, which was very forward, but miscarried by being too near a savin.

An old maid of honour in wormwood.

A topping Ben Jonson in laurel.

Divers eminent modern poets in bays, somewhat blighted, to be disposed of a pennyworth.

A quick-set hog shot up into a porcupine, by its being forgot a week in rainy weather.

A lavender pig with sage growing in his belly.

Noah's Ark in holly, standing on the mount; the ribs a little damaged for want of water.

A pair of Maidenheads in fir, in great forwardness.

Alexander Pope, Essay

Of Horn-beam, and for what it is proper in a Garden

I shall not treat here of the manner of raising Horn-beam,* for Nature her self has provided enough for us to make what Compartments we please with it in our Gardens.

The Plants of the Horn-beam, made use of in that Case, are small and rooted, about an Inch big at the Foot, for you should never chuse them bigger.

The best for your turn is, that which has a smooth shining Rind, and a

---

Carpinus betulus or Common hornbeam is a deciduous tree with elegant foliage and excellent autumn colour. Its ability to withstand hard pruning makes it a versatile hedging species. Ed.

great many Roots. It comes up well in all sorts of Earth, but better in good Soils, than bad.

When you put these Plants into the Ground, you must always dig a little Trench along the compartments where you set them; Plant them four Inches deep in the Ground, and at three Distance from one another, after having them cut to Eight or ten Inches high.

This being done, and the Plants put in those Trenches, along a Line drawn strait, you must supply the Roots with loose Ground; and to find out such, you must chuse the finest Day you can get for it.

This Work is to be done from *November* to the end of *March*, when the Sap begins to act in those Plants, and then the Course of it must not be interrupted, for fear you lose your Plants by it.

That the Horn-beam may grow to your liking, you must dig it four times a Year, in *March*, *May*, *July*, and *September*.

According as it comes up, you should keep it shear'd, that it may grow in the Form of an even Palisade; and when 'tis of a good Height, you make use of a Hook. If the Palisade runs up very high, you should get a Cart made on purpose, and the Man who Shears it gets up in it, and is drawn by one or two Horses, according as the Workman advances his Work.

Of the Use of Horn-beam in a Garden

Horn-beam is commonly made use of for Palisades, some of which are very high, and others as high as one can lean on, like a sort of Hedge, mingled with Trees at equal Distances.

These Palisades of Horn-beam serve to divide Compartments, and to give them what Figure we would have them have. These Compartments are diversify'd into the Star, or the Goose-foot, Walks winding variously for the greater Ornament of Parks, Labyrinths and Groves.

Of the Star

I shall not explain here what is meant by the Star and the Goose-foot, having sufficiently done it in the Dictionary of Gardeners Terms which I publish'd, and to which I refer the Reader: But since to define a Word is not enough to make one entirely comprehend what is understood by it, I have drawn the Figure, which will render the thing more intelligible.

Before we come to that Demonstration, I believe 'twill not be amiss to say something concerning the Plot of a Garden.

A Star has its Walks of Gravel which are roll'd, and in the Middle is compos'd of Grass-Plots, which are to be mowe'd once a Year, or oftner, as occasion requires: On the side of these Grass-Plots are Two Walks, broad, or narrow, according to the Breadth and Width of the Plots, and in every thing else made as the Gardener's Fancy dictates.

The Entrance into this Star is by another Walk that bounds it there; or all at once by its own Walks: But after I have said all this of the Star, I believe the best way of Explaining it will be by a Figure.

Of the Goose-foot

When a Man understands this Compartment well, 'tis a very fine Ornament to a Garden.

It has always Avenues leading to it; and these Avenues, as well as other Alleys that form the Goose-foot, are either Green-Plots, or roll'd Walks, with Trees in Ranks along the Sides of them.

The Middle of the Goose-foot is commonly a Grass-Plot, round or oval, with a roll'd Walk about it, of what Breadth you please.

Of a Labyrinth

A Labyrinth is a place cut into several Windings, set off with Horn-beam, to divide them one from another. In great Gardens we often meet with them; and the most valuable Labyrinths are always those that wind most, as that of *Versailles*, the Contrivance of which has been wonderfully lik'd by all that have seen it.

The Palisades, of which Labyrinths ought to be compos'd, should be Ten, Twelve, or Fifteen Foot high; some there are that are no higher than one can lean on; but those are not the finest.

The Walks of a Labyrinth ought to be kept roll'd, and the Horn-beams in them shear'd, in the Shape of Half-Moons; the Figure annex'd to this Page will demonstrate better what farther may be said on this Ornament of a Garden.

Of Groves

Bosquets or Groves are so call'd from Bouquet a Nosegay; and I believe that Gardeners never meant any thing else by giving this Term to this Compartment, which is a sort of green Knot, form'd by the Branches and Leaves of Trees that compose it, plac'd in Rows opposite to each other.

A Grove, in this Sense, is a Plot of Ground, more or less, as you think fit, enclos'd in Palisades of Horn-beam, the Middle of it fill'd with tall Trees, as Elms or the like, the Tops of which make the Tuft or Plume.

At the Foot of the Elms, which should grow along the Palisades at equal Distances, other little Wild Trees should be planted, and the Tuft that will by this means be form'd in the Inside, will resemble that of a Copse.

There are several ways of drawing out these Groves; some in regular Forms, the Plots being one answerable to another; and some in irregular, or the meer effect of Fancy, such as are mingled among other Compartments of a Garden, which are also mark'd out in various Figures.

Groves are only proper for spacious Gardens, belonging to Men of the highest Quality, for 'tis a very great Expence to keep them up.

There are other sorts of Groves, that are neither enclos'd by Borders of Horn-beam in Palisades, nor tufted within; but consisting only of Trees with high Stems, such as Elms planted in right Angles. Some make use of the Horse Chestnut-tree for this Purpose, which being plac'd in the same Order, forms a sort of a little Forest. The Superficies of the Ground should be kept very smooth, and well roll'd, or cover'd with Grass after the manner of Green-Plots.

Regular Groves should be planted only to adorn the fine Apartment of a Palace that has every thing regular about it: Those that are irregular are not less esteem'd; for the Variety of them, in great Parks, is what pleases most.

The Walks that run along these Groves ought always to be kept roll'd, unless being extreamly broad, you put some *Spanish* Trefoil, or common Grass-Plots in the middle of them, yet you should leave roll'd Walks on both Sides.

Of Galleries, and Portico's, or Arches

I have nam'd a great many sorts of Compartments, in which Horn-beam is made use of; yet methinks none of them look so beautiful and magnificent as a Gallery with Arches. *Note, That in* England *we cover our Portico-Galleries with Limes, which do very well.*

This Work seems very difficult to be done to most Spectators, and yet 'tis quite otherwise.

You remember that we have shewn how naturally the Horn-beam serves for Palisades, and where Nature has not furnish'd it with Qualities proper for your Operation, you must supply that Deficiency with Art. Suppose, then, you intend to raise a Gallery with Arches.

The first thing you must do, is to draw a Line as long as you design your Gallery to be, plant your Horn-beam on it, as I have directed you before to do. These Horn-beams thus planted, are to be the Foundation of your Gallery, when they are grown to a proper Height; the Management of them is not very difficult, you need only dig them a little, and shear them when they want it. As to what relates to the Forepart of the Gallery, you must be careful about it, because the forming of the Arches depends upon it.

The Gallery should be eight or ten Foot broad, that there may be room to walk in it, and twelve or fifteen Foot high, each Pillar four Foot distance from one another. When your Horn-beams are grown three Foot high, the Distance of each Pillar well regulated, and the Ground-work of the Gallery finish'd as I have inform'd you, the next Work is the Frontispiece; to make which you must stop the Horn-beam between the two Pillars at that Height, and run it up a Trellis made on purpose, which forms the Arcade; Do this as artificially as you can.

According as it grows up, if any of the Boughs out-shoot the other, you must even them with your Shears. Arcades thus manag'd will by Degrees grow strong in the Order you set them, and when once they have acquir'd the Shape that agrees best with them, 'tis easie to keep them so by the Shear, if you use it with Care and Industry.

Louis Liger, trans. George London & Henry Wise, *The Retir'd Gardener*

Of Statues

Amongst the several Methods made use of to convey the memorable Actions and great Personages of Antiquity to these times, this of *Statues*, is not the least, being the most publick and durable Memoirs of Virtue, Honour, and Valour.

For tho' there be many fabulous Relations of the Heathen Deities, which compose a great Part of this History, as of *Jupiter, Mars, Apollo,* and the rest of the Capital Deities; yet the most modest Accounts are, that some of them were Persons of Heroick and Valiant Behaviour, while others were Generous, Just, and Liberal, great Encouragers of Learning, and all virtuous Amusements; and this drew the Eyes of the Heathens upon them so much, as to Deifie them: And from a Contemplation of their Virtues, 'tis possible for any Thoughtful Person to extract many useful Things for the Conduct of this Life. But leaving that, the Grace and Majesty they give a Country Seat is very great; the Modern as well as the Ancient *Romans*, the greatest and politest People of the World, have fill'd almost every High-way and Publick Place with the Statues of their *Patres Patriæ*, as a grateful Tribute to their Merit; but their Gardens, as well as those of France, abound so much in them, that 'tis in that point They are still likely to out-doe Us.

I shall not here pretend to give an Historical Account of these illustrious Hero's, nor of their Virtual Attributes and Hieroglyphical Significations, leaving that to the skilful Mythologist; nor yet of their Shape, Lineament, or Articulate and Corporeal Dimensions, that being the Business of the ingenious Statuary. My Intent, in this Place, being to rectifie some Mistakes in their Local Proportion.

It cann't but be an unpleasant Sight (as common as it is) to view *Jupiter, Mars, Neptune*, and the rest of the Capital Deities of Heaven, misplac'd, and by a meanness of spirit below a good Designer, set perching upon a little Pedestal; one like a Citizen; a second with a Pike in his Hand, like a Foot-Soldier; and the third upon dry Land with a Trident, like a Cart-filler. These are certainly great Diminutions to the Politeness of the Statuary, as they are to the Noble Personages they hieroglyphically represent.

Others, perhaps, err in another respect, by placing *Pan* as a Tutelar God in the Flower-Garden, whilst *Ceres* and *Flora* are the silent Inhabitants of Woods and Groves. To this may be often join'd an Impropriety in the Gesture and Habiliments of these Gods, which ought to differ, as the Actions they are representing do: *Neptune* in the Management of his Sea-Affairs, embracing *Amphitrite*; and *Mars* in his Armorial Array in his Amour with *Venus*; are such Incongruities as the Statuary should always avoid: Since one would be as useless and troublesome a Companion in the guiding and taming his Sea-Horses as the

Warlike Habiliments of the other would be in the Embraces of a Fair Lady.

But to return: *Jupiter* and *Mars* should possess the largest Open Centres and Lawns of a grand Design, elevated upon Pedestal Columnial, and other Architectonical Works, according to the Model of the best Designer, with their immediate Servants and Vassels underneath; *Jupiter* with his *Mercurius*, *Mars* with *Fame*, and the rest of their Attendants; whilst the Niches ought to be fill'd with *Dii Minores* for one, or the Warlike Heroes of Antiquity, aswel as Modern, for the other, every one accoutred and ready to execute the Commands of their great Masters.

Neptune should possess the Centre of the greatest body of Water, (be it either Fountain, Bason, or whatever that kind) in his Chariot, attended by the *Naiades*, *Tritons*, and other his Sea-Attendants.

Venus ought to be placed among the *Graces*, *Cupid*, &c. And in all the lesser Centres of a Polygonar Circumscription, it would be proper to place *Apollo* with the *Muses* in the Niches, *Minerva* with the *Liberal Sciences*, &c.

Then *Vulcan* with the *Cyclops* in a Centre of less note, and all the rest of the Deities dispers'd in their particular Places and Order. *Flora*, *Ceres* and *Pomona*, to their several Charges; and the *Faunes* and *Sylvans*, to the more remote and Rural Centres and Parts of the Wood-work.

If such a Cruel Piece as *Andromeda* fasten'd to a Rock, should be brought into a Garden, it might be proper to place it near the Water, where she might always weep and lament her sad Fate. Thus *Niobe*, &c.

To be more plain: *Venus*, *Diana*, *Daphne*, and *Flora*, with their Attendants, may be compleat Furniture for the Flower-Garden; but they ought not to be too small, but bigger than the Life, especially in large Gardens, and elevated upon an accumulation of Architecture or Masonry, (as I have before mention'd) whilst *Mars* and *Neptune* be placed in the larger Centres; *Apollo* amongst the *Muses*; and *Minerva* amongst the *Liberal Sciences*, (as before.) That noble Grace that abundance of these Figures, placed all over our Rural Gardens and Plantations, will afford, is charming to consider. But the farther Disquisition of this Point is deferr'd till the next Volume.

Before I conclude this Chapter, I cann't but say a word or two concerning the farther Encouragement of *Statuary*, which seems at present as much or more neglected than any other Art whatsoever.

I cann't but think it a Work worthy of the Royal Munificence, to erect an Academy, as is common in other Countries, especially *Italy* and *France*, for its Improvement, and for a Nursery for young ingenious Men; which when they have learnt to Draw and Carve well, might be distributed amongst the Nobility and Gentry, who most of them stand in great need of these noble Decorations of Statues about their Country-Seats.

Stephen Switzer, *Ichnographica Rustica*

General Directions, &c.

I That the grand Front of a Building lie open upon an elegant Lawn or Plain of Grass, adorn'd with beautiful Statues, (of which hereafter in their Place,) terminated on its Sides with open Groves.

II That grand Avenues be planted from such large open Plains, with a Breadth proportionable to the Building, as well as to its Length of View.

III That Views in Gardens be as extensive as possible.

IV That such Walks, whose Views cannot be extended, terminate in Woods, Forests, misshapen Rocks, strange Precipices, Mountains, old Ruins, grand Buildings, &c.

V That no regular Ever-Greens, &c. be planted in any Part of an open Plain or Parterre.

VI That no Borders be made, or Scroll-Work cut, in any such Lawn or plain Parterre; for the Grandeur of those beautiful Carpets consists in their native Plainness.

VII That all Gardens be grand, beautiful, and natural.

VIII That shady Walks be planted from the End-Views of a House, and terminate in those open Groves that enclose the Sides of the plain Parterre, that thereby you may enter into immediate Shade, as soon as out of the House, without being heated by the scorching Rays of the Sun.

IX That all the Trees of your shady Walks and Groves be planted with Sweet-Brier, White Jessamine, and Honey-Suckles, environ'd at Bottom with a small Circle of Dwarf-Stock, Candy-Turf, and Pinks.

X That all those Parts, which are out of View from the House, be form'd into Wildernesses, Labyrinths, &c.

XI That Hills and Dales, of easy Ascents, be made by Art, where Nature has not perform'd that Work before.

XII That Earths cast out of Foundations, &c. be carried to such Places for raising of Mounts, from which, fine Views may be seen.

XIII That the Slopes of Mounts, &c. be laid, with a moderate Reclination, and planted with all Sorts of Ever-Greens in a promiscuous Manner, so as to grow all in a Thicket; which has a prodigious fine Effect.

In this very Manner are planted two beautiful Mounts in the Gardens of the Honourable Sir *Fisher Tench* at *Low-Layton* in *Essex*.

XIV That the Walks leading up the Slope of a Mount, have their Breadth contracted at the Top, full one half Part; and if that contracted Part be enclosed on the Sides with a Hedge whose Leaves are of a light Green, 'twill seemingly add a great Addition to the Length of the Walk, when view'd from the other End.

XV That all Walks whose Lengths are short, and lead away from any Point of View, be made narrower at their further Ends than at the hither Part; for by the Inclination of their Sides, they appear to be of a much greater Length than they really are; and the further End of very long Walk, Avenue, &c. appears to be much narrower than that End where you stand.

And the Reason is, that notwithstanding the Sides of such Walks are parallel to each other, yet as the Breadth of the further End is seen under a lesser Angle, than the Breadth of that Part where you stand, it will therefore appear as if contracted, altho' the Sides are actually parallel; for equal Objects always appear under equal Angles, Q.E.D.

XVI That the Walks of a Wilderness be never narrower than ten Feet, or wider than twenty five Feet.

XVII That the Walks of a Wilderness be so plac'd, as to respect the best Views of the Country.

XVIII That the Intersections of Walks be adorn'd with Statues, large open Plains, Groves, Cones of Fruit, of Ever-Greens, of Flowering Shrubs, of Forest Trees, Basons, Fountains, Sun-Dials, and Obelisks.

XIX That in those serpentine Meanders, be placed at proper Distances, large Openings, which you surprisingly come to; and in the first are entertain'd with a pretty Fruit-Garden, or Paradice-Stocks, with a curious Fountain; from which you are insensibly led through the pleasant Meanders of a shady delightful Plantation; first, into an oven Plain environ'd with lofty Pines, in whose Center is a pleasant Fountain, adorn'd with *Neptune* and his Tritons, &c. secondly, into a Flower-Garden, enrich'd with the most fragrant Flowers and beautiful Statues; and from thence through small Inclosures of Corn, open Plains, or small Meadows, Hop-Gardens, Orangeries, Melon-Grounds, Vineyards, Orchards, Nurseries, Physick-Gardens, Warrens, Paddocks of Deer, Sheep, Cows, &c. with the rural Enrichments of Hay-Stacks, Wood-Piles, &c.

These agreeable surprising Entertainments in the pleasant Passage thro' a Wilderness, must, without doubt, create new Pleasures at every Turn: And more especially when the Whole is so happily situated, as to be bless'd with small Rivulets and purling Streams of clear Water, which generally admit of fine Canals, Fountains, Cascades, &c. which are the very Life of a delightful rural Garden.

And to add to the Pleasure of these delightful Meanders, I advise that the Hedge-Rows of the Walks be intermix'd with Cherries, Plumbs, Apples, Pears, Bruxel Apricots, Figs, Gooseberries, Currants, Rasberries, &c. and the Borders planted with Strawberries, Violets, &c.

The most beautiful Forest-Trees for Hedges, are the *English* Elm, the *Dutch* Elm, the Lime-Tree, and Hornbeam: And altho' I have advis'd the Mixing of these Hedges of Forest-Trees with the aforesaid Fruits, yet you must not forget a Place for those pleasant and delightful Flowering-Shrubs, the White Jessamine, Honey-Suckle, and Sweet-Brier.

XX Observe, at proper Distances, to place publick and private Cabinets, which should (always) be encompass'd with a Hedge of Ever-Greens, and Flowering-Shrubs next behind them, before the Forest-Trees that are Standards.

XXI Such Walks as must terminate within the Garden, are best finish'd with Mounts, Aviaries, Grotto's, Cascades, Rocks, Ruins, Niches, or Amphitheatres of Ever-Greens, variously mix'd, with circular Hedges ascending behind one another, which renders a very graceful Appearance.

XXII Obelisks of Trellip-Work cover'd with Passion-Flowers, Grapes,

Honey-Suckles, and White Jessamine, are beautiful Ornaments in the Center of an open Plain, Flower-Garden, &c.

XXIII In the Planting of a Wilderness, be careful of making an equal Disposition of the several Kinds of Trees, and that you mix therewith the several Sorts of Ever-Greens; for they not only add a very great Beauty thereunto, by their different Leaves and Colours, in the Summer; but are a great Grace to a Garden in the Winter, when others have stood the Strip of their Leaves.

XXIV Canals, Fish-Ponds, &c. are most beautiful when environ'd with a Walk of stately Pines, and terminate at each End with a fine Grove of Forest-Trees, or Ever-Greens.

Or, if an extensive Canal terminate at one End in an elegant Piece of Architecture, with a Grove on each Side thereof, and the other End in a Wood, Grove, &c. 'twill have a noble and grand Aspect.

XXV Groves of Standard Ever-Greens, as Yew, Holly, Box, and Bay-Trees, are very pleasant, especially when a delightful Fountain is plac'd in their Center.

XXVI All Grass-Walks should be laid with the same Curvature as Gravel-Walks, and particularly in wet and cold Lands; for, by their being made flat or level from Side to Side, they soon settle into Holes in the Middle, by often walking on, and therein retain Wet, &c. which a circular surfaced Walk resists. The Proportion for the Heights of the Crown, or middle Part of any Grass or Gravel-Walk, is as five is to one, that is, if the Walk be five Foot in Breadth, the Height of the Middle, above the Level of the Sides, must be one Inch; if ten Foot, two Inches, fifteen Foot, three Inches, &c.

XXVII The Proportion that the Base of a Slope ought to have to its Perpendicular, is as three to one, that is, if the perpendicular Height be ten Feet, its Base must be thirty Feet; and the like of all others.

XXVIII Distant Hills in Parks, &c. are beautiful Objects, when planted with little Woods; as also are Valleys, when intermix'd with Water, and large Plains; and a rude Coppice in the middle of a fine Meadow, is a delightful Object.

XXIX Little Walks by purling Streams in Meadows, and through Corn-Fields, Thickets, &c. are delightful Entertainments.

XXX Open Lawns should be always in Proportion to the Grandeur of the

Building; and the Breadth of Avenues to the Fronts of Edifices, and their own Length also.

The entire Breadth of every Avenue should be divided into five equal Parts: Of which, the Middle, or grand Walk, must be three Fifths; and the Side, or Counter-Walks on each Side one Fifth each. But let the Length of Avenues fall as it will, you must always observe, that the grand Walk be never narrower than the Front of the Building.

The most beautiful and grand Figures for fine large open Lawns, are the Triangle Semicircle, Geometrical Square, Circle or Elipsis.

XXXI The Circle, Elipsis, Octagon, and mix'd Figures composed of Geometrical Squares, Paralellograms, and Arches of Circles, makes very beautiful Figures for Water, as may be seen in the several Parts of the Designs at the End hereof. But of them all, the Circle is the most grand and beautiful.

XXXII In the Planting of Groves, you must observe a regular Irregularity; not planting then according to the common Method like an Orchard, with their Trees in straight Lines ranging every Way, but in a rural Manner, as if they had receiv'd their Situation from Nature itself.

XXXIII Plant in and about your several Groves, and other Parts of your Garden, good Store of Black-Cherry and other Trees that Produce Food for Birds, which will not a little add to the Pleasure thereof.

XXXIV Where Water is easy to be had, always introduce a Basin or Fountain in every Flower and Fruit-Garden, Grove, and other pleasing Ornaments, in the several private Parts of your rural Garden.

XXXV The several Kinds of Forest-Trees make beautiful Groves, as also doth many Ever-Greens, or both mix'd together; but none more beautiful than that noble Tree the *Pine*.

XXXVI In the Disposition of the several Parts of Gardens in general, always observe that a perfect Shade be continued throughout, in such a Manner as to pass from one Quarter to another, &c. without being obliged at any Time to pass thro' the scorching Rays of the Sun.

XXXVII There is nothing adds so much to the Beauty and Grandeur of Gardens, as fine Statues; and nothing more disagreeable, than when wrongly plac'd; as Neptune on a Terrace-Walk, Mount, &c. or Pan, the God of Sheep, in a large Basin, Canal, or Fountain.

Batty Langley, *New Principles of Gardening*

Smoothness

The next property constantly observable in such objects is *Smoothness*: A quality so essential to beauty, that I do not now recollect any thing beautiful that is not smooth. In trees and flowers, smooth leaves are beautiful; smooth slopes of earth in gardens; smooth streams in the landscape; smooth coats of birds and beasts in animal beauties; in fine women, smooth skins; and in several sorts of ornamental furniture, smooth and polished surfaces. A very considerable part of the effect of beauty is owing to this quality; indeed the most considerable. For take any beautiful object, and give it a broken and rugged surface; and however well formed it may be in other respects, it pleases no longer. Whereas, let it want ever so many of the other constituents, if it wants not this, it becomes more pleasing than almost all the others without it. This seems to me so evident, that I am a good deal surprised, that none who have handled the subject have made any mention of the quality of smoothness, in the enumeration of those that go to the forming of beauty. For indeed any rugged, any sudden projection, any sharp angle, is in the highest degree contrary to that idea.

Edmund Burke, *A Philosophical Enquiry into the Origin*
of Our Ideas of the Sublime and Beautiful

Design in Gardening

The greatest fault of modern planners is their injudicious application of *Fir-trees*. – A quick growth and perpetual verdure have been the temptations for introducing them; but these advantages are very insufficient to justify the prevailing mode, which gives them an universal estimation. Trees of conic figure are by nature unsociable – not to be allow'd a place amid the luxuriant heads of oaks, or other noblest progeny of the forest; though they may sometimes join with the ash and poplar. They are beautiful as single objects – ill-suited to an extent of wood-land – serviceable however to particular swells of ground, if the size of the plantation be proportionable, and not (as Shenstone observes, and our artists execute) like coronets on an elephant's back. They may be loosely scatter'd on a wild heath: their *deep shades* may in many places be happily disposed: but when I see them in circular clumps choking up a meadow, or preposterously converted into shrubs under the branches of a forest-tree, they excite no other emotion, than contempt for the planter, – who perhaps may have acquired a singular degree of merit in smoothing lawns, and humouring every extension of inequality of surface. Indeed *Practice* is a necessary ingredient for modelling the surface of ground; or at least for an adequate *execution*. The difficulty attending this mechanical part of gardening has induced many proprietors to commit the whole of it to artists by profession, whose contracted geniuses (without the least *capability* of enlargement) have stampt an unmeaning sameness upon half the principal seat in the kingdom.

Uniting lawns is the chief purpose of *sunk fences*: – wherefore they should be *perfectly* concealed themselves, that we may not discover insufficiency in the execution: neither should unnatural swells be made use of in order to conceal them; for thus the very *purpose* is destroyed.

Shrubberies and *beds of flowers* demand limitation: – immoderately extended, they mark the triumph of luxury over elegance. The apparent waste of ground displeases us; and the plants themselves are too minute to admit of any considerable space being exclusively allotted them. (I say this, in regard to *beauty of disposition*, and mean not to interfere with the *vanity of collections*.) On spots, that have nothing observable in themselves, such profusion of ornament is generally bestowed; yet, however fashionably patronised, gaudy colouring is a poor compensation for natural deficiencies: with much more justice has POPE given the preference to that man's taste,

> Whose ample lawns are not asham'd to feed
> The milky heifer, and deserving steed.

An opinion prevails that *regularity is required in that part of a garden, which joins the dwelling-house*. The author, who asserts this maxim, shews at the same time the absurdity of extending it: but I rather take the rule itself to be a relict of the prejudice of habit. Hiding a good front – obstructing a prospect from the windows – rendering a mansion damp and unwholsome by too much shelter – are inconveniences to be avoid-

ed: but I see no connection between these cautions and positive regularity: there are indeed reasons for excluding it: a degree of wildness in the
garden contrasts the symmetry of the building; and the generality of edifices appear to greatest advantage

> Bosom'd high in tufted trees.

Fashion's dictates have subjected the *form* of planting to frequent variation: avenues, quincunxes, clumps, successively had the preference; *dot-
ting* (as they term it) is the present method, and the least exceptionable
of any. But a field for the exercise of genius should never be limited by
fashion.

Standing pools give offence to LORD BACON: - I have no partiality
for *the green mantle* they are sometimes covered with; but, without any
extraordinary clearness, properly placed, their effect may be admirable.
Gasper Poussin's landscapes prove the assertion. Ponds may be likewise
strung together, so as to gain a river-like appearance – or at least that of a
considerable lake. This junction of ponds is surprisingly executed at
HAGLEY: and, though an equal deception may not always be practicable, yet I think the experiment could not absolutely fail – but in the
hands of a mechanical artist, who would make their broad naked heads
the principal objects of view.

'Tis a common case with *garden-buildings*, to be strangely incoherent
in themselves – unconnected with the places they occupy: such are root-
houses in rosaries – hermitages richly ornamented – rustic seats marked
with a *formal vulgarity* by way of *rudeness*. As to pillars and obelisks, they
are generally erected to vanity. Had obelisks never stood upon classic
ground, one should be puzzled to account for their reception: other pillars may have greater beauty in themselves; yet I cannot recommend the
admission of either among rural objects, unless back'd by rising wood, or
in some small area surrounded by thickets.

The use of statues is another dangerous attempt in gardening – not
however impossible to be practised with success. How peculiarly happy is
the position of the *River-god* at STOURHEAD! How prettily group'd are
the *Sylvan Deities* near the temple of PAN on ENFIELD-CHACE! I
remember a figure at HAGLEY which one could fancy to be darting cross
an alley of a grove: the noble proprietor has since remov'd it – perhaps as

bordering upon puerile conceit – but I must confess myself much taken with the thought, and only wished the *pedestal* had been concealed.

There is an art in the management of grounds, little understood, and possibly the most difficult to be accomplished: 'tis analogous to what is called *keeping under* in painting: by some parts being seemingly neglected, the succeeding are more strikingly beautiful. The effect of this management is very apparent at the LEASOWES. I know not whether the same thing is intended at PAINE'S-HILL, when you are conducted to a view of the lake through specimens of *French* and *Italian* gardening: but *these* are too much labour'd to give an equal respite to the attention with natural negligences.

From a general view of our present gardens in populous districts, a stranger might imagine they were calculated for a race of LILLIPUTIANS. Are their shade, their ponds, or their islands proportionable to common mortals? Their winding walks – such as no human foot-step (except a reeling drunkard's) could have traced. Yet these, in the eyes of the proprietors, are perfect models of CHINESE; though the only part that can be called so, is their ridiculous style of architecture in rails and temples.

George Mason, *Design in Gardening*

On Modern Gardening

It is true we have heard much lately, as Sir William Temple did, of irregularity and imitations of nature in the gardens or grounds of the Chinese. The former is certainly true; they are as whimsically irregular as European gardens are formally uniform, and unvaried – but with regard to nature, it seems as much avoided, as in the squares and oblongs and straight lines of our ancestors. An artificial perpendicular rock starting out of a flat plain, and connected with nothing, often pierced through in various places with oval hollows, has no more pretension to be deemed natural than a lineal terrace or parterre. The late Mr. Joseph Spence, who had both taste and zeal for the present style, was so persuaded of the Chinese emperor's pleasure-ground being laid out on principles, resembling ours, that he translated and published, under the name of Sir Harry Beaumont, a particular account of that enclosure from the collec-

tion of the letters of the Jesuits. I have looked it over, and except a determined irregularity, can find nothing in it that gives me any idea of attention being paid to nature. It is of vast circumference and contains two
hundred palaces, besides as many contiguous for the eunuchs, all gilt,
painted and varnished. There are raised hills from twenty to sixty feet
high, streams and lakes, and one of the latter five miles round. These
waters are passed by bridges – but even their bridges must not be straight
– they serpentine as much as the rivulets, and are sometimes so long as
to be furnished with resting-places, and begin and end with triumphal
arches. Methinks a straight canal is as rational at least as a meandering
bridge. The colonnades undulate in the same manner. In short, this pretty gaudy scene is the work of caprice and whim; and when we reflect on
their buildings, presents no image but that of insubstantial tawdriness.
Nor is this all. Within this fantastic Paradise is a square town, each side a
mile long. Here the eunuchs of the court, to entertain his imperial
majesty with the bustle and business of the capital in which he resides,
but which it is not of his dignity ever to see, act merchants and all sorts
of trades, and even designedly exercise for his royal amusement every art
of knavery that is practised under his auspicious government. Methinks
this is the childish solace and repose of grandeur, not a retirement from
affairs to the delights of rural life. Here too his majesty plays at agriculture; there is a quarter set apart for that purpose; the eunuchs sow, reap,
and carry in their harvest in the imperial presence; and his majesty
returns to Peking, persuaded that he has been in the country.[*]

* The French have of late years adopted our style of gardening, but choosing to be fundamentally obliged to more remote rivals, they deny us half the merit, or rather the
originality of the invention, by ascribing the discovery to the Chinese, and by calling
our taste in gardening *le goût Anglo-Chinois*. I think I have shown that this is a blunder,
and that the Chinese have passed to one extremity of absurdity, as the French and all
antiquity had advanced to the other, both being equally remote from nature; regular
formality is the opposite point to fantastic Sharawadgis. The French, indeed, during
the fashionable paroxysm of philosophy, have surpassed us, at least in meditation on
the art. I have perused a great treatise of recent date, in which the author, extending his
views beyond mere luxury and amusement, has endeavoured to inspire his countrymen, even in the gratification of their expensive pleasures, with benevolent projects. He
proposes to them to combine gardening with charity, and to make every step of their
walks an act of generosity and a lesson of morality. Instead of adorning favourite
points with a heathen temple, a Chinese pagoda, a Gothic tower, or fictitious bridge, he

We have seen what Moor Park was, when pronounced a standard. But as no succeeding generation in an opulent and luxurious country contents itself with the perfection established by its ancestors, more perfect perfection was still sought; and improvements had gone on, till London and Wise had stocked our gardens with giants, animals, monsters, coats of arms and mottoes in yew, box and holly. Absurdity could go no farther, and the tide turned. Bridgman, the next fashionable designer of gardens, was far more chaste; and whether from good sense, or that the nation had been struck and reformed by the admirable paper in the Guardian, No.173, he banished verdant sculptures, and did not even revert to the square precision of the foregoing age. He enlarged his plans, disdained to make every division tally with its opposite, and though he still adhered much to straight walks with high clipped hedges, they were only his great lines; the rest he diversified by wilderness, and with loose groves of oak, though still within surrounding hedges. I have observed in the garden at Gubbins in Hertfordshire many detached thoughts, that strongly indicate the dawn of modern taste. As his reformation gained

---

proposes to them at the first resting-place to erect a school; a little farther to found an academy; at a third distance, a manufacture; and at the termination of the park to endow an hospital. Thus, says he, the proprietor would be led to meditate, as he saunters, on the different stages of human life, and both his expense and thoughts would march in a progression of patriotic acts and reflections. When he was laying out so magnificent, charitable, and philosophic an Utopian villa, it would have cost no more to have added a foundling hospital, a senate house, and a burying ground. – If I smile at such visions, still one must be glad that in the whirl of fashions, beneficence should have its turn in vogue; and though the French treat the virtues like everything else, but as an object of mode, it is to be hoped that they too will, every now and then, come into fashion again.

The author I have been mentioning reminds me of a French gentleman, who some years ago made me a visit at Strawberry Hill. He was so complaisant as to commend the place, and to approve our taste in gardens; but in the same style of thinking with the above-cited author, he said, 'I do like your imaginary temples and fictitious terminations of views: I would have real points of view with moving objects; for instance, here I would have – (I forget what) – and there a watering-place.' 'That is not so easy,' I replied, 'one cannot oblige others to assemble at such and such a spot for one's amusement – however, I am glad you would like a watering-place, for *there* happens to be one; in that creek of the Thames the inhabitants of the village do actually water their horses; but I doubt whether, if it were not *convenient* to them to do so, they would frequent the spot only to enliven my prospect.' – Such *Gallo-Chinois* gardens, I apprehend, will rarely be executed.

footing, he ventured farther, and in the royal garden at Richmond dared to introduce cultivated fields, and even morsels of a forest appearance, by the sides of those endless and tiresome walks that stretched out of one into another without intermission. But this was not till other innovators had broke loose too from rigid symmetry. But the capital stroke, the leading step to all that, has followed, was (I believe the first thought was Bridgman's) the destruction of walls for boundaries, and the invention of fossés - an attempt then deemed so astonishing, that the common people called them Ha! Ha's! to express their surprise at finding a sudden and unperceived check to their walk.

One of the first gardens planted in this simple though still formal style was my father's at Houghton. It was laid out by Mr. Eyre, an imitator of Bridgman. It contains three-and-twenty acres, then reckoned a considerable portion.

I call a sunk fence the leading step for these reasons. No sooner was this simple enchantment made, than levelling, mowing and rolling followed. The contiguous ground of the park without the sunk fence was to be harmonised with the lawn within; and the garden in its turn was to be set free from its prim regularity, that it might assort with the wilder country without. The sunk fence ascertained the specific garden, but that it might not draw too obvious a line of distinction between the neat and the rude, the contiguous outlying parts came to be included in a kind of general design: and when nature was taken into the plan, under improvements, every step that was made pointed out new beauties and inspired new ideas. At that moment appeared Kent, painter enough to taste the charms of landscape, bold and opinionated enough to dare and to dictate, and born with a genius to strike out a great system from the twilight of imperfect essays. He leaped the fence, and saw that all nature was a garden. He felt the delicious contrast of hill and valley changing imperceptibly into each other, tasted the beauty of the gentle swell, or concave scoop, and remarked how loose groves crowned an easy eminence in happy ornament, and while they called in the distant view between their graceful stems, removed and extended the perspective by delusive comparison.

Thus the pencil of his imagination bestowed all the arts of landscape on the scenes he handled. The great principles on which he worked were perspective, and light and shade. Groups of trees broke too uniform or too extensive a lawn; evergreens and woods were opposed to the glare of the champain, and where the view was less fortunate, or so much exposed as to be beheld at once, he blotted out some parts by thick shades, to divide it into variety, or to make the richest scene more enchanting by reserving it to a farther advance of the spectator's step. Thus selecting favourite objects, and veiling deformities by screens of plantation; sometimes allowing the rudest waste to add its foil to the richest theatre, he realised the compositions of the greatest masters in painting. Where objects were wanting to animate his horizon, his taste as an architect could bestow immediate termination. His buildings, his seats, his temples, were more the works of his pencil than of his compasses. We owe the restoration of Greece and the diffusion of architecture to his skill in landscape.

But of all the beauties he added to the face of this beautiful country, none surpassed his management of water. Adieu to canals, circular basins, and cascades tumbling down marble steps, that last absurd magnificence of Italian and French villas. The forced elevation of cataracts was no more. The gentle stream was taught to serpentize seemingly at its pleasure, and where discontinued by different levels, its course appeared to be concealed by thickets properly interspersed, and glittered again at a distance where it might be supposed to naturally arrive. Its borders were smoothed, but preserved their waving irregularity. A few trees scattered here and there on its edges sprinkled the tame bank that accompanied its meanders; and when it disappeared among the hills, shades descending from the heights leaned towards its progress, and framed the distant point of light under which it was lost, as it turned aside to either hand of the blue horizon.

Thus dealing in none but the colours of nature, and catching its most favourable features, men saw a new creation opening before their eyes. The living landscape was chastened or polished, not transformed. Freedom was given to the forms of trees; they extended their branches unrestricted, and where any eminent oak or master beech had escaped maiming and survived the forest, bush and bramble was removed, and all its honours were restored to distinguish and shade the plain. Where the united plumage of an ancient wood extended wide its undulating canopy, and stood venerable in its darkness, Kent thinned the foremost ranks, and left but so many detached and scattered trees as softened the approach of gloom and blended a chequered light with the thus lengthened shadows of the remaining columns.

Horace Walpole, On Modern Gardening

Oriental Gardening

Amongst the Chinese, Gardening is held in much higher esteem, than it is in Europe: they rank a perfect work in that Art, with the great productions of the human understanding; and say, that its efficacy in moving the passions, yields to that of few other arts whatever. Their Gardeners are not only Botanists, but also Painters and Philosophers; having a thorough knowledge of the human mind, and of the arts by which its strongest feelings are excited. It is not in China, as in Italy and France, where every petty Architect is a Gardener; neither is it as in another famous country, where peasants emerge from the melon grounds to take the periwig, and turn professors; as Sganarelle, the faggot-maker, quitted his hatchet, and commenced physician. In China, Gardening is a distinct profession, requiring extensive study; to the perfection of which few arrive. The Gardeners there, far from being either ignorant or illiterate, are men of high abilities, who join to good natural parts, most ornaments that study, travelling, and long experience can supply them with: it is in consideration of these accomplishments only that they are permitted to exercise their profession: for with the Chinese the taste of Oriental Gardening is an object of legislative attention; it being supposed to have an influence upon the general culture, and consequently upon the beauty of the whole country. They observe, that mistakes committed in this Art, are too important to be tolerated; being much exposed to view, and in a great measure irreparable: as it often requires the space of a century, to redress the blunders of an hour.

The Chinese Gardeners take nature for their pattern; and their aim is to imitate all her beautiful irregularities. Their first consideration is the nature of the ground they are to work upon: whether it be flat or sloping; hilly or mountainous; small or of considerable extent; abounding with springs and rivers, or labouring under a scarcity of water; whether woody or bare, rough or even, barren or rich; and whether the transitions be sudden, and the character grand, wild or tremendous; or whether they be gradual, and the general bent placid, gloomy or cheerful. To all which circumstances they carefully attend; choosing such dispositions as humour the ground, hide its defects, improve or set off its advantages, and can be executed with expedition, at a moderate expence.

They are also attentive to the wealth or indigence of the patron by whom they are employed; to his age, his infirmities, temper, amusements, connections, business and manner of living; as likewise to the season of the year in which the Garden is likely to be most frequented by him: suiting themselves in their composition to his circumstances; and providing for his wants and recreations. Their skill consists in struggling with the imperfections and defects of nature; and with every other impediment: and in producing, in spite of every obstacle, works that are uncommon, and perfect in their kind.

Though the Chinese artists have nature for their general model, yet they are not so attached to her as to exclude all appearance of art: on the contrary, they think it on many occasions, necessary to make an ostentatious show of their labour. Nature, say they, affords us but few materials to work with: plants, ground and water, are her only productions: and though both the forms and arrangements of these may be varied to an incredible degree, yet have they but few striking varieties; the rest being of the nature of changes rung upon bells, which, though in reality different, still produce the same uniform kind of jingling; the variation being too minute to be easily perceived.

Art must therefore supply the scantiness of nature; and not only be employed to produce variety, but also novelty and effect: for the simple arrangements of nature are met with in every common field, to a certain degree of perfection; and are therefore too familiar to excite any strong sensations in the mind of the beholder, or to produce any uncommon degree of pleasure.

It is indeed true, that novelty and variety may both be attained, by transplanting the peculiarities of one country to another; by introducing rocks, cataracts, impending woods, and other parts of romantic situations, in flat places; by employing much water where it is rare, and cultivated plains, amidst the rude irregularities of mountains: but even this resource is easily exhausted, and can seldom be put in practice, without a very great expence.

The Chinese are therefore no enemies to strait lines; because they are, generally speaking, productive of grandeur, which often cannot be attained without them: nor have they any aversion to regular geometric figures, which they say are beautiful in themselves, and well suited to small compositions, where the luxuriant irregularities of nature would fill up and embarrass the parts they should adorn. They likewise think them properest for flower-gardens, and all other compositions, where much art is apparent in the culture; and where it should therefore not be omitted in the forms.

Their regular buildings they generally surround with artificial temples, slopes, and many flights of steps; the angles of which are adorned with groups of sculpture and vases, intermixed with all sorts of artificial water-works, which, connecting with the architecture, spread the composition, serve to give it consequence, and add to the gaiety, splendour, and bustle of the scenery.

Round the main habitation, and near all their decorated structures, the grounds are laid out with great regularity, and kept with great care: no plants are admitted that intercept the view of the buildings; nor any lines but such as accompany the architecture properly, and contribute to the general symmetry and good effect of the whole composition: for they hold it absurd to surround an elegant fabric with disorderly rude vegetation; saying, that it looks like a diamond set in lead; and always conveys the idea of an unfinished work. When the buildings are rustic, the scenery which surrounds them is wild; when they are grand, it is gloomy; when gay, it is luxuriant: in short, the Chinese are scrupulously nice in preserving the same character through every part of the composition; which is one great cause of that surprising variety with which their works abound.

They are fond of introducing statues, busts, bas-reliefs, and every production of the chisel, as well in other parts of their Gardens, as round their buildings; observing, that they are not only ornamental, but, that by commemorating past events, and celebrated personages, they awaken the mind to pleasing contemplation; hurrying our reflections up into the remotest ages of antiquity: and they never fail to scatter ancient inscriptions, verses, and moral sentences, about their grounds; which are placed upon the backs of colossal tortoise and elephants; or large ruinated stones, and columns of marble; or engraved on trees and rocks: such situations being always chosen for them, as correspond with the sense of the inscriptions; which thereby acquire force in themselves, and likewise give a stronger expression to the scene.

They say, that all these decorations are necessary, to characterize and distinguish the different scenes of their compositions; among which, without such assistance, there would unavoidably be a tiresome similarity.

And whenever it is objected to them, that many of these things are unnatural, and ought therefore not to be suffered, they answer, that most improvements are unnatural; yet they are allowed to be improvements, and not only tolerated, but admired. Our vestments, say they, are neither of leather, nor like our skins, but formed of rich silks and embroidery; our houses and palaces bear no resemblance to caverns in the rocks, which are the only natural habitations; nor is our music either like thunder, or the whistling of the northern wind, the harmony of nature. Nature produces nothing either boiled, roasted or stewed; and yet we do not eat raw meat: nor doth she supply us with any other tools for all our purposes, but teeth and hands; yet we have saws, hammers, axes, and a thousand other implements: in short, there is scarcely any thing in which art is not apparent; and why should its appearance be excluded from Gardening only? Poets and painters soar above the pitch of nature, when they would give energy to their compositions. The same privilege, therefore, should be allowed to Gardeners: inanimate, simple nature, is too insipid for our purposes: much is expected of us; and therefore, we have occasion for every aid that either art or nature can furnish. The scenery of a Garden should differ as much from common nature, as an heroic poem doth from a prose relation; and Gardeners, like poets, should give a loose to their imagination; and even fly beyond the bounds of truth, whenever it is necessary to elevate, to embellish, to enliven, or to add novelty to their subject.

Sir William Chambers, *A Dissertation on Oriental Gardening*

Embellished Landscape

Among the peculiar features of English landscape, may be added also the embellished garden, and the park scene. In other countries the environs of great houses are yet under the direction of formality. The wonder-working hand of art, with its regular cascades, spouting fountains, flights of terraces, and other atchievements, hath still possession of the gardens of kings and princes. In England alone the pure model of nature is adopted.

This is a mode of scenery intirely of the sylvan kind. As we seek among the wild works of nature for the sublime, we seek here for the beautiful: and where there is a variety of lawn, wood, and water; and these naturally combined; and not too much decorated with buildings, nor disgraced by fantastic ornaments; we find a species of landscape, which no country, but England, can display in such perfection: not only because this just taste in decoration prevails no where else; but also, because no where else are found such proper materials. The want of English oak, as we have just observed, can never really be made up, in this kind of landscape especially. Nor do we any where find so close and rich a verdure. An easy swell may, every where, be given to ground: but it cannot every where be covered with a velvet turf, which constitutes one great beauty of the embellished lawn.

William Gilpin, *Observations, Relative Chiefly to Picturesque Beauty,*
Made in the Year 1772, On Several Parts of England; Particularly the Mountains,
and Lakes of Cumberland and Westmoreland

The Thirteenth Discourse

And here I must observe, and I believe it may be considered as a general rule, that no art can be grafted with success on another art. For though they all profess the same origin, and to proceed from the same stock, yet each has its own peculiar modes both of imitating nature, and of deviating from it, each for the accomplishment of its own peculiar purpose. These deviations, more especially, will not bear transplantation to another soil.

If a painter should endeavour to copy the theatrical pomp and parade of dress and attitude, instead of that simplicity which is not a greater beauty in life than it is in painting, we should condemn such pictures, as painted in the meanest style.

So also gardening, as far as gardening is an art, or entitled to that appellation, is a deviation from nature; for if the true taste consists, as many hold, in banishing every appearance of art, or any traces of the footsteps of man, it would then no longer be a garden. Even though we define it, 'Nature to advantage dressed', and in some sense it is such, and much more beautiful and commodious for the recreation of man; it is however, when so dressed, no longer a subject for the pencil of a landscape-painter, as all landscape-painters know, who love to have recourse to Nature herself, and to dress her according to the principles of their own art; which are far different from those of gardening, even when conducted according to the most approved principles; and such as a landscape-painter himself would adopt in the disposition of his own grounds, for his own private satisfaction.

Sir Joshua Reynolds, *Discourses Delivered to the Students of the Royal Academy*

The Picturesque Leasowes

The ascent from hence winds somewhat more steeply to another seat, where the eye is thrown over a rough scene of broken and furzy ground, upon a piece of water in the flat, whose extremities are hid behind trees and shrubs, amongst which the house appears, and makes upon the whole no unpleasing picture. The path still winds under cover up the hill, the steep declivity of which is somewhat eased by the serpentine sweep of it, till we come to a small bench, with this line of Pope's Eloisa:

'Divine oblivion of low-thoughted Care!'

The opening before it presents a solitary scene of trees, thickets, and precipice, and terminates upon a green hill, with a clump of firs on the top of it.

We now find the great use as well as beauty of the serpentine path in climbing up this wood, the first seat of which, alluding to the rural scene before it, has the following lines from Virgil:

Hic latis otia fundis
Speluncæ, vivique lacus, hic frigida Tempe,
Mugitusque bonum, mollesque sub arbores omni!

Here tranquil leisures in the ample field,
Here caves and living lakes their pleasures yield;
Here vales invite where sports the cooling breeze,
And peaceful sleep beneath embow'ring trees,
While lowing herds surround.

Here the eye looking down a slope beneath the spreading arms of oak and beech trees, passes first over some rough furzy ground, then over water to the large swelling lawn, in the centre of which the house is discovered among trees and thickets: this forms the fore ground. Beyond this appears a swell of waste furzy land, diversified with a cottage, and a road that winds behind a farm-house and a fine clump of trees. The back scene of all is a semicircular range of hills, diversified with woods, scenes of cultivation, and inclosures, to about four or five miles distance.

Still winding up into the wood, we come to a slight seat, opening through the trees to a bridge of five piers, crossing a large piece of water at about half a mile's distance. The next seat looks down from a considerable height, along the side of a steep precipice, upon irregular and pleasing ground. And now we turn upon a sudden into a long straight-lined walk in the wood, arched over with tall trees, and terminating with a small rustick building. Though the walk, as I said, be straight-lined, yet the base rises and falls so agreeably, as leaves no room to censure its formality. About the middle of this avenue, which runs the whole length of this hanging wood, we arrive unexpectedly at a lofty Gothick seat, whence we look down a slope, more considerable than that before mentioned, through the wood on each side. This view is indeed a fine one, the eye first travelling down over well-variegated ground into the valley, where is a large piece of water, whose sloping banks give all the appearance of a noble river. The ground from hence rises gradually to the top of Clent hill, at three or four miles distance, and the landscape is enriched with a view of Hales Owen, the late Lord Dudley's house, and a large wood of Lord Lyttleton's. It is impossible to give an adequate description of this view, the beauty of it depending on the great variety of objects and beautiful shape of ground, and all such a distance as to admit of being seen distinctly.

Here we proceed to the rustick building before mentioned, a slight and unexpensive edifice, formed of rough unhewn stone, commonly called here The Temple of Pan, having a trophy of the Tibia and Syrinx, and this inscription over the entrance:

Pan primus calamos cera conjungere plures
Edocuit; Pan curat oves, oviumque magistros.

Pan, god of shepherds, first inspir'd our swains
Their pipes to frame, and tune their rural strains;
Pan from impending harm the fold defends,
And Pan the master of the fold befriends.

Hence mounting once more to the right through this dark umbrageous walk, we enter at once upon a lightsome high natural terrace, whence the eye is thrown over all the scenes we have seen before, together with many fine additional ones, and all beheld from a declivity that approaches as near a precipice as is agreeable. In the middle is a seat with this description:

Divini gloria ruris

O glory of the sylvan scene divine!

To give a better idea of this, by far the most magnificent scene here, it were, perhaps, best to divide it into two distinct parts – the noble concave in the front, and the rich valley towards the right. – In regard to the former, if a boon companion could enlarge his idea of a punch-bowl, ornamented within all the romantick scenery the Chinese ever yet devised, it would, perhaps, afford him the highest idea he could possibly conceive of earthly happiness: he would certainly wish to swim in it. Suffice it to say, that the horizon, or brim, is as finely varied as the cavity. It would be idle here to mention the Clee hills, the Wreken, the Welsh mountains, or Caer Caradock, at a prodigious distance; which, though they finish the scene agreeably, should not be mentioned at the Leasowes, the beauty of which turns chiefly upon distinguishable scenes.

R. Dodsley, *A Description of the Leasowes*

A Tour of Some of the Gardens of England

(Memorandum made on a tour to some of the gardens in England, described by Whateley in his book on Gardening.)

While his descriptions, in point of style, are models of perfect elegance and classical correctness, they are as remarkable for their exactness. I always walked over the gardens with his book in my hand, examined with attention the particular spots he described, found them so justly characterized by him as to be easily recognized, and saw with wonder, that his fine imagination had never been able to seduce him from the truth. My inquiries were directed chiefly to such practical things as might enable me to estimate the expense of making and maintaining a garden in that style. My journey was in the months of March and April, 1786.

Chiswick. – Belongs to Duke of Devonshire. A garden about six acres; – the octagonal dome has an ill effect, both within and without: the garden shows still too much of art. An obelisk of very ill effect; another in the middle of a pond useless. [April 2]

Hampton-Court. – Old fashioned. Clipt yews grown wild. [April 2]

Twickenham. – Pope's original garden, three and a half acres. Sir Wm. Stanhope added one and a half acres. This is a long narrow slip, grass and trees in the middle, walk all around. Now Sir Wellbore Ellis's. Obelisk at bottom of Pope's garden, as monument to his mother. Inscription, 'Ah! Editha, matrum optima, mulierum amantissima, Vale.' The house about thirty yards from the Thames: the ground shelves gently to the water side; on the back of the house passes the street, and beyond that the garden. The grotto is under the street, and goes out level to the water. In the centre of the garden a mound with a spiral walk around it. A rookery. [April 2]

Esher-Place. – The house in a bottom near the river; on the other side the ground rises pretty much. The road by which we come to the house forms a dividing line in the middle of the front; on the right are heights, rising one beyond and above another, with clumps of trees, on the farthest a temple. A hollow filled up with a clump of trees, the tallest in the bottom, so that the top is quite flat. On the left the ground descends.

Clumps of trees, the clumps on each hand balance finely – a most lovely mixture of concave and convex. The garden is of about forty-five acres, besides the park which joins. Belongs to Lady Frances Pelham. [April 2]

Claremont. – Lord Clive's. Nothing remarkable.

Paynshill. – Mr. Hopkins. Three hundred and twenty-three acres, garden and park all in one. Well described by Whately. Grotto said to have cost £7,000. Whately says one of the bridges is of stone, but both now are of wood, the lower sixty feet high: there is too much evergreen. The dwelling-house built by Hopkins, ill-situated: he has not been there in five years. He lived there four years while building the present house. It is not finished; its architecture is incorrect. [April 2]

Woburn. – Belongs to Lord Peters. Lord Loughborough is the present tenant for two lives. Four people to the farm, four to the pleasure garden, four to the kitchen garden. All are intermixed, the pleasure garden being merely a highly-ornamented walk through and round the divisions of the farm and kitchen garden. [April 3]

Caversham. – Sold by Lord Cadogan to Major Marsac. Twenty-five acres of garden, four hundred acres of park, six acres of kitchen garden. A large lawn, separated by a sunk fence from the garden, appears to be part of it. A straight, broad gravel walk passes before the front and parallel to it, terminated on the right by a Doric temple, and opening at the other end on a fine prospect. This straight walk has an ill effect. The lawn in front, which is pasture, well disposed with clumps of trees. [April 4]

Wotton. – Now belongs to the Marquis of Buckingham, son of George Grenville. The lake covers fifty acres, the river five acres, the basin fifteen acres, the little river two acres – equal to seventy-two acres of water. The lake and great river are on a level; they fall into the basin five feet below, and that again into the little river five feet lower. A walk goes round the whole, three miles in circumference, and containing within it about three hundred acres: sometimes it passes close to the water, sometimes so far off as to leave large pasture grounds between it and the water. But two hands to keep the pleasure grounds in order; much neglected. The water affords two thousand brace of carp in a year. There is a Palladian bridge, of which, I think, Whatley does not speak. [April 5]

Stowe. – Belongs to the Marquis of Buckingham, son of George Grenville, and who takes it from Lord Temple. Fifteen men and eighteen boys employed in keeping the pleasure grounds. Within the walk are considerable portions separated by enclosures and used for pasture. The Egyptian pyramid is almost entirely taken down by the late Lord Temple, to erect a building there, in commemoration of Mr. Pitt, but he died before beginning it, and nothing is done to it yet. The grotto and two rotundas are taken away. There are four levels of water, receiving it one from the other. The basin contains seven acres, the lake below that ten acres. Kent's building is called the temple of Venus. The enclosure is entirely by ha-ha. At each end of the front line there is a recess like the bastion of a fort. In one of these is the temple of Friendship, in the other the temple of Venus. They are seen the one from the other, the line of sight passing, not through the garden, but through the country parallel to the line of the garden. This has a good effect. In the approach to Stowe, you are brought a mile through a straight avenue, pointing to the Corinthian arch and to the house, till you get to the arch, then you turn short to the right. The straight approach is very ill. The Corinthian arch has a very useless appearance, inasmuch as it has no pretension to any destination. Instead of being an object from the house, it is an obstacle to a very pleasing distant prospect. The Grecian valley being clear of trees, while the hill on each side is covered with them, is much deepened to appearance. [April 6]

Leasowes, in Shropshire. – Now the property of Mr. Horne by purchase. One hundred and fifty acres within the walk. The waters small. This is not even an ornamental farm – it is only a grazing farm with a path around it, here and there a seat of board, rarely anything better. Architecture has contributed nothing. The obelisk is of brick. Shenstone had but three hundred pounds a year, and ruined himself by what he did to this farm. It is said that he died of the heart-aches which his debts occasioned him. The part next to the road is of red earth, that on the further part grey. The first and second cascades are beautiful. The landscape at number eighteen, and prospect at thirty-two, are fine. The walk through the wood is umbrageous and pleasing. The whole arch of prospect may be of ninety degrees. Many of the inscriptions are lost. [April 7]

Blenheim. – Twenty-five hundred acres, of which two hundred is garden, one hundred and fifty water, twelve kitchen garden, and the rest park. Two hundred people employed to keep it in order, and to make alterations and additions. About fifty of these employed in pleasure grounds. The turf is mowed once in ten days. In summer, about two thousand fallow deer in the park, and two or three thousand sheep. The palace of Henry II was remaining till taken down by Sarah, widow of the first Duke of Marlborough. It was on a round spot levelled by art, near what is now water, and but a little above it. The island was a part of the high road leading to the palace. Rosamund's bower was near where is now a little grove, about two hundred yards from the palace. The well is near where the bower was. The water here is very beautiful, and very grand. The cascade from the lake, a fine one; except this the garden has no great beauties. It is not laid out in fine lawns and woods, but the trees are scattered thinly over the ground, and every here and there small thickets of shrubs, in oval raised beds, cultivated, and flowers among the shrubs. The gravelled walks are broad – art appears too much. There are but a few seats in it, and nothing of architecture more dignified. There is no one striking position in it. There has been a great addition to the length of the river since Whateley wrote. [April 9]

Enfield Chase. – One of the four lodges. Garden about sixty acres. Originally by Lord Chatham, now in the tenure of Dr. Beaver, who married the daughter of Mr. Sharpe. The lease lately renewed – not in good repair. The water very fine; would admit of great improvement by extending walks, etc., to the principal water at the bottom of the lawn.

Moor Park. – The lawn about thirty acres. A piece of ground up hill of six acres. A small lake. Clumps of spruce firs. Surrounded by walk – separately inclosed – destroys unity. The property of Mr. Rous, who bought of Sir Thomas Dundas. The building superb; the principle front a Corinthian portico of four columns; in front of the wings a colonnade, Ionic, subordinate. Back front a terrace, four Corinthian pilasters. Pulling down wings of building; removing deer; wants water.

Kew. –Archimedes' screw for raising water. [April 14]

Thomas Jefferson, *Garden Book*

The Summer of 1783

TO THE HONOURABLE DAINES BARRINGTON

As the effects of heat are seldom very remarkable in the northerly climate of England, where the summers are often so defective in warmth and sun-shine as not to ripen the fruits of the earth so well as might be wished, I shall be more concise in my account of the severity of a summer season, and so make a little amends for the prolix account of the degrees of cold, and the inconveniences that we suffered from late rigorous winters.

The summers of 1781 and 1783 were unusually hot and dry; to them therefore I shall turn back in my journals, without recurring to any more distant period. In the former of these years my peach and nectarine-trees suffered so much from the heat that the rind on the bodies was scalded and came off; since which the trees have been in a decaying state. This may prove a hint to assiduous gardeners to fence and shelter their wall-trees with mats or boards, as they may easily do, because such annoyance is seldom of long continuance. During that summer also, I observed that my apples were coddled, as it were, on the trees; so that they had no quickness of flavour, and would not keep in the winter. This circumstance put me in mind of what I heard travellers assert, that they never ate a good apple or apricot in the south of Europe, where the heats were so great as to render the juices vapid and insipid.

The great pests of a garden are wasps, which destroy all the finer fruits just as they are coming into perfection. In 1781 we had none; in 1783 there were myriads; which would have devoured all the produce of my garden, had not we set the boys to take the nests, and caught thousands with hazel twigs tipped with bird-lime: we have since employed the boys to take and destroy the large breeding wasps in the spring. Such expedients have a great effect on these marauders, and will keep them under. Though wasps do not abound but in hot summers, yet they do not prevail in every hot summer, as I have instanced in the two years above mentioned.

In the sultry season of 1783 honey-dews were so frequent as to deface and destroy the beauties of my garden. My honey-suckles, which were one week the most sweet and lovely objects that the eye could behold, became the next the most loathsome; being enveloped in a viscous substance, and loaded with black aphides, or smother-flies. The occasion of this clammy appearance seems to be this, that in hot weather the effluvia of flowers in fields and meadows and gardens are drawn up in the day by a brisk evaporation, and then in the night fall down again with the dews, in which they are entangled; that the air is strongly scented, and therefore impregnated with the particles of flowers in summer weather, our senses will inform us; and that this clammy sweet substance is of the vegetable kind we may learn from the bees, to whom it is very grateful: and we may be assured that it falls in the night, because it is always seen first in warm still mornings.

On chalky and sandy soils, and in the hot villages about London, the thermometer has been often observed to mount as high as 83 or 84; but with us, in this hilly and woody district, I have hardly ever seen it exceed 80; nor does it often arrive at that pitch. The reason, I conclude, is, that our dense clayey soil, so much shaded by trees, is not so easily heated through as those above-mentioned: and, besides, our mountains cause currents of air and breezes; and the vast effluvia from our woodlands temper and moderate our heats.

Gilbert White, *The Natural History & Antiquities of Selborne*

A Human Kindness

After breakfast walk in the gardens of the Tuileries, where there is the most extraordinary sight that either French or English eyes could ever behold at Paris. The King walking with six grenadiers of the *malice bourgeoise*, with an officer or two of his household and a page. The doors of the gardens are kept shut in respect to him, in order to exclude everybody but deputies or those who have admission tickets. When he entered the palace the doors of the gardens were thrown open for all without distinction, though the Queen was still walking with a lady of her court. She also was attended so closely by the *gardes bourgeoise*, that she could not speak, but in a low voice, without being heard by them. A mob followed her talking very loud, and paying no other apparent respect than that of taking off their hats wherever she passed, which was indeed more than I expected. Her Majesty does not appear to be in health; she seems to be much affected and shows it in her face; but the King is as plump as ease can render him. By his orders, there is a little garden railed off for the Dauphin to amuse himself in, and a small room is built in it to retire to in case of rain; here he was at work with his little hoe and rake, but not without a guard of two grenadiers.

Arthur Young, *Travels in France*

The Garden of Love

I went to the Garden of Love
And saw what I had never seen:
A chapel was built in the midst
Where I used to play on the green.

And the gates of this chapel were shut,
And 'Thou shalt not' writ over the door;
So I turned to the Garden of Love
That so many sweet flowers bore,

And I saw it was filled with graves
And tombstones where flowers should be;
And priests in black gowns were walking their rounds,
And binding with briars my joys and desires.

William Blake, *Songs of Experience*

How Far the Principles of Painting Have Been Applied to Improvements

Having now examined the chief qualities that in such various ways render objects interesting; having shewn how much beauty, spirit, and effect of landscape, real or imitated, depend on a due mixture of rough and smooth, of warm and cool tints; and of what extreme consequence variety and intricacy are in those, as well as in our other pleasures; having shewn too, that the general principles of improving are in reality the same as those of painting, I shall next enquire how far the principles of the last-mentioned art (clearly the best qualified to improve and refine our ideas of nature) have been attended to by improvers; and how far also those who first produced, and those who have continued the present system, were capable of applying them, even if they had wished to do so.

It appears from Mr. Walpole's very ingenious and entertaining Treatise on Modern Gardening, that Kent was the first who introduced that so much admired change from the old to the present system; the great leading feature of which change, and the leading character of each style, is very aptly expressed in half a line of Horace;

Mutat quadrata rotundis.

Formerly, every thing was in squares and parallelograms; now every thing is in segments of circles, and ellipses: the formality still remains; the character of that formality alone has changed. The old canal, for instance, has lost, indeed, its straightness and its angles; but it is become regularly serpentine, and the edges remain as naked, and as uniform as before: avenues, vistas, and strait ridings through woods, are exchanged for clumps, belts, and circular roads and plantations of every kind: strait alleys in gardens, and the platform of the old terrace, for the curves of the gravel walk. The intention of the new improvers was certainly meritorious; for they meant to banish formality, and so restore nature; but it must be remembered, that strongly marked, distinct, and regular curves, unbroken and undisguised, are hardly less unnatural or formal, though much less grand and simple, than strait lines; and that, independently of monotony, the continual and indiscriminate use of such curves, has an appearance of affectation and of studied grace, that always creates disgust.

The old style had indisputably defects and absurdities of the most obvious and striking kind. Kent, therefore, is entitled to the same praise as many other reformers, who have broken through narrow, inveterate, long established prejudices; and who, thereby, have prepared the way for more liberal notions, although, by their own practice and example, they may have substituted other narrow prejudices and absurdities in the room of those which they had banished. It must be owned at the same time, that like other reformers, he and his followers demolished, without distinction, the costly and magnificent decorations of past times, and all that had long been held in veneration; and among them (I speak solely of gardening) many things that still deserved to have been respected, and adopted. Such, however, is the zeal and enthusiasm with which, at the early period of their success, novelties of every kind are received, that the fascination becomes general; and those few, who may then see their defects, hardly dare to attack openly, what such a multitude is in arms to defend. It is reserved for those, who are farther removed from that moment of sudden change, and strong prejudice, to examine the merits and defects of both styles, in every particular of what is called improvement: But how are they to be examined? by the general and unchanging principles, to which the effects of all visible objects are to be referred, but which (for the reasons I before have mentioned) are very commonly called the principles of painting. These *general* principles, not those peculiar to the *practice* of the art, are, in my idea, universally to be referred to in every kind of ornamental gardening; in the most confined, as well as the most enlarged sense of the word: my business at present is almost entirely with the latter – with what may be termed the landscapes, and the general scenery of the place, whether under the title of grounds, lawn, park, or any other denomination.

With respect to Kent, and his particular mode of improving, I can say but little from my own knowledge, having never seen any works of his that I could be sure had undergone no alteration from any of his successors; but Mr. Walpole, by a few characteristic anecdotes, has made us perfectly acquainted with the turn of his mind, and the extent of his genius.

Sir Uvedale Price, *An Essay on the Picturesque*

A Poison Tree

I was angry with my friend;
I told my wrath, my wrath did end.
I was angry with my foe;
I told it not, my wrath did grow.

And I watered it in fears,
Night and morning with my tears;

And I sunned it with smiles,
And with soft deceitful wiles.

And it grew both day and night
Till it bore an apple bright;
And my foe beheld it shine,
And he knew that it was mine.

And into my garden stole
When the night had veiled the pole –
In the morning glad I see
My foe outstretched beneath the tree.

William Blake, *Songs of Experience*

Objections to Modern Gardening

OBJECTION NO. 1

There is no error more prevalent in modern gardening, or more frequently carried to excess, than taking away hedges to unite many small fields into one extensive and naked lawn, before plantations are made to give it the appearance of a park; and where ground is subdivided by sunk fences, imaginary freedom is dearly purchased at the expense of actual confinement.

No. 2

The baldness and nakedness round a house is part of the same mistaken system, of concealing fences to gain extent. A palace, or even an elegant villa, in a grass field, appears to me incongruous; yet I have seldom had sufficient influence to correct this common error.

No. 3

An approach which does not evidently lead to the house, or which does not take the shortest course, cannot be right.

No. 4

A poor man's cottage, divided into what is called *a pair of lodges*, is a mistaken expedient to mark importance in the entrance to a Park.

No. 5

The entrance gate should not be visible from the mansion, unless it opens into a court yard.

No. 6

The plantation surrounding a place, called a *Belt*, I have never advised; nor have I ever willingly marked a drive, or walk, completely round the verge of a park, except in small villas where a dry path round a person's own field, is always more interesting to him than any other walk.

No. 7

Small plantations of trees, surrounded by a fence, are the best expedients to form groupes, because trees planted singly seldom grow well; neglect of thinning and of removing the fence, has produced that ugly deformity called a *Clump*.

No. 8

Water on an eminence, or on the side of a hill, is among the most common errors of Mr. Brown's followers: in numerous instances I have been allowed to remove such pieces of water from the hills to the valleys; but in many my advice has not prevailed.

No. 9

Deception may be allowable in imitating works of NATURE; thus artificial rivers, lakes, and rock scenery, can only be great by deception, and the mind acquiesces in the fraud after it is detected: but in works of ART every trick ought to be avoided. Sham churches, sham ruins, sham bridges, and every thing which appears what it is not, disgusts when the trick is discovered.

No. 10

In buildings of every kind the *character* should be strictly observed. No incongruous mixture can be justified. To add Grecian to Gothic, or Gothic to Grecian, is equally absurd; and a sharp pointed arch to a garden gate, or a dairy window, however frequently it occurs, is not less offensive than Grecian architecture, in which the standard rules of relative proportion are neglected or violated.

The perfection of landscape gardening consists in the fullest attention to these principles, *Utility*, *Proportion*, and *Unity*, or harmony of parts to the whole.

Humphry Repton,
Observations on The Theory and Practice of Landscape Gardening

Neatness, Freshness, Lightness, Symmetry, Regularity, Uniformity and Propriety

Are not, therefore, new buildings beautiful? Unquestionably they are; and peculiarly so: for neatness, freshness, lightness, symmetry, regularity, uniformity, and propriety are undoubtedly beauties of the highest class; though the pleasure, which they afford, is not simply a pleasure of the sense of seeing; nor one received by the mind through the medium of painting. But, upon the same principle, as the association of ideas renders those qualities in visible objects, which are peculiarly pleasing to those conversant in that art; so like wise does it render those qualities, which are peculiarly adapted to promote the comforts and enjoyments of social life, pleasing to the eye of civilized man; though there be nothing, in the forms of colours of the objects themselves, in any degree pleasing to the sense; but, perhaps, the contrary. Hence neatness and freshness will always delight, if not out of character with the objects, in which they appear; or with the scenery, with which they are connected: for the mind requires propriety in every thing; that is, it requires that those properties, the ideas of which it has been invariably habituated to associate, should be associated in reality; otherwise the combinations will appear to be unnatural, incoherent, or absurd.

DRESS AND CULTURE. CONSISTENCY AND PROPRIETY

For this reason we require, immediately adjoining the dwellings of opulence and luxury, that every thing should assume its character; and not be, but appear to be dressed and cultivated. In such situations, neat gravel walks, mown turf, and flowering plants and shrubs, trained and distributed by art, are perfectly in character; although, if the same buildings were abandoned, and in ruins, we should, on the same principle of consistency and propriety, require neglected paths, rugged lanes, and wild uncultivated thickets; which are, in themselves, more pleasing, both to the eye and the imagination, but, unfit accompaniments for objects, not only originally produced by art, but, in which, art is constantly employed and exhibited. Nevertheless a path with the sides shaggy and neglected, or a picturesque lane between broken and rugged banks, may be kept as clean, and as commodious for the purpose of walking, as the neatest gravel walk; wherefore it is not upon any principle of reason, that the preference is, in such situations, justly given to the latter; but merely upon that of the habitual association of ideas.

In Houses and Gardens

This sort of neatness should, on the same principle, be confined to the immediate appendages of the house; that is, to the grounds, which are so connected with it, as to appear the necessary adjuncts to the dwelling, and therefore to be under the influence of the same character, which is a character of art. On this account, I think the avowed character of art of the Italian gardens preferable, in garden scenery, to the concealed one now in fashion; which is, in reality, rather counterfeited than concealed; for it appears in every thing; but appears in a dress, that does not belong to it: at every step we perceive its exertions; but, at the same time, perceive that it has laboured much to effect little; and that while it seeks to hide its character, it only, like a prostitute who affects modesty, discovers it the more. In the decorations, however, of the ground adjoining a house, much should depend upon the character of the house itself: if it be neat and regular, neatness and regularity should accompany it; but if it be rugged and picturesque, and situated amidst scenery of the same character, art should approach it with more caution: for though it be, in itself, an avowed work of art; yet the influence of time, with the accompaniments of trees and creepers, may have given it a character of nature, which ought to be as little disturbed, as is consistent with comfort: for, after all, the character of nature is more pleasing than any that can be given by art.

In Parks and Forests

At all events the character of dress and artificial neatness ought never to be suffered to encroach upon the park or the forest; where it is contrary to propriety as it is to beauty; and where its introduction, by our modern landscape gardeners, affords one of the most memorable instances of any recorded in the history of fashions, of the extravagant absurdity, with which an insatiate passion for novelty may infect a whole nation.

In Decorations of Grounds

Since the introduction of another style of ornamental gardening, called at first oriental, and afterwards landscape gardening (probably from its efficacy in destroying all picturesque composition) Grecian temples have been employed as decorations by almost all persons, who could afford to indulge their taste in objects so costly: but, though executed, in many instances, on a scale and in a manner suitable to the design, disappointment has, I believe, been invariably the result. Nevertheless they are unquestionably beautiful, being exactly copied from those models, which have stood the criticism of many successive ages, and been constantly beheld with delight and admiration. In the rich lawns and shrubberies of England, however, they lose all that power to please which they so eminently possess on the barren hills of Agrigentum and Segesta, or the naked plains of Pæstum and Athens. But barren and naked as these hills and plains are, they are still, if I may say so, their native hills and plains – the scenery, in which they sprang; and in which the mind, therefore, contemplates them connected and associated with numberless interesting circumstances, both local and historical – both physical and moral, upon which it delights to dwell. In our parks and gardens, on the contrary, they stand wholly unconnected with all that surrounds them – mere unmeaning excrescences; or, what is worse, manifestly meant for ornament, and therefore having no accessory character, but that of ostentatious vanity: so that, instead of exciting any interest, they vitiate and destroy that, which the naturalised objects of the country connected with them would otherwise excite. Even if the landscape scenery should be rendered really beautiful by such ornaments, its beauty will be that of a vain and affected coquette; which, though it may allure the sense, offends the understanding; and, on the whole, excites more disgust than pleasure. In all matters of this kind, the imagination must be conciliated before the eye can be delighted.

SITUATIONS

In choosing a situation for a house of this kind, which is to be a principal feature in a place, more consideration ought to be had of the views towards it, than of those fromwards it: for, consistently with comfort, which ought to be the first object in every dwelling, it very rarely happens that a perfect composition of landscape scenery can be obtained from a door or window; nor does it appear to me particularly desirable that it should be; for few persons ever look for such compositions, or pay much attention to them, while within doors. It is in walks or rides through parks, gardens, or pleasure grounds, that they are attended to and examined, and become subjects of conversation; wherefore the seats, or places of rest, with which such walks and rides are accommodated, are the points of sight, to which the compositions of the scenery ought to be principally adapted. To them, picturesque foregrounds may always be made or preserved, without any loss of comfort or violation of propriety: for that sort of trim neatness, which both require in grounds immediately adjoining a house, is completely misplaced, when employed on the borders of a ride or walk through a park or plantation. If the house be the principal object or feature of the scene from these points of view, the middle ground will be the properest situation for it as will clearly appear from the landscapes of the painters above cited (Claude and Poussin): this is also the situation, which considerations of domestic comfort will generally point out; as being the middle degree of elevation, between the too exposed ridges of the hills, and the too secluded recesses of the vallies. In any position, however, above the point of sight, such objects may be happily placed; and contribute to the embellishment of the adjoining scenery: but there are scarcely any buildings, except bridges, which will bear being looked down upon; a foreshortening from the roof to the base being necessarily awkward and ungraceful.

Sir John Vanbrugh

Sir John Vanbrugh is the only architect, I know of, who has either planned or placed his houses according to the principle here recommended; and, in his two chief works, Blenheim and Castle Howard, it appears to have been strictly adhered to, at least in the placing of them. The views from the principal fronts of both are bad, and much inferior to what other parts of the grounds would have afforded; but the situations of both, as objects to the surrounding scenery, are the best that could have been chosen; and both are certainly worthy of the best situations, which, not only the respective places, but the island of Great Britain could afford.

Mr. Brown

The direct reverse may be said of the late Mr. Brown; who, in the only place, in which he was employed both as architect and improver, with unlimited powers of design and expence in both, has built a house which no situation could adapt to any scenery, except that of a square or a

street; and placed it where no house could have served as an embellishment to the scenery, which does surround it. Such ever has, and ever will
be the difference between the works of artists of genius, who consult
their feelings, and those of plodding mechanics, who look only to their
rules. The former will necessarily be unequal and irregular; and produce
much to blame and ridicule, as well as much to applaud and admire;
whereas the latter, howsoever extolled by the fashions of the day, will
never rise above negative merit.

Richard Payne Knight, *An Analytical Enquiry into the Principles of Taste*

To Lady Beaumont

Lady! the songs of Spring were in the grove
While I was shaping beds for winter flowers;
While I was planting green unfading bowers,
And shrubs – to hang upon the warm alcove
And sheltering wall; and still, as Fancy wove
The dream, to time and nature's blended powers
I gave this paradise for winter hours,
A labyrinth, Lady! which your feet shall rove.
Yes! when the sun of life more feebly shines,
Becoming thoughts, I trust, of solemn gloom
Or of high gladness you shall hither bring;
And these perennial bowers and murmuring pines
Be gracious as the music and the bloom
And all the mighty ravishment of spring.

William Wordsworth

'Improvements'

'Oh! for shame!' cried Mrs Norris. 'A prison, indeed! Sotherton Court is
the noblest old place in the world.'

'It wants improvement, ma'am, beyond any thing. I never saw a place
that wanted so much improvement in my life; and it is so forlorn, that I
do not know what can be done with it.'

'No wonder that Mr Rushworth should think so at present,' said Mrs Grant to Mrs Norris, with a smile; 'but depend upon it, Sotherton will have *every* improvement in time which his heart can desire.'

'I must try to do something with it,' said Mr Rushworth, 'but I do not know what. I hope I shall have some good friend to help me.'

'Your best friend upon such an occasion,' said Miss Bertram, calmly, 'would be Mr Repton, I imagine.'

'That is what I was thinking of. As he has done so well by Smith, I think I had better have him at once. His terms are five guineas a day.'

'Well, and if they were *ten*,' cried Mrs Norris, 'I am sure *you* need not regard it. The expense need not be any impediment. If I were you, I should not think of the expense. I would have every thing done in the best style, and made as nice as possible. Such a place as Sotherton Court deserves every thing that taste and money can do. You have space to work upon there, and grounds that will well reward you. For my part, if I had any thing within the fiftieth part of the size of Sotherton, I should be always planting and improving, for naturally, I am excessively fond of it. It would be ridiculous for me to attempt any thing where I am now, with my little half acre. It would be quite a burlesque. But if I had more room, I should take a prodigious delight in improving and planting. We did a vast deal in that way at the parsonage; we made it quite a different place from what it was when we first had it. You young ones do not remember much about it, perhaps. But if dear Sir Thomas were here, he could tell you what improvements we made; and a great deal more would have been done, but for poor Mr Norris's sad state of health. He could hardly ever get out, poor man, to enjoy any thing, and *that* disheartened me from doing several things that Sir Thomas and I used to talk of. If it had not been for *that*, we should have carried on the garden wall, and made the plantation to shut out the churchyard, just as Dr Grant has done. We were always doing something, as it was. It was only the spring twelve-month before Mr Norris's death, that we put in the apricot against the stable wall, which is now grown such a noble tree, and getting to such perfection, sir,' addressing herself then to Dr Grant.

'The tree thrives well beyond a doubt, madam,' replied Dr Grant. 'The soil is good; and I never pass it without regretting that the fruit should be so little worth the trouble of gathering.'

'Sir, it is a moor park, we bought it as a moor park, and it cost us – that is, it was a present from Sir Thomas, but I saw the bill, and I know it cost seven shillings, and was charged as a moor park.'

'You were imposed on, ma'am,' replied Dr Grant; 'these potatoes have as much the flavour of a moor park apricot, as the fruit from that tree. It is an insipid fruit at the best; but a good apricot is eatable, which none from my garden are.'

'The truth is, ma'am,' said Mrs Grant, pretending to whisper across the table to Mrs Norris, 'that Dr Grant hardly knows what the natural taste of our apricot is; he is scarcely indulged with one, for it is so valuable a fruit, with a little assistance, and ours is such a remarkably large, fair sort, that what with early tarts and preserves, my cook contrives to get them all.'

Mrs Norris, who had begun to redden, was appeased, and, for a little while, other subjects took place of the improvements of Sotherton. Dr Grant and Mrs Norris were seldom good friends; their acquaintance had begun in dilapidations, and their habits were totally dissimilar.

After a short interruption, Mr Rushworth began again. 'Smith's place is the admiration of all the country; and it was a mere nothing before Repton took it in hand. I think I shall have Repton.'

'Mr Rushworth,' said Lady Bertram, 'if I were you, I would have a very pretty shrubbery. One likes to get out into a shrubbery in fine weather.'

Mr Rushworth was eager to assure her ladyship of his acquiescence, and tried to make out something complimentary; but between his submission to *her* taste, and his having always intended the same himself, with the super-added objects of professing attention to the comfort of ladies in general, and of insinuating, that there was one only whom he was anxious to please, he grew puzzled; and Edmund was glad to put an end to his speech by a proposal of wine. Mr Rushworth, however, though not usually a great talker, had still more to say on the subject next to his heart. 'Smith has not much above a hundred acres altogether in his grounds, which is little enough, and it makes it more surprising that the place can have been so improved. Now, at Sotherton, we have a good seven hundred, without reckoning the water meadows; so that I think, if so much could be done at Compton, we need not despair. There have been two or three fine old trees cut down that grew too near the house, and it opens the prospect amazingly, which makes me think that Repton, or any body of that sort, would certainly have the avenue at Sotherton down; the avenue that leads from the west front to the top of the hill you know,' turning to Miss Bertram particularly as he spoke. But Miss Bertram thought it most becoming to reply:

'The avenue! Oh! I do not recollect it. I really know very little of Sotherton.'

Fanny, who was sitting on the other side of Edmund, exactly opposite Miss Crawford, and who had been attentively listening, now looked at him, and said in a low voice,

'Cut down an avenue! What a pity! Does it not make you think of Cowper? "Ye fallen avenues, once more I mourn your fate unmerited."'

He smiled as he answered, 'I am afraid the avenue stands a bad chance, Fanny.'

Jane Austen, Mansfield Park

Gardens are so full of growth and life that it seems perverse to see only the decay and death. This, however, seems to have been the fixation of the poets and novelists of the time. No wonder they are all melancholy. This distemper is not confined to the British Isles either; the East and America join in. Thankfully, Charlotte Brontë, Guy de Maupassant, and the happy folk singers of Chhattisghar are more concerned with the beginning of life than its end.

Eden has a renaissance, but, once more, the troubles of the place rather than the joys attract the attention. Eve, or her suffering, is more popular than Adam, and Lilith, who was also in vogue at the time, makes a guest appearance (Lilith is, variously, Adam's first wife, a demon who attacks children, or a witch).

To counter the depression there is a taste for whimsy. Lewis Carroll gives flowers characters and voices, whilst Hans Andersen blesses them with souls. Neither imagines flowers to be particularly pleasant creations. A generation of children must have been scared to set foot outside, especially as the gardeners they might meet were such severe characters.

J. C. Loudon's account of the different classifications of gardener and how each status was achieved is an interesting piece of social history. The fluidity of horticultural employment, or 'servitude' as he puts it, and, presumably, its insecurity, must have made gardens watchful and suspicious places.

It is the great age of the kitchen garden and of specialist glasshouses devoted to, and managed for, the cultivation of particular groups of plants. I have included three pieces just to show the seriousness and depth with which these subjects are treated: Thomas Rivers debunks the myth that *grapes are challenging and George Don tells you everything you might need to know about glasshouse cultivation. It is difficult to imagine any gardener today breeding a culinary dandelion 'more vigorous' than the common sort, yet that is what Vilmorin-Andrieux describes.*

The controversy over design in gardens discovered two fresh protagonists in Sir Reginald Blomfield and William Robinson. Blomfield, an architect, argued, much like Richard Payne Knight at the start of the century, for the area around the house to be an obvious work of art; the house and garden to be a coherent unity. Robinson advocated informal planting, and for gardens to be left to gardeners. The debate found a certain, temporary, synthesis through the working partnership of Lutyens and Jekyll, but Robinson is ahead in the long game. Blomfield is worth reading though, and his passionate advocacy for some intelligent, sympathetic design to be applied to London's squares is as apposite now as it was in 1892.

Ode on Melancholy

No, no, go not to Lethe, neither twist
Wolfsbane, tight-rooted, for its poisonous wine;
Nor suffer thy pale forehead to be kissed
By nightshade, ruby grape of Proserpine;
Make not your rosary of yew-berries,
Nor let the beetle, nor the death-moth be
Your mournful Psyche, nor the downy owl
A partner in your sorrow's mysteries;
For shade to shade will come too drowsily,
And drown the wakeful anguish of the soul.

But when the melancholy fit shall fall
Sudden from heaven like a weeping cloud,
That fosters the droop-headed flowers all,
And hides the green hill in an April shroud;
Then glut thy sorrow on a morning rose,
Or on the rainbow of the salt sand-wave,

Or on the wealth of globed peonies;
Or if thy mistress some rich anger shows,
Imprison her soft hand, and let her rave,
And feed deep, deep upon her peerless eyes.

She dwells with Beauty – Beauty that must die;
And Joy, whose hand is ever at his lips
Bidding adieu; and aching Pleasure nigh,
Turning to poison while the bee-mouth sips.
Aye, in the very temple of Delight
Veiled Melancholy has her sovran shrine,
Though seen of none save him whose strenuous tongue
Can burst Joy's grape against his palate fine;
His soul shall taste the sadness of her might,
And be among her cloudy trophies hung.

John Keats

The Sensitive Plant

PART II

There was a power in this sweet place,
An Eve in this Eden; a ruling Grace
Which to the flowers, did they waken or dream,
Was as God is to the starry scheme.

A Lady, the wonder of her kind,
Whose form was upborne by a lovely mind,
Which, dilating, had moulded her mien and motion
Like a seaflower unfolded beneath the ocean,

Tended the garden from morn to even:
And the meteors of that sublunar heaven,
Like the lamps of the air when Night walks forth,
Laughed round her footsteps up from earth.

She had no companion of mortal race;
But her tremulous breath and her flushing face

Told, whilst the morn kissed the sleep from her eyes,
That her dreams were less slumber than paradise.

As if some bright Spirit for her sweet sake
Had deserted heaven while the stars were awake,
As if yet around her he lingering were,
Though the veil of daylight concealed him from her.

Her step seemed to pity the grass it pressed:
You might hear, by the heaving of her breast,
That the coming and going of the wind
Brought pleasure there, and left passion behind.

And, wherever her airy footstep trod,
Her trailing hair from the grassy sod
Erased its light vestige with shadowy sweep,
Like a sunny storm o'er the dark-green deep.

I doubt not the flowers of that garden sweet
Rejoiced in the sound of her gentle feet;
I doubt not they felt the spirit that came
From her glowing fingers through all their frame.

She sprinkled bright water from the stream
On those that were faint with the sunny beam;
And out of the cups of the heavy flowers
She emptied the rain of the thunder-showers.

She lifted their heads with her tender hands,
And sustained them with rods and osier-bands;
If the flowers had been her own infants, she
Could never have nursed them more tenderly.

And all killing insects and gnawing worms,
And things of obscene and unlovely forms,
She bore in a basket of Indian woof
Into the rough woods far aloof; –

In a basket of grasses and wildflowers full,
The freshest her gentle hands could pull

For the banished insects, whose intent,
Although they did ill, was innocent.

But the bee, and the beamlike ephemeris
Whose path is the lightning's, and soft moths that kiss
The sweet lips of the flowers, and harm not, did she
Make her attendant angels be.

And many an antenatal tomb
Where butterflies dream of the life to come
She left clinging round the smooth and dark
Edge of the odorous cedar-bark.

The fairest Creature from earliest Spring
Thus moved through the garden ministering
All the sweet season of summertide:
And, ere the first leaf looked brown, she died.

Percy Bysshe Shelley

Of the different Conditions of Men engaged in the Practice or Pursuit of Gardening

OF OPERATORS OR SERVING GARDENERS

The lowest grade in the scale of this class is garden labourers. These are occasionally employed to perform the common labours of gardening, as trenching, digging, hoeing, weeding, &c. Men for the more heavy, and women for the lighter employments. They are not supposed to have received any professional instruction, farther than what they may have obtained by voluntary or casual observation. In all gardens where three or four professional hands are constantly employed, some labourers are required at extraordinary seasons.

Apprentice. Youths intended for serving, or tradesmen gardeners, are generally articled or placed under master or tradesmen gardeners, for a given period on terms of mutual benefit; the master contracting to supply instruction, and generally food and lodging, or a weekly sum as an equivalent; and the parents of the apprentice granting the services of the latter during his apprenticeship as their part of the contract. The term agreed on is generally three years; or more if the youth is under sixteen years of age, but whatever may be the period, by the laws as to apprentices it must extend beyond that at which the youth attains the age of manhood.

No one can ever expect to attain to the rank either of master gardener or tradesman, who has not served an apprenticeship to the one or the other. In general it is preferable to apprentice youths to master gardeners, as there the labour is less than in tradesmen's gardens, and the opportunities for instruction generally much greater.

Journeyman. The period of apprenticeship being finished, that of journeyman commences, and continues, or ought to continue till the man is at least twenty-five years of age. During this period, he ought not to remain above one year in any one situation; thus, supposing he has completed his apprenticeship in a private garden at the age of twenty-one, and that his ultimate object is to become a head-gardener, he ought first to engage himself a year in a public botanic garden; the next year in a public nursery; that following, he should again enter a private garden, and continue making yearly changes in the most eminent of this class of gardens, till he meets with a situation as head-gardener. The course to be followed by an apprentice intended for a tradesmen gardener is obvious; having finished his period in a private garden, let him pass through a botanic and nursery-garden, and then continue in the most eminent of the class of public or tradesmen's gardens, to which he is destined.

Foreman (before-man, or first man). In extensive gardens where a number of hands are employed, they are commonly grouped or arranged in divisions, and one of the journeymen of longest standing employed as foreman, or sub-master, to the rest. Whenever three or more journeymen are employed, there is commonly a foreman, who has a certain extent of authority at all times, but especially in the absence of the masters. This confers a certain degree of rank for the time being, but none afterwards.

Master Gardener. A journeyman has attained the *situation* of master-gardener, when he is appointed to the management of a garden, even if he has no labourer, apprentice, or journeyman under him; but he has not attained the *rank* of master-gardener, till after being a year in such situation. Afterwards should he be obliged to work as journeyman, he still retains the rank and title of master-gardener, but not of head-gardener.

A *Head-Gardener* or *Upper-Gardener*, is a master who has apprentices or journeymen employed under him. Out of place and working as a journeyman, he retains the rank and title of master-gardener but not of head-gardener.

Nursery Foreman. This is an important situation, the foreman being entrusted with the numbered and priced catalogues of the articles dealt in; authorised to make sales; intrusted to keep an account of men's time, &c; and in consequence it entitles the holder to the rank of head-gardener while so engaged, and to that of master-gardener ever afterwards; the same may be said of foremen to public botanic gardens, and royal or national gardens.

A *Travelling Gardener* is one sent out as gardener, or collector of plants, along with scientific expeditions; he is generally chosen from a botanic garden; and his business is to collect gardening productions of every kind, and to mark the soil, aspect, climate, &c. to which they have been habituated.

Botanic Curator. This is the highest situation to which a serving gardener can attain next to that of being the royal or government gardener. He superintends the culture and management of a public botanic garden; maintains an extensive correspondence with other botanic curators; exchanges plants, seeds, and dried specimens, so as to keep up or increase his own collection of living plants, and *herbarium siccum*. Abroad, for want of sufficiently intelligent practical gardeners, they have what are called *directors*, and inspectors of botanic or other government gardens; but no such office is requisite in this country.

Royal Gardener, Court Gardener, or *Government Gardener; Jardinier de la Cour,* Fr.; *Hoffgartner,* Ger.; and *Giardiniaro de la Corte,* Ital. This is the highest step, the *summum bonum* of garden servitude. In foreign countries, the court-gardener wears an appropriate livery, as did formerly the head-gardeners of the principal nobility, as well as the court gardeners of this country. At present this remnant of feudal slavery is laid aside in every grade of garden servitude.

J. C. Loudon, An Encyclopedia of Gardening

Shrubberies

On this part of my subject it is not agreeable to my plan to be very minute, except as to the several kinds of shrubs and flowers, the lists of which I shall make as complete as I can: it is not for the use of florists that I pretend to write; but for the use of persons who have the means of forming pretty gardens, and who have a taste for making use of these means; a taste which, I am sorry to say, has been declining in England for a great many years.

As to the form of shrubberies, or pleasure grounds, that must greatly depend upon adventitious circumstances so various that particular directions must be inapplicable in nine cases out of ten. There are some things, however, which are general to all situations, and, with respect to these, I shall offer my opinion. Shrubberies should be so planted, if they be of considerable depth, as for the tallest trees to be at the back, and the lowest in front; if one could have one's will, one would go, by slow degrees, from a dwarf Kalmia to a Catalpa or a Horse-chestnut. Such a slope, however, would require the depth of a mile; and, therefore, that is out of the question. But some attention may be paid anywhere to the placing in proper relative position those trees which are likely to combine well with one another in the most dreary part of the year; so as to have cheerful colours as long as possible. For this purpose, no shrubbery should be without evergreens, such as the smaller kind of firs, tree box and laurel; and a little observation will in one autumn teach the planter what colours the leaves of our deciduous trees become at that season, and also which are the trees that retain their leaves the longest. He will find that, in situations very much sheltered, some will carry their leaves till very late indeed, and that others, be they where they may, will soon lose them. The poplars, the ash, and the elm, will retain their leaves well throughout the autumn if the situation be sheltered and the weather tolerably dry, and these die a very *bright yellow*. The oak, the beech, and the sycamore, die *red*, but the oak and the beech retain their leaves longest, the latter of these two, indeed, when young, retains them all the winter, but they become brown before the spring. The lime, the birch, the horse-chestnut, turn a *dingy brown* and fall soon, but particularly the last, which becomes an unsightly tree early in September. If the shrubbery be of narrow space, the best way is to have no very tall shrubs at all, and to be content with an outside border of lilacs or laurels. The walks, to be beautiful and convenient, should be a gravel of a deep yellow, well-sifted and laid down in the substantial manner directed for the walks of the kitchen-garden. Such walks cannot be kept in neat order without box edgings.

Gravel walks are not to be kept in neat order without being broken up once a year; and that once ought to be about the middle of the month of May. They are broken up with a pick-axe, newly raked over, and rolled with a stone-roller immediately after the raking, and not the whole walk at once; but a bit at a time, so that the top be not dry when the roller comes upon it: for, if it be, it will not bind. So nice a matter is this, that, if a part be prepared for rolling, and if the hands be called off to dinner before it be rolled, mats are laid on to shade it from the sun until their return to work. This is a matter of the greatest nicety: a very good eye is required in those who rake previous to the rolling, and the rollers must have a very steady hand, or there will be unevenness in the walk, which, when properly laid, is certainly one of the most beautiful objects in the world. If proper care have been taken in laying the foundation of the walk, few or no weeds will come even on its edges; but, if they should, they must be eradicated as soon as they appear. Some leaves will fall even in summer, and the walk must be swept with a soft broom once in the week, at least.

But *grass* is another great ornament, and, perhaps, if kept in neat order, the greatest of all. If grass be about to be laid down, the ground should be well prepared: if too poor to keep the grass fresh through a hot summer, it should be made richer, and always deeply moved. The next thing, is, to keep the ground, whether on the sides of terraces, on a slope, or on a level, perfectly smooth and even on the surface. To *sow* grass is not the way to have fine grass plats; but to cut the turf from a common or from some very ancient and closely-pressed pasture where the herbage is fine. From our finest Downs, or from spots in our Commons, the turf is generally taken; and, short grass, as the gardeners call it, is seen in perfection, I believe, nowhere but in England. The old DUKE OF ORLEANS, showing SIR FREDERICK EDEN his gardens at Chantilly, coming to a grass-plat, said, Here is something that you will like, at any rate; and then he told him that the turf of which the plat was formed was actually imported from England, and cut upon Epsom Down. The grass cut with a turfing-iron made for the purpose, is rolled up, just like a piece of cloth, green-sward inwards, the strips are cut by a line: and cut into pieces of from two to four feet long. These are laid down in the fall of the year on the place where they are to grow: they are placed and pressed up very closely together, being well beaten down with the back of the spade as the workman proceeds; and when the whole is laid, a roller of iron or of stone, of sufficient weight, is passed over the plat. During the next winter, care must be taken to roll again when the ground is in a dry state, after every frost. In the month of April, it will be necessary to begin to mow; for the grass will grow very well. Grass-plats are the greatest beauties of pleasure grounds if well managed; but, unless you are resolved not to spare the necessary expense for this purpose; if you think that you cannot have the perseverance to prevent your plat from becoming a sort of half meadow at certain times, the best way is not to attempt the thing at all. During the month of May, grass must be mowed once a week. From the first of June, to the middle of July, and especially if the weather be wet, twice a week may be necessary; or, one mowing and one swarding or poling, and sweeping. The mower can operate only in the *dew*: he must be at his work by daylight, and the grass must be swept up before it be dry. It is the general practice to mow every Saturday morning, and to pole or sward the grass in the middle of the week, to knock or cut off the heads of the daisies, and to take away the castings of the worms, which are very troublesome in the greater part of grass-plats. Where the thing is well done, the wormcasts are rubbed off by a pole or rod the evening before the mowing is performed, otherwise they interrupt the progress of the scythe and take off its edge. A good short-grass mower is a really able workman; and, if the plat have a good bottom, he will leave it very nearly as smooth and as even as the piece of green cloth which covers the table on which I am writing: it is quite surprising how close a scythe will go if in a hand that knows how to whet it and use it. If, however, you do not resolve to have the thing done in this manner, it is much better not to attempt it at all. The decay of gardening in England in this respect is quite surprising.

It is very much the fashion to have clumps of shrubs, or independent shrubs, upon grass-plats: people must follow their own taste; but, in my opinion, nothing is so beautiful as a clear carpet of green, surrounded with suitable shrubs and flowers, separated from it by walks of beautiful gravel. The edges of grass, whether against walks or against shrubberies, are sure to grow out, and ought, therefore, to be kept in by trimming or paring off very frequently; for the whole ought to be as smooth as a piece of cloth. If thistles or dandelions, or even daisies, come amongst the grass, the mowing of them is not enough, for each will make a circle round the crown of its root and will overpower the grass. This, however, is easily cured by cutting these roots off deeply with a knife, and pulling them up. This done during two summers successively, will destroy the dandelions and the thistles; and, as to the daisies, which have a shallow root, they may easily be kept down, if not extirpated.

In the fall of the year, all shrubberies (in the month of November) should be digged completely with a fork: all suckers should be taken away, all dead wood taken out: for if digged, they make the ground hollow, and harbour slugs and other vermin. The ground should be made smooth, therefore, when it is digged: all hares and rabbits kept out, for they are very mischievous in shrubberies, barking during the winter many of trees of the most valuable kind. During the summer, there should be two or three hoeings to prevent weeds from growing, and a nice raking once a week to take up any leaves that may have fallen; for no trees or flowers will be seen to advantage unless they stand upon a spot that is in neat order. Shrubs should not be too much crowded by any means; it cramps them in their growth, makes their shoots feeble, makes their bloom imperfect, and they hide one another: a shrubbery should not be a mass of indistinguishable parts; but an assemblage of objects each clearly distinguished from the other. The distribution should be such as to ensure bloom in every season that bloom can be had; and, though shade is in some cases desirable, flowering shrubs to be beautiful must not be shaded, except in instances so few as not to warrant the supposition that there is ever to be a departure from the general rule.

If there be water, every eye tells you that it ought to be bordered by grass; or, if of larger dimension, by trees the boughs of which touch its very edge: bare ground and water do not suit at all. It was formerly the fashion to have a sort of canal with broad grass-walks on the sides, and with water coming up to within a few inches of the closely-shaven grass;

and certainly few things were more beautiful than these. SIR WILLIAM TEMPLE had one of his own constructing in his gardens at MOOR PARK. On the outsides of the grass-walks were borders of beautiful flowers. I have stood for hours to look at this canal, for the good-natured manners of those days had led the proprietor to make an opening in the outer wall in order that his neighbours might enjoy the sight as well as himself; I have stood for hours, when a little boy, looking at this object; I have travelled far since, and have seen a great deal; but I have never seen anything of the gardening kind so beautiful in the whole course of my life.

The present taste is on the side of irregularity: straight walks, straight pieces of water, straight rows of trees, seem all to be out of fashion; but, it is also true that neatness; that really fine shrubberies and flower-gardens, have gone out of fashion at the same time. People, however, must follow their own tastes in these respects; and it is useless to recommend this or that manner of laying out a piece of ground.

William Cobbett, *The English Gardener*

Mariana

Mariana in the Moated Grange
(*Measure for Measure*)

1

With blackest moss the flowerpots
Were thickly crusted, one and all,
The rusted nails fell from the knots
That held the peach to the garden wall.
The broken sheds looked sad and strange,
Unlifted was the clinking latch,
Weeded and worn the ancient thatch
Upon the lonely moated grange.
She only said, 'My life is dreary,
He cometh not,' she said;
She said, 'I am aweary, aweary –
I would that I were dead!'

Alfred, Lord Tennyson, *Poems, Chiefly Lyrical*

General Management of Plants Grown Under Glass

Although we have given an account of the propagation and culture of the various GENERA in the body of work, we think it expedient to describe the general management of ornamental plants grown under glass, such as *greenhouse, stove,* or *hothouse,* as well as *alpine plants.*

1. *Alpine plants* are such as will not grow in the open ground to any perfection, and must be protected during winter by a frame; they are mostly natives of high situations, among rocks and on the tops of mountains, and consequently of low growth, seldom, if ever, exceeding six inches. They should be grown in small pots, and will thrive well in a mixture of loam, peat, and sand, the pots to be always well drained with potsherds; they should be shifted at least twice every season, and divided if the plant has grown too large; the mould which has been shaken from the pots, if not exhausted, to be mixed with new earth, and the plants potted afresh, after which they require a little water. If these instructions are attended to, alpine plants will always look healthy and neat.

2. *Greenhouse plants* are such as are natives of the Canary Islands, New Holland, and the Cape of Good Hope, and other countries in the same latitudes, which only require to be protected from frost in this country; therefore they are kept under glass during the winter. No fire is requisite, unless a strong frost is expected during the night. In winter they should have plenty of air given them upon fine days, as early in the day as the weather will permit; the house to be shut up very early in the afternoon, if cold. If the weather continues damp and wet, then a little fire is requisite to expel the damp, as greenhouse plants are more likely to be injured by damp than cold. The plants should be looked over every day, taking off any dead leaves, and watering those that are dry; this should be done early in the forenoon, and if the surface of the mould in the pots becomes green, it should be removed with a flat stick, but not so deep as to injure the roots, and a little fresh mould laid on instead. Towards spring they require a more plentiful supply of air and water, and when frost is not apprehended some of the sashes should be left a little open all night, and the air gradually admitted as the weather advances towards summer, until the time of setting the plants out of doors: in some sea-

sons this may be about the middle of May, in others not until the end. Calm cloudy weather is the best time for setting them out, when the most sheltered situation should be chosen, where a bed of ashes should previously have been prepared for them. There are various opinions as to the best time of shifting greenhouse plants into fresh pots and mould, but we think that the earliest spring time should be preferred; some shift them before they are set out of doors, some when they first set them out, others in the autumn, which last time is of all the most improper. The pots should be always well drained with sherds. If any of the plants have grown too straggling or tall, they should be cut back early in the spring, that they may become good bushy plants before autumn. In summer, while the plants are out of doors, if the weather is dry, they should be regularly and plentifully supplied with water, as late as possible every afternoon. The mould intended for shifting or potting off plants should never be sifted, but merely chopped up finely with a spade with the turf, for the turf and its roots are the best parts of the mould, keeping the soil light and loose, and allowing the roots of the plants to spread and the water to penetrate; sifted mould, on the other hand, hardens and becomes sour. The cuttings of greenhouse plants require to be put in at various seasons. From Christmas to the end of May is generally the best time, but this will depend entirely upon the state of the shoots required to make the cuttings; for instance, if the cuttings require to be ripened, they should be planted early in the spring; but if they require to be young, the time to plant them is when the shoots have grown a sufficient length for that purpose. In potting off plants raised from cuttings, care is requisite not to injure the young fibres; at first they should be placed in very small pots, and afterwards shifted into pots of increasing size, as they grow, but care should be taken not to plant them in too large pots, or to give them too much water. The seeds of greenhouse plants should always be sown in pots as early as possible in the spring, placed in a little bottom heat; and the seedlings should be potted off separately when they have grown about an inch in height.

3. *Frame plants* require exactly the same treatment as greenhouse plants, excepting that they do not require any fire during winter, but only to be protected by mats from the frost.

4. *Stove plants* are such as are natives within the tropics, therefore

require a great degree of heat and plenty of moisture at certain seasons of the year. They are usually of easy culture. The house in which they are grown should be very closely glazed, in order that the temperatures may be very regular during winter, or in cold windy nights. The temperature of the house should never be allowed to fall below 60° Fahrenheit in winter; and in fine days, when it rises to 70°, a little air may be given; but early in the afternoon it should be shut up close. Formerly the pots of stove plants were plunged in tan, but this method is now entirely exploded, and a bed of gravel or sand is substituted, which is greatly preferable for the health of the plants, as well as the diminution of expense. The houses may be either heated with hot water, or with steam conveyed through pipes, or by means of fires; but we consider the first two methods preferable, as giving a more congenial heat. As stove plants are apt to be infested by insects, such as the green fly, the red spider, and the mealy bug, the first may be destroyed by the smoke of tobacco, the second by sulphur-vivum, mixed up in a pail of quick lime, with which the flues should be washed all over, which is a certain means of exterminating them. The mealy bug and scaly bug are only to be got rid of by removing them with a small hair brush; for this purpose the plants should be examined as often as possible. The plants should be washed from an engine in fine weather, and the house kept warm, by which means they will always be kept clean and healthy. Air should be admitted as early as possible in the morning, in warm weather, taking care to shut up early in the afternoon, that the house may be kept to a proper temperature during the night. The time for re-potting them is early in the spring, and the pots always require to be drained with sherds, which keeps the mould loose and free from being soddened with water. The time at which cuttings should be planted is the same as that for greenhouse plants when the wood is fit, but these require heat. Seeds of stove plants should be sown immediately on their arrival from abroad, although the general time of sowing should be early in spring. A gentle hot-bed is the best for raising tropical seeds, but some few will come up better on a shelf or flue in the hothouse, and the sooner seedlings are potted off separately the better.

5. *Succulent plants*, so called, are such as have a fleshy nature; these are called dry greenhouse or dry stove plants, and consequently require to be grown in the same temperature as greenhouse and stove plants, being

natives of the same latitudes. In some gardens there are houses entirely appropriated for these plants, where they are placed on stages or shelves, and kept rather dry throughout the winter: but in gardens where there are not houses entirely appropriated for them, they should be kept on shelves erected for this purpose in a stove or greenhouse.

George Don, *A General History of the Dichlamydeous Plants*

Ghazal of Mira

The world passes, nothing lasts, and the creation of men
Is buried alive under the vault of Time.

Autumn comes pillaging gardens;
The bulbuls laugh to see the flowers falling.

Wars start up wherever your eye glances,
And the young men moan marching on the batteries.

Mira is the unkempt old man you see on the road;
He has taken his death-wound in battle.

Afghan folk song

Dress Grounds

The dress ground immediately connected with the house should be considered as the foreground of the picture, which the whole scene, taken together, presents to the eye, and should be treated as such. The groups, and single trees upon it, should be planted with reference to the scenery beyond, so as to lead the eye into the remote parts of the picture; excluding, as far as may be, whatever might injure the general composition.

In the formation, then, of the dress ground, I should recommend the making a slight sketch from the leading points of view, (usually the windows of the library or drawing-room), of the general scene as it exists; and then add to your sketch such groups of trees and shrubs, and such detached trees, as would hide the less interesting parts of the landscape, and, by breaking the uniformity of other parts, produce that connection so essential to composition. In forming such groups, particularly of larger trees, it should be well considered, whether a massive or a lighter group is requisite; whether the most distant scenery is to be caught through the stems of those trees, or to be altogether excluded by them. I would plant all the larger features with this reference to the general scene, before proceeding to the lesser embellishments of the lawn, as flower-beds, &c. which should be formed with reference to those features.

The groups of larger trees will usually be accompanied by shrubs of various size and character, to connect them with the lawn: rhododendrons, savine, and other of the pendant evergreens, are very useful for such purpose, when the turf, being carried under them, leaves no cutting line of border. Shrubs, in my opinion, should not be accompanied, in the same bed, by such flowers as require digging; the line of border above mentioned destroying that repose and that variety of form which ought to characterise the former. In a lawn of small dimensions, the loosing of the turf under the shrubs is of the utmost importance, as it gives an appearance of extent to its limited proportion. Pæonies, roses, hollyhocks, and other flowers that are of sufficient height or size to mingle with the shrubs, may be fairly united with them, if it can be effected without showing the mould. In the first formation of these plantations of shrubs, the borders must be dug, and, for a time, kept so; but every opportunity should be taken to break the edgy line, till it can be finally obliterated: to help this end, even in the first instance, periwinkle, St. John's wort, and other ground creepers, may be planted with the shrubs; and, by uniting them with the lawn, will tend to diminish the hard line of the border: a thing that cannot be too strongly insisted upon, as essential to continuity and repose.

It is impossible to lay down rules that may regulate the size, situation, or character of these plantations of shrubs, which will depend upon the shape, character, and extent of the grounds they are to embellish: some hints, however, as in other cases, may be suggested, to direct the unskilful hand in an operation of no small importance.

And first, as before observed, the plantations should be marked out from the principal point of view, so as to agree with the general scene. The size of each mass will depend partly upon what is to be excluded or broken in the remote landscape, and partly upon the character and size of the ground. If the situation to be planted be of small dimensions, one mass of tolerable size may be better than dividing it: but, if the ground admit of it, a variety of masses is preferable, as producing more intricacy and greater appearance of extent. In this case, the masses of shrubs will be so disposed as to show portions of lawn intersecting them in glades of different size and form. The general inclination of these masses of shrubs should tend, though in different degrees, towards the most interesting part of the scene, either within or without the dress ground, as circumstances may be. A horizontal line of plantation can rarely have a good effect. Though there will be a variety in the forms of plantations, there should be a general harmony of outline between them when they approach each other; the more swelling part of one opposing itself to the recess of the other. The nearer masses should generally be of lower material than the more remote, that the one may occasionally be seen over the other. Where the dress ground is of such dimensions as to allow these masses upon a large scale, the variety of their respective forms should be boldly marked, as, in the course of a few years, they ought to be broken. A few of the choicest plants will then occupy the space that present effect requires to be filled up with common material. For this purpose, care should be taken, in the first instance, to dispose of the choice plants before the mass is filled up, so that the former shall hereafter stand where they ought; whereas, for want of this precaution, a cedar of Lebanon may, when grown up, destroy the composition which, had it been rightly placed, it would have materially improved. For places where a cedar of Lebanon, or any of the larger firs, might be thought too big, the Virginia cedar or the hemlock spruce is well adapted: the latter is, in my opinion, the most beautiful of that class of evergreens; it likes shade and a moist ground, though I have seen it flourish in drier and more exposed situations.

When I said that these masses of shrubs, &c. should be marked out from the principal point of view, I did not mean that they need not be studied from any other point: on the contrary, it is essentially necessary that they be examined from every situation from which they are to be seen, that no beauty, as far as can be avoided, may be lost through inattention.

In order to assist the arrangement of these plantations, I should recommend forming them on the ground, with branches of various lengths, with the leaves on, which gives a far better idea of the intended effect than can be given by stakes: the branches, being laid on the ground, can be turned in any direction, till the best forms are obtained, which may then be marked on the turf with the edging-iron. Larger branches, stuck in the ground, will direct the placing of trees with the same advantage over a mere stake. Good hints for such planting of a lawn may be found on any common, where furze, broom, &c. furnish endless varieties of form and grouping. Having disposed the masses of trees, shrubs, &c. with reference to the general effect of the whole scene, we come now to the finishing touches of decoration – flowers.

William S. Gilpin, *Practical Hints upon Landscape Gardening*

The Elf of the Rose

In the middle of a garden grew a rose tree which was quite full of blossoms, and in one of these, the prettiest of them all, lived an Elf: he was such a little tiny thing that no human eye could see him. Behind every petal in the rose he had a bedroom. He was as well shaped and as handsome as any child could be, and had wings reaching from his shoulders right down to his feet. Oh! what a sweet smell there was in his room! And how bright and pretty were the walls of it! They were the pale pink, delicate rose leaves.

All day he enjoyed himself in the hot sunshine, flying from flower to flower, dancing on the wings of the butterfly as it flew, and measuring how many steps it took to go over all the roads and paths on a single lime-leaf. It was what we call the veins of the leaf that he reckoned as roads and paths: an enormous distance he had to go, and before he had finished, the sun set. He had begun very late for another thing.

It got very cold, the dew fell, the wind blew. It would be best to go home. He made all the haste he could, but the rose was shut, and he could not get in, not a single rose was open. The poor little Elf was terribly frightened: he had never spent the night out of doors before, but he had always slept sweetly, snug among the rose leaves. Oh dear! It would be the death of him for certain!

At the other end of the garden, he knew, there was a summerhouse with beautiful honeysuckle on it, whose flowers looked like large coloured horns: he would get into one of them and sleep till morning. Thither he flew. Hush! There were two people inside, a handsome young man and the prettiest of girls. Side by side they sat, and wished they might never be parted, so fond they were of each other, far fonder than the best of children can be of its father and mother.

'Yet we must part,' said the young man; 'your brother wishes us no good: that is why he is sending me on a mission far away beyond the mountains and lakes. Farewell, my sweetest bride, for my bride you are!'

They kissed one another: the young girl wept and gave him a rose, but before she put it in his hand she printed a kiss on it so fond and tender that the flower opened, and into it the little Elf flew and nestled his head against the delicate fragrant walls. But he could plainly hear 'Farewell, farewell!' said, and feel that the rose was placed in the young man's bosom. Oh how the heart in it beat! The little Elf could not get to sleep, so fast it beat. Not long did the rose lie quiet on his heart: the young man drew it out, and as he went alone through the dark wood he kissed it so often and so hard that the little Elf was in danger of being squeezed to death. Through the leaf he could feel how the man's lips burned: the very rose had opened itself as under the hottest sun of noonday.

There came another man, gloomy and passionate, the fair girl's evil brother. He drew a long sharp knife, and while the other kissed his rose the wicked man stabbed him to death, cut off his head, and buried it, with the body, in the soft earth under a lime tree.

'He's gone and forgotten now,' said the wicked brother; 'he will come back no more. A long journey he was to go, over mountains and lakes, where a man can easily lose his life; and he's lost his. He won't come back, and my sister will never dare ask me about him.' With that he spread the dead leaves over the disturbed earth with his foot, and went home in the dark night, but not alone, as he supposed. The little Elf kept him company, sitting in a withered rolled-up lime-leaf that had fallen on the bad man's hair as he dug the grave. His hat was over it now, and very dark it was in there, and the Elf quivered with horror and wrath at the foul deed.

The bad man got home at dawn. He took off his hat and went into his sister's bedroom. There she lay, the pretty young maid, dreaming of him whom she held so dear, who now, she thought, was travelling over hills and through forests: and the wicked brother stooped over her and laughed horribly, as a devil might laugh. The withered leaf fell from his hair upon the counterpane, but he did not notice it; he went out to sleep – he too – for a little in the early morning. But the Elf stole out of the withered leaf, crept into the ear of the sleeping girl, and told her, as in a dream, of the frightful murder; described to her the place where her brother had killed him and laid his body, told of the flowering lime tree hard by, and said: 'That you may see this is no dream that I have told you, you will find a withered leaf on you bed.' And so she did when she woke.

Oh what bitter tears she wept! Yet to no one dared she confide her trouble. The window stood open all day, and the little Elf might easily have gone out into the garden to the roses and all the other flowers, but he cared not to leave her in her sorrow. In the window stood a tree of monthly roses, and in one of these he sat and watched the poor girl. Several times her brother came into the room: he was in high spirits, and unkind – but she dared not to say a word of her great sorrow. As soon as night came she stole out of the house and into the wood to the place where the lime tree stood: she cleared the leaves away from the soil, dug down into it and found the murdered man. Oh, how she wept and prayed God that she might die soon! She longed to bear the body home with her, but that she could not. So she took the pale head with the closed eyes, kissed the cold mouth and shook the earth from the fair hair. "This shall be mine!" said she. So when she had laid earth and leaves over the dead body she took the head home with her, and a little branch of jessamine which was flowering in the wood where he was killed. As soon as she was in her room again, she fetched the largest flower-pot she could find, and in it she laid the dead man's head, put earth over it, and planted the sprig of jessamine.

'Farewell! farewell!' whispered the little Elf; he could not bear to look on all this sorrow any longer, and flew out into the garden, to his rose. But it had faded; only a few pale petals hung to the green fruit. 'Ah, how quickly passes all that is fair and good!' sighed he. At last he found another rose, which became his house; among its delicate scented leaves he could live and make his home.

Every morning he would fly to the poor girl's window, where she would always be standing by her flower-pot, weeping. The salt tears fell on the sprig of jessamine, but day by day as she grew paler and paler, the sprig grew yet more fresh and green; one twig after another was put forth, and little white buds came and turned to flowers, and she would kiss them. But her wicked brother reviled her and asked if she were going crazy: he could not bear it, and could not understand why she was always weeping over the flower-pot. He little knew what closed eyes, what red lips, had turned to earth there: and she would bow her head over the flower-pot, and there the little Elf found her slumbering. Into her ear he crept, and told her of the evening in the summer-house, and of the sweet smell of the roses and the loving kindness of the Elves, and she slept sweetly, and while she slept her life faded: a quiet death was hers, and now she was in heaven with whom she loved.

But the wicked brother looked at the beautiful flowering shrub and took it for himself as a legacy, and put it in his room, near the bed, for it was pleasant to look at, and the smell was sweet and fresh. The little Elf went there too, and flew from one flower to another – in each of them dwelt a little soul – and to them he told the story of the murdered youth whose head was now earth in earth, and of the wicked brother and the wretched sister. 'We know it!' said each of the souls in the flowers. 'We know it! Did we not grow out of the slain man's eyes and lips? We know! We know!' and they nodded their heads in a strange fashion. The Rose Elf could not understand how they could be so calm, and he flew out to the bees, who were gathering honey, and told them the story of the wicked brother; and the bees told their Queen, who gave orders that next morning they should join and kill the murderer.

But the night before – that is, the first night after the death of his sister, as the wicked brother slept in his bed close by the sweet-smelling jessamine – every flower cup opened, and, unseen, but each one bearing a poisoned spear, the flower souls came forth: and first they settled at his ear and told him dreadful dreams, and then they flew to his lips and pricked his tongue with the poisoned spears. 'Now we have avenged the dead!' they said, and home they went into the white bells of the jessamine. When morning came and the window was all at once thrown open, the Rose Elf hastened in with the Queen Bee and all the swarm to kill him. But he was dead already, and people were standing about him saying: 'The smell of the jessamine has killed him.' Then the Rose Elf understood the vengeance of the flowers and told it to the Queen of the Bees, and she hummed about the flower-pot with all her swarm. And as the bees could not be driven away, a man took the flower-pot, and one of the bees stung him on the hand, and he let the pot fall and it broke.

Then they saw the white skull; and they knew that he who lay dead in the bed was a murderer.

And the Queen Bee hummed in the fresh air and sang of the vengeance of the flowers and the Elf of the Rose, and how behind every last petal dwells one who can tell of evil deeds and avenge them.

Hans Christian Andersen

Ballad of Nurshali

Come in haste this dusk, dear child. I will be on the water path
When your girl friends go laughing by the road.
'Come in haste this dusk; I have become your nightingale,
And the young girls leave me alone because of you.
I give you the poppy of my mouth and my fallen hair.'
Come in haste this dusk, dear child.

'I have dishevelled and spread out my hair for you;
Take my wrist, for there is no shame
And my father has gone out.
Sit near me on this red bed quietly.'
Come in haste this dusk, dear child.

'Sit near me on this red bed, I lift the poppy to your lips;
Your hand is strong upon my breast;
My beauty is a garden and you the bird in the flowering tree.'
Come in haste this dusk, dear child.

'My beauty is a garden with crimson flowers.'
But I cannot reach over the thicket of your hair.
This is *Nurshali* sighing in the garden;
Come in haste this dusk, dear child.

Afghan folk song

An Evening Stroll

A splendid Midsummer shone over England: skies so pure, suns so radi-
ant as were then seen in long succession, seldom favour, even singly, our
wave-girt land. It was as if a band of Italian days had come from the
South, like a flock of glorious passenger birds, and lighted to rest them
on the cliffs of Albion. The hay was all got in; the fields round Thornfield
were green and shorn; the roads white and baked; the trees were in their
dark prime; hedge and wood, full-leaved and deeply tinted, contrasted
well with the sunny hue of the cleared meadows between.

On Midsummer-eve, Adèle, weary with gathering wild strawberries in
Hay Lane half the day, had gone to bed with the sun. I watched her drop
asleep, and when I left her, I sought the garden.

It was now the sweetest hour of the twenty-four: 'day its fervid fires
had wasted', and dew fell cool on panting plain and scorched summit.
Where the sun had gone down in simple state – pure of the pomp of
clouds – spread a solemn purple, burning with the light of red jewel and
furnace flame at one point, on one hill-peak, and extending high and
wide, soft and still softer, over half heaven. The east had its own charm of
fine, deep blue, and its own modest gem, a rising and solitary star: soon
it would boast the moon; but she was yet beneath the horizon.

I walked a while on the pavement; but a subtle, well-known scent – that
of a cigar – stole from some south window; and I saw the library casement
open a hand-breadth; I knew I might be watched thence; so I went apart
into the orchard. No nook in the grounds more sheltered and more Eden-
like; a very high wall shut it out from the court on one side; on the other
a beech avenue screened it from the lawn. At the bottom was a sunk fence,
its sole separation from lonely fields: a winding walk, bordered with laurels and terminating in a giant horsechestnut, circled at the base by a seat,
led down to the fence. Here one could wander unseen. While such honey-
dew fell, such silence reigned, such gloaming gathered, I felt as if I could
haunt such shade for ever; but in treading the flower and fruit parterres at
the upper part of this more open quarter, my step is stayed – not by
sound, not by sight, but once more by a warning fragrance.

Sweet-briar and southernwood, jasmine, pink, and rose have long been yielding their evening sacrifice of incense: this new scent is neither shrub nor flower; it is – I know it well – it is Mr Rochester's cigar. I look round and listen. I see trees laden with ripening fruit. I hear a nightingale warbling in a wood half a mile off: no moving form is visible, no coming step audible; but that perfume increases: I must flee. I make for the wicket leading into the shrubbery, and I see Mr Rochester entering. I step aside into the ivy recess; he will not stay long: he will soon return whence he came, and if I sit still he will never see me.

But no – eventide is as pleasant to him as to me, and this antique garden as attractive; and he strolls on, now lifting the gooseberry-tree branches to look at the fruit, large as plums, with which they are laden; now taking a ripe cherry from the wall; now stooping towards a knot of flowers, either to inhale their fragrance or to admire the dew-beads on their petals. A great moth goes humming by me; it alights on a plant at Mr Rochester's foot: he sees it, and bends to examine it.

'Now he has his back towards me,' thought I, 'and he is occupied too; perhaps, if I walk softly, I can slip away unnoticed.'

I trod on an edging of turf that the crackle of the pebbly gravel might not betray me: he was standing among the beds at a yard or two distant from where I had to pass; the moth apparently engaged him. 'I shall get by very well,' I meditated. As I crossed his shadow, thrown over the long garden by the moon, not yet risen high, he said quietly, without turning –

'Jane, come and look at this fellow.'

I had made no noise: he had not eyes behind – could his shadow feel? I started at first, and then I approached him.

'Look at his wings,' said he; 'he reminds me rather of a West Indian insect; one does not often see so large and gay a night-rover in England; there! he is flown.'

The moth roamed away. I was sheepishly retreating also; but Mr Rochester followed me, and when we reached the wicket he said –

'Turn back: on so lovely a night it is a shame to sit in the house; and surely no one can wish to go to bed while sunset is thus at meeting with moonrise.'

Charlotte Brontë, *Jane Eyre*

A Jealous Mistress

Art is a jealous mistress, and, if a man have a genius for painting, poetry, music, architecture, or philosophy, he makes a bad husband, and an ill provider, and should be wise in season, and not fetter himself with duties which will embitter his days, and spoil him for his proper work. We had in this region, twenty years ago, among our educated men, a sort of Arcadian fanaticism, a passionate desire to go upon the land, and unite farming to intellectual pursuits. Many effected their purpose, and made the experiment, and soon became downright ploughmen; but all were cured of their faith that scholarship and practical farming (I mean, with one's own hands) could be united.

With brow bent, with firm intent, the pale scholar leaves his desk to draw a freer breath, and to get a juster statement of his thought, in the garden-walk. He stoops to pull up a purslain, or a dock, that is choking the young corn, and finds there are two: close behind the last is a third; he reaches out his hand to a fourth; behind that are four thousand and one. He is heated and untuned, and, by and by, wakes up from his idiot dream of chickweed and red-root, to remember his morning thought, and to find, that, with his adamantine purposes, he has been duped by a dandelion. A garden is like those pernicious machineries we read of, every month, in the newspapers, which catch a man's coat-skirt or his hand, and draw in his arm, his leg, and his whole body to irresistible destruction. In an evil hour he pulled down his wall, and added a field to his homestead. No land is bad, but land is worse. If a man own land, the land owns him. Now let him leave home, if he dare. Every tree and graft, every hill of melons, row of corn, or quickset hedge, all he has done, and all he means to do, stand in his way, like duns, when he would go out of his gate. The devotion to these vines and trees he finds poisonous. Long free walks, a circuit of miles, free his brain, and serve his body. Long marches are no hardship to him. He believes he composes easily on the hills. But this pottering in a few square yards of garden is dispiriting and drivelling. The smell of the plants has drugged him, and robbed him of energy. He finds a catalepsy in his bones. He grows peevish and poor-spirited. The genius of reading and of gardening are antagonistic, like resinous and vitreous electricity. One is concentrative in sparks and shocks: the other is diffuse strength; so that each disqualifies its workman for the other's duties.

Ralph Waldo Emerson, *The Conduct of Life: Wealth*

The Gao Flower

I am the Gao flower high in a tree,
You are the grass Long Mai on the path-side.
When heat comes down after the dews of morning
The flower grows pale and tumbles on the grass,
The grass Long Mai that keeps the fallen Gao.

Folk who let their daughters grow.
Without achieving a husband
Might easily forget to fence their garden,
Or let their radishes grow flower and rank
When they could eat them ripe and tender.

Come to me, you that I see walk
Every night in a red turban;
Young man with the white turban, come to me.
We will plant marrows together in a garden,
And there may be little marrows for your children.

I will dye your turban blue and red and yellow,
You with the white turban.
You that are passing with a load of water,
I call you
And you do not even turn your head.

Annamese folk song

Grapes

For some few years it has been the fashion for gardeners in lordly places to grow grape vines in pots, which, after bearing one crop of fruit, are destroyed. Now these pots are generally of such large dimensions as to be quite out of character for our orchard houses, and totally unfit for the amateur who wishes to be master 'of all he surveys', as such immense pots are utterly unportable. Induced by observing in the land of the vine that grapes, and good grapes, could be grown on very small bushes, and in crevices containing but a scanty portion of earth, I tried their culture in comparatively small pots, without destroying them after giving their first produce, continuing their culture without shifting, but simply suffering their roots to feed in the border: this has succeeded admirably, and my vine bushes, this last season, have been beautiful objects, bearing from four to six bunches of nicely ripened grapes.

To form these bushes but little care is requisite: a vine one or two years from the eye, with a single stem, must be selected, and potted into an 11-inch pot, in the same compost as recommended for other fruit trees, adding to each pot a quart of 1-inch bones, well mixed with the mould, the bottom of the pot prepared and drained; then cut the vine down to within eight buds of its base: the three lower buds must go for nought; the five upper buds, if the wood be well ripened, will give each a bunch. The lower shoots should be stopped, their tops pinched off as soon as they are four inches long: the upper five shoots may be suffered to grow till the bunch is perceptible; these may then be stopped one bud above the bunch; and all lateral shoots which will afterwards come forth may be stopped at two buds from the base. No other will be required the first season than this finger-and-thumb pruning. It is quite possible that some of these five buds may fail to give a bunch; no matter, stop them of the same length as the fruit-bearing shoots, so as to make a uniform pretty bush; for the vine in all sites and situations, and in all stages of its growth, is a beautiful object. The second season, if it be desirable to make a very dwarf bush, the plant may be cut down partially, so as to bring the lowest shoots into action. Cut down through the main stem, below the second or third fruit-bearing spur of the former year: it will thus have five or six spurs. Now, on the pruning of these spurs depends success; they will, of course, from being grown under glass, be well ripened, and the buds well developed. Begin at the main stem, and count four or five buds from the base of the spur or divergent branch; the fourth or fifth will, in all probability, be nice and plump. This must be your fruit-bud.

Cut down to it closely; then, with a sharp pen-knife, *cut out* two or three buds, leaving the terminal bud, and one only, at the base of the spur close to the stem. This will give you a shoot, which is to be your fruit-bearing shoot for the following year. You will thus have on each spur two buds, one for fruit, the other for wood. In autumn, that part of the spur which has borne fruit must be cut down close to the shoot, which is to bear fruit the following season, and this shoot must be pruned in the same manner for one fruit bud and one shoot bud. This pruning should be done early in October, as the buds are then fully developed, and much is gained by autumnal pruning. A vine treated thus will last for many years, and may always be kept as a dwarf bush: the main stem, in time, will swell, and not require the support of a stick. The first season the cultivator must be content with three, four, or five bunches; but as his vine gathers strength, which it will rapidly do, if every spring a portion – say two or three inches – of the surface mould is removed from the pot, and the compost bountifully applied, even heaped around the stem; for it is so porous that it will not throw off the water; and if the vines are constantly watered with manure-water, they will soon be able to bear eight or ten bunches. They must also, after the fruit is set, be syringed twice a day in the summer. As soon as the fruit is gathered, prune off the roots which have fed them so bountifully all the summer, withhold water, and put them to rest for the winter. I may add, that vines do not need the extreme ventilation recommended for stone-fruits: a warm part of the orchard house will suit them best; or if a small house with a brick Arnott's stove can be entirely appropriated to them, so as to force them, and by having a succession of plants, to have two, or even three, crops in the season, much interest will accrue from their culture. To do this, if forcing be commenced in January, do not fill your house, put in, say one-third of your plants, early in March another third, and then in May the remainder.

The varieties best adapted for this bush culture are those that are very prolific; none are more so than the following: the Purple Frontignan, a most abundant bearer; the Prolific Sweet Water; the Purple Fontainebleau, also abundantly prolific; the Black Esperione; the Grove End Sweet Water; the Cambridge Botanic Garden, a variety of the Black Prince, and a great bearer; the Black Frontignan; the Purple Constantia; the Chasselas Musqué; the Chasselas Rose; the August Muscat, a perfect miniature vine, which gives fruit of fine flavour; and the Chaptal, which gives large and most beautiful bunches. It must not be forgotten that the bunches must all be thinned when the fruit have attained the size of small peas, otherwise the berries will become crowded and inferior.

Thomas Rivers, *The Orchard House*

The Heart of a Man, Broken

The next day, Charles went to sit on the bench, in the arbour. The sunlight was coming through the trellis; the vine-leaves threw their shadows over the gravel, jasmine perfumed the air, the sky was blue, cantharides beetles were droning round the flowering lilies, and Charles was choking like an adolescent from the vague amorous yearnings that swelled up in his aching heart.

At seven o'clock, little Berthe, who had not seen him that afternoon, came to fetch him in for dinner.

He had his head back against the wall, his eyes closed, his mouth open, and in his hand was a tress of long black hair.

– Come on, daddy! she said.

And, thinking that he was only playing, she gave him a gentle push. He fell to the ground. He was dead.

Thirty-six hours later, at the apothecary's request, Monsieur Canivet arrived. He opened him up and found nothing.

Gustave Flaubert, *Madame Bovary*

A Daughter of Eve

A fool I was to sleep at noon,
And wake when night is chilly
Beneath the comfortless cold moon;
A fool to pluck my rose too soon,
A fool to snap my lily.
My garden plot I have not kept;
Faded and all-forsaken,

I weep as I have never wept:
Oh it was summer when I slept,
It's winter now I waken.

Talk what you please of future Spring
And sun-warmed sweet tomorrow:–
Stripped bare of hope and everything,
No more to laugh, no more to sing,
I sit alone with sorrow.

Christina Rossetti

The Wild Garden

About a generation ago a taste began to be manifested for placing a number of tender plants in the open air in summer, with a view to the production of showy masses of decided colour. The subjects selected were mostly from sub-tropical climates and of free growth; placed in the open air of our genial early summer, and in fresh rich earth, every year they grew rapidly and flowered abundantly during the summer and early autumn months, and until cut down by the first frosts. The brilliancy of tone resulting from this system was very attractive, and since its introduction there has been a gradual rooting out of all the old favourites in favour of the bedding system. This was carried to such an extent that of late it has not been uncommon, indeed it has been the rule, to find the largest gardens in the country without a single hardy flower, all energy and expense being devoted to the production of the many thousand exotics required for the summer decoration. It should be distinctly borne in mind that the expense for this system is an annual one; that no matter what amount of money may be spent in this way, no matter how many years may be devoted to perfecting it, the first sharp frost of November merely prepares a yet further expense and labour.

Its highest results need hardly be described; they are seen in all our great public gardens; our London and many other city parks show them in the shape of beds filled with vast quantities of flowers, covering the ground frequently in a showy way, and not unfrequently in a repulsively gaudy manner: every private garden is taken possession of by the same beauties. Occasionally some variety is introduced. We go to Kew or the Crystal Palace to see what looks best there, or the weekly gardening papers tell us; and the following season sees tens of thousands of the same arrangements and patterns scattered all over the country. I will not here enter into the question of the comparative advantages of the two systems; it is enough to state that even on its votaries the system at present in fashion is beginning to pall. Some are looking back with regret to the old mixed-border gardens; others are endeavouring to soften the harshness of the bedding system by the introduction of fine-leaved plants, but all are agreed that a great mistake has been made in destroying all our sweet old border flowers, from tall Lilies to dwarf Hepaticas, though very few persons indeed have any idea of the numbers of beautiful subjects in this way which we may gather from every northern and temperate clime.

What is to be done? Every garden should have a mixed border, but except in the little cottage gardens before alluded to – 'umbrageous man's nests', as Mr.Carlyle calls them, gardens dependent on it solely are quite out of the question. It is also clear that, base and frightfully opposed to every law of nature's own arrangement of living things as is the bedding system, it has yet some features which deserve to be retained on a small scale. My object is now to show how we may, without losing the better features of the mixed bedding or any other system, follow one infinitely superior to any now practised, yet supplementing both, and exhibiting more of the varied beauty of hardy flowers than the most ardent admirer of the old style of garden ever dreams of. We may do this by naturalizing or making wild innumerable beautiful natives of many regions of the earth in our woods, wild and semi-wild places, rougher parts of pleasure grounds, etc., and in unoccupied places in almost every kind of garden.

I allude not to the wood and brake flora of any one alp or chain of alps, but to that which finds its home in the innumerable woodlands that fall in furrowed folds from beneath the hoary heads of all the great mountain chains of the world, whether they rise from hot Indian plains or green European pastures. The Palm and sacred Fig, as well as the Wheat and the Vine, are separated from the stemless plants that cushion under the snow for half the year, by a zone of hardier and not less beautiful life, varied as the breezes that whisper on the mountain sides, and as the little rills that seam them. I allude to the Lilies, and Bluebells, and

Foxgloves, and Irises, and Windflowers, and Columbines, and Aconites, and Rock-roses, and Violets, and Cranesbills, and countless Pea-flowers, and mountain Avens, and Brambles, and Cinquefoils, and Evening Primroses, and Clematises, and Honeysuckles, and Michaelmas Daisies, and Feverfews, and Wood-hyacinths, and Daffodils, and Bindweeds, and Forget-me-nots, and sweet blue Omphalodes, and Primroses, and Day Lilies, and Asphodels, and St. Bruno's Lilies, and the almost innumerable plants which form the flora of regions where, though life is yet rife on every inch of ground, and we are enjoying the verdure and the temperature of our lowland meadows, there is a 'sense of a great power beginning to be manifested in the earth, and of a deep and majestic concord in the rise of the long low lines of piny hills; the first utterances of those mighty mountain symphonies, soon to be more loudly lifted and wildly broken along the battlements of the Alps. But their strength is as yet restrained, and the far-reaching ridges of pastoral mountains succeed each other, like the long and sighing swell which moves over quiet waters, from some far-off stormy sea. And there is a deep tenderness pervading that vast monotony. The destructive forces, and the stern expression of the central ranges, are alike withdrawn. No frost-ploughed, dust-encumbered paths of the ancient glacier fret the soft Jura pastures; no splintered heaps of ruin break the fair ranks of her forests; no pale, defiled, or furious rivers rend their rude and changeful ways among her rocks. Patiently, eddy by eddy, the clear green streams wind along their well-known beds; and under the dark quietness of the undisturbed pines there spring up, year by year, such company of joyful flowers as I know not the like of among the blessings of the earth. It was spring-time, too; and all were coming forth in clusters crowded for very love. There was room enough for all, but they crushed their leaves into all manner of strange shapes, only to be nearer each other. There was the Wood Anemone, star after star, closing every now and then into nebulae; and there was the Oxalis, troop by troop, like virginal processions of the Mois de Marie, the dark vertical clefts in the limestone choked up with them as with heavy snow, and touched with Ivy on the edges – Ivy as light and lovely as the Vine; and, ever and anon, a blue gush of Violets and Cowslip bells in sunny places; and in the more open ground, the Vetch, and Comfrey, and Mezereon, and the small sapphire buds of the alpine

Polygala, and the Wild Strawberry, just a blossom or two, all showered amidst the golden softness of deep, warm, amber-coloured moss.'*

   This is a picture of but one of innumerable and infinitely varied scenes in the wilder parts of all northern and temperate regions, at many different elevations. The loveliness and ceaselessly varying charms of such scenes are indeed difficult to describe or imagine; the essential thing to bear in mind is that the plants that go to form them *are hardy, and will thrive in our climate as well as native plants.*

   Such beauty may be realised in every wood and copse and wild shrubbery that screens our 'trim gardens'. Naturally our woods and wilds have no small loveliness in spring; we have here and there the Lily-of-the-valley and the Snowdrop wild, and everywhere the exquisite Primrose and Cowslip; the Bluebell and the Foxglove sometimes take nearly complete possession of whole woods, and turn them into paradises of vernal beauty; but, with all our treasures in this way, we have no attractions in semi-wild places compared to what it is within our power to create. A certain number of beautiful plants occur amongst the weeds in our woods, and there we stop. But there are many countries with winters as cold as, or colder than, our own, possessing a rich flora; and by taking the best hardy exotics and establishing them with the best of our own wild flowers in wild or half-wild spots near our houses and gardens, we may produce the most charming results ever seen in such places. To most people a pretty plant in the wild state is more attractive than any garden denizen. It is free, and taking care of itself, it has had to contend with and has overcome weeds which, left to their own sweet will in a garden, would soon leave very small trace of the plants therein; and, moreover, it is usually surrounded by some degree of graceful wild spray – the green above, and the moss and brambles and grass around. Many will say with Tennyson, in 'Amphion', –

> Better to me the meanest weed
> That blows upon its mountain,
> The vilest herb that runs to seed
> Beside its native fountain –

But by the means presently to be explained, numbers of plants, neither 'mean' nor 'vile', but of the highest order of beauty and fragrance, and clothed with the sweetest associations, may be seen to greater perfection,

*A passage from John Ruskin, *The Lamp of Memory*. Ed.

wild as weeds, in the spaces now devoted to rank grass and weeds in our shrubberies, ornamental plantations, and by wood walks, than ever they were in our gardens.

William Robinson, *The Wild Garden*

Three Songs about the Bee

The bee flies around and settles on my breast
It sips the juice and buzzes as it goes
It flies round and round and settles on my head
It sips the juice and buzzes as it goes
The bee buzzes in the garden
It flies round and round and sits between my thighs
It sips the juice and buzzes as it goes
To the eyes the bee is ugly, but its words are sweet
If I could meet that bee I would clasp it to my heart
I would keep it in my thighs and give it my honey
The bee buzzes in the garden.

*

My marigold, you made me love you
Then you forgot me, filling your hair with flowers
When I remember your dear ways
Pain fills my heart
My diamond
Your pure body will one day be mixed with dust
Love you have broken
You have made me drunk with poison
How beautiful
Are two mates like a pair of bees
I would become a bee
I would turn you into a flower
But this pure body
Will be earth and turn to dust.

*

At the bottom of the garden

The black bee
Hides in the temple of flower-buds
In youth
What enormous joys there are
In age
The hour of death draws near.

Folk songs of Chhattisgarh

This Compost

Something startles me where I thought I was safest,
I withdraw from the still woods I loved,
I will not go now on the pastures to walk,
I will not strip the clothes from my body to meet my lover the sea,
I will not touch my flesh to the earth as to other flesh to renew me.

O how can it be that the ground itself does not sicken?
How can you be alive you growths of spring?
How can you furnish health you blood of herbs, roots, orchards, grain?
Are they not continually putting distemper'd corpses within you?
Is not every continent work'd over and over with sour dead?

Where have you disposed of their carcasses?
Those drunkards and gluttons of so many generations?
Where have you drawn off the foul liquid and meat?
I do not see any of it upon you to-day, or perhaps I am deceiv'd,
I will run a furrow with my plough, I will press my spade through the
    sod and turn it up underneath,
I am sure I shall expose some foul meat.

Behold this compost! behold it well!
Perhaps every mite has once form'd part of a sick person – yet behold!
The grass of spring covers the prairies,
The bean bursts noiselessly through the mould in the garden,
The delicate spear of the onion pierces upward,
The apple-buds cluster together on the apple-branches,
The resurrection of the wheat appears with pale visage out of its graves,

The tinge awakes over the willow-tree and the mulberry-tree,
The he-birds carol mornings and evenings while the she-birds sit on
    their nests,
The young of poultry break through the hatch'd eggs,
The new-born of animals appear, the calf is dropt from the cow, the
    colt from the mare,
Out of its little hill faithfully rise the potato's dark green leaves,
Out of its hill rises the yellow maize-stalk, the lilacs bloom in the door-
    yards,
The summer growth is innocent and disdainful above all those strata of
    sour dead.

What chemistry!
That the winds are really not infectious,
That this is no cheat, this transparent green-wash of the sea which is so
    amorous after me,
That is safe to allow it to lick my naked body all over with its tongues,
That it will not endanger me with the fevers that have deposited them-
    selves in it,
That all is clean forever and forever,
That the cool drink from the well tastes so good,
That blackberries are so flavorous and juicy,
That the fruits of the apple-orchard and the orange-orchard, that mel-
    ons, grapes, peaches, plums, will none of them poison me,
That when I recline on the grass I do not catch any disease,
Though probably every spear of grass rises out of what was once a
    catching disease.

Now I am terrified at the Earth, it is so calm and patient,
It grows such sweet things out of such corruptions,
It turns harmless and stainless on its axis, with such endless successions
    of diseas'd corpses,
It distils such exquisite winds out of such infused fetor,
It renews with such unwitting looks its prodigal, annual, sumptuous
    crops,
It gives such divine materials to men, and accepts such leavings from
    them at last.

Walt Whitman, Autumn Rivulets

The Garden of Live Flowers

This time she came upon a large flower-bed, with a border of daisies, and a willow-tree growing in the middle.

'O Tiger-lily,' said Alice, addressing herself to one that was waving gracefully about in the wind, 'I *wish* you could talk!'

'We *can* talk,' said the Tiger-lily: 'when there's anybody worth talking to.'

Alice was so astonished that she couldn't speak for a minute: it quite seemed to take her breath away. At length, as the Tiger-lily only went on waving about, she spoke again, in a timid voice – almost in a whisper. 'And can *all* the flowers talk?'

'As well as *you* can,' said the Tiger-lily. 'And a great deal louder.'

'It isn't manners for us to begin, you know,' said the Rose, 'and I really was wondering when you'd speak! Said I to myself, "Her face has got *some* sense in it, though it's not a clever one!" Still, you're the right colour, and that goes a long way.'

'I don't care about the colour,' the Tiger-lily remarked. 'If only her petals curled up a little more, she'd be all right.'

Alice didn't like being criticised, so she began asking questions: 'Aren't you sometimes frightened at being planted out here, with nobody to take care of you?'

'There's the tree in the middle,' said the Rose. 'What else is it good for?'

'But what could it do, if any danger came?' Alice asked.

'It could bark,' said the Rose.

'It says "Bough-wough!"' cried a Daisy: 'that's why its branches are called boughs!'

'Didn't you know *that*?' cried another Daisy, and here they all began shouting together, till the air seemed quite full of little shrill voices. 'Silence, every one of you!' cried the Tiger-lily, waving itself passionately from side to side, and trembling with excitement. 'They know I can't get at them!' it panted, bending its quivering head towards Alice, 'or they wouldn't dare to do it!'

'Never mind!' Alice said in a soothing tone, and stooping down to the daisies, who were just beginning again, she whispered, 'If you don't hold your tongues, I'll pick you!'

There was silence in a moment, and several of the pink daisies turned white.

'That's right!' said the Tiger-lily. 'The daisies are worst of all. When one speaks, they all begin together, and it's enough to make one wither to hear the way they go on!'

'How is it you can all talk so nicely?' Alice said, hoping to get it into a better temper by a compliment. 'I've been in many gardens before, but none of the flowers could talk.'

'Put your hand down, and feel the ground,' said the Tiger-lily. 'Then you'll know why.'

Alice did so. 'It's very hard,' she said, 'but I don't see what that has to do with it.'

'In most gardens,' the Tiger-lily said, 'they make the beds too soft – so that the flowers are always asleep.'

This sounded a very good reason, and Alice was quite pleased to know it. 'I never thought of that before!' she said.

'It's *my* opinion that you never think *at all*,' the Rose said in a rather severe tone.

'I never saw anybody that looked stupider,' a Violet said, so suddenly that Alice quite jumped; for it hadn't spoken before.

'Hold *your* tongue,' cried the Tiger-lily. 'As if *you* ever saw anybody. You keep your head under the leaves, and snore away there till you know no more what's going on in the world, than if you were a bud!'

'Are there any more people in the garden besides me?' Alice said, not choosing to notice the Rose's last remark.

'There's one other flower in the garden that can move like you,' said the Rose. 'I wonder how you do it –' ('You're always wondering,' said the Tiger-lily), 'but she's more bushy than you are.'

'Is she like me?" Alice asked eagerly, for the thought crossed her mind, 'There's another little girl in the garden somewhere!'

'Well, she has the same awkward shape as you,' the Rose said: 'but she's redder – and her petals are shorter, I think.'

'They're done up close, like a dahlia,' said the Tiger-lily: 'not tumbled about, like yours.'

'But that's not *your* fault,' the Rose added kindly: 'you're beginning to fade, you know – and then one can't help one's petals getting a little untidy.'

Alice didn't like this idea at all: so, to change the subject, she asked, 'Does she ever come out here?'

'I dare say you'll see her soon,' said the Rose. 'She's one of the kind that has nine spikes, you know.'

'Where does she wear them?' Alice asked, with some curiosity.

'Why, all round her head, of course,' the Rose replied. 'I was wondering *you* hadn't got some too. I thought it was the regular rule.'

'She's coming!' cried the Larkspur. 'I can hear her footstep, thump, thump, along the gravel walk!'

Alice looked round eagerly, and found that it was the Red Queen. 'She's grown a good deal!' was her first remark. She had indeed; when Alice first found her in the ashes, she had been only three inches high – and here she was, half a head taller than Alice herself!

'It's the fresh air that does it,' said the Rose: 'wonderfully fine air it is, out here.'

'I think I'll go and meet her,' said Alice, for, though the flowers were interesting enough, she felt that it would be far grander to have a talk with a real Queen.

Lewis Carroll, Through the Looking-Glass

Adam, Lilith, and Eve

One day it thundered and lightened.
Two women, fairly frightened,
Sank to their knees, transformed, transfixed,
At the feet of the man who sat betwixt;
And 'Mercy!' cried each – 'if I tell the truth
Of a passage in my youth!'

Said This: 'Do you mind the morning
I met your love with scorning?
As the worst of the venom on my lips,
I thought "If, despite this lie, he strips
The mask from my soul with a kiss – I crawl
His slave, – soul, body and all!"'

Said That: 'We stood to be married;
The priest, or someone, tarried;
"If Paradise-door prove locked?" smiled you.
I thought, as I nodded, smiling too,
"Did one, that's away, arrive – nor late
Nor soon should unlock Hell's gate!"'

It ceased to lighten and thunder.
Up started both in wonder,
Looked round and saw that the sky was clear,
Then laughed 'Confess you believed us, Dear!'
'I saw through the joke!' the man replied
They re-seated themselves beside.

Robert Browning

Dandelion

Leontodon Taraxacum, L. *Compositae*
French, Pissenlit, Dent-de-lion. *German*, Löwenzahn.
Flemish, Molsalaad. *Italian*, Dente di leone.

Native of Europe. – Perennial. – Leaves all radical, spreading into a rosette, smooth, oblong, runcinate, with triangular-lanceolate lobes, and entire towards the extremity; youngest leaves often brownish at the commencement of their growth. Flower-stalks hollow, one-flowered; flower-heads large with florets of golden-yellow. Seeds compressed, oblong, rough or scaly, and prickly at the top; their germinating power lasts for two years.

People contented themselves with gathering Dandelions in the meadows or fields until, as they became an important article of commerce in the Central Market of Paris, it occurred to some that it could be cultivated and improved by the selection of seed from choice plants. Thus the plant was improved to a remarkable degree, as may easily be seen by comparing the produce of seeds gathered from the wild plant with that of seeds obtained from the cultivated plants.

CULTURE. – The seed may be sown in March or April, either where the plants are to stand, or in a seed-bed, from which the seedlings are to be pricked out, in May or June, in rows, which should be 14 to 16 in. apart. The plants are extremely hardy, and require no attention beyond occasional hoeings and waterings. In autumn they commence to yield, and will continue to do so all through the winter, if they are looked after. The quality of the Dandelion is much improved by blanching, which may be effected either by covering the bed with a layer of sand, or by placing an inverted flower-pot over each plant, having previously gathered the leaves up together. The pot should be large enough to cover the plant without pressing the leaves too closely against one another. In winter the plants lose most of their leaves, but an abundant new growth takes place in spring, and any plants which have not yielded much the first year do so plentifully in the spring of the second.

USES. – The whole of the plant is used for salad; if blanched, so much the better.

Large Green Montmagny Dandelion. – This, now largely grown in the vicinity of Paris, is a more vigorous form of the Common Dandelion. It blanches well.

Thick-leaved, or *Cabbaging, Dandelion.* – A very distinct variety, obtained by cultivation, and surpassing the wild plant not so much in the size as in the very great number of its leaves, which form a regular tuft or clump, instead of a plain rosette. It yields a very abundant crop without taking up much ground, and blanches very easily and, indeed, almost naturally. It appears to us to be the best variety that has been obtained up to the present.

Improved Very Early Dandelion. – Increasing the breadth of the leaves of Dandelions has resulted in fewer leaves being produced. The variety known as *Improved Broad-leaved Dandelion*, forms a simple rosette of very large and broad leaves, sometimes 20 in. across. Its productiveness not being in proportion to the amount of space it occupies, it has been almost completely superseded by a sub-variety called the *Improved Very Early Dandelion*, in which less productiveness is compensated for by greater earliness. Its leaves are large, and are formed as soon as the winter is over. They make a delicate salad.

Improved Giant Erect Dandelion. – A distinct variety which, instead of forming into a rosette, like other Dandelions, grows in erect, strong, thickly set tufts. The leaves are long, stout, toothed, and slightly brown. It is very early, vigorous, and more prolific than most of the other Dandelions.

Moss-leaved Dandelion. – A distinct variety of Curled-leaved Dandelion, much denser and more compact than the Common kind, and apparently permanent in its characteristics. The blade of the leaf is divided and, as it were, slashed into narrow strips. The plant can be easily blanched, and in that condition affords a salad not unlike Curled Endive, but coming in in spring, when it is very difficult to have any Endive fit for table use.

MM. Vilmorin-Andrieux, *The Vegetable Garden*

Love Comes Calling

The notary's house faced on to the square. Behind it there was a pleasant, well-kept garden stretching as far as the Passage des Piques, an alley which was always deserted and from which it was separated by a wall.

It was at the bottom of this garden that Maître Moreau's wife had given a rendezvous, for the first time, to Captain Sommerive, who had been paying attentions to her for a long time.

Her husband had gone to Paris for a week, so she was free for the whole of that time. The captain had pressed her so hard, had implored her with such persuasive words; she was so convinced that he was passionately in love with her; and she felt so isolated, so misunderstood, so neglected in the midst of all the contracts which seemed to be her husband's only interest, that she had given away her heart without asking herself whether she would give anything more one day.

Then, after months of platonic love, of squeezed hands, of brief kisses stolen behind doors, the captain had declared that he would leave town straight away and apply for a posting unless she gave him a rendezvous, a real rendezvous under the trees, during her husband's absence.

She had given way; she had promised a meeting.

Now she was waiting for him, huddled against the wall, her heart pounding wildly, and starting at the slightest sound.

Suddenly she heard somebody clambering over the wall and she nearly ran away. What if it weren't the captain? What if it were a thief? But no – a voice called out softly: 'Mathilde!' She replied: 'Étienne!' And a man dropped on to the path with a clatter of metal.

It was he! And what a kiss they exchanged!

For a long time they remained clasped in each other's arms, their lips pressed together. But suddenly a fine drizzle began to fall and the raindrops dripping from one leaf to another produced a rippling sound of water in the darkness. She gave a start as the first drop fell on her neck.

'Mathilde,' he said, 'my darling, my love, my sweet, my angel, let's go indoors. It's midnight; we have nothing to fear. Let's go inside, please.'

Guy de Maupassant, *The Matter with André*

Winter Comes

Winter scourges his horses
Through the North,
His hair is bitter snow
On the great wind.
The trees are weeping leaves
Because the nests are dead,
Because the flowers were nests of scent
And the nests had singing petals
And the flowers and nests are dead.

Your voice brings back the songs
Of every nest,
Your eyes bring back the sun
Out of the South,
Violets and roses peep
Where you have laughed the snow away
And kissed the snow away,
And in my heart there is a garden still
For the lost birds.

Folk Song of Daghestan

The Formal Garden in England

The disregard of conditions which the landscape gardener shows in dealing with the house and garden is even more conspicuous in his treatment of public grounds. For some inscrutable reason the laying out of public grounds is usually left either to the engineer or to the landscape gardener. The engineer is, no doubt, a man of ability and attainment, but there is nothing in his training to qualify him to deal with a problem which is in the main artistic; and the landscape gardener makes it his business to dispense with serious design. The result is that our public spaces are seldom laid out on any principle at all. For instance, a London square is an entirely artificial affair. It is bounded by rectangular blocks of buildings, and straight roads and fences. It would only be reasonable to adhere to this simple motive; but hand this over to the landscape gardener and he will at once set to work to contradict the whole character of the place by means of irregular curves and irrelevant hummocks. His dislike of a simple straight line and a plain piece of grass amounts almost to a mania. In Bloomsbury, till within the last few years, there existed a good old-fashioned square garden, laid out in four grass plots, with a lime walk and a border of flowers running round the sides. It was restful and pleasant to look at. The grass plots were good for lawn-tennis and the lime walks kindly to the citizen; but the landscape gardener appeared on the scene and speedily put all this to rights. He cut up the grass plots and destroyed two sides of the lime walk, and he heaped up some mounds, and made the most curiously unreasonable paths; and went his way, having destroyed one of the few square gardens in London with any pretence to design. Instead of trying to treat the square as a whole, or, better still, instead of leaving it alone, he deliberately turned his back on the adjacent architecture, and produced a result which has no distinction but that of immense vulgarity.

Much more might be done in the way of planting avenues of trees along the approaches to towns and in the towns themselves. Evelyn mentions the road from Heidelberg to Darmstadt, which was planted all the way with walnuts, and an avenue of 4 leagues long and 50 paces wide, 'planted with young oaklings, as straight as a line, from the city of Utrecht to Amersfoort.' The road from Hoorn to Alkmaar, in North Holland, and from Hoorn to Enkhuizen, passes for miles under an avenue of elms. 'Is there,' Evelyn says, 'a more ravishing or delightful object, than to behold some entire streets and whole towns planted with these lime-trees in even lines before their doors, so as they seem like cities in a wood?' Mr. Robinson's views to the contrary are significant. In his *Garden Design*, he asserts that 'the ugliest things in the fair land of France are the ugly old lines of clipt limes which deface many French towns.' In regard to this assertion, I would only repeat, that the depth of colour, the play of reflected light, the extreme brilliancy of the isolated spots of sunshine, which result from these close-clipt masses of leafage, must surely appeal to a person of quite ordinary sensibility. But the point of serious moment in Mr. Robinson's pronouncement is its hopeless modernism in the worst sense. It shows an insensibility to what has been done in the past, and an unconsciousness of a whole world of thought, which together constitute one of the most fatal tendencies of modern design. Out of a mind well stored with knowledge and tradition good original ideas may come, but what are we to expect from a mind stored with the ideas of the Great Exhibition of 1851? We are to expect exactly what we have got in most of our modern parks and public gardens, and we cannot feel very sanguine as to any prospects of improvement. The London County Council have shown a wise anxiety to secure public spaces whenever possible, but when they have got them their advisers seem very uncertain as to how they should deal with them. They waste the public money in humps and earthworks, and economise in kiosques and cast-iron fountains, and this, though there are admirable models to follow in the gardens of the Luxembourg and the Tuileries and in most of the important cities of Europe. Nowhere is the provincialism of modern English thought more clearly shown than in our State and municipal dealings with art.

In dealing with great spaces the landscape gardener seems to have little idea of mass. He is for ever breaking up the outline with little knots of trees, and reducing the size of his grounds by peppering them all over with shrubs. The consequence is that though one may feel weary with traversing his interminable paths, no permanent impression of size is left on the mind. Such a place, for instance, as Battersea Park is like a bad piece of architecture full of details which stultify each other. The only good point in it is the one avenue, and this leads to nowhere. If this park had been planted out with groves and avenues of limes, like the boulevard at Avallon, or the squares at Vernon, or even like the east side of Hyde Park between the Achilles statue and the Marble Arch, at least one definite effect would have been reached. There might have been shady walks, and noble walls of trees, instead of the spasmodic futility of Battersea Park, and without pedantry the principles of formal design should be applied to public grounds and parks. A dominant idea should control the general scheme. Merely to introduce so many statues or plaster casts is to begin at the wrong end. These are the accidents of the system, not the system itself, and this is why the attempt at formal gardening at the head of the Serpentine was such a failure. The details were not particularly well designed, but even if they had been, it was essentially inartistic to plump them down in the midst of incongruous surroundings.

Perhaps of all the unsatisfactory public places in England the worst is the public cemetery. Here again one finds the same disregard of decent order, the same hatred of simplicity, the same meanness of imagination. Here, if anywhere, all pettiness, all banalities should be avoided. We want rest, even if it is sombre in its severity; but instead we are offered narrow winding roads and broken pillars under weeping willows, everything that can suggest the ghastly paraphernalia of the undertaker. Why not have long walks of yew at once, with cypress-trees or junipers? But the landscape gardener is nothing if not 'natural', and so he gives us a bad copy of an ill-chosen subject.

. . . As was pointed out in an earlier chapter, the landscape gardener attempts to establish a sort of hierarchy of nature, based on much the same principle as that which distinguishes a gentleman by his incapacity to do any useful work. Directly it is proved that a plant or a tree is good for food, it is expelled from the flower garden without any regard to its intrinsic beauty. The hazel-hedge has gone, and the apple-tree has long been banished from the flowers. Of all the trees an apple-tree in full bloom, or ripe in autumn is perhaps the loveliest. Trained as an espalier it makes a beautiful hedge, and set out as in an orchard it lets the sun play through its leaves and chequer with gold the green velvet of the grass in a way that no other tree will quite allow. Nothing can be more beautiful than some of the walks under the apple-trees in the gardens at Penshurst. Yet the landscape gardener would shudder at the idea of planting a grove or hedge of apple-trees in his garden. Instead of this he will give you a conifer or a monkey-puzzler, though the guilder-rose grows wild in the meadow and the spindle-tree in the wood, and the rowan, the elder, and the white-thorn; and the wild cherry in autumn fires the woodland with its crimson and gold. Every one admires these as a matter of proper sensibility to nature, but it does not seem to occur to people that they would grow with as little difficulty in a garden, and at the very smallest expense. It would undoubtedly injure the business of the nursery gardener to allow that they were possible. Again, the pear-tree and chequer-tree, the quince, the medlar, and the mulberry are surely entitled by their beauty to a place in the garden. It is only since nature has been taken in hand by the landscapist and taught her proper position that these have been excluded. When there was no talk about nature, and man had not learnt to consider himself as something detached from nature and altogether superior, the fruit-tree was counted among the beauties of the garden. It is of fruit-trees that Homer tells us in the garden of Alcinous: 'Without the palace, near the doors, was a great garden, four acres by four, and round it on every side was driven a fence. There grew tall trees and beautiful pears and pomegranates, and apple-trees with gleaming fruit, and luscious figs and teeming olive-trees.' Or again, in the ground of a mediæval tapestry all beautiful flowers and fruits grow together, the strawberry next the violet, and columbines among the raspberries, and fair roses twine among the apple boughs. So again with flowers: 'The dahlia has banished the hollyhock, with its old friend the sunflower, into the cottage garden, where it still flanks the little walk that leads from the wicket to the porch – not the only instance in which our natural taste has been redeemed by the cottage against the vulgar pretensions of luxury and wealth.' [James, *The Carthusian*.] It is more of this unsophisticated liking for everything that is beautiful that ought to be allowed full play in the gardens; less of the pedantry that lays down rules about nature and is at heart indifferent to the beauty about which it preaches.

If there were any truth in his cant about nature would the landscape gardener bed out asters and geraniums, would he make the lawn hideous with patches of brilliant red varied by streaks of purple blue, and add his finishing touch in the magenta of his choicest dahlia? Would he plant them in patterns of stars and lozenges and tadpoles? Would he border them with paths of asphalt? Would he not rather fill his borders with every kind of beautiful flower that he might delight in? It is impossible to take his professions seriously when he flies in the face of nature, when he transplants exotics into impossible conditions, when rarity, difficulty, and expense of production are his tests of the value of a flower. The beauty that he claims for his garden is not his but that of the flowers, the grass, the sunlight, and the cloud, which no amount of bad design can utterly destroy.

Reginald Blomfield, *The Formal Garden in England*

The Virtues of Soil

Contact with the brown earth cures all diseases, mitigates all troubles and anxieties, smooths the wrinkles that city cares have engraved on the face; and restores, even in the later days of a man's life, some touches of the joy that made gold and honey and music, and ever-changing aspirations and fancies of the simplest facts, and, indeed, of all the facts of human existence in the happy days of youth. Do you remember the doll's garden the girls made next to yours, and took up your sprouting mustard seed to make a hedge all around it to keep the dog out? Do you remember which side up to place the scarlet runner seed, and the frantic delight with which you saw green shoots appear on the willow sticks you stole from the gardener's shed, and employed to make a terrific palisade to your own garden when there were three clumps of crocuses in flower, and some wallflowers almost out, and a rose tree nearly dead through being five times transplanted, and the girls broke in again and called you greedy for having all the tops of the pine-apples swathed in wool and planted in front of the cottage you had made out of a cigar box? You do remember these things? Of course you do; you will never forget them; but this garden you are now thinking about will bring the flower of youth to beautify your grave experiences, and *health*, the foundation of happiness, will come as a distillation from the earth and its leafy garniture. The fable of Antaeus is an epitome of the life of man, and illustrates, in its own heroic way, the spiritual and material tonic that may be derived from farming and gardening.

SOILS. – In determining what to grow and how to manage, you will have to face this difficulty – that no garden, however favourable in a general way the soil and climate and surroundings may be, is equally adapted for all the kinds of vegetables and fruits you will wish to derive from it. The consequence is that you will have to effect compromises and make shifts, and in the end, perhaps, make yourself content with inferior products of some kinds, while, let us hope, you will have plenty of superior products of other kinds to compensate abundantly. Moreover, it matters not how well versed you may be in geology and chemistry and the requirements of plants, you will have to learn much on the spot, and you will have to respect the *genius loci*, and be in no haste to regard as nonsense the 'wise saws' of your neighbours who may tell you that yours is a wonderful land for parsley, but won't do for asparagus; or that it suits cauliflowers beyond all expectation, but will not produce potatoes fit to eat. A deep sandy loam will suit almost every crop you can think of as proper for a kitchen garden, and deep retentive clay may be made one of the best soils in the world by means of hard work and judicious manuring and cropping. If you are located on clay, you ought to embrace every opportunity of carting in at a cheap rate lime-rubbish and sandy road drift. If on peat, lime-rubbish and clay will be valuable materials, and bone the best of manures. If on chalk or gravel, clay, turf, pond-mud, and fat manure will be of immense advantage. There is scarcely a soil to be found that does not need the occasional help of good stable manure, but it certainly does tend to make light soils lighter, so that it is possible in some cases its employment may be less advantageous than others.

But it is nevertheless a golden rule that to use manure in excess is scarcely possible, and the market gardens in the neighbourhood of London may always be pointed to in illustration of the rule. It is scarcely an exaggeration to say that for every load of vegetables taken off the ground a load of good stable manure is put on. The waggon that goes to market with a load of cabbages calls on the way home at some brewery or omnibus yard for a load of manure, and thus the supply is sustained at little cost, and the fertility of the land is kept at a high pitch.

In the management of the soil scientific knowledge is of some value. For example, chemistry tells us that the potato contains a considerable proportion of potash, salts, and phosphates. Geology tells us that sandy soils, which consist largely of silica, are often deficient of those minerals, while granitic soils are usually rich in potash, and limestone soils are rich in phosphates. What shall we do, then, to prepare our sand for the production of potatoes? Good stable manure will help it immensely, and, wanting that, phosphor-guano may answer admirably, and wanting that, muriate of potash and superphosphate may suffice. The most useful of what are called 'artificial manures' are phosphor-guano, superphosphate of lime, bone-dust, kainit (a cheap, rough kind of potash); muriate of potash, a better and apparently more expensive manure, that in many instances would prove cheaper than kainit; nitrate of soda, and common salt.

It is worthy to remark that deep fertile soils in first-rate condition are not in the least degree benefited by 'artificials', whereas on thin poor soils that have been badly managed they frequently – indeed commonly – produce results that may be described as more than satisfactory and that actually approach the wonderful. Everything depends on what is done and how it is done, but this may be averred with safety, that it will always pay well to manure the land liberally and keep it in the highest possible condition of productiveness. To be afraid to bury money in the soil is to forfeit your right to take money out. The deep strong clays and loams need the help of good stable manure, but artificials will be of little service to them, except to thin the crop and so ensure more room for the plants that survive. It is a fact to be borne in mind that artificial manures, even if of so mild a nature as ivory dust and superphosphate, kill a considerable proportion of seed; so that it is advisable to put these fertilisers out of the immediate reach of the young plants, for it is better to thin them ourselves than have them thinned by a process of poisoning. The mode of application we find answers best is to have the artificials powdered on the soil in the trench as the digging proceeds, as they are then covered with soil, and the plants do not reach them until they are strong enough to derive benefit from high living.

Earth-work is generally well understood by the class likely to be employed in the rougher kinds of garden labour. We shall suppose the reader to regard the handling of the spade as *infra dig.*, and this will save expenditure of space in describing the noble art of turning the turf topsy-turvy. It will soon be discovered by the observant amateur that human nature has a greater liking for scratching than for digging, and hence to ensure for a piece of ground what a gardener would call a 'good doing' is not an easy matter. But there is great virtue in stirring, not withstanding Hood's assertion that it is the action of a spoon. It is rather the exception than the rule for the kitchen garden to be as deeply stirred and knocked about as it ought to be. Ordinary flat digging answers for most crops, but a certain extent of ground ought every year to be trenched, so that in the course of five or six years or so, all the plots devoted to rotation cropping may be turned over to the depth of two spits. If the crop to be put on will allow it, a good body of manure should be put in the trench, between the two spits, as the work proceeds, but it may be advisable to put the manure at the bottom of the trench below both spits, or to trench without manure and finish by pricking in a coat of manure on the top. If gigantic parsnips, carrots, and salsify are wanted, put the manure at the bottom; if fine peas, beans, cauliflowers, broccolis, and cabbages are your desire, put the manure between the two spits; if the ground is intended for a seed bed, prick the manure into the top crust about half a spit deep. It is a common experience of those who enter into possession of old gardens to find the growth of everything stunted and the soil apparently worn out. Nine times in ten, or even ninety-nine times in a hundred, when this is the case, the land may be rendered capable of almost anything by the simple process of trenching and putting a good body of fat manure between the two spits. In all probability the kind of tillage that has been followed has been founded on scratching instead of digging, and hence the second spit, perhaps the whole body, of soil from a depth of six inches downward is in the state of maiden earth, never touched by plough or spade, with all the elements of fertility still locked up in it as in the times far back when the soil was made by the deposition of grain upon grain at the bottom of the sea. As the value of trenching depends on the quality of the subsoil, it follows of course that where the subsoil consists of unkind stuff it may not be advisable to bring it to the surface. In very many such cases bastard trenching, in which the second or under spit is broken, but is not thrown up, improves the ground considerably, and it may happen that a subsoil of a most unpromising appearance and texture proves of the greatest value when mixed with the surface soil, and exposed for a time to the atmosphere. A mixture of soils generally results in the production of a staple more fertile than either were separately; but caution must of course be exercised, whenever the subsoil is not obviously suitable. In the case of a deep yellow loam or nut-brown clay showing a tendency to mellow into loam, there can be no question for doubt, and the spirited cultivator will ensure that some of the second spit shall see the daylight.

Shirley Hibberd, *The Amateur's Kitchen Garden, Frame-ground and Forcing-Pit*

Blood-letting

The time arrived for killing the pig which Jude and his wife had fattened in their sty during the autumn months, and the butchering was timed to take place as soon as it was light in the morning, so that Jude might get to Alfredston without losing more than a quarter of a day.

The night had seemed strangely silent. Jude looked out of the window long before dawn, and perceived that the ground was covered with snow – snow rather deep for the season, it seemed, a few flakes still falling.

'I'm afraid the pig-killer won't be able to come,' he said to Arabella.

'O, he'll come. You must get up and make the water hot, if you want Challow to scald him. Though I like singeing best.'

'I'll get up,' said Jude. 'I like the way of my own county.'

He went downstairs, lit the fire under the copper, and began feeding it with bean-stalks, all the time without a candle, the blaze flinging a cheerful shine into the room; though for him the sense of cheerfulness was lessened by thoughts on the reason of that blaze – to heat water to scald the bristles from the body of an animal that as yet lived, and whose voice could be continually heard from a corner of the garden. At half-past six, the time of appointment with the butcher, the water boiled, and Jude's wife came downstairs.

'Is Challow come?' she asked.

'No.'

They waited, and it grew lighter, with the dreary light of a snowy dawn. She went out, gazed along the road, and returning said, 'He's not coming. Drunk last night, I expect. The snow may be deep in the valley.'

'Can't be put off. There's no more victuals for the pig. He ate the last mixing o' barleymeal yesterday morning.'

'Yesterday morning? What has he lived on since?'

'Nothing.'

'What – he has been starving?'

'Yes. We always do it the last day or two, to save bother with the innerds. What ignorance, not to know that!'

'That accounts for his crying so. Poor creature!'

'Well – you must do the sticking – there's no help for it. I'll show you how. Or I'll do it myself – I think I could. Though as it is such a big pig I had rather Challow had done it. However, his basket o' knives and things have been sent on here, and we can use 'em.'

'Of course you shan't do it,' said Jude. 'I'll do it, since it must be done.'

He went out to the sty, shovelled away the snow for the space of a couple of yards or more, and placed the stool in front, with the knives and ropes at hand. A robin peered down at the preparations from the nearest tree, and, not liking the sinister look of the scene, flew away, though hungry. By this time Arabella had joined her husband, and Jude, rope in hand, got into the sty, and noosed the affrighted animal, who, beginning with a squeak of surprise, rose to repeated cries of rage. Arabella opened the sty-door, and together they hoisted the victim onto the stool, legs upward, and while Jude held him Arabella bound him down, looping the cord over his legs to keep him from struggling.

The animal's note changed its quality. It was not now rage, but the cry of despair; long-drawn, slow and hopeless.

'Upon my soul I would sooner have gone without the pig than have had this to do!' said Jude. 'A creature I have fed with my own hands.'

'Don't be such a tender-hearted fool! There's the sticking-knife – the one with the point. Now whatever you do, don't stick un too deep.'

'I'll stick him effectually, so as to make short work of it. That's the chief thing.'

'You must not!' she cried. 'The meat must be well bled, and to do that he must die slow. We shall lose a shilling a score if the meat is red and bloody! Just touch the vein, that's all. I was brought up to it, and I know. Every good butcher keeps un bleeding long. He ought to be eight or ten minutes dying, at least.'

'He shall not be half a minute if I can help it, however the meat may look,' said Jude determinedly. Scraping the bristles from the pig's upturned throat, as he had seen the butchers do, he slit the fat; then plunged in the knife with all his might.

"Od damn it all!' she cried, 'that ever I should say it! You've over-stuck un! And I telling you all the time –'

'Do be quiet, Arabella, and have a little pity on the creature!'

'Hold up the pail to catch the blood, and don't talk!'

However unworkmanlike the deed, it had been mercifully done. The blood flowed out in a torrent instead of in the trickling stream she had desired. The dying animal's cry assumed its third and final tone, the shriek of agony; his glazing eyes riveting themselves on Arabella with the eloquently keen reproach of a creature recognising at last the treachery of those who had seemed his only friends.

'Make un stop that!' said Arabella. 'Such a noise will bring somebody or other up here, and I don't want people to know we are doing it ourselves.' Picking up the knife from the ground whereon Jude had flung it, she slipped it into the gash, and slit the windpipe. The pig was instantly silent, his dying breath coming through the hole.

'That's better,' she said.

'It is a hateful business!' said he.

'Pigs must be killed.'

The animal heaved in a final convulsion, and, despite the rope, kicked out with all his last strength. A tablespoonful of black clot came forth, the trickling of red blood having ceased for some seconds.

'That's it; now he'll go,' said she. 'Artful creatures – they always keep back a drop like that as long as they can!'

The last plunge had come so unexpectedly as to make Jude stagger, and in recovering himself he kicked over the vessel in which the blood had been caught.

'There!' she cried, thoroughly in a passion. 'Now I can't make any blackpot. There's a waste, all through you!'

Jude put the pail upright, but only about a third of the steaming liquid was left in it, the main part being splashed over the snow, and forming a dismal, sordid, ugly spectacle – to those who saw it as other than an ordinary obtaining of meat. The lips and nostrils of the animal turned livid, then white, and the muscles of his limbs relaxed.

'Thank God!' Jude said. 'He's dead.'

'What's God got to do with such a messy job as a pig-killing, I should like to know!' she said scornfully. 'Poor folks must live.'

'I know, I know,' he said. 'I don't scold you.'

Suddenly they became aware of a voice at hand.

'Well done, young married volk! I couldn't have carried it out much better myself, cuss me if I could!' The voice, which was husky, came from the garden-gate, and looking up from the scene of slaughter they saw the burly form of Mr. Challow leaning over the gate, critically surveying their performance.

Thomas Hardy, *Jude the Obscure*

The Gardener

The gardener does not love to talk,
He makes me keep the gravel walk;
And when he puts his tools away,
He locks the door and takes the key.

Away behind the currant row
Where no one else but cook may go,
Far in the plots, I see him dig,
Old and serious, brown and big.

He digs the flowers, green, red, and blue,
Nor wishes to be spoken to.
He digs the flowers and cuts the hay,
And never seems to want to play.

Silly gardener! summer goes,
And winter comes with pinching toes,
When in the garden bare and brown

You must lay your barrow down.

Well now, and while the summer stays,
To profit by these garden days,
O how much wiser you would be
To play at Indian wars with me!

Robert Louis Stevenson, A Child's Garden of Verses

Presumption of wealth and time run through these (mostly) Edwardian texts. Any author, such as Gertrude Jekyll, who advises planting Scotch fir (Pinus sylvestris) 'in quantity', is not writing for suburbia. The mood is one of lightness, curiosity, and summer days after the long Victorian winter. Despite biographies to the contrary, I cannot but imagine these authors as middle-aged, slightly overweight aunties and uncles, who never had children of their own. They look on the world around them with indulgent good humour and bright intelligence.

That is not to claim they do not have their faults. S. Reynolds Hole strikes me as pompous; Gertrude Jekyll has such a tone of unnecessary superiority that I dislike her almost as much as the later Marion Cran. But even snobs can be good gardeners, and I admire the spirit with which Jekyll's attention has shifted, as her eyesight fails, to the many sounds of a garden. I wonder at her partnership with Lutyens, who reveals a warm and likeable personality in his letter from a client's house.

The emotional and spiritual benefits of being in gardens are expressed in different ways by Eden Phillpotts and Alfred Austin. Austin, a rather forgettable poet laureate, has left several interesting accounts of his unconventional household and garden. All are rich in the sort of casual, incidental detail which reveals much about the thoughts and attitudes of a time. This piece is also a model of the type of foresight and circumspection which we need to relearn if water is to be managed more effectively.

The civilising influence of gardens makes them essential elements in the new cities imagined by Ebenezer Howard. His manifesto for the inclusion of *nature in cities, and the exclusion of pollution, would make cities more pleasant, without a doubt. But there is something tiresomely prescriptive about utopians, and their accumulation of rules soon precludes the very element which is most desirable of all, freedom.*

Sir George Sitwell's flight of fancy, by contrast, is all about the plurality of possibility: mediocrity, ignorance, and failure of imagination are the vices he would exclude from his perfect world. His meditation on time in respect to place, his exploration of ageing in relation to gardens, are so very humane and affirmative, and the more precious for being rare.

A different engagement with time is explored in The Secret Garden. *It seems prophetic now – so many walled gardens, so many stove-houses, were about to lose their men and slide into the dereliction which Frances Hodgson Burnett describes here in 1911.*

The Enjoyments of a Garden

I asked a schoolboy, in the sweet summertide, 'what he thought a garden was for?' and he said, *Strawberries.* His younger sister suggested *Croquet,* and the elder *Garden-parties.* The brother from Oxford made a prompt declaration in favour of *Lawn Tennis and Cigarettes,* but he was rebuked by a solemn senior, who wore spectacles, and more back hair than is usual with males, and was told that 'a garden was designed for botanical research, and for the classification of plants.' He was about to demonstrate the differences between the *Acoty-* and *Monocoty-ledonous* divisions, when the collegian remembered an engagement elsewhere.

I repeated my question to a middle-aged nymph, who wore a feathered hat of noble proportions over a loose green tunic with a silver belt, and she replied, with a rapturous disdain of the ignorance which presumed to ask – 'What is a garden for? For the soul, sir, for the soul of the poet! For visions of the invisible, for grasping the intangible, for hearing the inaudible, for exaltations' (she raised her hands, and stood tiptoe, like jocund day upon the misty mountain top, as though she would soar into space) 'above the miserable dullness of common life into the splendid regions of the imagination and romance.' I ventured to suggest that she would have to do a large amount of soaring before she met with anything more beautiful than the flowers, or sweeter than the nightingale's note; but the flighty one still wished to fly.

A capacious gentleman informed me that nothing in horticulture touched him so sensibly as green peas and new potatoes, and he spoke with so much cheerful candour that I could not be angry; but my indignation was roused by a morose millionaire, when he declared that of all his expenses he grudged most the outlay on his confounded garden.

Dejected, I sought solace from certain ladies and gentlemen, who had expressed in my hearing their devoted love of flowers. They were but miserable comforters. Their devotion was superficial, their homage conventional: there was no heart in their worship. I met with many who held flowers in high estimation, not for their own sake, not for the loveliness and perfect beauty of their colour, their fragrance, and their form, not because even Solomon in all his glory was not arrayed like one of these, but because they were the most effective decorations of their window-sills, apartments, and tables, and the most becoming embellishments for their own personal display. I found gentlemen who restricted their enthusiasm to one class of plants, ignoring all the rest; and even in this their valuation was regulated by the rarity and the cost of the flower. 'I can assure you, my dear sir,' they said, 'that there is only one other specimen in the country, and that the happy possessor is my friend, Lord Lombard.' And I shall never forget the disastrous results which followed, when I informed one of these would-be monopolists, that I knew a third party, who had duplicates. He favoured me with a scowl during the remainder of our interview, and became my bitter enemy for life.

Others were quite as exclusive, but with a difference of intention. They not only desired to possess, but that the public should know that they possessed, something out of the common; and from their love of renown, or their 'sacra auri fames', they competed for prizes which were awarded to their favourite flower. It seemed to me that they derived much more gratification from the cups and stakes than from the horses, who had won the race.

The unkindest cut of all, so common that it makes one callous, comes from those visitors who 'would be so delighted to see our garden!' and they come and see, and forget to be delighted. They admire the old city walls which surround it, they like to hear the cawing of the rooks, they are pleased with the sun-dial and the garden-chairs, but as for horticulture they might as well be in Piccadilly! They would be more attracted by the fruit in Solomon's shop than by all the flowers in the border. I heard a lady speaking to her companion of 'the most perfect gem she had ever seen', and when, supposing that reference was made to some exquisite novelty in plants, I inquired the name and habitation, I was informed that the subject under discussion was 'Isabel's new baby!' 'Ladies,' I remarked, with a courteous but scathing satire, 'I have been a baby myself, and am now a proprietor, but I am constrained to inform you that this is a private, and not a nursery, garden.'

Thus disappointed, deceived, disheartened, I began to fear that my intense love of a garden might be a mere hallucination, an idiosyncrasy, a want of manliness, a softening of the brain. Nevertheless I persevered with my inquiries, until I found that which I sought – the sympathy of an enthusiasm as hearty as my own, a brotherhood and a sisterhood, who, amid all the ignorance and pretence of which I have given examples, were devoted to the culture of flowers, and enjoyed from this occupation a large portion of the happiness, which is the purest and the surest we can know on earth, the happiness of Home.

S. Reynolds Hole, *Our Gardens*

Things Worth Doing

I think it is a fair test of the genuineness of the profession of the many people who now declare that they love plants and gardens, to see if they are willing to take any trouble of this kind for themselves. For though there are now whole shelves-full of the helpful books that had no existence in my younger days, yet there are many things that can only be ascertained by careful trying in individual gardens.

Now that there is so much to choose from, we should not let any mental slothfulness stand in the way of thinking and watching and comparing, so as to arrive at a just appreciation of the merits and uses of all our garden plants.

It is not possible to use to any good effect all the plants that are to be had. In my own case I should wish to grow many more than just those I have, but if I do not find a place where my critical garden conscience approves of having any one plant I would rather be without it. It is better to me to deny myself the pleasure of having it, than to endure the mild sense of guilt of having placed it where it neither does justice nor accords with its neighbours, and where it reproaches me every time I pass it.

I feel sure that it is in a great measure just because this is so little understood, that gardens are so often unsatisfactory and uninteresting. If owners could see, each in their own garden, what is the thing most worth doing, and take some pains to work out that one idea or group of ideas, gardens would not be so generally dull and commonplace.

Often in choosing plants and shrubs people begin the wrong way. They know certain things they would like to have, and they look through catalogues and order these, and others that they think, from the description, they would also like, and then plant them without any previous consideration of how or why.

Often when I have had to do with other people's gardens, they have said: 'I have bought a quantity of shrubs and plants; show me where to place them;' to which I can only answer: 'That is not the way in which I can help you; show me your spaces and I will tell you what plants to get for them.'

Many places that would be beautiful if almost left alone are spoiled by doing away with some simple natural feature in order to put in its place some hackneyed form of gardening. Such places should be treated with the most deliberate and careful consideration. Hardly a year passes that I do not see in my own neighbourhood examples of this kind that seem to me extremely ill-judged. Houses great and small are being built on tracts of natural heath-land. A perfect undergrowth of wild Heaths is there already. If it is old and overgrown, it can be easily renewed by clearing it off and lightly digging the ground over, when the Heaths will quickly spring up again. Often there are already thriving young Scotch Firs and Birches.

Where such conditions exist, a beautiful garden can be easily made at the least possible cost, jealously saving all that there is already, and then using in some simple way such plants as I have recommended in the chapter on Plants for Poor Soils. The presence of the Scotch Fir points to that being the best tree to plant in quantity; and the few other trees that will do admirably in dry light soils, Birch, Spanish Chestnut, Holly, and Juniper, will give as much variety as can be wanted by a sober mind that understands the value of temperance in planting.

There are many people who almost unthinkingly will say, 'But I like variety.' Do they really think and feel that variety is actually desirable as an end in itself, and is of more value than a series of thoughtfully composed garden pictures? There are no doubt many to whom, from want of a certain class of refinement of education or natural gift of teachable aptitude, are unable to understand or appreciate, at anything like its full value, a good garden picture, and to these no doubt a quantity of individual plants give a greater degree of pleasure than such as they could derive from the contemplation of any beautiful arrangement of a lesser number. When I see this in ordinary gardens, I try to put myself into the same mental attitude, and so far succeed, in that I can perceive that it represents one of the earlier stages in the love of a garden, and that one must not quarrel with it, because a garden is for its owner's pleasure, and whatever the degree or form of that pleasure, if only it be sincere, it is right and reasonable, and adds to human happiness in one of the purest and best of ways. And often I find I have to put upon myself this kind of drag, because when one has passed through the more elementary stages which deal with isolated details, and has come to a point when one feels some slight power of what perhaps may be called generalship; when the means and material that go to the making of a garden seem to be within one's grasp and awaiting one's command, then comes the danger of being inclined to lay down the law, and of advocating the ultimate effects that one feels oneself to be most desirable in an intolerant spirit of cocksure pontification. So I try, when I am in a garden of the ordinary kind where the owner likes variety, to see it a little from the same point of view; and in the arboretum, where one of each of a hundred different kinds of Conifers stand in their fine young growth, to see and admire the individuals only, and to stifle my longing to see a hundred of one sort at a time, and to keep down the shop-window feeling, and the idea of a worthless library made up of odd single volumes where there should be complete sets, and the comparison of an inconsequent jumble of words with a clearly-written sentence, and all such naughty similitudes, as come crowding through the brain of the garden-artist (if I may give myself a title so honourable), who desires not only to see the beautiful plants and trees, but to see them used in the best and largest and most worthy of ways.

There is no spot of ground, however arid, bare, or ugly, that cannot be tamed into such a state as may give an impression of beauty and delight. It cannot always be done easily; but there is no place under natural conditions that cannot be graced with an adornment of suitable vegetation.

More than once I have had pleasure in taking in hand some spot of ground where it was said 'nothing would grow'. On two occasions it was a heap of about fifty loads of sand wheeled out of the basement of a building, in one case placed under some Scotch Firs, in another under Oaks and Chestnuts. Both are now as well covered with thriving plants and shrubs as any other parts of the garden they are in, clothed in the one case with Aucubas, hardy Ferns, Periwinkles, and Honesty, and in the other with Aucubas, Ferns, and the two grand Mulleins, *Verbascum olympicum* and *V. phlomoides*. It should be remembered that the Aucuba is one of the few shrubs that enjoys shade.

Throughout my life I have found that one of the things most worth doing was to cultivate the habit of close observation. Like all else, the more it is exercised the easier it becomes, till it is so much a part of oneself that one may observe almost critically and hardly be aware of it. A habit so acquired stands one in good stead in all garden matters, so that in an exhibition of flowers or in a botanic garden one can judge of the merits of a plant hitherto unknown to one, and at once see in what way it is good, and why, and how it differs from those of the same class that one may have at home.

And I know from my own case that the will and the power to observe does not depend on the possession of keen sight. For I have sight that is both painful and inadequate; short sight of the severest kind, and always progressive (my natural focus is two inches); but the little I have I try to make the most of, and often find that I have observed things that have escaped strong and long-sighted people.

As if by way of compensation I have very keen hearing, and when I hear a little rustling rush in the grass and heath, or in the dead leaves under the trees, I can tell whether it is a snake or lizard, mouse or bird. Many birds I am aware of only by the sound of their flight. I can nearly always tell what trees I am near by the sound of the wind in their leaves, though in the same tree it differs much from spring to autumn, as the leaves become of a harder and drier texture. The Birches have a small, quick, high-pitched sound; so like that of falling rain that I am often deceived into thinking it really is rain, when it is only their own leaves hitting each other with a small rain-like patter. The voice of Oak leaves is also rather high-pitched, though lower than that of Birch. Chestnut leaves in a mild breeze sound much more deliberate; a sort of slow slither. Nearly all trees in a gentle wind have a pleasant sound, but I confess to a distinct dislike to the noise of all the Poplars; feeling it to be painfully fussy, unrestful, and disturbing. On the other hand, how soothing and delightful is the murmur of Scotch Firs both near and far. And what pleasant muffled music is that of a wind-waved field of corn, and especially of ripe barley. The giant Grasses, Reeds, and Bamboo sound curiously dry. The great Reed, *Arundo Donax*, makes more noise in a moderate breeze than when the wind blows a gale, for then the long ribbon-like leaves are blown straight out and play much less against each other; the Arabs say, 'It whispers in the breeze and is silent in the storm.' But of all the plants I know, the one whose foliage has the strangest sound is the Virginian Allspice (*Calycanthus floridus*), whose leaves are of so dry and harsh a quality that they seem to grate and clash as they come together.

Gertrude Jekyll, *Home and Garden*

The Structure of Garden City

I will not cease from mental strife,
Nor shall my sword sleep in my hand,
Till we have built Jerusalem
In England's green and pleasant land.

– *Blake*

Thorough sanitary and remedial action in the houses that we have; and then the building of more, strongly, beautifully, and in groups of limited extent, kept in proportion to their streams and walled round, so that there may be no festering and wretched suburb anywhere, but clean and busy street within and the open country without, with a belt of beautiful garden and orchard round the walls, so that from any part of the city perfectly fresh air and grass and sight of far horizon might be reachable in a few minutes' walk. This the final aim.

– John Ruskin, 'Sesame and Lilies'

The reader is asked to imagine an estate embracing an area of 6,000 acres, which is at present purely agricultural, and had been obtained by purchase in the open market . . .

The objects of this land purchase may be stated in various ways, but it is sufficient here to say that some of the chief objects are these: To find for our industrial population work at wages of *higher purchasing power*, and to secure healthier surroundings and more regular employment. To enterprising manufacturers, co-operative societies, architects, engineers, builders, and mechanicians of all kinds, as well as to many engaged in various professions, it is intended to offer a means of securing new and better employment for their capital and talents, while to the agriculturists at present on the estate, as well as to those who may migrate thither, it is designed to open a new market for their produce close to their doors. Its object is, in short, to raise the standard of health and comfort of all true workers of whatever grade – the means by which these objects are to be achieved being a healthy, natural, and economic combination of town and country life, and this on land owned by the municipality.

Garden City, which is to be built near the centre of the 6,000 acres, covers an area of 1,000 acres, or a sixth part of the 6,000 acres, and might be of circular form, 1,240 yards (or nearly three-quarters of a mile) from centre to circumference.

Six magnificent boulevards – each 120 feet wide – traverse the city from centre to circumference, dividing it into six equal parts or wards. In the centre is a circular space containing about five and a half acres, laid out as a beautiful and well-watered garden; and, surrounding this garden, each standing in its own ample grounds, are the larger public buildings – town hall, principal concert and lecture hall, theatre, library, museum, picture-gallery, and hospital.

The rest of the large space encircled by the 'Crystal Palace' is a public park, containing 145 acres, which includes ample recreation grounds within very easy access of all the people.

Running all round the Central Park (except where it is intersected by the boulevards) is a wide glass arcade called the 'Crystal Palace', opening on to the park. This building is in wet weather one of the favourite resorts of the people, whilst the knowledge that its bright shelter is ever close at hand tempts people into Central Park, even in the most doubtful of weathers. Here manufactured goods are exposed for sale, and here most of that class of shopping which requires the joy of deliberation and selection is done. The space enclosed by the Crystal Palace is, however, a good deal larger than is required for these purposes, and a considerable part of it is used as a Winter Garden – the whole forming a permanent exhibition of a most attractive character, whilst its circular form brings it near to every dweller in the town – the furthest inhabitant being within 600 yards.

Passing out of the Crystal Palace on our way to the outer ring of the town, we cross Fifth Avenue – lined, as are all roads of the town, with trees – fronting which, and looking on to the Crystal Palace, we find a ring of very excellently-built houses, each standing in its own ample grounds; and, as we continue our walk, we observe that the houses are for the most part built either in concentric rings, facing the various avenues (as the circular roads are termed), or fronting the boulevards and roads, which all converge to the centre of the town. Asking the friend who accompanies us on our journey what the population of this little city may be, we are told about 30,000 in the city itself, and about 2,000 in the agricultural estate, and that there are in the town 5,500 building lots of an *average* size of 20 feet x 130 feet – the minimum space allotted for the purpose being 20 x 100. Noticing the very varied architecture and design which the houses and groups of houses display – some having common gardens and co-operative kitchens – we learn that general observance of street line or harmonious departure from it are the chief points as to house-building over which the municipal authorities exercise control, for, though proper sanitary arrangements are strictly enforced, the fullest measure of individual taste and preference is encouraged.

Walking still toward the outskirts of town, we come upon 'Grand

Avenue'. This avenue is fully entitled to the name it bears, for it is 420 feet wide, and, forming a belt of green upwards of three miles long, divides that part of the town which lies outside Central Park into two belts. It really constitutes an additional park of 115 acres – a park which is within 240 yards of the furthest removed inhabitant. In this splendid avenue six sites, each of four acres, are occupied by public schools and their surrounding play-grounds and gardens, while other sites are reserved for churches, of such denominations as the religious beliefs of the people may determine, to be erected and maintained out of the funds of the worshippers and their friends. We observe that the houses fronting on Grand Avenue have departed from the general plan of concentric rings, and, in order to ensure a longer line of frontage on Grand Avenue, are arranged in crescents – thus also to the eye yet further enlarging the already splendid width of Grand Avenue.

On the outer ring of the town are factories, warehouses, dairies, markets, coal yards, timber yards, etc., all fronting on the circle railway, which encompasses the whole town, and which has sidings connecting it with a main line of railway which passes through the estate. This arrangement enables goods to be loaded direct into trucks from the warehouses and workshops, and so sent by railway to distant markets, or to be taken direct from the trucks into the warehouses or factories; thus not only effecting a very great saving in regard to packing and cartage, and reducing to a minimum loss from breakage, but also, by reducing traffic on the roads of the town, lessening to a very marked extent the cost of their maintenance. The smoke fiend is kept well within bounds in Garden City; for all machinery is driven by electric energy, with the result that the cost of electricity for lighting and other purposes is greatly reduced.

Ebenezer Howard, *Garden Cities of To-Morrow*

24 July 1904

I got to Thakeham about eight. A most divine evening. The great Downs bathed in reflected light and the garden wonderfully good. Blackburn is very slow apparently, but is really an artist and he does little at a time but what he does is singularly good I think. He has made the pergola delight-ful – in a way quite his own – with hollyhocks – and to enjoy the effect he postpones planting the more permanent things. His attitude is so unlike the general of people – like leaving a picture unfinished to enjoy the ini-tial stages.

The children's gardens are very amusing. The four of them. There is no place for the fifth. I retorted they could all be divided and so make eight. Aileen's garden was dull but tidy and fairly full. Sylvia's garden was rather wayward, Barbara's absolutely neglected, Aubrey's garden, aged 4 is really wonderful, he watches things grow, knows the names of all his plants and is thrilled and thrilling over it, so wise and sensible, picks off dead things, weeds, waters, propagates with sense and care. He has a row of sweet peas and roared with laughter at the idea of their climbing sticks, he put them in under protest, now in transport of delight, they climb! The lawn is covered with guinea pigs. I do wish we could have a garden and a country house and if only we could do that combined with sea and river it would be perfect.

Edwin Lutyens, Letter to Lady Emily Lutyens

The Pond

We take ourselves too seriously; our neighbours not seriously enough. This I believe to be true of life, and it is also true of gardens. Too often I have felt scornful of other gardens, and too often my neighbours have scoffed at mine. Behind my back they call my compound a 'stuffy little nursery', and I speak of theirs lightly as howling wildernesses. This is wrong and unkind. We must give and take in visiting other people's gar-dens, and try to see from the standpoint of the owners. The motive is everything. Some men merely garden for health. In that case, you must look at the gardener rather than the garden, to see whether his end has been attained.

If we are to be sane and contented and possible company for our kind, a toy is necessary to each one of us. A garden is a very good toy, and, as in the case of sportsmen, one destroys nature's rarest and most ferocious creations at the cost to himself of perhaps fifty pounds a head, while another, quite as keen, has to be content with an annual fortnight among the partridges; so in gardening, one man may play with everything that grows, and keep fifty gardeners to look after them, while another is reduced to a window-garden up three flights of steps.

Most of our gardens lie between these extremes; but if the thing were practicable I would plant pinetums for posterity, and do my gardening in the grand manner. I would secure half a county, and plan forests, lakes, islands in the lakes, and marble temples to Ceres and Pomona on the islands. I would emulate the princes of the ancient time, and my garden should resemble those classic and stately plantations of the past, wherein 'noble spirits contented not themselves with trees, but by the attendance of aviaries, fishponds, and all variety of animals; they made their gardens the epitome of the earth, and some resemblance of the secular shows of old.'

One cannot cram the epitome of the earth into an acre, but birds, beasts, and even reptiles occur in my garden from time to time. The little pond is the centre of fascination for most of them. Here the human boy shall be found harassing the newts and water-man beetles, and the human girl also appears, to the discomfort of dragon-flies and dismay of water-snails. My higher vertebrates are, however, better treated under the chapter devoted to garden pests.

Of respectable wild beasts the hedgehog occurs. He goes his nightly rounds and, I think, does good according to his lights. If we meet, as sometimes happens, in the dusk, he salaams very respectfully, bows his head down between his paws, and remains motionless in that somewhat servile attitude until I have passed by. Squirrels cross my garden constantly, with that little undulating run of theirs; but they do not stay, as I have nothing to offer them. Field-mice, on the contrary, are very fond of half-hardy Cape-bulbs – with a fondness different to mine. They build their nests in the rockeries, and have to be destroyed. Frogs, toads, and newts all increase and multiply here and are encouraged; and once I saw a large grass-snake apparently regarding a water-lily, but he poured himself away, like a stream of amber and silver, among my marsh irises and never appeared again. Dogs enter, though not by invitation. The large dogs stroll around in a gentlemanly way and work no harm; the smaller sorts do evil, and tear and scratch and refuse to keep to the paths. When discovered, they bark insolently to hide their own uneasiness, and dash about over the borders and lose their heads, and forget how they got in. There is little use for a dog or a cat in a garden, though a cat certainly occurs here. His name is 'Gaffer', and he is a brindled or tabbied beast of courteous disposition but colourless character. He does neither harm nor good. I have heard of him that he once caught a young thrush, who was sitting with his back turned waiting for his mother; but even that is in the nature of legend.

We count the usual birds, but only a few have ever called for any special admiration. A pair of missel-thrushes, with very great judgment, built their nest in a large araucaria imbricate. From this lofty point they commanded the situation; and to see them dash out if any jay or jackdaw dared even to pass by, was an amusing sight. With harsh invective they would flash from their nest like brown arrows, and flicker about the intruder and scream their indignation until he was far away. Then they flew back, talked together about the dreadful characters there are in the world, cooled down gradually, and so returned to their young. No watch-dogs were ever more energetic or more fierce. Jackdaws fled before them, and when they came down to the lawn for food, even blackbirds, who hesitate not to send the ordinary thrush about his business, raised no sort of argument with them. They reared a brood of two, and the party quickly disappeared.

Our champion visitor, however, was a kingfisher. What possessed this distinguished fowl to visit us I could never understand. I suppose that he knew the place for a 'resort', and fancied a change from the seclusion of Dart or Teign rivers. He came in December and stayed a fortnight. The goldfish held indignation meetings – in deep water – but he caught a good many, and they suited him well. To study his methods was exceedingly instructive. He sat on arundo donex at first, but it was not quite convenient, and so I arranged a stick for him hanging over the pond. From this point he enjoyed excellent sport. Suddenly, like a gem falling, he would drop with a splash and then return ashore – a young goldfish in his beak. My daughter sided with the fish, while I ranged myself beside the fisher. She hated death, as the young will, with all her might, and told me that it was a cruel and abominable thing that these fish, in the security of their home, should thus be cut off by a ferocious murderer. I explained that kingfishers were much rarer and lovelier and more interesting than any gold carp whatsoever; and I added that we might get plenty more goldfish for twopence each, whereas another kingfisher could hardly be hoped for. She answered that to buy more goldfish might be all right from my point of view, but would not prove the least comfort to those that the bird had eaten, and very likely not much to those he had left. This, in its small way, was true; but I dwelt on the laws of hospitality, explained that the kingfisher must live, and also made it clear that life for him inevitably meant death for something else. In reply she argued that I had never asked the kingfisher, that he came without an invitation, and that I owed no obligation to anybody who broke this first and simple law of society. To come and stop with people unasked struck my daughter as the unpardonable sin. Indeed, she has not forgiven the kingfisher unto this day. At the end of his fortnight he went as he had come, sans ceremony. I hoped when winter returned that he might pay me a second visit, but he did not do so. Probably, when the novelty has worn off, goldfish are a poor substitute for trout.

Eden Phillpotts, *My Garden*

The Garden That I Love

I wandered round the garden for neutral company, and fell to wondering whether it is more attractive in late spring or in the early days of autumn. I saw it affirmed in print the other day that the writers who say a beautiful flower-garden can be had for eight, and sometimes for nine, months of the year, are misleading people. I can only reply that the person who made that statement has but an imperfect acquaintance with gardening and its possibilities. Should there come a heavy and continuous fall of snow at the beginning of March, and should it lie for the whole of that month, then I grant the ordinary course of nature has been for once interrupted. But when, in the south or west of England, does that happen? I have known something like it, but only something like it, occur just once in a now pretty long experience. For the rest, I am prepared not only to do battle for the 'eight or nine months' period, but to go still farther, and to plead that no month in the year is out of doors wholly flow-

erless, at least, in the south, south-east, south-west, and west of England.
I speak only of what I know, and what the Garden That I Love has taught
me. New Year's Day, let us say, has come and gone, and January is moving slowly on. Choose but the aspect aright, and prepare the soil with due
knowledge, and what is there to prevent the winter-aconites from greeting the New Year, and accompanying it till January be spent? Do not suppose this will infallibly happen the very first January after you put the
bulbs into the ground, though even then it may. You must not, however,
count on it. But the year after that, and for every succeeding January, the
winter-aconites will illuminate with their golden cressets the spot where
you have placed them. We have two little nooks for them immediately on
either side of the entrance-door that looks south-east, and they never fail
to come forth and show themselves in the very first month of the year,
signalling to their brethren in the turf under the old oak to be up and
about, and not long laggard after these early risers. The most effective
clump of them, no doubt, is in a small round open bed under a tulip-
tree, as yet of moderate dimensions, though it has already begun to flower in the late summer. But these winter-aconites open a little later, by
reason of the partial shade above them given by the pretty thick branches of the tulip-tree, even when still bare of leaves. That little round space
serves a double purpose; for, while the winter-aconites in full flower
there cover the whole of it, below them and out of sight are colchicum
bulbs, which the ignorant call winter-crocuses, given me many years ago
by the wife of a famous Field-Marshal and a woman of exquisite taste.
They are of the pale lavender colour, much more rare and difficult to get
than the larger, deep-coloured ones, which we also have; and when their
foliage fades, and can be carefully cut or pulled away, up come, to replace
them, the strong, vigorous leaves of the *Colchicum*. But only the leaves;
which in summer themselves wax wilted and fade, and then leafless flowers of the most delicate colour and dainty beauty come up, and look like
Fairyland under the then lavishly furnished tulip-tree. And does the horticultural sceptic I refer to suppose it is impossible to coax yellow crocuses – for the yellow ones are the hardiest – to face the perils of the early
days of the year, or to get snowdrops to do the same without any coaxing
at all? And the primrose? I do not speak of garden primulas, but of the
wild and simple native of the woodlands. Is it beneath one's notice, and

undeserving of a place in the garden? In the one we love there is always a place allotted to it, and more than one place; and it must be a very peculiar January, one deep in snow, or hard frost-bound, for a certain number of these unaffected flowers not to be awake and up somewhere then. I will not engage that on your rockery you shall have *Cyclamen coum* in bloom, but you may, and with it the small, modest, but clustering and effective flowers of the *Potentilla*.

But, like a prudent general, I keep my best and bravest battalion for the final charge; and I ask this sceptic of gardens whether he has ever seen the *Iris stylosa*? I saw them first in a but-little-cared-for garden at Bordighera pretty long ago, and I stood wondering under the spell of enchantment. I brought some home with me, or, rather, had them sent to me late in the spring when they had finished flowering, and for the first two years made a deplorable misuse of them. They showed ample leafage, but did not flower; and then it struck me that they had not been accustomed to high living, and I had been overfeeding them, and the muzzle must be put on by giving them the leanest of fare. In plain words, the soil was much too rich for them. I took them up, broke them into small pieces, and planted them in a sheltered yet sunny position, and in a mass of rubble mixed with light poor soil. Since then they have produced an uninterrupted succession of flowers from the beginning of December till the coming of the first swallow. Veronica delights in them, and some are always taken to her boudoir, where freesias also are welcome, but from which flowers of strong perfume are rigidly excluded.

But this is not winter, whose contribution to the 'nine months in the year' I think I have established; nor yet spring, whose floral reputation needs no defending, for no one would dream of assailing it. We are, at the time at which I write, at the parting of the ways between a prodigious summer and an equally splendid but less ostentatious autumn; or, to put it differently, October is protecting the rear of departing summer. I cannot help a little self-complacency just now, since the garden has this year had a conspicuous triumph. The unbroken drought of July and August had dealt irreparable desolation in every other garden I have seen or heard of; and the ruin was completed by the hurricane of wind that accompanied the advent of showers, even then not too bountiful. Never before has the Garden That I Love been in greater beauty. There is a vacuum, a failure, nowhere; and even Veronica is unreserved in her admiration. She was away during August, and returned only in the early days of September. I had abstained from all report of its condition, and my silence led her to conclude, not that no news was good news, but very bad news indeed. In order to keep up the comedy, I arranged that on her return she should enter from the lane, in order that what there was to show should burst upon her nearly all at once.

'I suppose,' she said, 'the Garden is a wreck, like all that I have seen elsewhere.'

'It has been a sadly trying time,' I replied evasively.

In another moment we emerged from the plantation near the well, and suddenly the Garden was in sight. She stopped full short, as the phrase is, held up both hands, and exclaimed –

'Oh!'

That was all, but how much it was, and one was more than rewarded for all one had done to baffle the long-continued drought. Let me say once more that due digging and manuring in May ought to furnish a garden with protection against Fate in any ordinary year. But I had misgivings that this was going to be an extraordinary one; and as, two winters ago, we made, under the old Manor Pound, a good large tank to receive the rain-water from all the guttering round the old red-roofed farm buildings still remaining near the house, including those of the house itself, there was an ample supply at the beginning of June. Not to everything, but only to the beds and borders stocked with things planted in them at the end of May, we began at once applying rain-water after the sun had gone off them. Many persons will assert that watering does no good, and sometimes does serious hurt. But that depends on the nature of the water. If the water be hard, or, indeed, other than *bona-fide* rain-water, that would be so; for, of course, watering has a tendency to bring roots and rootlets to the surface in expectation of what they like so much; and the process, once started, must be persisted in. Persist we did; and we followed up the watering with periodical hoeing. By the end of the month everything looked wonderfully forward, and then the nine weeks' drought began. Confident in the resources of the tank, we continued our evening labours with excellent effect. But, by the middle of August, the gardener said the tank was very low. In a few more days it was empty, and the drought and sun-heat were more pitiless than ever. In our resolve not to be beaten there was no slackening; and though our modest resources can produce only hand water-barrels, these were trundled down to the river and back for three or four hours every day. I felt, however, that, though no complaint had been uttered, the 'grind' was too much in such weather, and so reverted to another device. There is another tank, which Cowper, perhaps, who introduces into his verse such a realistic line as 'The stable yields a stercoraceous heap', would have described more minutely, but of which I will content myself with saying that it yielded some three to four hundred gallons a day of soft, but not quite so savoury, a liquid. Needs must when 'the devil of a drought' drives; and, as Veronica and Lamia were absent, it did not much matter.

After three days, clouds began to muster on the horizon; rumblings were heard in the distance, and, finally, down came the rain. The situation, as they say, had been saved. But that represents very inadequately what had happened. Coming on the top – you see, I cannot help adopting the language of the grateful and triumphant gardener and his help – of the use of the unsavoury tank, the rain put the finishing touch to our efforts, and produced the effect that caused Veronica to halt in astonishment, and exclaim –

'Oh!'

Alfred Austin, The Garden That I Love

On the Making of Gardens

To make a great garden, one must have a great idea or a great opportunity; a cypress causeway leading to a giant's castle, or a fountain cave where a ceaseless iris plays on a river falling through the roof, or a deep clear pool with an underworld fantasy of dragon-guarded treasure caves lit by unearthly light, or a mighty palace quadrangle lined with hanging gardens of arcaded terraces, or a great galleon in a lake whose decks are dropping with jasmine and myrtle, or a precipitous ravine with double bridges and a terrace on either hand. But it is possible to introduce a touch of imaginative beauty into almost any garden by finding the most perfect form for one of its features, or by giving expression to the soul of some particular flower or tree, as with the Virginian vine on the trellis arcades at Schwetzingen and the cypress in the Giusti avenue at Verona.

So, if it is to be a rose-garden, do not choose those stunted, unnatural, earth-loving strains, which have nothing of vigour and wildness in them, nor banish other flowers which may do homage to the beauty of a rose as courtiers to a queen. Let climbing roses drop in a veil from the terrace and smother with flower-spangled embroidery the garden walls, run riot over vaulted arcades, clamber up lofty obelisks of leaf-tangled trellis, twine themselves round the pillars of a rose-roofed temple, where little avalanches of sweetness shall rustle down at a touch and the dusty gold of the sunshine shall mingle with the summer snow of the flying petals. Let them leap in a great bow or fall in a creamy cataract to a foaming pool of flowers. In the midst of the garden set a statue of Venus with a great bloom trained to her hand, or of Flora, her cornucopia overflowing with white rosettes, or a tiny basin where leaden *amorini* seated upon the margin are fishing with trailing buds. If the place be away from the house and surrounded by forest trees, let there be a rose balloon weighed down by struggling cupids, or the hollow ribs and bellying curves of an old-world ship with ruddy sail and cordage flecked with ivory blossom, or one of those rose-castles which the French romance gave to the garden for a mimic siege in May, low towers of carpenter's work with flanking turrets and iron-studded postern. Such a *Château d'Amour* is represent-ed on many a mediæval casket and mirror-case. Ponderous mangonels are bombarding the fortress with monstrous blossoms, while from the battlements fair ladies hurl down roses still heavy with morning dew full in the faces of the attacking knights.

Gardens consecrated to the worship of some particular flower have been in favour since the Ancient Sages devoted their old age to the cul-ture of chrysanthemum or peony, but who has yet worked out the utmost beauty of blue iris or silver-chaliced water-lily, of sweet pea or pansy, or, sacred to the Queen of Heaven, the 'flower and plant of light'? Who has realised to the full glory of the vine, or clematis, or honeysuck-le, wisteria, or bougainvillea? If it be sculpture that you seek, try the effect of a fountain court of *amorini*, where baby loves are climbing the obelisks and the flower-vases, playing and splashing each other upon the water-edge, swimming out to a marble Nef whose mast and sail and homing bows are festooned with clambering cupids. Turn into marble Watteau's dream, 'L'Embarquement pour l'Île de Cythère' or Fragonard's 'Fontaine d'Amour'. Let there be a children's corner, the Good Shepherd of the Catacombs with a lamb upon His shoulder standing amongst the little beds, or a Garden of the Happy Hours, where Time by the sun-dial is fast asleep, his hands and feet fettered with rose-wreaths, while on the steps below him the children are weaving their flower-garlands, wrestling, reading, singing, playing at war and art and marriage. If it be colour that you desire, let the view from the low parlour window be a flash of lavender-blue, centred with gold, remembering that wild Nature's loveliest effects are in this key of colour, as witness the hyacinths that repeat the sky, the purple tide of the heather, the Alpine anemones, the dark-blue gentians of the Jura pastures; if a wall garden, throw round it a grey ring of castle walls, for in art it is only appearances that matter and forgery is not a crime unless it fails to deceive. Of historic motives for laying out there can never be a lack. The fruit trees and vine-covered trellises that tempered the sunshine in the late Roman gardens, the pergolas and vaulted pavilions of the Normans in Sicily, the green tunnels of the fourteenth century, the stately arched hedges of Bacon's essay, are well suited to any country where the summer heat is oppressive. How interesting to re-constitute a forgotten type, the garden of Queen Ultrogoth, the flower-orchard of the Dark Ages, the Paradise of William the Bad, the Gothic pleasaunce of Crescentius, of the 'Roman de la Rose', of Chaucer, of the 'King's Quair'! In every land there are countless old houses still disfigured by the bare lawn and tortuous ways of the landscape gardener, and no one will have lived in vain who is able to restore to one of them the melodious beauty of which Pope and Rousseau robbed it.

But we are not forced to confine ourselves to imaginative reproductions of the past. Invention was not exhausted in the eighteenth century when design went out of fashion. I know no reason why we should not have subtly curving terrace fronts and courts that sweep outward like the mouth of a trumpet to enlarge the view, and indeed but for the intrusion of the unhallowed *Giardino Inglese*, this might have been the natural development of the Rococo garden. How many flowering realms there are yet to conquer! Who has yet sought the summer coolness of a water labyrinth with rose-bordered canals, where a great pool serves for a lawn in front of the house and boats may pass among the fruit trees and the flowers; or the quaintness of a garden of autumn fruit, where purple grapes hang in jewelled clusters upon the wall, dwarf pears and fairy apples are touched with quivering gold; where gourds and pumpkins like strange reptiles have crept out of the flower-beds to sun themselves upon the pavers, some great as the wheels of Cinderella's coach, some shaped by nature as punch-bowls or urns or bottles or balloons or writhing serpents, some moulded for sport into dragon's heads and laughing masks and monstrous baroque faces? Who has yet realised the poetry, the forlorn and elfish beauty of a deserted garden? Who has worked out the possibilities of a sea-shore demesne, or of an amphitheatre in a quarried cliff, or – except at Syracuse – of flowery paths that wind their way across stony abysses? Who has made for himself the knots and pergolas of a roof terrace where, as in Seneca's day, orchids may be planted upon the highest towers and whole forests may shake upon the tops and turrets of the house? The false perspective which Nero introduced about his Golden House, giving across the lawns and lakes prospects of far-off cities, might, if the limitations be frankly accepted, be developed into a minor art, as indeed it is in Japan. Flattened curves and contrasts of foliage are often used to give the illusion of distance, and the method can be carried further, for with flowering shrubs one may represent a distant waterfall, or turn a commonplace hill, like that at Scarborough, into a snow-capped mountain.

But whatever the garden is to be, whether its roses are to clamber up the eaves of a cottage or the towers of a palace, this at least is necessary, that it should be made with a care for the future and a conviction of the importance of the task. According to Bacon, gardens are for refreshment; not for pleasure alone, nor even for happiness, but for the renewing rest that makes labour more fruitful, the unbending of a bow that it may shoot the stronger. In the ancient world it was ever the greatest of the emperors and wisest of the philosophers that sought peace and rest in a garden. By the olive groves and flower-bordered canals of the *Academia* Plato discussed with his followers the supremacy of reason, the identity of truth and goodness. Among the roses and myrtles and covered walks of the Lyceum Aristotle taught that perfect happiness is to be found in contemplation, in the divine intuitions of reason. Theophrastus left to his pupils the shady theatre of their studies, and amidst the fruit and flowers Epicurus pondered how by wise conduct to attain happiness. In the garden of the Bamboo-Grove Buddha taught the conquest of self, and in the Garden of Sorrows a greater teacher was found, for we know that Jesus ofttimes resorted thither with His disciples. The cloistered paradises of Sicily and of the Arabs may have been made for fairer, frailer flowers, but the rose-tangled orchards of the Middle Ages and the great gardens of the Renaissance did not serve for pleasure alone. In the romances we find the company playing chess in the apple-garden, singing, weaving garlands, dancing the carol, looking on at the play of jugglers, tumblers and dancing-girls, but here also they listen to the lay of the troubadour, and here part of the business of government is carried on. In the 'Chanson de Roland', Charlemagne gives audience in a *verger* to the ambassadors of the Pagan King of Spain, seated on a golden chair of state beside a bush of eglantine under the shadow of a pine tree, and in 'Garin le Loherain', Count Fremont, one of the great barons, receives a messenger sitting in a garden surrounded by his friends. Some of the great pleasure-grounds of the Renaissance were ever crowded with a great retinue of priests and lawyers, architects and painters, doctors and men of letters, to whom they offered change and rest and freedom. Others were the homes of a court, where laws were considered, finance was regulated, envoys were received; where in one arbour the Poet Laureate might be paying his addresses to the Muse, in another the Treasurer be grappling with his budget, while by the fountain under the shadow of the cypresses the Prince and his companions were discussing the doctrines of Plato and the greatness of the ancient world. Many of the letters of René d'Anjou are dated from the garden at Aix, and a century later we find Queen Elizabeth giving audience in her garden at Hampton and one of her courtiers attesting a charter in his *viridarium* at Edzell. The garden, like beauty in landscape, is inimical to all evil passions: it stands for efficiency, for patience in labour, for strength in adversity, for the power to forgive. Perhaps at the last, in contemplation of the recurring miracle of spring and of that eternal stream of life which is ever flowing before our eyes, we may find that it stands for something more – one of the three things the Greek philosopher thought it was law-

ful to pray for, hope to the dying; for along the thread of time and consciousness the individual is never severed from the race; he is but a leaf
on a tree, a blossom on a flowering plant; to the ocean of life he goes, and
from the ocean he may return again. Gardens have coloured every dream
of future life, every hope of happiness in this, and he who can make them
more beautiful has helped to exalt the sentiment of religion, poetry and
love. The older descriptions of Paradise are simple renderings of the
pleasure-grounds of the Persians and the flower-orchards of the Dark
Ages, imagination being able to picture itself things more perfect than
the eye ever saw, but not things diverse in kind. The mind cannot antici-
pate an unknown sensation; the deaf mute cannot form an idea of a
sound, nor the man who is blind from birth have a mental vision. Every
impression, whatever its elements may be, is an indivisible whole, differing from its parts and even from the sum of them as a chord in music
from the notes of which it is composed, or a new flower from the plants
that gave it birth, and it is thus always in the power of the artist to give us
a fresh creation, something different in kind, as different as were the
fountain courts of the Renaissance from the gardens of the Arabs, or the
terraces of Helmsley from the alleys of Versailles.

St Carlo's unjust judgment on Cardinal Gambra – that the revenues
laid out upon his villa would have been better employed in good works
– has even now its defenders, and we have yet with us the 'practical man'
who, visiting the dream-gardens of Italy, can see nothing in the cypresses but bundles of faggots, in the flower-beds but baskets of vegetables, in
the statues and fountains but heaps of road-metal, and goes away sor-
rowful at heart over the selfishness of these aristocrats, who waste on
pride and luxury what might have been given to the poor. Yet in truth
such a garden as that of Lante is a world-possession, and the builder of it
like a great poet who has influenced the life of thousands, putting them
in touch with the greatness of the past, lifting their thoughts and aspirations to a higher level, revealing to them the light of their own soul,
opening their eyes to the beauty of the world. Architecture, the most
unselfish of arts, belongs to the passer-by, and every old house and garden in which the ideal has been sought is a gift to the nation, to be
enjoyed by future generations who will learn from it more of history and
art and philosophy than may be found in books. Thus the garden-maker

is striving not for himself alone but for those who are to come after, for the unborn children who shall play on the flowery lawns and chase each other through the alleys, filling their laps with treasure of never-fading roses, weaving amidst the flowers and the sunshine dream-garlands of golden years. They too will share the joys and sorrows of the garden, will learn to love even the humblest tribes of its inhabitants: the prodigal weeds that carry the banners of spring in procession upon the cornices, and the dwarf trees, dead to the world, that have rooted themselves like anchorites in the crevices; the tinted lichen which feed on pure air and sunshine and outlast the stubborn oaks, and the lowly mosses which drink in the dewdrops and the blue shadows of the mighty trees; the sweet-sighing herbs of the twilight; and the pale stars of earth which, stirred from their slumbers when night is dropping dew into the mouths of the thirsty flowers, call the outcast moths to a honeyed banquet. They too will know bare winter's hidden hoard, when the earth under their feet is full of dreams – dim memories of misty morns and dewy eves, of the slumberous warmth of the golden sunshine, the soft caresses of the life-giving breezes, the nuptial kisses of the bees. They too will feel the rhythmic breath of wakening life from the countless millions of beings in earth and air and dewdrop and rivulet, with the rising murmur of insect delight, the scent of the sun-kissed grasses – all the mystery and music, the riot and rapture of the spring, and the passion of the flaming roses, and that strange thrill of autumn sadness when the flowers that have mingled their perfumes through the summer are breathing out to each other the grief of a last farewell.

It is not given to every man, when his life's work is over, to grow old in a garden he has made, to lose in the ocean roll of the seasons little eddies of pain and sickness and weariness, to watch year after year green surging tides of spring and summer break at his feet in a foam of woodland flowers, and the garden like a faithful retainer growing grey in its master's service. But for him who may live to see it, there shall be a wilder beauty than any he has planned. Nature, like a shy wood-nymph, shall steal softly back on summer nights to the silent domain, shading with tenderest pencillings of brown and grey and ripened stone, scattering wood-violets in the grassy alleys and wreathing vine and ivy the trellised arbour, painting with cloudy crusts of crumbly gold the long balustrades, inlaying the cornices with lines of emerald moss, planting little ferns within the fountain basin and tiny patches of green velvet upon the Sea-God's shoulder. As the years pass by and no rude hand disturbs the traces of her presence, Nature becomes more daring. Flower-spangled tapestries of woven tendrils fall from the terrace, strange fleecy mottlings of silver-grey and saffron and orange and greeny-gold make the wall a medley more beautiful than broidered hangings or than painted pictures, the niches are curtained with creepers, the pool is choked with water-plants, blossoming weeds are in every crevice, and with pendent crystals the roof of the grotto is fretted into an Arab vault. Autumn has come at last, and the harvest is being gathered in. Flying shafts of silvery splendour fall upon the fountain, and all the house is dark, save for the strange light that is burning yet in the chamber window. Softly the Triton mourns, as if sobbing below his breath, alone in the moon-enchanted fairyland of a deserted garden.

Sir George Sitwell, On the Making of Gardens

The Secret Garden

It was the sweetest, most mysterious-looking place anyone could imagine. The high walls which shut it in were covered with the leafless stems of climbing roses, which were so thick that they were matted together. Mary Lennox knew they were roses because she had seen a great many roses in India. All the ground was covered with grass of a wintry brown, and out of it grew clumps of bushes which were surely rose-bushes if they were alive. There were numbers of standard roses which had so spread their branches that they were like little trees. There were other trees in the garden, and one of the things which made the place look strangest and loveliest was that climbing roses had run all over them and swung down long tendrils which made light swaying curtains, and here and there they had caught at each other or at a far-reaching branch and had crept from one tree to another and made lovely bridges of themselves. There were neither leaves nor roses on them now, and Mary did not know whether they were dead or alive, but their thin grey or brown branches and sprays looked like a sort of hazy mantle spreading over everything, walls, and trees, and even brown grass, where they had fallen from their fastenings and run along the ground. It was this hazy tangle from tree to tree which made it look so mysterious. Mary had thought it must be different from other gardens which had not been left all by themselves so long; and, indeed, it was different from any other place she had ever seen in her life.

'How still it is!' she whispered. 'How still!'

Then she waited a moment and listened to the stillness. The robin, who had flown to his tree-top, was still as all the rest. He did not even flutter his wings; he sat without stirring, and looked at Mary.

'No wonder it is still,' she whispered again. 'I am the first person who has spoken here for ten years.'

She moved away from the door, stepping as softly as if she were afraid of awakening someone. She was glad that there was grass under her feet and that her steps made no sounds. She walked under one of the fairy-like arches between the trees and looked up at the sprays and tendrils which formed them.

'I wonder if they are all quite dead,' she said. 'Is it all a quite dead garden? I wish it wasn't.'

If she had been Ben Weatherstaff she could have told whether the wood was alive by looking at it, but she could only see that there were only grey or brown sprays and branches, and none showed any signs of even a tiny leaf-bud anywhere.

But she was *inside* the wonderful garden, and she could come through the door under the ivy at any time, and she felt as if she had found a world all her own.

Frances Hodgson Burnett, The Secret Garden

The Rock Garden

Times have wholly changed for the rock-garden. Fifty years ago it was merely the appanage of the large pleasure ground. In some odd corner, or in some dank, tree-haunted hollow, you rigged up a dump of broken cement blocks, and added bits of stone and fragments of statuary. You called this 'the Rockery', and proudly led your friends to see it, and planted it all over with Periwinkle to hide the hollows in which your Alpines had promptly died. In other words, you considered only the stones, and not the plants that were to live among them. No wonder, then, that the rockery came soon to be looked on as the rich man's extravagant fad: that a poor one would as readily have thought of having a French chef: and that between 1870 and 1890 there should have been an almost general slump in the noble and exquisite art of cultivating Alpine plants.

Thanks, however, to the insistent crying in the wilderness of a few ardent evangelists a revolutionary change has passed over the scene in the last twenty years. The personalities of the Alpine plants have come to engross the attention of their cultivators, and the actual rock of the structure has lost almost all of its importance, except as the stage on which the children of the wild hills are to be made to play out their captive life. And as such, of course, its main point is that it shall be so built as to help them play it out with the utmost brilliancy and happiness of which captivity is capable.

With this change of thought there has come another, of even more importance to the gardener at large, and one which has ultimately had the privilege of causing this book to be written. For, as soon as the rock-garden began to be looked on only as the best way of growing rock-plants to perfection, it became obvious that, instead of being the most expensive, it really was by far the cheapest and most repaying form of gardening. It has become accordingly, and is hourly still more universally becoming, the pet passion of the man who has small means, and only a small plot of ground to play with. In older days he had to content himself with a little pimply bed of Pelargoniums in a lawn like a handkerchief, with a Monkey-Puzzle in the centre: or, if his opportunities were yet smaller, and his ambitions keener, he could wrestle with Roses in a back-yard.

But now the truth has dawned, and its full daylight is approaching: for much less cost of time and money, you can have a much more brilliant show than even Pelargoniums can give; and of plants whose personality has far more interest and charm than any bedding Annual. Nothing, in fact, could possibly fill the small garden plot with perennial delight, so adequately, cheaply and appropriately as a constellation of rock-plants.

The old ideas of the rock-garden itself are to be set aside: no expensive Drunkard's Dream of stony spikes and pinnacles is wanted. If you wish to grow Alpines with joy and glory you cannot be too simple and inexpensive in your preparations. Very little stone indeed is needed; it is far easier to have too much than too little: a lovely rock-garden is often made without any visible stone at all. For the only essential part of stone, from an Alpine's point of view, is that it should be buried under the ground, so that one's roots may run gripping along its sides, and penetrate underneath in search of the moisture that is always there. So that, with a few little blocks well sunk into the soil, some quite small slope, or gently elevated bed in a cottage or villa garden can show, for practically no cost of money or trouble, as splendid a display as anything that the Alps themselves could afford.

This scheme, of course, is only the very baldest and cheapest beginning. The gardener who has thus achieved wide stretches of Mossy Phlox or Mazarine Speedwell won't be content to stay at that point for ever. Gradually his ambitions will swell, with the more ambitious exactions of the haughtier plants to which he soon aspires; appetite grows by success; and not the smallest owner of the rubbliest back-yard in Birmingham need fail of those initial successes if once he makes a profitable start.

And it is for the smaller grower that I am now especially writing; it is still possible, indeed, and with increasing enlightenment, to build royal landscape-rockeries of peak and valley and boulder, at any cost up to five-and-twenty thousand pounds or more. But the essential nature of rock-plants, and the whole meaning of this book, is, that for five-and-twenty shillings, it is no less possible for you, in a tiny and ill-favoured space, amid untoward surroundings, to have exactly the same quality of beauty, from exactly the same plants – yes, and very possibly achieve a patch of *Dianthus alpinus* or *Gentiana verna* that would make the twenty-five-thousand-pounder go green with envy. For Alpines, being really noble, are the most democratic of plants, and know no distinction of rank or wealth; all that they know and care for are their friends, whether from pithead or palace. Their instincts are unerring, and they have no respect for persons.

Now, then, for the creation of your rock-garden. The two absolute essentials, in the first place, are these: an open situation, and perfect drainage. You must never try to grow Alpines anywhere under the influence of trees. A dank hollow is doom; drip is damnation. It is imperative to choose a place where sun and air have all the play they can. It need not matter if the sunlight only falls for a few hours; the essential point is that your Alpines must not be darkened *immediately overhead*, by any malignant presences. Overhanging branches must be hewn well away; encroaching bushes cut back until they know their place.

But, even more important than that, if possible, is the necessity of perfect drainage. For Alpines, though usually sweet-tempered, are easily irritated by clogging damp. Therefore, you must be sure and lay your fundamental precautions well and thoroughly against such damages. It is easily done; I only warn you so passionately, to make sure that it is done. What you have to do when getting ready your bed for rock-plants, be it big or little, is, instead of merely taking out two foot of soil in preparation, to take out three. You then, at the bottom, lay a foundation of rough clinkers, brick oddments, broken stone, etc., for the depth of 9 inches or a foot. Then in on top of that goes your made soil; and you have perfect drainage. This applies, of course, most closely, to a bed made on the level, or in a hollow, if it has to be made there. But even on a bank or slope, though so much precaution is not so vital, it can never do harm, and always good. And it applies quite as urgently, even if you are able to think of making even the tiniest of bog gardens, such as by sinking the sawn half of a tub some quarter of an inch below the ground level, excavating a two-foot deep trench round it, and filling up with first 6 inches of drainage, and then a good mixture which will be kept damp, according as the tub is filled to overflowing.

I talked of making soil. This, I think, it is *always* as well to do, if you can, though Alpines grow luxuriantly in any rich, well-fed, and well-matured ground, such as the soil of an old kitchen-garden. In point of fact, though crude manure is loathsome to their delicate taste, all mountain plants fairly revel in ripe and very rich conditions. (Some of them, even – a few – overeat themselves, and become too torpid to flower.) Therefore, it is best to give them something good, and better suited to their need in the way of food and drainage, than the ordinary soil of the border. One's ambition is to get a mixture rich yet light, not dusty in summer droughts, nor caky and ponderous in winter rains. My own prescription is, to take two parts of the best loam you can get (that of your own garden may do very well), which should, for choice, be fibrous, clean, and on the heavy side. Dig well into this one part of powdered leaf-mould, and another part of fairly coarse silver sand. This will give you an ideal mixture. But of course this is *only* an ideal (and only a general suggestion); you may not be able, or willing, to make so much fuss; and then your ordinary garden soil *may* do very well for you, if your drainage be perfect and your position open, and your ambition not inclined to rise beyond the commoner things; only nothing ever does quite so well as that which does best. And I mean to take it for granted that the very best is what you will ultimately aim at.

Another important point that I urgently recommend, is that, when you have got your mixture ready, you dig into it (two spadefuls to a barrow load, or a little more) some coarsely powdered lime-rubble, such as mortar from an old wall. The enormous majority of Alpine plants, some 95 per cent., I should say, crave and clamour for abundant lime in the soil. In the case of the rare exceptions, which I shall notice if they are really beyond conversion (for very often a plant peculiar to granite hills is perfectly happy with lime in the garden), you will, of course, omit the lime, and substitute peat, or at all events one part of peat, for the loam in your mixture. And the last acme of perfection is reached, if, to either peaty or limy concoction, you add (to each barrowful) two or three spadefuls of finely broken road metal (anything but flint) – rough chips about the size of your finger tips. Besides enormously helping the drainage, these keep moisture too, and provide gripping-hold for the fibres of your treasures. So, with this composition, you have an absolute certainty of success with your choicest Alpines. I repeat that none of these fine fussments are necessary for a dazzling sixpenny show of Arabis and Alyssum: but, with this mixture prepared and laid down from the beginning you will be justified at any moment in going on later to *Primula Allionii* and *Saxifraga diapensioeides*. It is always easier to do good work, if you begin doing it from the very start.

Reginald Farrer, *The Rock Garden*

The Merging of Spring and Summer

At this point I should like to analyse and define the essence of Summer, and decide when the moment arrives that one bids farewell to Spring and feels Summer has come. But there can be no hard and fast line, no definite boundary, unless we make an arbitrary one of the name of the month, for much of Summer has appeared by the middle of May, and Spring is ever present in any garden, where tender young growth and promise of flower are continually springing from the ground. Certain scents and sounds mean Summer to me; taken singly, like specific characters, they are insufficient, but in combination they spell a certain season. The snoring drawl of a contented greenfinch and the mowing machine whirring over the lawns, turning them into parallel-striped carpets of two shades of green, the scent of the bruised and cut grass drying in the sun, initiate the summer feeling, and constitute the prelude; but the monotoned double croon of a turtle-dove, with its well-trilled R's, and the high-pitched rattle of the hay-cutter in the meadows, followed by the aroma of new-mown hay, with a whiff of the clean fragrance of a Dog Rose, build up the real article, and guarantee the presence of Summer as surely as the facts that you can cast clouts without missing them, and go out after dinner without further clothing than the meal demands.

There is so gradual a transition from Spring to Summer that one only notices the invasion of the warmer season here and there at first; it is as though these sister-queens agreed to rule together for a spell, and their courtiers and servants mingled freely; a Rose or a Lily appears among the tall, over-blown Tulips, which daily lay down some of their vernal banners as they drop their petals. A little later we must look in quiet, shady corners for the courtiers of Queen Spring, whilst everywhere may be seen those of Summer in rose-laden bushes and tropical flowers, returned with the reign of the new monarch from their exile to the greenhouses. It generally happens that the feeling that Spring has lost the upper hand comes over me when I get back to my garden after an arduous day's work on the first day of what was once the Temple, and is now the Chelsea Show. The masses of Roses and Rhododendrons and Azaleas seen there under canvas are not somehow convincing arguments for Summer's rule, at least not sufficiently strong to overcome the display made by the banks of well-preserved Tulips that in most seasons come from the fields of two or three great growers. Even the presence of Sweet Peas and Chrysanthemums, Dahlias and forced fruit, produces no sensation of Summer, for they all have an untimely, forced appearance. But, on my return, a stroll around the garden before it is time to dress for dinner, shows that the Tulips that looked respectable yesterday, are now shabby and faded, and disappointing at close quarters, and I go to look for bloom on summer-flowering plants that I have been reminded of by the forced specimens at the show. There is so much to be done, and to be looked at, in the garden at this time of year that I often miss the show of buds appearing upon some treasure until reminded by flowers in an exhibit that I have not called upon mine this season, and I enjoy the visit of inquiry, especially if it is rewarded by a promise of abundance. It does one good to lift the leaves of a *Paeonia lutea* and find clusters of plump buds hidden beneath them, or to discover a goodly number of flowering shoots just starting out sideways from the rosettes of *Gentiana Kurroo*, and so to be assured that both the beginning and end of Summer will give their widely different charms.

When Spring is merging into Summer in the last days of May, I like to watch the daily progress of *Wisteria multijuga*, which increases almost hourly in beauty, until the full display of the lavender cascade of flowers is reached in June. Many of the flower-clusters are by then a yard, or even more, in length, and the older flowers at the upper end do not fall until the last few buds are opening at the tips of the bunches, so that the effect is as striking as that produced by any flowering shrub that can be grown in the open air. I have often heard complaints that the *multijuga* forms are rather shy flowerers, and I think that is true of plants that are trained on walls or on anything that encourages the slender shoots to wander on and still find support, and that it is necessary to induce woody growths to stand away free from any support before a really profuse flowering can be expected. This habit fits them for use as standards, and I know of few things better for sheltered positions on lawns. My oldest specimen was turned out of its pot into its present position some dozen of years ago, and it soon threw out wild arms seeking for something to twine around beyond its central stake. The aspirations of these tentacles were cut short; they thickened into self-supporting branches about a yard in length, and after three seasons of this treatment commenced to bear flowers, and every year up to and including 1912 the flower display increased in wealth. Then it was so lavish that the foliage that followed was thinner than usual, and I half expected this season's flowering would be poor, but was sadly disappointed when I found no more than three flowering buds which dried up and fell off at an early stage of development. I hope and trust its absolute barrenness is of the nature of a rest cure, and that next season it will be strong and well again, and appear at Queen Summer's State Ball clad in a court train of greater length than ever.

When buying *W. multijuga* it is wise to see plants in flower, and choose those that please your taste in colour and form; for it is raised very easily from seed, even in the warmer parts of this country, and seedlings vary enormously. Further, we can hardly expect the altruism of the Japanese gardener to so thoroughly overpower his commercial instincts that he should export his largest and longest flowered and best coloured varieties at the same price as the ordinary seedlings; so it is he who keeps a wary, wide-open eye in the show tent and nursery that will be best pleased with *Wisteria multijuga* in his garden.

This is especially true of the white variety, which in its best form is one of the loveliest things that can excite an optic nerve. When the flowers of the racemes are open on rather more than half their length, that upper portion is snowy white, and the rest is a wonderfully shaded series of tints of the softest emerald green, of course deepest at the tapered tip, as though the paint had been allowed to run down.

I unfortunately bought the white one I wished to grow into a standard in unenlightened days, and I do not believe it will ever be a startling object, for its racemes are short, and the unopened buds more nearly resemble aquamarines, or broken soda-water bottles, than the emeralds I had hoped for. The poor plant stands higher up the gravelly bank than the lilac form, and is often thirsty about flowering time, and flings the baby buds off the central rachis as crabs are said to do with their legs and claws unless packed too closely for kicking in the boiling pot.

A little disappointment such as this provides a text for a Jeremiad on the uncertainty of success in gardening, the a-gley-ganging tendency of your best-laid plans that comes so aft that, though it may enhance your rare triumphs, still lets you feel that you are gambling against all the forces of Nature with those of Chance thrown in.

E. A. Bowles, *My Garden in Summer*

It was, perhaps, unfair of me to associate these writers with not one, but two world-wide conflicts, with a pandemic of Spanish flu and the Great Depression, thrown in. Hindsight can lead to a sense of pressing tragedy when, actually, the hopes of the time were genuine. Le Corbusier was not to know that the stars of his modernist vanity were about to fall to pieces as he criticised those of the Sun King at Versailles. Or Frank Kingdon Ward's gentle appeal to moderation and peace, achieved by the 'soothing effect of flowers on the spirit of man', was a sandcastle confronting a bitter sea.

Indeed, there is a sense of the appreciation of gardens for their stability. Gardens may be subject to change but these changes are universal and eternal and reassuring, not unpredictable and destructive like politics or the free market. Gardeners can still find satisfaction and joy in their gardens, no matter how small the areas have become. And, to a certain extent, garden writing still attracts its obsessives who do not see beyond the shrubbery.

Marion Cran, lecturing after her motor tour of England, lingers over flower-swathed villages, and the innate good taste of the earth-bound peasants. Britain may just have fought a war, but England has come through unscarred, and the world will be fine for as long as this vision remains uncorrupted. In less than twenty years, the battlefield has come to these gardens, vegetables displacing flowers, as if victory could be won by the turning of a spade.

Far away in California, in what could be another century, Florence Yoch gracefully, succinctly, sets out her design principles for 'A Little Garden of Gaiety' – an investment which all city councils might consider.

The poets had a mixed time, as poets will, but it is a good interlude for the variety of gardens taken as inspiration. In the garden of love, Rilke is poised, reclaiming the rose as arch-metaphor. Sadly, having made it through the cull of poets in World War I, he died of leukaemia in 1926, the year of these poems. Yeats makes the rose the prize in a political garden; this too is fed with blood, as if the world had not seen enough. Gethsemane, least favoured of all the historic-mythic gardens, inspires Kipling, who, being intensely personal, becomes Everyman. Eden is re-imagined by Dylan Thomas as a parched and unforgiving place. E. E. Cummings has two verses of lucidity, recalling Spenser's Garden of Adonis. But truth was found by Patrick Kavanagh in an Irish Hesperides, 'Where the sun was always setting on the play.' The lights are going out.

❧

Digging (1)

Today I think
Only with scents, – scents dead leaves yield,
And bracken, and wild carrot's seed,
And the square mustard field;

Odours that rise
When the spade wounds the root of tree,
Rose, currant, raspberry, or goutweed,
Rhubarb or celery;

The smoke's smell, too,
Flowing from where a bonfire burns
The dead, the waste, the dangerous,
And all to sweetness turns.

It is enough
To smell, to crumble the dark earth,
While the robin sings over again
Sad songs of Autumn mirth.

Edward Thomas

Mino, Lord of the Garden

The young cat trotted lordly down the path, waving his tail. He was an ordinary tabby with white paws, a slender young gentleman. A crouching, fluffy, brownish-grey cat was stealing up the side of the fence. The Mino walked statelily up to her, with manly nonchalance. She crouched before him and pressed herself on the ground in humility, a fluffy soft outcast, looking up at him with wild eyes that were green and lovely as great jewels. He looked casually down on her. So she crept a few inches further, proceeding on her way to the back door, crouching in a wonderful, soft, self-obliterating manner, and moving like a shadow.

He, going statelily on his slim legs, walked after her, then suddenly, for pure excess, he gave her a light cuff with his paw on the side of her face. She ran off a few steps, like a blown leaf along the ground, then crouched unobtrusively, in submissive, wild patience. The Mino pretended to take no notice of her. He blinked his eyes superbly at the landscape. In a minute she drew herself together and moved softly, a fleecy brown-grey shadow, a few paces forward. She began to quicken her pace, in a moment she would be gone like a dream, when the young grey lord sprang before her, and gave her a light handsome cuff. She subsided at once, submissively.

'She is a wild cat,' said Birkin. 'She has come in from the woods.'

The eyes of the stray cat flared round for a moment, like great green fires staring at Birkin. Then she rushed in a soft swift rush, half way down the garden. There she paused to look round. The Mino turned his face in pure superiority to his master, and slowly closed his eyes, standing in statuesque young perfection. The wild cat's round, green, wandering eyes were staring all the while like uncanny fires. Then again, like a shadow, she slid towards the kitchen.

In a lovely springing leap, like a wind, the Mino was upon her, and had boxed her twice, very definitely, with a white delicate fist. She sank and slid back, unquestioning. He walked after her, and cuffed her once or twice, leisurely, with sudden little blows of his magic white paws.

'Now why does he do that?' cried Ursula in indignation.

'They are on intimate terms,' said Birkin.

'And that is why he hits her?'

'Yes,' laughed Birkin, 'I think he wants to make it quite obvious to her.'

'Isn't it horrid of him!' she cried; and going out into the garden she called to the Mino:

'Stop it, don't bully. Stop hitting her.'

The stray cat vanished like a swift, invisible shadow. The Mino glanced at Ursula, then looked from her disdainfully to his master.

'Are you a bully, Mino?' Birkin asked.

The young slim cat looked at him, and slowly narrowed its eyes. Then it glanced away at the landscape, looking into the distance as if completely oblivious of the two human beings.

'Mino,' said Ursula, 'I don't like you. You are a bully like all males.'

'No,' said Birkin, 'he is justified. He is not a bully. He is only insisting to the poor stray that she acknowledge him as a sort of fate, her own fate: because you can see she is fluffy and promiscuous as the wind. I am with him entirely. He wants superfine stability.'

'Yes, I know!' cried Ursula. 'He wants his own way – I know what your fine words work down to – bossiness, I call it bossiness.'

The young cat again glanced at Birkin in disdain of the noisy woman.

'I quite agree with you, Miciotto,' said Birkin to the cat. 'Keep your male dignity, and your higher understanding.'

Again the Mino narrowed his eyes as if he were looking at the sun. Then, suddenly affecting to have no connection at all with the two people, he went trotting off, with assumed spontaneity and gaiety, his tail erect, his white feet blithe.

'Now he will find the belle sauvage once more, and entertain her with his superior wisdom,' laughed Birkin.

Ursula looked at the man who stood in the garden with his hair blowing and his eyes smiling ironically, and she cried:

'Oh it makes me so cross, this assumption of male superiority! And it is such a lie! One wouldn't mind if there were any justification for it.'

'The wild cat,' said Birkin, 'doesn't mind. She perceives that it is justified.'

'Does she!' cried Ursula. 'And tell it to the Horse Marines.'

'To them also.'

'It is just like Gerald Crich with his horse – a lust for bullying – a real

Wille zur Macht – so base, so petty.'

'I agree that the Wille zur Macht is a base and petty thing. But with the Mino, it is a desire to bring this female cat into a pure stable equilibrium, a transcendent and abiding *rapport* with the single male. Whereas without him, as you see, she is a mere stray, a fluffy sporadic bit of chaos. It is a volonté de pouvoir, if you like, a will to ability, taking pouvoir as a verb."

'Ah –! Sophistries! It's the old Adam.'

'Oh yes. Adam kept Eve in the indestructible paradise, when he kept her single with himself, like a star in its orbit.'

D. H. Lawrence, *Women in Love*

Potatoes and Rattlesnakes

The garden, curiously enough, was a quarter of a mile from the house, and the way to it led up a shallow draw past the cattle corral. Grandmother called my attention to a stout hickory cane, tipped with copper, which hung by a leather thong from her belt. This, she said, was her rattlesnake cane. I must never go to the garden without a heavy stick or a corn-knife; she had killed a good many rattlers on her way back and forth. A little girl who lived on the Black Hawk road was bitten on the ankle and had been sick all summer.

I can remember exactly how the country looked to me as I walked beside my grandmother along the faint wagon-tracks on that early September morning. Perhaps the glide of long railway travel was still with me, for more than anything else I felt motion in the landscape; in the fresh, easy-blowing morning wind, and in the earth itself, as if the shaggy grass were a sort of loose hide, and underneath it herds of wild buffalo were galloping, galloping . . .

Alone, I should never have found the garden – except, perhaps, for the big yellow pumpkins that lay about unprotected by their withering vines – and I felt very little interest in it when I got there, I wanted to walk straight on through the red grass and over the edge of the world, which could not be very far away. The light air about me told me that the world ended here: only the ground and sun and sky were left, and if one went a little farther there would be only sun and sky, and one would float off into them, like the tawny hawks which sailed over our heads making slow shadows on the grass. While grandmother took the pitchfork we found standing in one of the rows and dug potatoes, while I picked them up out of the soft brown earth and put them into the bag, I kept looking up at the hawks that were doing what I might so easily do.

When grandmother was ready to go, I said I would like to stay up there in the garden awhile.

She peered down at me from under her sunbonnet. 'Aren't you afraid of snakes?'

'A little,' I admitted, 'but I'd like to stay, anyhow.'

'Well, if you see one, don't have anything to do with him. The big yellow and brown ones won't hurt you; they're bull-snakes and help to keep the gophers down. Don't be scared if you see anything look out of that hole in the bank over there. That's a badger hole. He's about as big as a big 'possom, and his face is striped, black and white. He takes a chicken once in a while, but I won't let the men harm him. In a new country a body feels friendly to the animals. I like to have him come out and watch me when I'm at work.'

Grandmother swung the bag of potatoes over her shoulder and went down the path, leaning forward a little. The road followed the windings of the draw; when she came to the first bend, she waved at me and disappeared. I was left alone with this new feeling of lightness and content.

I sat down in the middle of the garden, where snakes could scarcely approach unseen, and leaned my back against a warm yellow pumpkin. There were some ground-cherry bushes growing along the furrows, full of fruit. I turned back the papery triangular sheaths that protected the berries and ate a few. All about me giant grasshoppers, twice as big as any I had ever seen, were doing acrobatic feats among the dried vines. The gophers scurried up and down the ploughed ground. There in the sheltered draw-bottom the wind did not blow very hard, but I could hear it singing its humming tune up on the level, and I could see the tall grasses wave. The earth was warm under me, and warm as I crumbled it through my fingers. Queer little red bugs came out and moved in slow squadrons around me. Their backs were polished vermilion, with black spots. I kept as still as I could. Nothing happened. I did not expect anything to happen. I was something that lay under the sun and felt it, like the pump-kins, and I did not want to be anything more. I was entirely happy. Perhaps we feel like that when we die and become a part of something entire, whether it is sun and air, or goodness and knowledge. At any rate, that is happiness; to be dissolved into something complete and great. When it comes to one, it comes as naturally as sleep.

Willa Cather, *My Ántonia*

Gethsemane

1914-1918
The Garden called Gethsemane
In Picardy it was,
And there the people came to see
The English soldiers pass.
We used to pass – we used to pass
Or halt, as it might be.
And ship our masks in case of gas
Beyond Gethsemane.

The Garden called Gethsemane,
It held a pretty lass,
But all the time she talked to me
I prayed my cup might pass.
The officer sat on the chair,
The men lay on the grass,
And all the time we halted there
I prayed my cup might pass.

It didn't pass – it didn't pass –
It didn't pass from me.
I drank it when we met the gas
Beyond Gethsemane!

Rudyard Kipling

The Rose Tree

'O words are lightly spoken,'
Said Pearse to Connolly,
'Maybe a breath of politic words
Has withered our Rose Tree;
Or maybe but a wind that blows
Across the bitter sea.'

'It needs to be but watered,'
James Connolly replied,
'To make the green come out again
And spread on every side,
And shake the blossom from the bud
To be the garden's pride.'

'But where can we draw water,'
Said Pearse to Connolly,
'When all the wells are parched away?
O plain as plain can be
There's nothing but our own red blood
Can make a right Rose Tree.'

W. B. Yeats

The Dormouse and the Doctor

There once was a Dormouse who lived in a bed
Of delphiniums (blue) and geraniums (red),
And all the day long he'd a wonderful view
Of geraniums (red) and delphiniums (blue).

A Doctor came hurrying round, and he said:
'Tut-tut, I am sorry to find you in bed.
Just say "Ninety-nine," while I look at your chest . . .
Don't you find that chrysanthemums answer the best?'

The Dormouse looked round at the view and replied
(When he'd said "Ninety-nine") that he'd tried and he'd tried,
And much the most answering things that he knew
Were geraniums (red) and delphiniums (blue).

The Doctor stood frowning and shaking his head,
And he took up his shiny silk hat as he said:
'What the patient requires is a change,' and he went
To see some chrysanthemum people in Kent.

The Dormouse lay there, and he gazed at the view
Of geraniums (red) and delphiniums (blue),
And he knew there was nothing he wanted instead
Of delphiniums (blue) and geraniums (red).

The Doctor came back and, to show what he meant,
He had brought some chrysanthemum cuttings from Kent.
'Now *these*,' he remarked, 'give a *much* better view
Than geraniums (red) and delphiniums (blue).'

They took out their spades and they dug up the bed
Of delphiniums (blue) and geraniums (red),
And they planted chrysanthemums (yellow and white).
'And *now*,' said the Doctor, 'we'll *soon* have you right.'

The Dormouse looked out, and he said with a sigh:
'I suppose all these people know better than I.
It was silly, perhaps, but I *did* like the view
Of geraniums (red) and delphiniums (blue).'

The Doctor came round and examined his chest,
And ordered him Nourishment, Tonics, and Rest.
'How very effective,' he said, as he shook
The thermometer, 'all these chrysanthemums look!'

The Dormouse turned over to shut out the sight
Of the endless chrysanthemums (yellow and white).
'How lovely,' he thought, 'to be back in a bed
Of delphiniums (blue) and geraniums (red).'

The Doctor said, 'Tut! It's another attack!'
And ordered him Milk and Massage-of-the-back,
And Freedom-from-worry and Drives-in-a-car,
And murmured, 'How sweet your chrysanthemums are!'

The Dormouse lay there with his paws to his eyes,
And imagined himself such a pleasant surprise:
'I'll *pretend* the chrysanthemums turn to a bed
Of delphiniums (blue) and geraniums (red)!'

The Doctor next morning was rubbing his hands,
And saying, 'There's nobody quite understands
These cases as I do! The cure has begun!
How fresh the chrysanthemums look in the sun!'

The Dormouse lay happy, his eyes were so tight
He could see no chrysanthemums, yellow or white.
And all that he felt at the back of his head
Were delphiniums (blue) and geraniums (red).

A. A. Milne, *When We Were Very Young*

Garden-Night

Mist-like through the arching roses hover,
roses for the living intertwined,
those who, still imperfectly resigned,
out of recent death come billowing over . . .

They, whose oneness with it's so entire,
greet this earth's cool surface once again, –
hope to scratch themselves against the briar
with a long-forgotten pain.

Hand of one through trellised vine goes stealing
for the leaf's detected green . . .
Leaf denies . . . now with her cheek she's feeling . . .
But the night-wind comes between . . .

Rainer Maria Rilke

This is the Garden

this is the garden: colours come and go,
frail azures fluttering from night's outer wing
strong silent greens serenely lingering,
absolute lights like baths of golden snow.
This is the garden: pursed lips do blow
upon cool flutes within wide glooms, and sing
(of harps celestial to the quivering string)
invisible faces hauntingly and slow.

This is the garden. Time shall surely reap
and on Death's blade lie many a flower curled,
in other lands where other songs be sung;
yet stand They here enraptured, as among
the slow deep trees perpetual of sleep
some silver-fingered fountain steals the world.

E. E. Cummings

The Peasant Woman's Garden

I have lately been taken on a motor trip through unfrequented England, from the southern part of Kent up to the Great Wall of the North and down again, travelling through the byways of this our Garden Island. By noon and by sunset, and by the colourless light of moon and stars, the way has led, through rain and shine, warm and cool, along unfrequented roads; from the wooded Weald to high bare wolds, through fruitful vales and wind-swept moor, by river, lake, and dewpond: and all the way, wherever it went, the road was garden-set. Whether of grey Cotswold stone, of warm red brick, or historic oak and plaster, the people of our country spell 'home' with flowers. When we have learned to plant more thoughtfully, there will be few places in the world to compare with the garden isle of Britain.

All through the book I have been trying to resist repeating to you an idea. Every time it nagged and bit at me I would hush it quiet again. I would say to myself: 'They want to know how to grow their flowers; they want helpful advice and cultural hints; they don't want *ideas*. Don't bother the people. They are friendly; why upset them?'

And so I played the coward's trick, and talked of what I was told you wanted to hear, instead of what was in my heart – which is all that really matters. For it is only what people *feel* that counts in the end, you know: textbook advice is never thronged with feeling. Perhaps that is why it is such a bore.

So here is the tale of the village of lilies. It was evening, and we had been motoring all day. You know how the light seems to slip away at twilight. There is one moment of evening when it seems to slip out of your eyes so that you can feel it go, like grains of sand slip and slip through your fingers – do you know that moment? We were going down the road from Salisbury Plain, the sunset fading out, the moon up, and a grey softness over the hard edges of the world.

It had been a hot, dusty day; it was like dipping in a cool well to feel the aching daylight give way to calm night. And then, in that wide-eyed hour, the road went down into a village I can never forget. A village of grey stone houses – *old* houses, full of the beauty of peace – and every garden there had its Madonna lilies. For some reason, either because they suited the soil and grew well there, or because some garden-lover with genius lived there, every garden, small or great, had at least *one* tall clump of lilies; and some were full of them.

How can I make you see that picture as I saw it? Out of the naked plain we dropped in the hour of moonlight and grey mist into a grey old lovely village all lit up with the pale lamps of the scented lilies. They were beside me on every hand – luminous, tall. My friends slowed the car and went slowly – slowly – through a spirit-village lit with white flame of lilies.

I must not grow fantastic as I tell you my tale; I make you see it real, as indeed it was real. But I assure you that I was transported there into a world of unearthly beauty. The misty shadows hid the earth and the roots of the plants – softened them away, so that the pale flowers rose round me like the sweet, strong things rise from the souls of men to blossom in the gardens of God – love and patience, and loyalty, aspiring. So ethereal it was, there under the moon shadows, the village of lilies.

Thinking it all over, I knew I had been very fortunate to happen upon the place in its beautiful moment – at the hour of sunset and moonrise, at the time of their fullest bloom. In the time when everything is glamoured, I happened to find that place where every one loves and grows Madonna lilies.

These happy accidents do come our way now and again. They make the worth-while moments in life – the moments of pure happiness – but they are not very common. And so we treasure them. The best of life is only moments. The rest is waiting for them. Anyway, one thing was sure. Neither moonlight nor sunset fading could have given me that thrill of sheer wonder if the gardens of that place had not grown the lilies.

And it was at this point in memory that my idea was born. Could we begin to plant a little more for each other, a little less for ourselves? Britain might become fairer if other places would do something like that – a village of roses, for instance, in some place where roses grow very well, another of irises, of Michaelmas daisies. The day may come when we shall hear people say, "Let us go to B— this week-end; all the irises will be out'; or,

'Can't we arrange our trip to pass through H— and lunch among the roses?'; or,

'It is lupin time; let us go to W—.'

There are some parts in the Eastern States of America where lilacs grow better than in any other part of the world, and the people know it so well that they take pride in their lilacs and grow every species and every hybrid in great profusion. A hard-headed business man said to me one day: 'It's remarkable, Mrs. Cran, but those lilacs divert traffic. Thousands travel east every spring to see them at Long Island and Rochester.'

So America has waked to the idea of making a district famous for the beauty of one flower, as the South Africans did long ago when they planted Pretoria with blue Jacaranda trees.

Now and then, in travelling the countryside, one comes across the touch of individual genius which seizes simple material and makes of it a compelling picture. Imagine a tiny whitewashed cottage standing up over the roadside, reached by a few worn stone steps. Of the utmost poverty, the utmost sparkling cleanliness. A stout old dear in the doorway watching the car come by, and watching, too, with gratification, our undisguised admiration of her garden. We stopped to look: a rosy-mauve mass of willowherb by one white wall; and depth on depth of blue geranium on the other; and she – wide, expansive, benevolent, intelligent – in the doorway between them in a gingham dress. I asked her what made her plant those flowers.

'Nice colours they be,' she said, 'and they things grow well hereabouts – a body need not buy such as they. See the '*sweets*?'

She led me back of the house, where a ditch ran below a hedge of hazel. It was fragrant with meadowsweet – nothing else – under the dark green hedge a foam of fragrance, growing in just the damp place that meadowsweets and all the spiraeas love best. In the horticultural world they call the meadowsweets spiraea; and when one orders from catalogues it is just as well to know under what name to look for them. It is a funny habit we humans have of muddling everything up as much as possible with a lot of difficult names. If I had my way, everything should be as simple as possible; but that would upset the scholars very much. *She* called them 'sweets', the fat old dear.

Poor, but undefeated, she had gone into the nursery-bed of nature, and made from its ungrudged bounty a garden-picture of wild flowers about her home. She had put blue geranium and rosy willowherb where colour was needed, against the cool white walls of her tiny house; and ivory feather plumes where the dark hedge called for light. Here were native intelligence and native taste making a lovely picture, with the restraint that is the true mark of genius.

Rare sweetness flourished in the wide, unlikely body of that country-woman whose cottage lies somewhere between the Severn and the Avon: love of beauty, love of flowers, love of home, and the sensitive fastidiousness of a true artist. I believe that the word 'artist' holds in itself the essence of the word 'lover'. I am sure that the best gardens are made by those who approach their land as lovers; but that matter can wait for a leisured talk another day.

Taste is not always a natural gift; but it can be acquired. There are a great many garden-lovers who are but now beginning to enjoy the nature world and hardly know what they want, and certainly do not know how to get it. These are the people who love flowers and want to grow them – love every kind and then make the mistake of wanting to grow some of everything.

'It is such a *mess*; it never seems to mean anything.'

The reason is always the same: confused planting. Some of everything; and so, in effect, nothing. If these gardens were planted out with a seedling of this, a cutting of that, and a bush of something else for the purpose of satisfying the owner's love of botany, love of variety, love of *anything*, the whole medley would fall together under the touch of sympathy. But when it has all come about through the beginner's lack of restraint, the garden is a bore.

The first thing to realize is that space, dignity, and perspective are essential to a tasteful garden. Taste means controlled choosing, elimination, self-discipline. It is no use expecting a spotty, scrappy jumble of plants to give the balanced effect of a single variety planted in mass. Consider a picture of hydrangeas in a Cornish garden, or the simplicity of irises growing along a river bank.

Just before Christmas I was asked to lend a hand to two raw amateurs in making plans for their little suburban London gardens. With great enthusiasm we drew up a couple of plans. One varied her plan as she planted, putting two or three hollyhocks there, a bush of lupins here, linum and campion, a Madonna lily, a bush of feathery *Thalictrum dipterocarpum*, a *Heuchera* from the tennis club, and so on. The plan disappeared altogether when Chelsea Flower Show came on and she saw the dazzling enticements of a hundred beguiling flower-merchants. The result was a featureless muddle.

The other adhered strictly to plan. Every edging to bed and border was Mrs. Sinkins pink, crocuses and muscari just behind for the spring; then *Nepeta Mussini* and antirrhinum Nelrose; above and behind that were standard bushes of Red Letter Day, and last of all a string of American Pillar roses all around. In the centre of this surround, a small flagged rose-garden, with four beds edged with the same variety of pinks, and a bird-table in the midst. There were two beds of rose Ophelia, two of the red rose Etoile de Hollande. Between the stones of the little rose-garden she planted the pretty thymes, and Arenaria, and Raoulia. Round the windows of her bungalow grew rose Zephyrine Drouhin, because it was sweet to smell and had no thorns to tear the curtains when they blew about in gusty summer-time.

It was, is, an extremely pretty garden. When the pinks are out it seems as if one had come to a very large garden, the scent is so warm and sweet. She gathers sheaves of blooms for friends, and still the borders look full of the white flowers with their green shadows. People wonder at the size of her garden when they see her offerings; but it is a little garden. Only it grows a *few* things, and grows them well. The design of it is marked out admirably by the white flowering and grey foliage of the pinks. The warm reds of the roses and antirrhinums are tempered and refreshed, too, by the broad bands of *Nepeta* – no flower is so generous in its length of bloom and vigour of growth, or a softer blue than *Nepeta Mussini*.

There is nothing ambitious in this planting: no rare and costly plants, no startling new colour-scheme. But it arrests the eye of every wayfarer passing by because it has that rare quality, that secret of beauty – restraint. The little garden anyone may have, but very few attain. They want too much! The old peasant woman knew better; she had the knowledge we of the world, who care for the spirit, spend our lives in learning. She knew the grandeur of simplicity.

Marion Cran, Garden Talks

Counterweight

Garden by gathering rain almost tenderly sombered,
garden under the lingering hand.
As though in their beds the species more earnestly pondered
how by a gardener's thought they were ever outscanned.

For they think of him; some of his painstaking mood has remained in
their innocent freedom and some of his limiting fate.
They are tugged at as well by the two-ness we are so strikingly trained in;
even in the lightest we waken a counterweight.

Rainer Maria Rilke

Versailles

Louis XIV is no longer the successor of Louis XIII. He is the ROI-SOLEIL. Immense vanity! At the foot of the throne, his architects brought him plans drawn from a bird's-eye view which seem like a chart of stars; immense axes, formed like stars. The Roi-Soleil swells with pride; and gigantic works are carried out. But a man has only two eyes at a level of about 5 feet 6 inches above the ground, and can only look at one point at a time. The arms of the stars are only visible one after the other, and what you have is really a right angle masked by foliation. A right angle is not a star; the stars fall to pieces. And so it goes on: the great basin, the embroidered flower-beds which are outside the general panorama, the buildings that one can only see in fragments and as one moves about. It is a snare and a delusion. Louis XIV deceived himself of his own free will. He transgressed the truths of architecture because he did not work with the objective elements of architecture.

Le Corbusier, *Towards a New Architecture*

The Little Garden of Gaiety

In the East even gaiety may slumber. California, however, has a twelve months' responsibility to keep the garden gay and charming. Decay has no charm. For the fundamental lines of our design we must employ only plants that remain thrifty and interesting throughout the year, avoiding the opposite pitfall of monotony which is never conducive to gaiety. Some of our most obligingly evergreen things become very monotonous and most of the easily attained and long enduring garden color becomes wearisome.

As elsewhere, design is our friend and comforter. It dictates feeling, guides choice of material and tides over the lean season. Given simple, satisfying lines worked out in substantial materials and interesting shapes and leaf texture, we have the framework on which to apply the everchanging element of color.

The first burst of spring is the one constantly recurring thrill that never palls and unless fully featured a garden fails one of its foremost purposes. The colors expressing spring are crystal clear and gentle harmonies. In summer gaiety takes a higher pitch and the full gamut of effulgent brilliant discord is surprisingly satisfying. For autumn, rich minor notes, purple, mauve, smoky gold, and burnt rose embody the mood. In southern California there are quite a number of things which flower blithely on into winter and it is always surprising how a least flicker of color can light up an evergreen garden.

Some things that hold full beauty to the end – like Salvia leucantha and Lantanas – become important, but it is the few hardy souls like the earliest Acacias, Jasminum primulinum and Winter Peas and Bignonias which are cheerfully starting their new careers, bringing forth fresh color, while everything else is relinquishing the ghost. Though often obscured during the more colorful seasons, it is in winter that design comes into its own.

Of course, the voice of the garden is water and in the tiniest garden it is possible to get a maximum of effect by the simplest means – a central location, no coping, and an exaggeratedly high spray, can be almost dramatic.

Contrast is the foil of color, light, and music, so here we surround our gay little garden by rather a prim solid green hedge along the sides. At the rear we look into the shadowy depth of pleached trees. The borders are planted to things of woodsy character, few flowers, and delicate shades.

Florence Yoch, *The Little Garden of Gaiety*

On Gardens and Gardening

How Little Gardens Are Laid Out

There are several different ways in which to lay out a little garden; the best way is to get a gardener. The gardener will put up a number of sticks, twigs, and broomsticks, and will assure you that these are maples, hawthorns, lilacs, standard and bush roses, and other natural species; then he will dig the soil, turn it over and pat it again; he will make little paths of rubble, stick here and there into the ground some faded foliage, and declare that these are perennials; he will sow seeds for the future lawn, which he will call English rye grass and bent grass, fox-tail, dog's-tail, and cat's-tail grass; and then he will depart leaving the garden brown and naked, as it was on the first day of the creation of the world; and he will warn you that every day you should carefully water all this soil of the earth, and when the grass peeps out you must order some gravel for the paths. Very well then.

One would think that watering a little garden is quite a simple thing, especially if one has a hose. It will soon be clear that until it has been tamed a hose is an evasive and dangerous beast, for it contorts itself, it jumps, it wriggles, it makes puddles of water, and dives with delight into the mess it has made; then it goes for the man who is going to use it and coils itself round his legs; you must hold it down with your foot, and then it rears and twists round your waist and neck, and while you are fighting with it as with a cobra, the monster turns up its brass mouth and projects a mighty stream of water through the windows on to the curtains which have been recently hung. You must grasp it firmly, and hold it tight; the beast rears with pain, and begins to spout water, not from the mouth, but from the hydrant and from somewhere in the middle of its body. Three men at least are needed to tame it at first, and they all leave the place of battle splashed to the ears with mud and drenched with water; as to the garden itself, in parts it has changed into greasy pools, while in other places it is cracking with thirst.

If you do this every day, in a fortnight weeds will spring up instead of grass. This is one of Nature's mysteries – how from the best grass seed most luxuriant and hairy weeds come up; perhaps weed seed ought to be sown and then a nice lawn would result. In three weeks the lawn is thickly overgrown with thistles and other pests, creeping, or rooted a foot deep in the earth; if you want to pull them out they break off at the root, or they bring up whole lumps of soil with them. It's like this: the more of a nuisance the more they stick to life.

In the meantime, through a mysterious metamorphosis of matter, the rubble of the paths has changed into the most sticky and greasy clay that you can imagine.

Nevertheless, weeds in the lawn must be rooted out; you are weeding and weeding, and behind your steps the future lawn turns into naked and brown earth as it was on the first day of the creation of the world.

Only on one or two spots something like a greenish mould appears, something like mist, and scanty, and very like down; that's grass, certainly. You walk round it on tiptoe, and chase away the sparrows; and while you are peering into the earth, on the gooseberry and currant bushes the first little leaves have broken forth, all unawares; Spring is always too quick for you.

Your relation towards things has changed. If it rains you say that it rains on the garden; if the sun shines, it does not shine just anyhow, but it shines on the garden; in the evening you rejoice that the garden will rest.

One day you will open your eyes and the garden will be green, long grass will glisten with dew, and from the tangled tops of the roses swollen and crimson buds will peep forth; and the trees will be old, and their crowns will be dark and heavy and widely spread, with a musty smell in their damp shade. And you will remember no more the slender, naked, brown little garden of those days, the uncertain down of the first grass, the first pinched buds, and all the earthy, poor and touching beauty of a garden which is being laid out.

Very well, but now you must water and weed, and pick the stones out of the soil.

On the Art of Gardening

While I was only a remote and distracted onlooker of the accomplished work of gardens, I considered gardeners to be beings of a peculiarly poetic and gentle mind, who cultivate perfumes of flowers listening to the birds singing. Now, when I look at the affair more closely, I find that a real gardener is not a man who cultivates flowers; he is a man who cultivates the soil. He is a creature who digs himself into the earth, and leaves the sight of what is on it to us gaping good-for-nothings. He lives buried in the ground. He builds his monument in a heap of compost. If he came into the Garden of Eden he would sniff excitedly and say: 'Good Lord, what humus!' I think he would forget to eat the fruit of the tree of knowledge of good and evil; he would rather look round to see how he could manage to take away from the Lord some barrow-loads of the paradisaic soil. Or he would discover that the tree of knowledge of good and evil has not a nice dishlike bed, and he would begin to mess about with the soil, innocent of what is hanging over his head. 'Where are you, Adam?' the Lord would say. 'In a moment,' the gardener would shout over his shoulder; 'I am busy now.' And he would go on making his little bed.

If gardeners had been developing from the beginning of the world by natural selection they would have evolved into some kind of invertebrate. After all, for what purpose has a gardener a back? Apparently only so that he can straighten it at times, and say: 'My back does ache!' As for legs, they may be folded in different ways; one may sit on the heels, kneel on the knees, bring the legs somehow underneath, or finally put them around one's neck; fingers are good pegs for poking holes, palms break clods or divide the mould, while the head serves for holding a pipe; only the back remains an inflexible thing which the gardener tries in vain to bend. The earthworm also is without a back. The gardener usually ends above in his seat; legs and arms are straddled, the head somewhere between the knees like a grazing mare. He is not a man who would like 'to add at least a cubit to his stature'; on the contrary, he folds his stature into half, he squats and shortens himself by all possible means; as you find him he is seldom over one metre high.

Tilling the soil consists, on the one hand, in various diggings, hoeings, turnings, buryings, loosenings, pattings, and smoothings, and on the other in ingredients. No pudding could be more complicated than the preparation of a garden soil; as far as I have been able to find out, dung, manure, guano, leafmould, sods, humus, sand, straw, lime, kainit, Thomas's powder, baby's powder, saltpetre, horn, phosphates, droppings, cow-dung, ashes, peat, compost, water, beer, knocked-out pipes, burnt matches, dead cats, and many other substances are added. All this is continually mixed, stirred in, and flavoured; as I said, the gardener is not a man who smells a rose, but who is persecuted by the idea that 'the soil would like some lime', or that it is heavy (as lead the gardener says) and 'would like some sand'. Gardening becomes a scientific affair. A rose in flower is, so to speak, only for dilettanti; the gardener's pleasure is deeper rooted, right in the womb of the soil. After his death the gardener does not become a butterfly, intoxicated by the perfumes of flowers, but a garden worm tasting all the dark, nitrogenous, and spicy delights of the soil.

Now, in spring gardeners are irresistibly drawn to their gardens; as soon as they lay the spoon down, they are on the beds, presenting their rumps to the splendid azure sky; here they crumble a warm clod between their fingers, there they push nearer the roots a weathered and precious piece of last year's dung, there they pull out a weed, and here they pick up a little stone; now they work up the soil round the strawberries, and in a moment they bend to some young lettuce, nose close to the earth, fondly tickling a fragile tuft of roots. In this position they enjoy spring, while over their behinds the sun describes his glorious circuit, the clouds swim, and the birds of heaven mate. Already the cherry buds are opening, young foliage is expanding with sweet tenderness, blackbirds sing like mad; then the gardener straightens himself, eases his back, and says thoughtfully: 'in autumn I shall manure it thoroughly, and I shall add some sand.'

But there is one moment when the gardener rises and straightens himself up to his full height; this is in the afternoon, when he administers the sacrament of water to his little garden. Then he stands, straight and almost noble, directing the jet of water from the mouth of the hydrant; the water rushes in a silver and kissing shower; out of the puffy soil wafts a perfumed breath of moisture, every little leaf is almost wildly green, and sparkles with an appetising joy, so that a man might eat it. 'So, and now it is enough,' the gardener whispers happily; he does not mean by 'it' the little cherry-tree covered with buds, or the purple currant; he is thinking of the brown soil.

And after the sun has set he sighs with deep content: 'I have sweated to-day!'

Karel Čapek, *The Gardener's Year*

Ash-Wednesday

Part 2

Lady, three white leopards sat under a juniper-tree
In the cool of the day, having fed to satiety
On my legs my heart my liver and that which had been contained
In the hollow round of my skull. And God said
Shall these bones live? shall these
Bones live? And that which had been contained

In the bones (which were already dry) said chirping:
Because of the goodness of this Lady
And because of her loveliness, and because
She honours the Virgin in meditation,
We shine with brightness. And I who am here dissembled
Proffer my deeds to oblivion, and my love
To the posterity of the desert and the fruit of the gourd.
It is this which recovers
My guts the strings of my eyes and the indigestible portions
Which the leopards reject. The Lady is withdrawn
In a white gown, to contemplation, in a white gown.
Let the whiteness of bones atone to forgetfulness.
There is no life in them. As I am forgotten
And would be forgotten, so I would forget
Thus devoted, concentrated in purpose. And God said
Prophesy to the wind, to the wind only for only
The wind will listen. And the bones sang chirping
With the burden of the grasshopper, saying

>Lady of silences
>Calm and distressed
>Torn and most whole
>Rose of memory
>Rose of forgetfulness
>Exhausted and life-giving
>Worried reposeful
>The single Rose
>Is now the Garden
>Where all loves end
>Terminate torment
>Of love unsatisfied
>The greater torment
>Of love satisfied
>End of the endless
>Journey to no end
>Conclusion of all that
>Is inconclusible

Speech without word
Word of no speech
Grace to the Mother
For the Garden
Where all love ends.

Under a juniper-tree the bones sang, scattered and shining
We are glad to be scattered, we did little good to each other,
Under a tree in the cool of the day, with the blessing of sand,
Forgetting themselves and each other, united
In the quiet of the desert. This is the land which ye
Shall divide by lot. And neither division nor unity
Matters. This is the land. We have our inheritance.

T. S. Eliot

Atrophied and Faintly Rotten

Feeling good from the rosy wine at lunch, Nicole Driver folded her arms high enough for the artificial camellia on her shoulder to touch her cheek, and went out into her lovely grassless garden. The garden was bounded on one side by the house, from which it flowed and into which it ran, on two sides by the old village, and on the last by the cliff falling by ledges to the sea.

Along the walls on the village side all was dusty, the wriggling vines, the lemon and eucalyptus trees, the casual wheelbarrow, left only a moment since, but already grown into the path, atrophied and faintly rotten. Nicole was invariably somewhat surprised that, by turning in the other direction past a bed of peonies, she walked into an area so green and cool that the leaves and petals were curled with tender damp.

Knotted at her throat she wore a lilac scarf that even in the achromatic sunshine cast its colour up to her face and down around her moving feet in a lilac shadow. Her face was hard, almost stern, save for the soft gleam of piteous doubt that looked from her green eyes. Her once fair hair had darkened, but she was lovelier now at twenty-four than she had been at eighteen, when her hair was brighter than she.

Following a walk marked by an intangible mist of bloom that followed the white border stones, she came to a space overlooking the sea where there were lanterns asleep in the fig trees and a big table and wicker chairs and a great market umbrella from Siena, all gathered about an enormous pine, the biggest tree in the garden. She paused there a moment, looking absently at a growth of nasturtiums and iris tangled at its foot, as though sprung from a careless handful of seeds, listening to the plaints and accusations of some nursery squabble in the house. When this died away on the summer air, she walked on, between kaleidoscopic peonies massed in pink clouds, black and brown tulips and fragile mauve-stemmed roses, transparent like sugar flowers in a confectioner's window – until, as if the scherzo of colour could reach no further intensity, it broke off suddenly in mid-air, and moist steps went down to a level five feet below.

Here there was a well with the boarding around it dank and slippery even on the brightest days. She went up the stairs on the other side and into the vegetable garden; she walked rather quickly; she liked to be active, though at times she gave the impression of repose that was at once static and evocative. This was because she knew few words and believed in none, and in the world she was rather silent, contributing just her share of urbane humour with a precision that approached meagreness. But at the moment when strangers tended to grow uncomfortable in the presence of this economy she would seize the topic and rush off with it, feverishly surprised with herself – then bring it back and relinquish it abruptly, almost timidly, like an obedient retriever, having been adequate and something more.

As she stood in the fuzzy green light of the vegetable garden, Dick crossed the path ahead of her going to his work house. Nicole waited silently till he had passed; then she went on through lines of prospective salads to a little menagerie where pigeons and rabbits and a parrot made a medley of insolent noises at her. Descending to another ledge she reached a low, curved wall and looked down seven hundred feet to the Mediterranean Sea.

She stood in the ancient hill village of Tarmes. The villa and its grounds were made out of a row of peasant dwellings that abutted on the cliff – five small houses had been combined to make the house and four destroyed to make the garden. The exterior walls were untouched, so that from the road far below it was indistinguishable from the violet grey mass of the town.

For a moment Nicole stood looking down at the Mediterranean, but there was nothing to do with that, even with her tireless hands.

F. Scott Fitzgerald, *Tender is the Night*

Incarnate Devil

Incarnate devil in a talking snake,
The central plains of Asia in his garden,
In shaping-time the circle stung awake,
In shapes of sin forked out the bearded apple,
And God walked there who was a fiddling warden
And played down pardon from the heavens' hill.

When we were strangers to the guided seas,
A handmade moon half holy in a cloud,
The wise men tell me that the garden gods
Twined good and evil on an eastern tree;
And when the moon rose windily it was
Black as the beast and paler than the cross.

We in our Eden knew the secret guardian
In sacred waters that no frost could harden,
And in the mighty mornings of the earth;
Hell in a horn of sulphur and a cloven myth,
All heaven in a midnight of the sun,
A serpent fiddled in the shaping-time.

Dylan Thomas

The Perverseness of Plants

In these days of doubt we ought surely to be thankful for trees and flowers and all green and growing things. The great popularity enjoyed by gardening, and the increasing numbers who visit flower shows proves that in fact we are. Bacon's idea of the 'greater perfection' of gardening seems true. From the fact that God Almighty first planted a garden, he deduced that it was the purest of human pleasures; and from the fact that civilised man builds stately palaces before he ever gardens finely, he argued that gardening must be the most civilised of all the arts, and would necessarily be the last attained. We have now reached a stage in our civilisation sufficiently advanced to be able to garden finely; so perhaps the slump has done some good after all, guiding our attention towards simpler pleasures. One may be unconscious of any direct healing power possessed by gardens; but no one will deny the soothing effect of flowers on the spirit of man. They are symbols of peace and tranquillity. The perpetual miracle of growth, the yearly cycle of change, so gradual yet so profound and apparently final, the unfolding of bud to leaf and flower, involving adjustments so infinitely finer than anything man can compass, are a source of joy and wonder. The absolute assurance that it will be repeated next year, and the year after, and for ever, gives us a confidence which nothing else gives. We see the Buddhist cycle of rebirth going on under our eyes in the garden. Even in the tropics there is a rhythm. After the day's labour in the teeming city, there is no balm like the peace of an English garden in the scented summer twilight. Certainly it is more pleasant to be surrounded by beautiful colours harmoniously arranged, by quick and challenging shapes, than by sad grey lifeless earth and torpid forms and dead brick walls and smoking chimneys, by pots and dust and all the litter and tatter of a garish civilisation!

There is always hope for the man who loves flowers, and I for one will never believe that the bottom has fallen right out of England so long as there are gardens, and men to tend them faithfully. First the planning, then the making and planting, finally the blossoming. There are many ways of making a garden, or rather there are many styles of garden, formal and informal; and the elements of a garden, the plants themselves, are legion. Now these are the bare elements of a garden: form and colour, scent and sound, and the surprise of contrast; and it needs an elegant blending of all to make a perfect garden.

Anyone who seeks that 'peace which passeth all understanding' or, as the Buddhist calls it, Nirvana, might well turn to his garden to distract his mind from the daily anxieties of life. We all love flowers for the graciousness of form, no less than for their delicious colours, and sweet fragrance; and there is nothing which gives so great a return for the labour and money expended on it as a small garden. Thanks to quick transport from the scene of our daily labours, few of us are without some sort of garden, if we can afford to live only a few miles out in the country; even for those who are forced to live in the city, there are public parks where they can enjoy vicariously the gardener's craft. When the city man comes home, tired after his day's work, it is to his garden that he turns, not only for recreation but for comfort. Sitting outside after supper one warm June night he watches the shadows lengthening on the lawn as the sun drops slowly in the west; a great peace descends on him. We can picture the scene, as he sits there drinking in the richness of the earth, while the outlines of the trees melt into the lilac dusk. One by one the colours are eclipsed, first the reds, then the blues, last of all the yellows. But the scent of the rose lingers. A faint breeze stirs the leaves; and a bat wheels swiftly overhead, and is gone like a spirit. Now it is dark; and presently without warning the trees begin to cast shadows anew, faintly at first and on the far side of the lawn. A rich glow suffuses the east; the full moon has risen. Thus he sits, bathed in the golden radiance; and as he dozes his troubles slip from him like a garment, and he dreams of the flowers which have sprung up at the touch of his hands. There they stand in royal array, a tribute to his skill and patience; Roses, Irises, Larkspurs, Paeonies, Lupins, and many more, in tumultuous colours and shapes. He has watched over them in their infancy, tended them in sickness, gloried over them in their prime. He has made of them that worth while thing, a garden; and in blossoming time the garden has been as balm to his soul. So, even in these hard times, let us not neglect our gardens, but rather sacrifice much else, that we may enjoy the purest and most exquisite pleasure in life: the yield of mother earth in all its strange forms. Truly the cultivation of flowers is something more than a luxury; it is a religion.

But many of us live too near the city to be able to possess a real garden. We have only a small plot of mother earth; it is level as a billiard table, and there is no tumbling water to thrill the air; nor are there song birds at dawn and dusk, but rather the everlasting throb of the hurtling machine. A niggard nature has denied form, so it would seem; *our* world is void.

But the truth is, nature gave us the flat places of the earth to till the soil and cultivate plants, and we have abused the gift. In a mechanical age we have built our cities on the plains, which were given to us for our crops, and left the hills gutted and abandoned. How much more thrilling life would be if our cities were in the hills. What scope for the engineer, for the architect! A city set on a hill! The hanging gardens of Babylon would be elementary compared with what our bold designers might achieve! Of course, we have been utterly lured away by false gods – the rapid accumulation of pelf – things which you may touch or see. Wordsworth, standing on Westminster Bridge, was dazzled by the glitter of wealth like the rest of us. If he had seen Simla, which is the beginning of a new earth, if not of a new heaven, or Gyantse, or Tsela Dzong, he might have written a lyric rather than a sonnet. Form is lacking, by nature, and peace has been murdered by man, and we are left with the raw material to build again as best we may. Yet we need not despair, for we have the last elements of which a garden consists, without which form is but naked shape, coldly geometrical, and sound and colour and scent are never born at all; we have our flowers and shrubs – even trees, if we are fortunate. And for the rest, if we cannot have more – and all men do not desire a garden – there are our public parks and gardens and playing fields, well laid out, which minister to our needs, though we take no more than a communal interest in public parks over which we have no direct control. Now the more in contact with the city we are, the more we tend to cultivate foreign plants. I cannot say why, but so it is. If you live in the country, and have a large garden, you are certain to grow many English trees at least; but the nearer you come to the city, the more your plot of earth dwindles in size as it rises in price, the more dependent you are on foreign plants. Perhaps few of us realise how many of our commonest garden flowers *are* foreign. It is not until we ask ourselves seriously whether such and such a plant *is*, in sober fact, English (that is whether it grows wild in the woods or the hedgerows of England) that we come to the conclusion that it cannot be English. We may perhaps fall back upon the theory that it was born and bred here; but it is simpler to assume that it grows wild possibly in some part of Europe, say by the shores of the Mediterranean or in the Alps or the Balkans, or on Mount Olympus. It is true that in its wild state we might not recognise it: nurserymen have 'improved' our Wallflowers, Stocks, Pinks, Michaelmas

Daisies, Violas, Tulips, Delphiniums, Irises, and scores of other flowers, sometimes out of all knowledge. But their humbler forefathers at all events grow wild still, unimproved, and after a little practice we could easily recognize them for what they are. Near towns, where the atmosphere is full of gases which are no ingredients of pure air, the emanations from factories and engines, few plants can live, still fewer thrive. One need only examine the leaves of evergreen trees after a London winter fog to realise this. Every leaf is covered with a glutinous black film. This presently hardens into a crust which defies even the rain to wash it off. The trunks and branches of the trees are likewise blackened, and as this foul deposit gradually wears off, it goes into the soil and poisons the living roots. Small wonder that gardening in the neighbourhood of a big manufacturing town, or even near a big arterial road, is heartbreaking; the one smirching the clean air with smoke and acids, the other belching forth fumes of petrol and charred oil, and filling the air with the finest particles of dust. No wonder but few deciduous trees which shed their leaves at the beginning of the most perilous season can thrive in such polluted air.

Frank Kingdon Ward, The Romance of Gardening

Gardens of the Ashikaga Age

When the Ashikaga Shogunate was set up in 1338, the political centre of the country was restored again to Kyoto, the ancient city of beauteous hills. The Ashikaga period may be called the greatest age of our garden art, producing remarkably original works of exquisite artistic quality. This was the time when the Shogun and the rest of the military aristocracy vied with one another as enthusiastic and generous patrons of art, demanding high excellence in architecture, garden, painting, and other fine and decorative arts. Both the temple garden and the garden of the *samurai* mansion grew rapidly.

Zen Buddhism, which had been spreading fast since the previous period, reached the height of its ecclesiastical development during the Ashikaga period under the patronage and adherence of the military aristocracy, and completely swayed the mind and life of the ruling class. This tremendous religion of Nature and Self-Knowledge brought about an extremely subjective tendency in the Japanese people's attitude toward Nature and initiated them into the ultimate beauty of the plain, the simple, and the unassertive. The garden under the Zen influence became an expression of meditative thought on Nature, the Ultimate. Never in the other ages before or after were our garden art and landscape painting so intimately related both in spirit and form as during this period. They were the twin arts embodying the very essence of the Zen thought of the Ashikaga age. Sesshu, the greatest landscape painter of Japan (1420–1506) designed gardens; Soami (15th cent.), who was a kind of art adviser to Yoshimasa, the eighth Shogun of the Ashikaga family, versed in every branch of contemporary art, was a famous garden architect. Even today, looking at the fragmentary remains of these fifteenth-century gardens, we feel as if brought into the presence of one of the most forceful India-ink drawings of rugged mountains and trees handed down to us from this age.

The Ashikaga garden presents two distinct types. One is the continuous growth of the Lake-and-Island Style coming down through the past centuries and destined to develop further in later periods. In the Ashikaga period it retained many phases of the Heian and Kamakura Palace Style. One great departure, however, was, as the relics of this period show, the detachment of the garden from the house to form by itself an independent architectural whole, with a central, dominant garden architecture of its own. This necessarily brought about considerable changes in the ground-plan and in the composing techniques, for from the older plan of the one-faced construction to be looked at from the front of the house, now the garden had to be so built as to look perfect from various angles of view, for the observer here was to walk in the garden and sit in the central garden house looking all around. However, this sort of composite planning and setting was still in the experimental stage during this period, its full growth being attained only in the Yedo period.

We have several very notable specimens of the Ashikaga period garden of the Lake-and-Island Style still comparatively well preserved. We shall now briefly discuss their individual features.

First in the list comes the garden of the Kitayama Palace, built by Yoshimitsu, the third Shogun of the Ashikaga family, at the foot of Kinugasa Hill outside the city of Kyoto. The palace has long since been made into a temple and called Rokuon-ji, but because of the gorgeous pavilion-like building in the centre of its garden, it is popularly called the Kinkaku-ji (Temple of the Golden Pavilion). This so-called Golden Pavilion is a three-storeyed structure, of which the uppermost storey was originally covered with gold leaf rising conspicuously in such a way as to command the whole garden. It is the first instance of a three-storeyed building ornamenting a Japanese garden. We suspect that the idea was suggested by contemporary Chinese garden architecture, though its form and design are more in the traditional Japanese style, and also in the details we see strong influences of Zen temple architecture. It was certainly a noteworthy innovation in our garden setting, and the building with its stately elegance is regarded as a very fine work of the kind.

This edifice stands by a lake of considerable size, which, when compared with the lake of the Silver Pavilion – to be discussed later – is much more open and sunny, retaining the spacious air of the Heian Palace Style. In the lake are several islets, some of which have the form of the turtle. This formalism comes from the old tradition of the Holy Isle of the Eastern Sea, which is said to have the shape of a turtle and to be covered with pine trees, both the turtle and the pine tree being symbols of longevity. However, these symbolical meanings are of no significance at all in the design of this garden. The pavilion, the lake, the islets, and the masterly planting are entirely free from such traditional symbolism and make up a perfect landscape picture, so warranting its recognition as an artistic composition of a high order.

As for the details of the garden, we do not find many that show the original work, since the long lapse of time has worn away the ornamented surface of the composition. Only in the rockwork do we discover a few valuable pieces of original construction, and from them we can get some idea of the technique of the time, which seems to have been of bold simplicity quite unlike the high elaboration of the later periods. Another feature is that upright rocks were in more abundant use than horizontal ones, the characteristic which prevailed in the rock art through the Kamakura to the Ashikaga period (13th–16th cent.).

Almost a twin to the Temple of the Golden Pavilion in our historical associations as well as in the study of our garden art is the Jisho-ji or so-called Ginkaku-ji (Temple of the Silver Pavilion).

Here, too, we have an example of central garden architecture, in the form of a building of two storeys, the upper one of which was originally planned to be overlaid with silver, though the plan was not realised. Besides this piece of architecture, there is facing the garden another and larger building, intended for residence and known as the Togu-do. This was selected as a place where the dilettante Shogun Yoshimasa could pass his days, enjoying to his heart's content the beautiful, costly garden, and drinking tea in the tea-ceremony room built in the house. This room of his is the oldest specimen of all tea-ceremony rooms, being a four and a half mat room (nine feet square).

This garden appears to have been planted with these two pieces of architecture to be the viewing points. It can of course be enjoyed while rambling through it, but its composition was clearly based on the two central features, the pavilion and the Togu-do. The garden is smaller in area than that of the Golden Pavilion, but quite apart from its actual size it gives an effect of seclusion and delicacy, thereby well expressing the characteristic taste of the period.

The garden has a lake somewhat complicated in form with two turtle-formed islets in it. The rich rockwork around the lake and the islets retain much of the original construction, showing the very elaborate and stiff rock art of this age. When compared with that of later periods it has a much more formal and decorative effect, corresponding, one might say, to what was called *shin* in the later classification of styles of rock arrangement. That was when many conventions grew up around garden art, and in the elaboration of details the three degrees of *shin* (formal), *gyo* (semi-formal) and *so* (informal) were distinguished. This garden, like many others, has come through vicissitudes of fortune, suffering much alteration. Some of the buildings in the garden were destroyed by fire, and only traces of these can be seen today.

Let us now discuss the other of the two types originated in the Ashikaga period, that is, the Flat Garden.

The most famous of the kind is the Stone Garden of the Ryoan-ji. This temple was formerly the villa of Hosokawa Katsumoto (1430–1473), and its wonderful flat garden which is found in the *hojo* (superior's quarters) was designed probably by Soami, the artist of the Garden of the Silver Pavilion. In type it shows direct descent from the Hojo Court of the Kamakura period, which was what had developed out of the Senzai

Court of the Heian palace architecture. It is a little enclosed garden tucked away in the recess of a building, resembling in nature the castle court or the cloister court of medieval Europe. In Japan even such a little space was made into a natural landscape, though not conformed at all in theme as in the case of the Lake-and-Island style; and this Ryoan-ji garden is especially noted for its originality of design and perfect beauty of composition.

The entire garden ground is covered with white sand, and not a tree, not a bush, is seen on it. On the sand, fifteen stones, choice in every respect, are set in groups of five, two, three, two and three. The space is enclosed with a low plaster wall, which bounds the sandy garden from the richly wooded land outside. In olden times, so the records tell us, through the tree branches beyond the garden wall were seen Otoko-yama Hill and the long winding bed of the River Yodo, although at present the vista is almost closed by the overgrowth of the woods. This is all that there is in the composition of this garden. There is no lake, nor stream, the ground being perfectly level, from which characteristic came the type name 'Flat Garden'.

The Flat Garden is certainly a wonderful achievement of this age. Its principle is to create, on a narrow flat piece of ground, with some rock-work and planting, any kind of natural scenery the heart can wish. No one now knows for certain what sort of scenery these fifteen stones make up; but whatever the motif there can be no doubt as to the beauty of its spatial composition, formed by sand-covered level ground, divided by a low wall from the green traceries of tree boughs beyond, and with its various stones exquisitely spaced on the enclosed whiteness of sand. Here one sees the most artistic attitude man can attain toward stones, the subtlest of Nature's beauties, into which the artists of this age threw their heart and soul, revelling in the joy of stone spacing, just as some artists in later years came to discover the art of flower spacing, which we now call flower arrangement. Here is indeed the greatest work of Ashikaga rock art and maybe of all Japanese landscape art, without seeing which, no one has the right to discuss the Japanese garden.

Tsuyoshi Tamura, *Art of the Landscape Garden in Japan*

Grasping the Nettle

Of these two species (Great Nettle, *Urtica dioica*; Small Nettle, *Urtica urens*) the first only is a serious nuisance. The second is an annual and it must be included among the annual weeds which require different treatment.

No other weed is allowed to infest hedges, shrubberies, and even our gardens and meadows with such impunity as the nettle. What with its unpleasant mode of defence above ground and its strong yellow spreading roots below, many who dislike it exceedingly are afraid of it, and find it a hopeless task to dig it up with all its roots. Indeed in a shrubbery this is impossible. And so it is a common sight to see hedges fringed with a yard or more of compactly growing nettles, reaching to a height of five or six feet, or great banks in the middle of grass fields where one annual mowing is the only attack on them. And yet there is no real difficulty in getting rid of them altogether. The treatment must differ according to their environment and mode of growth.

It is commonly said, and it may be true, that with nettles in a field, if you cut them three times a year for three years they will be finished. I have wondered whether this is a fairy tale. The three threes make it sound like a magic or a nostrum and fairly safe to advise as so few people would ever see it through. It sounds like bathing in the Jordan three times. However, knowing of this and employing my wits I exterminated nettles which pervaded a shrubbery in a single year. When I took possession of my present house I determined to leave the borders alone the first year to see what there might be in them. In a shrubbery close to the house the ground became covered with tall and prosperous stinging nettles, so the next year I started my experiment which was suggested by the three three story above. At the end of February or the beginning of March I went all over the shrubbery looking for the first nettle shoots to appear. When these were two of three inches high I got them low down between my finger and thumb and just pulled them off. I found gloves such a nuisance that I used my bare hand and the stings from the tender nettles left only a rather pleasant tingling sensation. Every week without fail I went all over the ground pulling off the tender growth. This required some patience because they seemed to come as strong and as often every week. However by July a marked falling off became apparent and then, in August, when I tried to pull off the weakly growth, I pulled out in places a long wire which was all that was left of what had been a thick yellow root. It had shrunk to a thread in providing the material for so many young shoots, and it no longer filled the hole in the ground intersecting the roots of trees, and it just pulled out. After this the young nettle shoots became scarcer and scarcer and the battle was won. The next year a few seedlings only had to be pulled out and for all the years since I have not seen a nettle in this shrubbery. I have given this experience in very full detail because though there is a far quicker and easier way to destroy nettles by poison, this may be undesirable where nettles have established themselves in the roots of valuable fruit trees or shrubs, and it is not easy to confine the poison to the nettles. The principle is the same as that on which the three cuttings a year for three years depends, but it is far more drastically carried out. Obviously it is only practicable on a few precious spots. Some might prefer a hoe to their fingers but this would not pull out the long wires.

Sir Charles V. Boys, *Weeds, Weeds, Weeds*

Bloody Rhododendrons

The gates had shut to with a crash behind us, the dusty high-road was out of sight, and I became aware that this was not the drive I had imagined would be Manderley's, this was not a broad and spacious thing of gravel, flanked with neat turf at either side, kept smooth with rake and brush.

This drive twisted and turned as a serpent, scarce wider in places than a path, and above our heads was a great colonnade of trees, whose branches nodded and intermingled with one another, making an archway for us, like the roof of a church. Even the midday sun would not penetrate the interlacing of those green leaves, they were too thickly entwined, one with another, and only little flickering patches of warm light would come in intermittent waves to dapple the drive with gold. It was very silent, very still. On the high-road there had been a gay west wind blowing in my face, making the grass on the hedges dance in unison, but here there was no wind. Even the engine of the car had taken a new note, throbbing low, quieter than before. As the drive descended to the valley so the trees came in upon us, great beeches with lovely smooth white stems, lifting their myriad branches to one another, and other trees, trees I could not name, coming close, so close that I could touch them with my hands. On we went, over a little bridge that spanned a narrow stream, and still this drive that was no drive twisted and turned like an enchanted ribbon through the dark and silent woods, penetrating even deeper to the very heart surely of the forest itself, and still there was no clearing, no space to hold a house.

The length of it began to nag at my nerves, it must be this turn, I thought, or round that further bend, but as I leant forward in my seat I was forever disappointed, there was no house, no field, no broad and friendly garden, nothing but the silence and the deep woods. The lodge gates were a memory, and the high-road something belonging to another time, another world.

Suddenly I saw a clearing in the dark drive ahead, and a patch of sky, and in a moment the dark trees had thinned, the nameless shrubs had disappeared, and on either side of us was a wall of colour, blood-red, reaching far above our heads. We were amongst the rhododendrons. There was something bewildering, even shocking, about the suddenness of their discovery. The woods had not prepared me for them. They startled me with their crimson faces, massed one upon the other in incredible profusion, showing no leaf, no twig, nothing but the slaughterous red, luscious and fantastic, unlike any rhododendron plant I had seen before.

I glanced at Maxim. He was smiling. 'Like them?' he said.

I told him 'Yes', a little breathlessly, uncertain whether I was speaking the truth or not, for to me a rhododendron was a homely, domestic thing, strictly conventional, mauve or pink in colour, standing one beside the other in a neat round bed. And these were monsters, rearing to the sky, massed like a battalion, too beautiful I thought, too powerful, they were not plants at all.

Daphne du Maurier, *Rebecca*

The Long Garden

It was the garden of the golden apples,
A long garden between a railway and a road,
In the sow's rooting where the hen scratches
We dipped our fingers in the pockets of God.

In the thistly hedge old boots were flying sandals
By which we travelled through the childhood skies,
Old buckets rusty-holed with half-hung handles
Were drums to play when old men married wives.

The pole that lifted the clothes-line in the middle
Was the flag-pole on a prince's palace when
We looked at it through fingers crossed to riddle
In evening sunlight miracles for men.

It was the garden of golden apples,
And when the Carrick train went by we knew
That we could never die till something happened
Like wishing for a fruit that never grew,

Or wanting to be up on Candle-Fort
Above the village with its shops and mill.
The racing cyclists' gasp-gapped reports
Hinted of pubs where life can drink his fill.

And when the sun went down into Drumcatton
And the New Moon by its little finger swung
From the telegraph wires, we knew how God had happened
And what the blackbird in the whitethorn sang.

It was the garden of the golden apples,
The half-way house where we had stopped a day
Before we took the west road to Drumcatton
Where the sun was always setting on the play.

Patrick Kavanagh

The Dead Months

It is very easy to become sentimental over things that flower in winter. 'Ah, yes,' people say, 'snowdrops – so brave of them, the dear things.' Botanists rather tend to regard plants which flower in the winter as escapists – I beg your pardon for this last and worst outrage of the psychologists – which, unable to face the competition of other things with more normal habits, have taken refuge in a time of the year when their conquerors are still decently tucked up in their winter sleep. Some of them, in fact, go so far back that they get into the summer before, like the *Colchicums* and the autumn crocus. Here, in parenthesis, it must be remarked that *Colchicum* and autumn crocus are always being confused by bad gardeners and, worse, by bad nurserymen. *Crocus* has three stamens and narrow, grassy leaves, and there is not a bad member in the whole genus: *Colchicum* has six stamens, leathery leaves which smother everything within feet of them in the summer, is extremely poisonous, and is no plant for a small garden. Many of the species and hybrids are of dubious shades: and the only variety of real charm, a white seedling, has been lost to cultivation. I admit that I am prejudiced: but then I have lived where *Colchicum* is a poisonous weed. And, anyhow, I hold that people who write about plants should do their best to hoe out undesirables: our gardens and our catalogues are packed with species and varieties which should long since have been placed in an *Index Exparadisius*.

But plants have a sentimental value, as well as botanical interest: and the function of winter-flowering things in a garden is to cheer up the gardener with a reminder that spring cannot be far away. I can remember being considerably heartened by the sight of a *Mezereum* in the garden of a ruined cottage, near Laventie, and if anyone on a bleak January day suggests, 'Let's go down to the end of the garden and see if the *Thingumia* is in flower yet,' I will tear myself from the fire and go. *Thingumia* once turned out to be *Garrya elliptica*, which I detest. More usually it is three small ragged robins of yellow on a bush of witch-hazel, six feet across.

In this last remark lies a neglected truth. Winter-flowering plants and shrubs, with few exceptions, are not showy, or free-flowering, or uniform in their flowering date: they do not lend themselves to decorative display. It would be a waste of good space to devote any part of the garden entirely to them, even if you overlapped into spring and autumn. *Iris stylosa*, for instance, in two of the three forms which are commonly grown, is a lovely thing. It will grow and flower happily where a gravel path joins a wall, a test which it shares with Virginia creeper and Virginia stock – with *Hamamelis virginica* as well, one of the second-best witch-hazels. But you cannot make a decorative effect out of *Iris stylosa* any more than you can rely on its flowering at Christmas. It will go on producing buds for your vases out of its tangles of rusty herbage whenever the winter sun warms it, though it may not start doing it till March: and perhaps one afternoon in spring there will be such a show of bloom that you will forget that you must bear with its general untidiness for nine months before you see another bloom.

Plant winter jasmine where you can see it without going outdoors: it is always rather ragged and untidy at close quarters, but quite indispensable. It is worth a place on the south wall, but will give a show facing any point of the heavens if you prune it and tend it every year. All these winter-flowering shrubs should be pruned with at least as much care as you devote to your roses, and manured even more liberally with potash, phosphate, and mulch. Shrubs on walls must be kept hard back to the wall, and not allowed to grow out into bushes of old stems. It is not entirely a matter of the conservation of heat by the wall, but rather the keeping of the tender tissues out of the draught. Even in a gale the air an inch from the wall is scarcely moving, and growth is thus protected from the drying winds of early spring, which do so much more damage than the frost.

Winter-sweet, *Chimonanthus fragrans*, dowdiest of flowers, is just worth a place, so sweet of scent, so niggardly of bloom. The so-called large-flowered form is not worth having, and almost scentless. Is it worth no man's while to raise a few hundred seedlings in the hope of a better and more kindly variety? But of all the winter-flowering shrubs there is none to compare with the winter cherry (not to be confused with the winter cherry pie, winter heliotrope, most abominable and vulgar of the weeds still sold by unscrupulous nurserymen to novices). *Jugatsu Sakura*, the October cherry of Japan, is the most companionable of small

trees, always in flower in the winter months, with an apparently inex-
haustible supply of new buds continuing their succession of little pink,
rather fringed and campanulate flowers on the bare stems – an indispensable in any garden, large or small, and the best of the Higan or *sub-
hirtella* cherries. All the *Mezereums*, of course, you must have, and
Hamamelis mollis, if your conditions suit it, and the Glastonbury thorn,
less pious than its legend, and the double sloe, and *Pyrus japonica cardi-
nalis*, which gives a show all winter on a south wall.

So much for trees. At ground-level *Crocus*, naturally: starting with the
many forms of *speciosus* and ending with Cloth of Gold, there can never
be too many of these species and seedlings. You can get a collection for a
small sum from one of the great English bulb firms, and nurse the rarities in pans and a cold frame till you have a stock to play with. It is rather
interesting to compare the different species in their reaction to light and
temperature, for if you bring a pan of spring crocus in bud into a warm
room they open forthwith: but many of the autumn species need the
concentrated light of a reading-lamp as well. But, apart from rarities, you
need blocks and tufts of the cheaper species wherever they can be
squeezed in: *Sieberi* in the rose-beds, *Tommasinianus* in the grass, *sativus*
in the herb-patch. If you are lucky you will wake up to find seedling crocuses everywhere, even in your gravel paths. Snowdrops have not quite
the charm of crocuses, or so many species cheaply obtainable: but half a
dozen sorts, from the big *Elwesii* to the dainty charm of *viridiapice*,
ought to be in every garden – and an autumn variety if you like.

Winter irises, beyond *stylosa*, are not everybody's game – with lots of
glass and an alpine house perhaps! But now that *reticulata* is so cheap, it
is worth a few shillings a year to grow it in seed-pans and boxes for the
house – earth, of course, not 'fibre' – and to plant out as a kitchen garden
edging the moment it flags, to flower again two years later. There may be
some way of growing Christmas roses white and unmuddied without the
help of glass *cloches* or frames. I have yet to find it.

Looking back, I see that I have forgotten the best of all the winter flowers after the jasmine. Amid such a host of introductions from the east
and from the west, English cottage gardens continue to grow a
Mediterranean evergreen which, for all I know, may have come in with
the Romans. This is *Viburnum Tinus*, the Laurustinus so much despised

by the *cognoscenti*. It may be bettered by the new Chinese introductions in the same genus – notably Farrer's *Viburnum fragrans*; but its behaviour after the drought years of 1933–34 should make any country-man hesitate before he condemns it as a Victorian evergreen. I have forgotten, too, the most steadfast of all winter flowers, *Lithospermum rosmarinifolium*, which I grow wedged in among tussocks of Iris stylosa under the thatch of my workroom, between the outward-sloping slabs that take the drip and the wall, a narrow strip of rubbly soil that never gets frostbound. The flowers are touched by every frost, but with unconquerable courage fresh trumpets of gentian-blue press out to mock the grey skies. It is the only constant flower I know for the dead season: it is apparently indifferent to limestone, and its only fault is that there is not enough of it, for it is 'a low and base bush', only a foot or eighteen inches high: and that, when one is wearing an overcoat and feeling rheumatic, is a long way down.

And the moral? Let your winter flowers point it. Take heart; winter is soon over, and the older you live the sooner spring comes.

> Non simper imbres nubibus hispidos
> Manant in agros . . .

The rain it rains not every day. If there is nothing in flower in the garden, and you do not possess *Lithospermum rosmarinifolium*, turn to Horace for advice once again:

> Dissolve frigus ligna super foro
> Large reponens: atque benignius
> Deprome quadrimum Sabina . . .

And when you are comfortable reach for the catalogues.

Humphrey John, *The Skeptical Gardener*

I Will Leave Your White House

I will leave your white house and tranquil garden.
Let life be empty and bright.
You, and only you, I shall glorify in my poems,
As a woman has never been able to do.
And you remember the beloved
For whose eyes you created this paradise,
But I deal in rare commodities –
I sell your love and tenderness.

Anna Akhmatova

Luxuries

In these critical times the wise gardener is thinking of the winter supplies, and concentrating his energies on getting plenty of the utility vegetables. Potatoes, carrots, onions, parsnips, swedes, artichokes, and
winter greens are of the first importance. But it doesn't follow that we
should deny ourselves everything in the nature of a luxury, especially as
some of the so-called luxury vegetables can be produced without inter-
fering with the general Dig for Victory plans.

Variety is good for us, and the vegetable diet can become a little
monotonous without the addition of an occasional novelty, just by way
of a change, and to add interest to the proceedings. Apparently a good
many of my listeners have been thinking along these lines, for I have had
quite a lot of letters lately about such things as mushrooms, melons, and
pumpkins: to say nothing of asparagus, peaches, and strawberries.

Now I am not going to advocate the growing of any of these in war-
time if it means neglecting the essential subjects; but where they can be
conveniently fitted into the scheme of things, to add variety, and make
life a little more worth living, I'm all for them, in moderation, of course.
Take mushrooms, for example. Many a savoury dish can be lifted from
the mediocre to the sublime by the addition of a mushroom or two; but
we can't all afford to pay seven shillings a pound for them, so why not

grow a few, or at least have a shot at it? There is no need to construct elaborate pits or sheds, or buy loads of expensive stable manure, unless you are making a serious business of it. You can have a little flutter on almost any grass patch, or even among the bushes in an odd corner, provided you regard it as a gamble and don't cry if nothing happens. You won't have lost much anyway. I grew a couple of dozen beauties under a group of shrubs, and a still better crop in a celery trench, where they appeared of their own accord. I had been trying to grow some in a dark shed in the orthodox way, where I made a bed with a couple of loads of nicely turned and seasoned stable manure, following all the rules to the letter, but nothing happened; not a smell of a mushroom did I get. The bed gradually got stale and sour and cold, and, in due course, I gave it up as a bad job, and used the manure for the celery, and then the mushrooms came up, hundreds of them, all over the sides of the trench. Mushrooms are like that – rather temperamental. They grow if they think they will, but they won't be dictated to. Now let us assume that you still have a bit of lawn or a grass patch, or a paddock of grass field. All you require is a barrow-load or a few buckets of fresh horse-droppings. If you are in the country you can usually manage that, if you watch your opportunities; in the town it is not so easy (sorry to talk about such things in the middle of the rhubarb and custard, but there's no getting away from it in a garden). You also require a carton of mushroom spawn, which you can get from any good seedsman. Get the sterilised spawn, if you can; it is much better, but if there is none available, get a brick of the ordinary spawn.

Now cut out a piece of turf, about nine inches square, and put on one side. Scoop out the soil underneath it with a trowel to make a hole six inches deep or rather more; fill this with horse manure, and make it fairly firm, then into the middle of this press a piece of mushroom spawn about the size of a walnut, and, finally, replace the turf and tread on it. You can make these holes a couple of feet apart all over the grass. Or if you do it in odd corners among the bushes where there is no turf, you merely cover it with a good inch of soil. Do this any time during the next month and then forget all about it. Perhaps nothing will happen, but, on the other hand, given favourable weather, by the end of August or early September, you may find mushrooms bobbing up all over the place, and then, of course, you will have to stop mowing the grass or using the hoe. You can also grow mushrooms in a cold frame, after you have finished raising seedlings in it. Only for this purpose you should move it into the shade, at the north side of the building, or somewhere like that, away from the hot sun. If it is a shallow frame, you will have to dig the soil out from under it for a foot or so to give sufficient depth. Get a load of fairly fresh stable manure which hasn't been out in the rain; it doesn't matter if there is a fair amount of straw with it, and if you've got a heap of dead leaves, mix them with it, about a third of the leaves to two-thirds stable manure. Turn and mix it two or three times to let it ferment, and then put it in the frame and tread it down firmly till it is about a foot deep. It will be hot and steamy, so you must leave it till it begins to cool down; when it is just comfortably warm (between 70 and 80 degrees, if you test it with a thermometer), you press bits of mushroom spawn into it, nine inches apart. Then you put the lights on, but keep them wedged up at the back with a bit of wood, so that they are open about half an inch to let the hot air out, and cover them completely with old sacks or straw or bracken to keep them dark and even in temperature. Have a look in about ten days; and as soon as you see little white threads of mycelium appearing, cover the bed with an inch of soil, and shut the frames up as before. If the bed is in good condition to start with, water shouldn't be necessary, and it is better if you can manage without, but if the soil gets dry, water it lightly with a rose-can in the morning, and leave enough ventilation to allow the moisture to evaporate. Be patient, and don't keep opening it every day to have a look. You won't get mushrooms for a month or two, and if they don't turn up trumps you won't have lost much; the manure will still be good for the garden.

Another way of using the frame in the summer is to grow melons in it. There are certain varieties of melons which grow quite well in a cold frame. Hero of Lockinge is a good one, as good as those grown in hot houses, and most well-known seedsmen offer one or two good varieties suitable for the frame, in addition to the Cantaloupe varieties.

Here again a barrow-load of stable manure is an asset, because it provides warmth to give the plants a good start. It should be put in the bottom of the frame, pressed down, and covered with six inches of soil. Three or four seeds can be sown now in a group in the middle of the frame, but if you can get young plants brought on in pots ready for planting, so much the better. You must keep the lights on, but give a chink of ventilation whenever the weather allows it, and shade from the strong mid-day sun by putting an old lace curtain or something similar over the glass. As the plants grow, train a shoot towards each corner of the frame, and when they have nearly reached it, pinch out the growing point to induce branching. During hot weather the plants must be syringed well every morning, and they must be kept watered as required. Give ventilation during the day, and close the lights in the evening. When the flowers appear, they must be hand-pollinated. The simplest way to do this is to pick off a male flower, that is one with a thin stalk, tear off or roll back the petals, and dust the pollen into the centre of the female flowers, which are the ones with the tiny melon already showing below the flower, and quite easy to distinguish; they are very much like marrow flowers, only smaller. Unless this pollinating is done, there won't be any melons, so don't forget it. And when the melons begin to form, put something under them to cock them up away from the soil.

That brings us to pumpkins, but I'm not sure that pumpkins can be classed with the luxury vegetables. A good pumpkin is worth having, if you save it for the winter. You can make pumpkin pie with it, or mix it with other fruits and vegetables; it makes them go further, and absorbs the flavours, either sweet or savoury. Pumpkins are grown in the same way as marrows. You can sow the seeds out of doors now, two or three seeds in a group, and put a glass cloche over them, or a box with a pane of glass over it does quite well to protect the young plants during their infancy. When the fruits appear, put a board or a heap of brushwood under them to prevent slugs spoiling them. Give them plenty of water, and something a little stronger if necessary, and you should have no difficulty in getting a few good pumpkins.

Nearly everyone likes to grow a few marrows, and it seems to be generally understood that the only place to grow vegetable marrows is on a muck heap. The marrow is certainly a very useful plant for covering up an unsightly heap, but it will grow just as well on the flat ground, provided there is some good soil for it to grow in, for marrows have a lot to do in a short time and they need plenty of nourishment. Last year I suggested covering the Anderson air-raid shelters with marrow plants. Most of these are covered with soil, and resemble a mound of earth which needs keeping out of sight. But I was surprised to find that a large number of people, in following this advice, planted the marrows on top of the shelter, where the soil was shallow, and dried out during the summer. They should, of course, be planted at the base of the mound, say a couple of plants each side in pockets of prepared soil, if necessary, with some good manure mixed with it. Then they won't get so dry, and the shoots can be trained over the shelter as they grow. I always think marrows are better if the shoots are trained over something, even if you have to build some sort of rough framework for them. It allows air to circulate round the fruits, and keeps them off the ground and away from slugs and other troubles. When there is nothing to train them over, and where space is limited, the bush varieties are more suitable; these make a compact plant which does not spread about, and can, therefore, be planted at the corners of the plot, or where there wouldn't be room for the wandering kinds.

C. H. Middleton, *Dig for Victory*

On my bookshelves at home Ariel and Wolfwatching sit cheek by jowl. I don't know if that would please Sylvia and Ted, but it pleases me. I have had similar pleasure re-uniting horticultural pairings and sparring over the course of this book: Robinson and Blomfield; Lutyens and Jekyll; Plath and Hughes; Gilpin and Gilpin; Repton and Price; Price and Payne Knight; Larkin and his lawnmower; Nicolson and Sackville-West. I mention this because gardens, like man, are not islands. On a practical level, gardens are often collaborative, working partners differentiating according to their skills. Sissinghurst is a successful example of this kind of partnership, although poor Harold's contribution is often neglected. The thought behind a garden can be refined through correspondence or argument. And a garden grows the gardener, who learns through success and failure, who learns just by observation through time, by acquiring experience directly and vicariously, by having patience. Like other human activities, gardens are a part of a tradition.

So, this is a useful point, before the end, at which to allow the writers of the modern period to review what has been learned through the centuries about these gardens that seem to be so essential to our humanity. Much of the writing I have chosen takes values which have been assumed and makes them explicit. Sylvia Crowe explains why statues might be desired in a garden and how they work; Russell Page provides a case study for the use of water. Christopher Lloyd considers light, and Mary Keen, the colour blue.

The tradition has not ceased, however, and continues to grow. With this in mind, there is writing to reflect changes in fashion over the period.

Graham Stuart Thomas eulogises heathers, although few would do so now. There has been a renewed interest in Robinsonian wild gardening and Penelope Hobhouse gives a succinct account of modern thinking. That greater radical, Francis Bacon, imagined his wilderness to include molehills just as a natural heath would, and finds an unlikely disciple in the state of Arizona.

Our gardens are still used by animals, whether invited or not, and still provide a fellowship of interest between their humans. I warmed to Eric Parker's enlightened attitude to poisons and gin traps, and his reasonable approach to pest control, distinguishing between the level of seriousness of damage and likelihood of damage, and acting accordingly.

I enjoyed too, letting the dreamers dream. The dreams for a private space such as Vita Sackville-West's green, white, and silver garden, a garden which came to be, or the more academic speculations of Geoffrey Grigson with his toxicological garden, although that too has had a legacy at Alnwick. Edward Hyams's concerns are global, positive, and no closer to coming about than when he wrote them down. Jellicoe's response to Israel's dream – just fascinating.

29 December 1946

In the afternoon I moon about with Vita trying to convince her that planning is an element in gardening. She wishes just to jab in the things which she has left over. The tragedy of the romantic temperament is that it dislikes form so much that it ignores the effect of colour. She wants to put in stuff which 'will give a lovely red colour in the autumn'. I wish to put in stuff which will furnish shape to the perspective. In the end we part, not as friends.

Harold Nicolson

Garden Nuisances

I have written elsewhere of my garden in Surrey; here, of the garden itself, it is enough to say that it forms the chief part of a plot of some twelve acres of what was originally Surrey woodland, and that it lies surrounded by Surrey woodland to-day. It was made by grubbing a large open space in larch woods and hazel coppice, and of the space so opened, part to-day is occupied by lawns, flower borders, orchards, a heather garden, and a rock garden.

And occupied, also, from time to time, and for periods of time varying in length, by various wild creatures; by the descendants of those that lived in and used the woodland out of which the garden was made. They still regard the place, doubtless, as their forerunners regarded it, as affording opportunities for obtaining food and for multiplying their own species; as their own property, in short, though perhaps containing surprising features. It is entirely surrounded by wire netting, except for the gate of the drive (we used to speak of a carriage drive, and do so now; why never of a car drive?), and through the gate, which it is impossible to keep shut by night, animals come into the garden. Hares lope up the drive and make nests for leverets in the herbaceous border; rabbits come the same way to dine on crocuses and carnations. Foxes leap the wire netting; badgers climb five-barred gates. As for moles, mice, rats, and hedgehogs, they have never left the place, and never will; there are grass snakes in the garden, and I have seen an adder or two; and if there are any newcomers, which we should not have been likely to see thirty or forty years ago, I can only think of cabbage butterflies, which in days past would not visit a wood where there were no cabbages.

But I am writing here of garden nuisances, and not all the creatures that visit the garden are nuisances. Badgers, I know, have dug in the lawns of my neighbours, three or four miles away, but badgers have never done me any harm, though I have found hairs from badgers' coats sticking to the bars of the garden gates. Hedgehogs are harmless, and so are snakes, which I like to see swimming in pools in the rock garden. But hares, rabbits, moles, rats, mice? And slugs and cockchafers and ants and cabbage butterflies? How shall I rate them, in what order of iniquity?

Perhaps I dislike rats most, but there are few of them, and they seldom damage flowers, though if a bird-table with food happens to be near to terrace beds, they will come for any food left over from the day, and perhaps scratch into the weeping-holes of terrace walls. Then they have to be dealt with by means of dogs, which means a mercifully quick end, or by wire traps – never steel gins. But rats I merely dislike; they are not a real or a regular nuisance. Mice, on the other hand – but I find it difficult to write dispassionately of mice. Mice climb tulip stems, bite off the flower heads and make caches of them under bushes. Mice tunnel among saxifrages and phloxes, and eat where they tunnel. It is difficult to set break-back traps for mice without the risk of catching birds. And mice are prolific. She-mice breed at the age of five months, carry their young for three weeks, and then breed again, giving birth to nine or ten; so that if a single pair of mice are left alone through a year – but fortunately gardeners do manage to deal with mice, using water-cans, birch-brooms, and other engines. But mice persist.

Next to mice, moles. There is a mole-run in my garden of which I do not know the length. It must be several hundred yards, for it runs almost round three sides of the garden, and travels out in ramifications into the orchard, but there is a place where I lose it near a wood, and there must be access to it from a further run, for fresh moles are continually arriving. If there is one part of the garden where moles are intolerable, it is the rock garden. Mole-hills are unsightly on the fringe of the lawn, or in the orchard, but they do no lasting harm to the grass. In the rock garden they do incalculable harm, for they tunnel under and through the roots of plants, and you cannot find the direction of the tunnel except by digging up the garden. I have heard of moles being smoked out by specially made 'candles' of damped powder of some sort, and I have read of worms treated with arsenic being placed in their runs, but I could not use poison, even for a rat, much less a mole, and I prefer to let others skilled in the setting of traps deal with moles in that way.

And hares, and rabbits? A hare that confides her leverets to the garden I can only regard as a guest though I like her to leave early, and try to persuade her to do so by picking up the leverets and looking at them. Then, when I have shown them to as many people as possible as the loveliest little creatures in the world, I put them down on the ground again, and the hare comes back when I am gone and takes them away into the wood.

There is no such simple way, unfortunately, of dealing with rabbits. The thing to do with rabbits is to find them and shoot them, or have them shot; perhaps to snare them if you can find the 'jumps', or the track by which they travel over grass; but even under the provocation of vanished carnations, I do not set, or allow to be set, the steel gin. There is no greater nuisance in a garden than a rabbit, and in a garden of any size, with herbaceous borders, shrubs, heather, and perhaps an orchard as a neighbour, there is no animal more difficult to find; but even so, he shall be spared the gin.

Lesser foes than hares and rabbits thrust themselves on the gardener's attention. Slugs, for example; and for slugs there are traps advertised, such as the Cambridge slug and snail trap, which costs a shilling, and there are various chemical destroyers, killers, and insecticides so named, sold by the tin, the pound, or the hundredweight. Personally I have been lucky with – or rather without – slugs, which do not trouble me overmuch; but a simple and cheap trap, in any case, is the skin of half an orange.

There are certain insects which seem to vary from year to year, sometimes to an extent difficult to understand, in numbers. I have known years in which the very beautiful but very tiresome bronze-green rose beetles have swarmed in the garden and eaten my dog-roses to tatters, and even flown and crawled in hundreds over the lawn; and then, for years together, not a beetle is to be seen. Cockchafers, again, in some seasons multiply enormously, and produce odd effects in garden paths with the large holes from which they emerge after their many months of underground existence. The worst experience I have had with cockchafers was a year in which the grubs ate the roots of the plants of a strawberry-bed; and the trouble there was that the grubs were not suspected till the mischief was done. I knew a gardener who once had a spaniel which could scent cockchafer grubs and dig them up – a useful companion. But the gardener did not name the grubs as those of cockchafers; he spoke of them, as they are always spoken of by gardeners in the countryside I know best, as 'Joe Bassetts'. How they got that name I have never been able to discover.

Ants I consider a nuisance, especially the Small Black Ant, or Garden Ant – it is really very dark brown instead of black – which makes nests under and among the bargate paving-stones of my terrace walks, hollows out the sand and pushes it up where it should not be, between the stones and among the roots and stalks of terrace plants. I have tried to get rid of these ants with cyanide of potassium, but I have come to the conclusion that boiling water is instantaneous and better.

And butterflies? Cabbage Whites, I am afraid, for all the grace of their flight, must be counted as among the chief enemies of the kitchen garden. Hand-picking of the caterpillars is one of the remedies; the butterfly net is another. But other butterflies – other than the Large and Small Garden Whites, the Cabbage Whites, which do feed on cabbage – would it be believed that any gardener could regard them as enemies? Could any gardener worthy of the name wish to destroy at sight Peacocks, Tortoiseshells, Painted Ladies, Brimstones, Commas, Red Admirals, the caterpillars of which feed in most cases on nettles, but in no case on garden plants? Recently a well-known writer on gardening subjects, in an article printed in the *Journal of the Royal Horticultural Society*, praised the advice of a well-known playwright who in a book years ago advised the destruction of all butterflies. He, apparently, still believes that all butterflies are dangerous enemies of gardeners:

'When horticulturalists, so-called, invite me to beam on these gorgeous insects, I know that I am dealing with ignorance. There is no place for butterflies in a properly kept border. Off with them! Down with them! . . . The females lay eggs in prodigal and generous spirit. They choose a specimen plant for every accouchement.'

The writer of this book, and the modern gardener who praises his advice, rightly remark that they are dealing with ignorance. But they do not realise that the ignorance is their own.

Eric Parker, The Gardener's Week-End Book

September

The garden is in mourning;
the rain sinks coolly on the flowers,
summertime shudders
quietly to its close.

Leaf upon golden leaf is dropping
down from the tall acacia tree.
Summer smiles amazed and exhausted
on the dying dream that was this garden.

Long by the roses,
it tarries, yearns for rest,
slowly closes its (great)
weary eyes.

Richard Strauss, *Four Last Songs*

22 January 1950

It is amusing to make one-colour gardens. They need not necessarily be large, and they need not necessarily be enclosed, though the enclosure of a dark hedge is, of course, ideal. Failing this, any secluded corner will do, or even a strip of border running under a wall, perhaps the wall of the house. The site chosen must depend upon the general lay-out, the size of the garden, and the opportunities offered. And if you think that one colour would be monotonous, you can have a two- or even a three-colour, provided the colours are happily married, which is sometimes easier of achievement in the vegetable than in the human world. You can have, for instance, the blues and the purples, or the yellows and the bronzes, with their attendant mauves and orange, respectively. Personal taste alone will dictate what you choose.

For my own part, I am trying to make a grey, green, and white garden. This is an experiment which I ardently hope may be successful, though I doubt it. One's best ideas seldom play up in practice to one's expectations, especially in gardening, where everything looks so well on paper and in the catalogues, but fails so lamentably in fulfilment after you have tucked your plants into the soil. Still, one hopes.

My grey, green, and white garden will have the advantage of a high yew hedge behind it, a wall along one side, a strip of box edging along another side, and a path of old brick along the fourth side. It is, in fact, nothing more than a fairly large bed, which has now been divided into halves by a short path of grey flagstones, terminating in a rough wooden seat. When you sit on this seat, you will be turning your backs to the yew hedge, and from there I hope you will survey a low sea of grey clumps of foliage, pierced here and there with tall white flowers. I visualise the white trumpets of dozens of Regale lilies, grown three years ago from seed, coming up through the grey of southernwood and artemisia and cotton-lavender, with grey-and-white edging plants such as *Dianthus Mrs. Sinkins* and the silvery mats of *Stachys Lanata,* more familiar and so much nicer under its English names of Rabbits' Ears or Saviour's Flannel. There will be white pansies, and white peonies, and white irises with their grey leaves . . . at least, I hope there will be all these things. I don't want to boast in advance about my grey, green, and white garden. It may be a terrible failure. I wanted only to suggest that such experiments are worth trying, and that you can adapt them to your own taste, and your own opportunities.

All the same, I cannot help hoping that the great ghostly barn-owl will sweep silently across a pale garden, next summer, in the twilight – the pale garden that I am now planting, under the first flakes of snow.

Vita Sackville-West, *In Your Garden*

A Toxicological Garden

Some commendably affected Plantations
of Venomous Vegetables

The Garden of Cyrus

I have no wish to poison my friends or my neighbours, and I do not wish to establish a trade in what were called once 'powders of inheritance', *les poudres de succession.* Nevertheless I think at times of making a toxicological garden or a poisoner's garden, of making a garden within the garden altogether confined to poisonous plants. It would be curious. It would be a reply to the mere chromatic hedonism of the flower border; and since poisonous plants are various in their needs, a poisoner's garden would pose a number of interesting difficulties – of soil, shade, damp, drainage, and light.

My own garden combines chalk with clay, so, unmodified, there could be a worse foundation for a poisonous assembly. A soil of this kind would do well for many of the more familiar species, the yew, the two native hellebores, monkshood (which was sacred to Hecate and was first vomited upon the earth by Cerberus, the dog of Hell, when Hercules forced him up from underground), lords-and-ladies – it is there already, the two native daphnes, hemlock, and meadow saffron and deadly night-shade. And you may be reminded by that list that there are poisonous and dangerous plants grown by every one of us without apprehension. Children have been killed by yew berries, by the scarlet berries of *Daphne Mezereum*, by the leaves and fruits of monkshood, which yield aconitin, the instrument of more than one celebrated murder. Children have been killed, too, by laburnum, of which the seeds, the leaves, the fruits, the bark and everything else are poisonous. So a poisonous garden, which was known to be poisonous, might be safer than its commonplace neighbour in which the possibilities of death hide more innocently. Such a garden would not be the first of its kind. King Attalus, Sir Thomas Browne writes in *The Garden of Cyrus*, 'lives for poisonous plantations of Aconites, Henbane, Hellebore, and plants hardly admitted within the walls of Paradise.' He was king of Pergamum, which was a cult centre of Asclepius or Aesculapius, the God of Medicine.

Some of the poison-plants are sombre enough, but the look of such a garden would not be gloomy at least to the eye. The poison year would begin with the purple flowers of Daphne mezereum, brilliant on the naked and crabbed branches, or with peach blossom (since peach ker-nels can be resolved into prussic acid). In high summer there would be foxgloves, now and then called dead man's bells; in autumn the scarlet of lords-and-ladies would shine in dark corners, and the coral of the yew berries would lie on the grass margins, filled in their turn with the naked purples of meadow saffron. It is a sound moral fable that poison should look gay, speckled, gorgeously coloured. Still, some degree of gloom would be appropriate and would certainly be supplied against the yews by another plant which would do well in a heavy, chalky soil, having at the same time plenty of nitrogen. So imagine in the half-shade a thicket of fleshy and deadly nightshade. There is no question that this plant is the essential poisoner. William Robinson's principle for introducing a native species into the garden would apply to it – that it should not be too familiar outside the garden. Deadly nightshade we do not see every day in most parts of Great Britain. With us it is less common than it is in

France and Central Europe, partly, I suppose, because in Great Britain it occurs mainly in soils with plenty of lime. Its whole life history has been summarised in a paper in the Journal of Ecology. Abroad, so one learns, it is found in rough country, in meadows and in clearings in wood and forest. With us it confines itself to lower ground and keeps more curious and select company, in an open community of vegetation in which its neighbours are likely to be elders, dog's mercury, nettles, and burdock. It likes shade and a damp atmosphere, and, best of all habitats, a steep slope on which the soil is friable and well drained. Indicative facts, all of these, if you wish to try it in the garden. Frost is inclined to scorch it, if the plants are too exposed. The seeds germinate slowly, and appear to do better if they are sown in March than if they are sown in the autumn.

Linnaeus celebrated the nightshade's deadliness by calling it *Atropa* after one of the Fates – Atropos, the third of the trio, who cut the thread of life with her shears and stood for the irremediable end of all things. The Fates lived in a marble cave, which suggests the English counterpart of a limestone cave with elders, nettles, and deadly nightshade growing at the mouth, and bats emerging in the twilight. The Fates wore robes with a purple border. Linnaeus would have known that and no doubt linked the purple border and the brownish-purple bells of the plant. On calcareous soils the nightshade grows wild from Yorkshire to Dorset; if you live on the Gloucestershire limestones, for example, you will have no difficulty in finding it. The Cotswolds must be the best area for it in Great Britain. Yet we cannot be quite sure that deadly nightshade is a native wilding. It has been known and used from early times, it has been tied up with magic and medicine – with magic, no doubt, because extracts of the plant will dilate the pupils of the eye, making the eyes not only more beautiful but more terrible. Yet the nightshade's likes and dislikes in the wild make one suspect it was introduced into Great Britain, a magical plant, perhaps, that early settlers could not do without. There is no geological record for it over here, and only one archaeological record, when seeds were discovered in the excavations of the Roman city of Silchester. So it may have come in during the Romanisation of the country, and then, like other plants, gone wild from cultivation. One individual plant, according to Sir Edward Salisbury's investigations, may ripen as many as sixty to eighty thousand seeds in the year; but for whatever reason (and this argues against its standing as a native) very few of the seeds mature into plants. It would be much commoner if they did.

Its poisonous alkaloid, hyoscyamine (less abundant in the devil's black cherries in August than in the young stem and young leaves in April) is converted into atropin for oculists and hyoscine, the poison which Crippen used on his wife; and when you think of the kindlier uses which doctors other than Crippen can make of deadly nightshade, do not forget that there is hyoscine in the tablets you buy from the chemist at Victoria for settling your inside as you cross a restless channel from Folkestone to Boulogne.

In the toxicological garden there are relatives of deadly nightshade which must be there as well, henbane, for one, and mandrake for another. But it may not be quite so easy to fit them in. I have tried henbane, and failed, which is a pity, for I agree with W. H. Hudson that it is one of the most curiously handsome of all English plants, either in flower or in fruit. Sulphur flowers streaked with purple are not to be met with every day. These flowers are spaced curiously along the stem, they smell half attractive, half repellent, and the pale green leaves have a softness like the feel of alpaca. My trouble, which a more energetic gardener would have settled, no doubt, is that henbane obviously needs a light soil. So, according to the older gardening books, does mandrake (*Mandragora officinarum*) – a light soil and some shade. In the forties and fifties of the last century four other species of mandrake and three other species of henbane, from Italy, the Canaries, and Egypt, are listed. For the poisonous garden it might be worth finding them all.

The various species mentioned so far are only a few of all the possible candidates. Several of them are plants with a European or Near Eastern range, whose poisonous or medical uses have spread outwards and westward from the parent centres of our civilisation. Thus in Babylonia henbane seeds were used against toothache, and they were still being used in that way by country people here and abroad so many hundreds of years later. I firmly hold that we should grow plants for their associations as well as for their possibly excellent appearance, so it would be right to fill most of the poison beds with these ancient and familiar species. We should have to include the opium poppy. We should allow into the poisonous garden at any rate one bush of the ordinary laurel (*Prunus*

Laurocerasus), which is now so much out of fashion, beautiful as it is with its black stems (rather as tree than bush) and ivory flowers and glittering leaves. Again it is a Near Eastern plant, though it came late into England in the seventeenth century; and it has been administered to kill more than butterflies of childhood in a jam-jar. One famous eighteenth-century murderer used the *aqua laurocerasi*, or cherry laurel water, which was included in the British pharmacopoeia.

Poison from the New World, nevertheless, ought not to be despised. If there was no room for any of the larger sumachs, I could not do without the grim *Rhus radicans*, the Poison Ivy from the United States. There it would be, its virulent leaves turning red, as the leaves of a proper sumach, in the autumn. We do not realise how lucky we are to have few plants which are a positive scourge to the human race. Plants may contain poisonous substances, but at least they keep the poison, for the most part, to themselves. They do not ask us to pick their leaves and chew them or to extract the poisons. In England we have nothing worse than plants which scratch, and nettles which sting. If it was the thorn of a rose (he had picked a rose for a young girl) which caused the death of Rainer Maria Rilke, it was Rilke's own fault that he gave himself a wound which could be infected, not the fault of any rosaceous venom. And if nettles stung sharply enough and gravely enough we should no doubt have exterminated them long ago; or tried to, which is a cautionary qualification required if we think of American experience with poison ivy. *Rhus radicans* is hardly less common now than when it surprised the first settlers on the eastern seaboard; and touching it, a light touch, has consequences, if you are susceptible, which no nettle-stung English child can imagine. That is a little exaggerated. I should have written that you have only to touch a broken leaf from which the sap had exuded, to learn the answer in a matter of hours or of days. The poison enters your skin. You go red, you blister, you itch intolerably. You are feverish and you may not be able to sleep. Scratch and then put your fingers elsewhere, and you infect some other part of your body. Suppose the poison gets to your face: it can swell you up, close your eyes, and turn you into an unrecognisable cross between a baboon and Neanderthal man. Fat people are supposed to be more susceptible than thin ones. You can catch the poison from logs out in the woodshed which have brushed against poison ivy, or by touching a pair of boots in which someone has been out shooting. You can catch it from a handshake, from towels, or clothes, or bedclothes. It has even been caught from picking up a croquet ball. Or you can be poisoned *inside* from the smoke of a bonfire in which there are the leaves of poison ivy. One of the first colonists who wrote of its existence made light of it, wishing perhaps not to deter others who might come out to the New World. It had a bad name, but was 'questionless of no very ill nature'. He may have been one of the fortunate tough-skinned creatures who can touch poison ivy without trouble. The Indians knew it well and were scared of it, hoping to turn away its wrath by talking to it kindly and calling it 'my friend'. And before the pathology of Rhus dermatitis, as the affliction is called, was investigated thoroughly in the nineteen-twenties so that sensible methods of treatment could be devised, all manner of 'cures' were in use. Indian herbal concoctions were tried, everything from a cream made of gunpowder to bruised nettles, onion poultices and a visit to a Turkish bath. Ointments often made things worse by dissolving the poison and spreading it round the body.

Perhaps I could do without this plant after all, in spite of its delicate twining habit, its shining leaves, triple-arranged, which turn so nobly scarlet in the autumn. Or if it goes into a poison corner, round it there must be an iron fence and on the fence a notice, as I once saw it in the Botanical Garden at Munich. It would be the nearest thing possible to having a upas tree casting a deathly shade around the garden.

That is not all. Irony would demand at least two species in the poison garden, alongside the poison ivy compound. Two species we regard as being almost the symbols of purity and innocence – cyclamen and lily-of-the-valley. Four drops of extract of lily-of-the-valley will suffice to kill a dog in ten minutes if you inject it (but why should you?) into the blood stream. I owe this select item to one of the more curious books about plants – *Des Plantes Vénéneuses*, by Ch. Cornevin, who was professor at the École National Vétérinaire in Paris and must have ranked high among the strange poisoners of the world. He did not himself inject the dangerous glucosides of lily-of-the-valley into the poor mongrel. But there was nothing he did not know about death by poison among cows, horses, pigs, sheep, goats, dogs, cats, fowls, ducks, pigeons, and the results of feeding to them corncockle seed, laburnum, hemlock, water dropwort, yew, oleander, meadow saffron, rhododendron, caper spurge (that fine cottager's plant, which should be in any garden, poisonous or no, for its bluish leaves and its geometric pattern). Cornevin will tell you that an injection of two and a half grains of the extract of dry flowers of oleander (those most emotive of southern flowers) will put finis to a cat, three grains to a dog or a pigeon, and five grains to a guinea-pig; or that a dozen berries of *Daphne mezereum* will kill a child, or exactly what happens when extract of laburnum is hypodermically injected into a hen: 'Cinq minutes après l'injection l'oiseau s'affaisse sur ses jambes, porte la tête en arrière, tombe, se relève, retombe sur son bec, bâille, raidit ses membres, il y a opisthotonus, la mandible inférieure s'agite convulsivement, les ailes battent – et l'animal meurt', thirty to forty minutes after the injection.

Perhaps it is most surprising of all to learn about cyclamen, since few of us are likely to have experience of injecting dogs with lily-of-the-valley or hens with laburnum. *Cyclamen europaeum* is the villain. You extract the juice from the tubers and use it for poaching trout. At a rate of a cubic centimetre of juice in two litres of water, it kills at once the small fish (and frogs and tadpoles) and after a while the bigger fish. And though cyclamen poison, an ancient one which was known to Pliny, can be used to kill you or me, it does not make the fish uneatable. It would take a good many guineas' worth of tubers of cyclamen from an English florist to kill one dish of trout out of the Test, so the method can be revealed safely in an English book, however common it is or may have been in the French Alps. And how difficult to associate the keen perfume of *Cyclamen europaeum* – to my nose the most exquisite of all flower scents – with the killing of any creature at all!

A dangerous man, this Professor Cornevin, one would think, if he had not worked off his poisoner's impulses in the interest of science and the farmer. Perhaps in the toxicological garden there should be statues of Cornevin, Crippen, and King Attalus.

Geoffrey Grigson, *Gardenage or The Plants of Ninhursaga*

Living and Learning

One of the most delightful things about gardening is the free-masonry it gives with other gardeners, and the interest and pleasure all gardeners get by visiting other people's gardens. We all have a lot to learn and in every new garden there is a chance of finding inspiration – new flowers, different arrangement or fresh treatment for old subjects. Even if it is a garden you know by heart there are twelve months in the year and every month means a different garden, and the discovery of things unexpected all the rest of the year.

I have never yet been to a garden that hasn't given me some new ideas, and it is surprising how you find most interesting things in gardens that you wouldn't suspect held any secrets. There was a tiny little slip of a garden in front of a cottage in this village that was full of *Corydalis solida*, something you normally find only in a connoisseur's garden. Once at a church fête in a rectory garden I came on a large bed of *Penstemon confertus caeruleus*.

It was in the garden that friends of mine rented in Charmouth that I first met my treasured othonnopsis, and that one small cutting has made hundreds of plants for me and my friends. Except for that unusual plant the garden was of no interest whatsoever. It was exciting to find that pink charmer, Felicia, in another friend's garden and better still when I was offered seedlings of it. Now I have to be rather firm with the lady as she thinks that parts of my garden belong to her and her only, but I'd hate to be without her.

One isn't always lucky enough to get plants but ideas are available for anyone who wants to take them. There is a garden I know nearly as well as my own. One day in the spring I noticed what I thought was a new plant. It was used as an edging and was covered with delicate little pale yellow flowers, on wiry stems. But on enquiry I found it was no newcomer but our old friend epimedium with the foliage cut off. We grow this plant for its lovely leaves and tend to forget how lovely the flowers can be. By the time they come out the foliage is tattered and shabby and it is sensible to remove it so that the full beauty of the flowers and the new leaves, in palest green, pink tinged, can have the stage.

In the same garden I realized how kind and softening stoechas lavender can be if planted to blur the hard lines of stone work. Here wide steps led up to a terrace on which is a large stone basin. The lazy growth and hazy colouring of the lavender give a peaceful feeling of permanence and grace. Stonework can be rather uncompromising at times but careful planting humanizes it.

I adopted this idea in my own garden. It was suggested to me that an old stone seat would look right on my terrace, and at the time all I could find for the purpose was an old stone sink. The front part was cut away and it was hoisted on two rather solid blocks of stone, but it looked clumsy and uncouth, and I really couldn't bear to look at it until it was partly hidden by growing things. A huge plant of *Statice latifolia* in the foreground gives bold foliage all the year round and in the summer a cloud of soft blue. Again rosemary has come to the rescue, and a prostrate cupressus makes a swirl of grey-green against the hard stone. A downy mat of *Stachys lanata* is spreading pleasantly towards the seat and, what is even better, I see tiny seedlings appearing in tinier cracks in the paving. Kind nature is doing the job for me, in a gentle haphazard way which is much more pleasing than my more deliberate efforts.

Another gardening friend gave me the idea for one of my most successful plantings. On the left of the little crazy path that leads to the barton the higher ground is held up by a stone wall. At one spot the ground behind is level with the wall, and it was here that I planted a *Cytisus kewensis* to spread across the bed and pour down the wall. I look forward each year to the moment when that corner becomes a sheet of deep cream, a haze of forget-me-nots nearby and nepeta and roses in the background, all smiling and shining in the spring sunshine. It even excites people who are not gardeners and know nothing about gardening.

The same friend suggested I plant *Euphorbia Wulfenii* in the top terrace, as a screen and for emphasis. Again it was a stroke of genius. Never have I seen this spurge so happy and luxuriant, and in that position none of the beauty of its magnificence is lost.

I could go on and on. But that is just what gardening is, going on and on. My philistine of a husband often told with amusement how a cousin when asked when he expected to finish his garden replied 'Never, I hope.' And that, I think, applies to all true gardeners.

Margery Fish, *We Made A Garden*

Heathers

The most important thing in designing a garden is to get the right shapes and balance between path and lawn and the planting space. The next most important thing is to introduce a style of planting which will embellish and furnish the whole during whatever period or periods the garden is called upon to serve; and the finishing touch to this is that the planting shall be knitted together with a permanent, if possible ever-green, underplanting.

This is a chapter on heathers, and the above remarks will serve to shew what importance should be attached to them. For they and their kind are the very plants that can make or mar a garden, by their arrangement. One hears so much about 'grouping' these days; everything must be planted in groups for effect, regardless of its character. To my mind this is utterly wrong. How can one group Japanese cherries, every tree and every variety of which has a singular individuality and mode of branching of its own? How group *Cotoneaster salicifolia* with its strong, virile lines? Why should we mass together striking shrubs like *Viburnum tomentosum* and *Azalea amoena*? How can we enjoy a mass of *Verbascum vernale*, whose great leaves and tower of yellow demand space around them? And even among the lowlier plants there are similar examples.

Let us see what alternative we can find for the above examples, chosen without any more thought and time than it takes to write them down. If in a big park a mass of colour is needed from a tree, *Malus* of the *floribunda* persuasion will be admirable: they have little stance and quality; again, we might select *Berberis stenophylla* with its thicket-forming branches or roses like *Rosa canina andersonii* for big groups of shrubs. In the flower border heleniums and gaillardias will knit themselves into groups and all will be well, but for the lowly foreground stretches choose heathers and sun roses, *Potentilla fruticosa*, dwarf rhododendrons, berge-nias, and others.

For grouping is right and vitally *necessary* in any garden if carried out with the right plants – those plants of a colonising tendency and of little individuality in regard to 'line'. In the winter garden especially, heathers stand out, to my mind, as the first essential to successful design, when

planted in drifts and stretches in front and around their larger neighbours. Without them any winter garden will be a collection of plants,
and of all gardens this is the most tedious to those who seek refreshment
from it.

There are fortunately no 'ifs and buts' about these drifts of pink winter-flowering heathers. Their roots are not dependent upon those bacte-
ria – peculiar to most Ericaceous plants – which die on exposure to lime,
and therefore cannot transmit the goodness from the ground to the
roots. *Erica carnea* and *E. mediterranea* and its hybrids – all we need for
our purpose – will grow in limy soil as well as in an acid one. A good light
loam suits them well, but in impoverished gardens the addition of leaf-
mould will be beneficial. Considering how much they benefit from wind
and sunshine, it is surprising how they thrive in sheltered and often
shady gardens.

For general purposes there is nothing, I think, so good as the ordinary
E. carnea. This, the mountain heath, also called *E. herbacea*, is a sturdy,
bushy plant up to 9 inches or so in height, making a close thicket of tiny
twigs set with tiny, bronze-green leaves, and by August the new season's
buds, arranged in closely packed spikes some 3 inches long, may be seen.
These usually open in December and the drift gradually takes on a rosy-
pink glow. Anything more fitting as a ground-cover for Hamamelis or
other open-growing shrubs, or for planting in drifts along the path I cannot imagine. This valuable plant has been segregated into a number of
forms, and that known as 'King George V' usually opens its flowers in
late December. It is a more compact type with deeper rosy blooms.
'Queen Mary', 'Mrs. Samuel Doncaster', 'Winter Beauty', and other old
varieties crowd the lists, and all give just that different tint that is needed
for a succession of groupings.

Of whites we have *E. carnea alba*, a compact little plant for small
spaces. Some few years ago a fine white was discovered in Italy and
named 'Springwood', after the discoverer's Scottish home. This has the
longest spikes of any and the long individual flowers are capped by their
protruding light brown stamens with finer effect than in the pink forms.
It is extremely vigorous and a first-class carpeter – it is nothing to find
single plants covering 12 or 20 square feet – but unfortunately it has an
almost horizontal habit, with the result that on flat ground its blooms
are not seen to best advantage; but when planted on slopes this habit

becomes an asset. Generally known as 'Springwood White', it has a love-ly pale pink counterpart, 'Springwood Pink'; this is slightly less vigorous, but both are most admirable weed-smothering plants. *E.c. rubra* is a richly coloured form, and a considerably darker one, *vivellii*, has coppery dark foliage and rich carmine-crimson flowers which do not open until March: it is of very compact, dwarf growth. A number of newer varieties should be watched; several have given an excellent account of themselves at Wisley. 'December Red' flowers both early and late, while 'Alan Coates' is a good plant for earliest spring. Both are vigorous yet compact. Another splendid variety in these darker shades is 'Ruby Glow'. As so often happens in almost any genus, the darker flowered forms are less vigorous than the paler forms, and I often wonder why this should be so.

Graham Stuart Thomas, Colour in the Winter Garden

The English Dream

I come back to Candide and Dr.Pangloss, and to Candide's conclusive reply to the doctor's philosophising: *all that is very well said, but let us cultivate our garden.* And I believe that men busy in the useful arts are, in fact, more harmlessly and contentedly engaged than others. There is, in all living creatures, a perfectly obvious motion towards order and away from chaos, towards pattern and rhythm, towards what we call beauty. Men, being also products of the natural order, share it; it is apparent in the play of both men and beasts, in art, in the crafts. This shaping of material, of sound and motion as well as matter, is not just something nice we like to do but can manage without: it is a deep, natural need, an attribute of life itself which we ignore at our peril.

Whether any animal but man applies the urge to order and rhythm to new ends is not yet clear; at all events men do this; they make new things. Those who do so we call artists and scientists, but I do not believe that there is any real distinction between them and practitioners of the useful arts, the craftsmen. It is sometimes argued that a pot, a basket, a bolt of cloth, an internal-combustion engine are primarily for use and only inci-dentally beautiful, whereas the fine arts need no justification in terms of use; they minister to the mind and spirit of man, not to his bodily needs.

This is nonsense: you cannot divide a man into bits, he is whole or he is nothing. The object of a pot is to keep liquid in; the object of a symphony or a painting or a poem is to reveal something about the universe which the artist can perceive but the rest of us cannot until he points it out to us. A work of fine art is beautiful for precisely the same reason that a work of craft is beautiful in a lesser degree, that is because by imposing order and making a pattern it serves a purpose; and it is quite beside the point to consider which part of a man is served by a particular piece of work.

If all this be true it might be interpreted as an argument in favour of a return to the manual making of things, a retreat from the machine. But this will never do. I would not even suggest that if and when industry really fulfils the promise of emancipation from tedious labour made in its name, and the problem of leisure becomes serious, we should turn to pottery and hand-loom weaving. I do not pretend to know why it is that there is a peculiarly distasteful falseness in continuing to do by hand what can be done by machinery; but there certainly is, and I have no doubt it accounts for the ugliness of the pots and cloth and other articles made by people who have simply escaped from the real world as it is to the practice of ancient crafts. It is to the point that when one does happen upon a pot or a pan as good to look at as it is serviceable, yet made by hand today, it is always in one of the few remaining places where there is an unbroken tradition of that kind of work; where, in short, the articles in question are being made as a matter of course, and not as cure for urban neuroses. No; there will perhaps be Cellinis and Chippendales in the future, but they will design cleverer machines and things for those machines to make.

There remains a field of work which does demand the direct application of man's hand and eye and mind to the material; which is so vast that it would not be overmanned if the entire population of the world entered it; and which, in the results obtained, ministers to all man's needs from the lowest to the highest. That is 'creative' horticulture.

Gardening, as practised by millions of people everywhere, is usually confined to the growing of vegetables, fruit, and flowers of kinds and varieties which have been bred by relatively few specialists and are propagated by commercial nurseries. A minority of gardeners specialise and produce prize specimens of well-known varieties. But only a very tiny minority indeed ever try to make new plants. Yet it is my belief that if only ten per cent of the world's gardeners interested themselves in plant-breeding and selection the result would be greater for the well-being and happiness of mankind, and much less dangerous than the most spectacular advances made in physics. I have a good reason for this belief.

First, the principal causes contributing to happiness are not difficult to determine. They are, in the first place, adequate food, clothing and shelter: nothing has contributed, and still does contribute, more towards the first two than plant breeding and selection. In the second place, an occupation ministering to the strong and universal desire to make patterns, rhythms, order out of chaos, in short to create something: and if what is created is a living plant, apt to endure longer, in its progeny, than works of paper, paint or stone, what could be more satisfying? In the third place there is, of course, the need for a satisfactory emotional life, which is to some extent ministered to by working in beautiful surroundings. I have deliberately put this condition third because I am convinced it need not be placed any higher.

The idea 'happiness' and the word itself, vague enough in the first place, have been bedevilled by the Occidental preoccupation with romantic love. It has long been the principal theme for literature and this, combined with the vulgar 'democratic' illusion that all human beings are capable and deserving of what some human beings can do and feel, has resulted in romantic love becoming something which, it is felt, everyone can and should experience, the outcome being 'happiness'. This is precisely as if we all laid claim to a right to the experience of composing the Emperor Concerto, commanding an army in the field, or dying of some rare and terrible disease.

Once we succeed in emancipating ourselves from the illusions imposed by literature – which is not to deprecate literature itself – it becomes clear that the emotional side of an ordinary man or woman's life is very adequately catered for by the satisfaction of a decided inclination for some other person: and that really far more important than this is the satisfaction of the need for occupation which ministers to self-respect, as well as to the fundamental need apparent in literally all living creatures, animal or vegetable, to make patterns and establish rhythms.

That being achieved, the illusory need for a demon lover or a dream girl will tend to vanish.

Unfortunately this cure for spleen and of part of our aesthetic and economic ills can be applied only to a minority; this is because of the wretched tendency which, since about 1800, the human race has shown to breed like vermin, and consequently to be treated as such by its leaders. Not everybody can have a garden. Well, not everybody would want one. In Britain something like a quarter of the population have a garden or allotment of some sort, which is a very great deal. The fraction could be larger in countries with more room. But consider what the results might be if only five or six million people, all over the world, set about their gardening as an art or science, instead of as a craft. In the past two hundred or so generations a tiny handful of people have made thousands of economic and ornamental plants out of wild ones. In our own lifetime food production per acre has been increased more than a hundred per cent by a few hundred plant-breeding specialists. It will be protested that these people were, are, trained scientific workers with large resources. But until late in the nineteenth century the work was being done by men who certainly were nothing of the kind, and these men produced what until very recently were, and in many cases still are, our best varieties of plants and cattle.

Any man or woman getting a living in skilled, semi-skilled, or even only deft, factory work, that is whose hands are accustomed to be used, can learn budding and grafting and plant-breeding techniques. Any person with the patience to add up a column of figures correctly can carry out a programme of selection for plant improvement. Any person who can read above the level of a tabloid newspaper can read and understand at least the simplest part of genetics. I am not by nature deft and I never learnt to use my hands until the Navy taught me to do so during the war, but I have very easily become a successful grafter of fruit trees and vines, and thousands of rose amateurs bud their own roses.

I believe that the number of people in our frustration-ridden civilisation, whose work merely serves to get them the bread by which man cannot live alone, aspire to be artists, or scientists: and rightly so, *naturally* so, for these are the occupations proper to mankind. It is by these means alone that man, being unspecialised in the biological sense, can fulfil the need manifest as universal in the shape of a snowflake, or the pattern of a cat's fur. But although for me the work of art properly so called is, as it were, a sublime by-product of a craft, yet the craftsmen to whom it is given to stand at the growing points of human consciousness, that is to be artists, are rare. There are quite enough indifferent poets, clumsy painters, and insignificant composers in the world. And as for the useful arts, for the reason already suggested only one, needlework, is still free from the reproach of futility; and, significantly, it is the only one which has not declined either in taste or in execution.

But there can never be too many people engaged in increasing the world's provision of generous food plants or beautiful ornamental ones, and this is work which cannot be mechanised, work which calls for intelligent thought issuing in deft manual operations. Nor need any man or woman fear that in taking to the making of a garden, or to the improvement, however small, of a variety, he or she is practising a lesser art when the great ones remain open to them – not, at least, in Britain.

In support of which contention here is what, not quite a century ago, Hippolyte Taine, the shrewdest, most critical and most thorough of all the foreigners who have ever made a careful study of the English, wrote of our gardens:

'Every original work, a garden quite as much as a book or a building, is a confidence revealing deep feelings. In my opinion their [the English] gardens reveal, better than any other of their works, the poetic dream in the English soul.'

Edward Hyams, The Speaking Garden

Union

An hour later he awoke refreshed and went down into the garden. The sun was already low and its rays, no longer overwhelming, were lighting amiably on the araucarias, the pines, the lusty ilexes which were the glory of the place. From the end of the main alley, sloping gently down between high laurel hedges framing anonymous busts of broken-nosed goddesses, could be heard the gentle drizzle of spray falling into the fountain of Amphitrite. He moved swiftly towards it, eager to see it again. The waters came spurting in minute jets, blown from shells of Tritons and Naiads, from noses of marine monsters, spattering and pattering on the greenish surface, bouncing and bubbling, wavering and quivering, dissolving into laughing little gurgles; from the whole fountain, the tepid water, the stones covered with velvety moss, emanated a promise of pleasure that would never turn to pain. Perched on an islet in the middle of the round basin, modelled by a crude but sensual hand, a vigorous smiling Neptune was embracing a willing Amphitrite; her navel, wet with spray and gleaming in the sun, would be the nest, shortly, for hidden kisses in subaqueous shade. Don Fabrizio paused, gazed, remembered, regretted. He stood there a long while.

'Uncle, come and look at the foreign peaches. They've turned out fine. And leave these indecencies which are not for men of your age.'

Tancredi's affectionate mocking voice called him from his voluptuous torpor. He had not heard the boy come; he was like a cat. For the first time he felt a touch of rancour prick him at the sight of Tancredi; this fop with the pinched-in waist under his dark blue suit had been the cause of those sour thoughts of his about death two hours ago. Then he realised that it was not rancour, just disguised alarm: he was afraid the other would talk to him about Concetta. But his nephew's approach and tone was not that of one preparing to make amorous confidences to a man like himself. Don Fabrizio grew calm again; his nephew was looking at him with the affectionate irony which youth accords to age. 'They can allow themselves to be a bit nice to us, as they're sure to be free of us the day after our funerals.' He went with Tancredi to look at the 'foreign peaches'. The grafting with German cuttings, made two years ago, had succeeded perfectly; there was not much fruit, a dozen or so, on the two grafted trees, but it was big, velvety, luscious-looking; yellowish, with a faint flush of rosy pink on the cheeks, like those of modest little Chinese girls. The Prince felt them with the delicacy for which his fleshy fingers were famous. 'They seem quite ripe. A pity there are too few for to-night. But we'll get them picked to-morrow and see what they're like.'

'There! that's how I like you, Uncle; like this, in the part of *agricola pius* – appreciating in anticipation of fruits of your own labours; and not as I found you a short while ago, gazing at all that shameless naked flesh.'

'And yet, Tancredi, these peaches are also products of love, of coupling.'

'Of course, but legal love, blessed by you as their master, and by Nino the gardener as notary. Considered, fruitful love. As for those,' he went on, pointing at the fountain whose shimmer could just be discerned through a veil of ilexes, 'd'you really think they've been before a priest?'

The conversation was taking a dangerous turn and Don Fabrizio hastily changed its direction. As they moved back up towards the house Tancredi began telling what he had heard of the love-life of Donnafugata: Menica, the daughter of Saverio the keeper, had let herself be put with child by her young man; the marriage would be rushed on now. Calicchio had just avoided being shot by an angry husband.

'But how d'you know such things?'

'I know, Uncle, I know. They tell me everything; they know I'll sympathise.'

When they reached the top of the steps, which rose from the garden to the palace with gentle turns and long landings, they could see the dusky horizon beyond the trees; over towards the sea huge, inky clouds were climbing up the sky. Perhaps the anger of God was satiated and the annual curse over Sicily nearly over? At that moment those clouds loaded with relief were being stared at by thousands of other eyes, sensed in the womb of the earth by billions of seeds.

'Let's hope the summer is over and that the rains are finally here,' said Don Fabrizio; and with these words the haughty noble to whom rain would only be a personal nuisance showed himself a brother to his roughest peasants.

Giuseppe Tomasi di Lampedusa, *The Leopard*

Sculptural Forms

The art of garden making and the sculptor's art have been complementary to each other ever since the days of Rome.

Some of the earliest gardens of the Renaissance were designed expressly for the display of statues and until the last century sculpture of different kinds was an essential part of the design of all the great gardens of the western world. Statues have been used in many different ways, but the underlying reasons for their use have been the same. They are the great humanizers, by which man projects his personality and his love of creation into the realm of nature. Lovingly he turned the tree trunk and acanthus leaves into the column and carved capital. In the classic statues he expressed his ideal of the human body, into the voluptuous curves of the baroque he put all the self-confident joy of life of the seventeenth century, and today the sculptor reflects the modern groping for the underlying unity of the world. Statues have always been an expression of man's mind and because of their obvious human origin they at once draw attention to themselves and stand out from their natural surroundings. For this reason they are natural focal points. From afar attention is projected to them, so that all the ground between them and the beholder is at once recognised as man's domain.

The English landscape gardens of the eighteenth century used this device to embrace the whole park and even the intervening farmlands into their picture by the placing of a temple or an obelisk on a distant hill. In the same way the statues in the rondells at Versailles make it plain that the allées and bosquets are part of the civilised world.

Just as the statue at a distance has an irresistible pull, making the eye and thoughts travel to it over intervening ground, so it allows the attention to rest in peace once it is reached; and this is the role it plays as the terminal feature of a classical vista or as the focal point of a small garden.

One or both of these qualities of drawing the eye irresistibly over intervening ground and of allowing it to rest content, can be seen in almost all well-placed statues; and the neglect of them is the cause of most ill siting. Because a statue is a natural focus of attention, it brooks no competition, and either one piece should hold the attention at a time or several together should form a complete and unified composition, or a natural progression.

The long vista at Bramham Park, Yorkshire, looks across a pool and the end is marked by a huge urn. The two do not compete, but are complementary, together forming one composition. The dominant vertical figure is completed by the calm horizontal pool which does nothing to prevent the eye travelling easily on its way to the terminal point.

But at the Villa Medici, in Rome, the dominating figure in the pool, which should be the focal point of the view, is confused by the second over-powering figure at the far end of the garden.

There are good reasons why the classical statue is an attribute of the Italian garden. The climate, with its bright light, not only conserves the whiteness of the marble, but shows it to the best advantage, especially when seen against the background of sombre evergreens. In England the climate discolours the stone and the misty light tends to blur the outlines. For this reason the bolder lines of the temples, bridges and obelisks of the eighteenth century gardens are more effective than the statues, while the massive forms of some modern sculpture, with their broad planes, are better suited to our misty climate and a better foil to the open texture of deciduous trees.

It is natural that abstract forms, which modern painting and sculpture have made familiar, should find their way into the garden, either in the selective form of *objets trouvés* or in the creative form of sculpture. There is historic precedent for the *objets trouvés* in the Japanese use of carefully selected stones for their garden compositions, and it is not only in this field that modern art has reached something closely akin to the art of the ancient east.

A seeing eye may recognize in many unexpected objects some form which evokes pleasure and expresses the feeling of the garden's character, bringing it to a point of interest and emphasis. Italian oil jars have a traditional place in the garden, but many of our native objects are quite as beautiful in form, including, for instance, certain types of buoy which might find a fitting place in a sea-side garden.

The opportunities for siting sculpture in gardens are more diverse than in any other environment and ideally there should be complete unity of intention between the sculptor and the garden designer. Either may take the lead or they may work in unison from the first. Usually it will be the garden architect who desires a particular type of work for a particular place, but it may equally well be that a garden is required as a setting for a predetermined work. In either case the background with its tone and texture, the lighting and the shadow, will become part of the composition of the sculpture, which in its turn may become the heart of the garden design.

The clear-cut, gleaming statues of Italy find their perfect foil in the dark, matt, low-toned walls of clipped *Quercus ilex*. And, in the same tradition, yew has long been recognized as the perfect background plant.

Where the effect is to be light against dark, modelling against a flat surface, this is a sound choice. But sometimes a different effect may be sought. It may be that work should be seen as a dark silhouette, in which case the sky makes the ideal background. A magnificent example of this is the fountain group at the Villa Lante. Or where broad mass is more important than fine detail, it may be better to replace the matt-surface background with a strong mosaic of patterned foliage. For instance, Henry Moore's reclining figure would look well against a background of *Viburnum davidii*, and the smooth form of Epstein's doves is accentuated by the interlaced pattern of the bamboo leaves. From its earliest days sculpture has derived patterns from plant form, and an alternative to using plants as a purely recessive background is to let them contribute to this pattern. The choice of a group of yuccas as the setting for Barbara Hepworth's vertical feature was inspired.

The colour relationship of sculpture to its setting may be either the simple contrast of light stone against dark foliage or some more subtle affinity, such as the green of bronze metal, harmonised with a background of glaucous foliage.

The position of a statue in relation to eye level can give completely different effects. Just as the eye is carried forward towards a man-made object, so it can be led upwards. The little lion perched high on its pillar at the Villa Marlia accentuates the depth of the hedge enclosure and pulls the eye and spirit up to the opening of the sky above.

Unless there is a deliberate intention to create some such effect, the sculpture should be placed at natural eye level. Scale-relationship to the human figure has a strong psychological effect. A statue far greater than life size is extrovert and draws the onlooker beyond himself; one less than the human scale leads rather to introspection. The miniature bust at Hidcote expresses intimacy and the quiet thought of the recluse. The great Fame at the Villa Garzoni is the epitome of the exuberance of Baroque man.

Since sculpture is an expression of the creative spirit of man, each work, to keep its value, must retain its individuality. Its force is lost if imitations are mass-produced, however good the original may have been. The interest of a focal point is gone as soon as it is realised that it is but one more copy of the Mercury which we have seen in a dozen other gardens. It cannot be the genius of the place if it has already been met in the same role elsewhere. The same stricture does not apply to the use of a classic pattern of vase or oil jars, or of the good modern designs of plant container. For here lies the difference between craftsmanship, which is the fashioning of a shape evolved through use and the character of its material and which loses nothing by repetition, and creative art, which is an individual expression, unique to one time, place and personality. Both have a place in gardens and sculpture, in particular, is needed in the gardens of today to bring interest into a small space and a strong, humanized focal point into the compositions of plant form.

Sylvia Crowe, *Garden Design*

Thrushes

Terrifying are the intent sleek thrushes on the lawn,
More coiled steel than living – a poised
Dark deadly eye, those delicate legs
Triggered to stirrings beyond sense – with a start, a bounce, a
stab
Overtake the instant and drag out some writhing thing.
No indolent procrastinations and no yawning stares.
No sighs or head-scratchings. Nothing but bounce and stab
And a ravening second.

Ted Hughes

The Search for a Paradise Garden

Israel recently placed before the Council of the International Federation of Landscape Architects the proposal that there should be an international garden on Mount Carmel. It is a good starting-point for deliberation on world affairs, for it leads on to a question of the most startling and challenging nature. Is it now possible to create a garden of universal appeal, a paradise not for one way of life, but for all ways of life that exist upon this complex globe? Is it possible to weave the different strands of mankind into one Paradise garden carpet after the manner of the ancient Persians?

Let us first make a study of history, watch how this merges into the modern world, and then examine the contemporary scene.

I

Since this idea emanated from Israel, and since the Garden of Eden is at least metaphorically the first garden, it is proper that we should begin here. But I fear that this garden would be of little help in our explorations; we know now that nature left to herself becomes a jungle, and that it is one of the purposes of our art to compose and order our environment to our particular requirements. Nevertheless, if we pass swiftly to the vast woodland scenery of Central Africa, we shall see natives sitting basking in the sun, themselves part of their natural environment. Unlike the European, the working African does not wish a bonus payment in cash; he prefers it in time, or rather in time off, in order that he may just sit in Paradise. How wise are those natives, and how odd must seem to them the rest of the world who cannot sit still, but must press on restlessly.

The flight back from Central Africa to the Mediterranean, if one follows the Nile from Khartoum to Alexandria, is probably the most prodigious in its comprehension of landscape of any comparable distance in the world. Far below lies the silver streak of river with its rich banks of variegated green patterns, sometimes wide, sometimes so narrow as almost to disappear; and on either side the hot arid desert disappearing as far as the eye can see (and this may be more than a hundred miles). This thin strip is the cradle of western civilisation: its architecture is magnificent; its man-made landscape, especially of Thebes and Luxor, probably the grandest in the world, ancient or modern; its houses and gardens must have been lovely. But we will not pause here to gather a contribution to our universal garden, for the whole of the architecture was based on suppression rather than enlightenment of the individual spirit, and it is with this only that we are concerned.

II

The three great forces in history on which the gardens and indeed the landscape of almost the whole world are based are the Chinese, the Western Asian, and the ancient Greek.

The first of these, the Chinese, sprang from its own land, spread to Japan, and began to influence Europe seriously from the middle of the eighteenth century. It was an art based upon a philosophy that man was a part of organic nature and just like nature did not change after having reached a 'climax'. It was undoubtedly extremely restful and contented. The only real excitements were the grotesque in nature, such as the storms, twisted trees, waterfalls, for these disturbed the quiet flow of life. The sense both here and in the tea-houses of Japan were brought to a state of sensitivity unknown to the western world. It is said, for instance, that trees were planted in order that the sound of the breezes through the leaves would be to the ear like music. My universal garden would remind us also that we are always a part of nature and would tune us to that delicate response to nature which has almost passed from our experience.

III

If the Chinese garden developed through centuries of reflection and meditation, the Persian garden of Western Asia had a shorter and stormier life. The two great civilisations of antiquity had both reached their summit unknown to each other at approximately the same time in the fifth century BC, the eastern in China, and the western in Greece. For centuries thereafter there was an area stretching from India to the Mediterranean which came first under one influence and then under the other.

This area, constantly on the boil within itself, occasionally produced great philosophy and great art. For a short while, for instance, the Arabs astonished the world and carried their Persian arts along the Mediterranean and across Spain to the Pyrenees. Spain is much enriched by having developed from two civilisations.

Similarly, the maritime city of Venice became, and remains today, the most interesting city of its kind in existence, cross-fertilizing on the one hand the garden arts of the Netherlands with those of Persia, and influencing on the other such purely Italian Renaissance painters as Giovanni Bellini. 'The Earthly Paradise' contains something of the arts of China, Persia, and Italy; that is to say, of most civilised countries.

The Persian conceived his garden as a small and fertile oasis set in a huge barren landscape. It was a kind of sanctuary, and its name, Paradise (a walled enclosure), soon came to acquire a wider association. Its design was simple, geometric, and based on the irrigation water channels of the desert. It inspired the design of the Paradise carpet, a reminder to us of the variety and wealth of detail that can be woven into a simple background. It is this basic simplicity that appeals to us as much today as it has in the past. What began as no more than an engineer's conception of a functional landscape, became in due course a work of art, and was endowed for very obvious reasons with an almost sacred character. The whole garden, including fruit trees and cypresses, was symbolic of life and death. It is certainly the clearest example in history of the progress of landscape from one of pure utility to one within the realms of metaphysics.

IV

If the Persian garden was somewhat limited in variety and generally passive and gentle, the garden arts springing from ancient Greece were very different. Western man set himself to adventure upon and conquer the resources of nature. He could never become static and there was no prophesying what he might not achieve nor when he might not destroy himself.

Not long ago my plane from Africa to England circled the Acropolis before leaving Athens for Rome. Even in its ruins the Parthenon is profoundly moving, and there is something both noble and tragic in the thought that this tiny beginning generated such tremendous forces. Set in the wild scenery of Greece, these tranquil temples seem to me to have attempted to draw down and establish upon earth the eternal rhythms of the heavens. To the Greek, man was something greater than a vegetable and must rise above his state; he found satisfaction not in the untidy environment upon the surface of the earth, but rather in the noble geometry and order of the universe.

Except only for groves of trees, the Greek was not interested in gardens, and the fountain source of all our classical garden art is Italy. The Italian of the Renaissance was the first individual in the world to realize that he and all like him had a mind and will of his own. He envisaged architecture as a projection of his personality, and his garden as a projection of his architecture. This accounts for the richness of variety, and if I were asked to study and report on the human mind through its response to geometry, the medium I should choose would be the Italian garden.

Within the formal shapes that play so agreeably upon the mind, are all the minor incidents of architecture, which are informed solely by the human figure.

When the Italian garden spread to Europe, it changed its character. At Versailles it became the expression of a monarch who wished to reflect not only his own aspirations, but those of a whole country. The great gardens of Le Nôtre have been a superb inspiration of town planning, there being no grander example than L'Enfant's plan for Washington.

In Austria the arts flowered for the brief period of rejoicing and relief following the raising of the siege by the Turks. The Baroque gardens of Austria are a climax of man's warmth of feeling and his splendid stature in the great scheme of things. Technically at least the Belvedere would in my opinion rank for a place in the first twelve classic gardens of the world. I should place Melk monastery in the first six of the romantic landscapes of the world. This is no small contribution to our study of history, and the fame of Austrian gardens is all the more enduring because of those paintings by Bellotto which are the finest of their kind. Observe particularly in that of the Liechtenstein Palace how the emotion of the human figure transmits itself to the vase and thence to the buildings. Here is the spirit of Baroque.

I have mentioned only a few of the countries concerned in the classic gardens, but when we conceive of the vast number, large and small, which have been made and enjoyed over the centuries in Europe and beyond the confines of Europe, and the peace and tranquillity they have brought to countless millions, then we can understand how it is that the Renaissance garden retains its charm although its significance may have changed. For every such garden is still a projection of that aspiring western mind, and carries with it that urge for ordering the affairs of nature which at last is beginning to fill us with alarm. Nevertheless, our universal garden shall contain a measure of the classic western garden, properly proportioned to the whole, for the individual mind of man, whose power is terrifying, is yet the most precious thing in the world . . .

VIII

We have before us a world seeking for peace and tranquillity. Landscape architects cannot lead the world, but they can interpret those feelings and urges that are within everyone and create the first need for the human being, a reconciliation between himself and his environment. As a matter of fact, by doing their work properly, they can do very much more. It seems to me that international landscape is like international humanity, and if we face the issue of the one, we face that of the other also.

There should be no such thing as an international style, such as was conceived in the 'thirties, for the reduction of all design to a pattern would be to reduce us to the animal state. The construction of an international landscape depends on three qualities: the quality of regionalism, which holds us to an environment; the quality of the universal, which holds us to an environment; and the quality of individuality, which is the separate human mind and soul.

This is in fact the echo of history, the legacy respectively of the Chinese, Persian, and Western philosophies. Peace in the modern world of landscape would seem to depend upon the recognition that none of these philosophies is sufficient in itself. If we are not wiser than our forefathers, we do at least seem to wish to be more tolerant; and this implies that our garden, like a good salad, must be composed of all these ingredients.

So diverse are the people, climate, and geography of this world, that our universal garden must, alas, remain an abstract idea.

G. A. Jellicoe, *Studies in Landscape Design*

Southern Gothic

for W.E.B. & P.R.
Something of the homing bee at dusk
Seems to inquire, perplexed, how there can be
No flowers here, not even withered stalks of flowers,
Conjures a garden where no garden is
And trellises too frail almost to bear
The memory of a rose, much less a rose.
Great oaks, more monumentally great oaks now
Than ever when the living rose was new,
Cast shade that is the more completely shade

Upon a house of broken windows merely
And empty nests up under broken eaves.
No damask any more prevents the moon,
But it unravels, peeling from the wall,
Red roses within roses within roses.

Donald Justice

Water in the Garden

Water in the garden, whether pond or stream, lakeside or artificial pool, offers the gardener temptations hard to resist. Before your inner eye float luscious pictures of groups of iris and primula, willows and water-lilies and a mirage of picturesque details culled from books and catalogues and exhibition gardens. Too much enthusiasm of this kind and you may quite likely damage your garden composition irretrievably. My own pleasure in finding water in a garden has so often led me into the wildest errors that I have learnt to stop and reflect very carefully before starting work. I have learnt to try always to contain my enthusiasm and see the site as a whole; water is only one factor, to be looked at just as impartially as the others. Then, I must consider whether I shall have to change the shape, the direction or the levels of the water. Its relationship to the other elements in the composition may be so dull that I may have to decide to give it greater prominence or else to reduce it to an incidental detail. Running water may involve a heightening of key, so that both design and planting should suggest light and gaiety and movement; still water demands a quieter and more static treatment. My thought is always 'How little can I do?', rather than how much, to achieve the most telling result.

Since running water implies changing levels, I like at the lowest point in a garden to widen and slow up a fast-running stream, whether natural or artificial. Water which runs fast and uninterruptedly through and out of a garden may seem to drain away the garden's character. In such a case I like to widen it into a pool and give it time to pause. Carefully arranged planting, too, can give the impression of steadying and slowing down the passage of a stream. Planting on both sides of a length of running water, however charming in detail, will only accentuate the sense of movement.

Plant thickly with high plants and bushes in a wide bed designed as a single unit and placed at an angle to the flow; or let the stream run through a group of flowering or other trees planted on both banks, so that there is an alternation of light and shadow, level lawns and heavy planting.

Slow-moving water, pools, canals and ponds, call for a different treatment. Trees, lawns and planting should be arranged to accentuate their static qualities. The shapes and colours reflected in the water will count for much even though you may not consciously absorb the impressions they make on you. You have to remember that every vertical accent, every rounded mass will be repeated by reflection.

Not far from Turin there is a magnificent mid-eighteenth-century villa in the high rococo manner. Being Piedmontese, its style is more classical than the rococo of the Veneto or Naples. A formal entrance court leads to the elaborate and splendid north façade, and the equally elaborate south front looks down a long lawn framed in trees. I was called in to see what could be done on the east side, where the main reception rooms on the first floor gave on to a piece of level ground devoted to vegetables, a few rose-beds and beyond, perhaps a hundred and fifty yards from the house, a disconsolate spinney of Canadian poplars reaching to the boundary wall. Here was a site which demanded a composition in the grand manner and I set to work.

Fired by the splendid architecture of the house I made sketch after sketch, seeing a garden to be developed in clipped hedges and pleached trees, with fountains and statues combined into the elaborate and baroque forms. My host who had retrieved the house from ruin and rearranged the interior with great discretion and taste considered my efforts with a sympathetic eye and finally said, 'Yes, but these are not for Piedmont.' So we set out over the rich levels of the Po valley, where the fields are squared off by countless irrigation channels bordered since the time of Virgil by pollarded willows and poplars, and I saw how the great houses are set in immense expanses of gravel with gardens merely sketched in by lines of trees or a hedge or a wall, and simplified beyond severity almost to dullness.

Now I saw that my garden should be classical rather than baroque in plan and that I could avoid any dullness and still remain in the spirit of this countryside by using spaces of water rather than of gravel. A further clue was offered me by the original name of the property, 'Il Carpeneto' – the place of hornbeams.

So from the house I designed a canal running across the level ground and through the poplars to the limit of the property, with two short lateral arms about half-way down. As the total length was relatively short this canal is narrowed at the far end and four Lombardy poplars planted at the four corners of the crossing with their reflections, add height and distance. The canal is set, without path or edging, in close-mown grass with a line of clipped lime trees on either side as far as the centre of the design. Beyond, through the wood where the canal is a little narrower, there are two lines of chestnuts on either side which will be allowed to grow freely and eventually form a green vault over the water.

From the house high hornbeam hedges frame the first part of the canal and the lateral arms. These hedges are doubled and between them lies a wide hidden gravel walk shaded by still another double line of clipped lime trees. In three years the hornbeams, planted quite small, have grown into thick hedges four feet through and twelve feet high. As all hedges should be, they are clipped rather wider at the base than at the top so as to give the impression of great solidity. This garden of grass, hedges, trees and water seems to me to have become timeless and inevitable. Is it because it is, in one sense, a synthesis and a symbol of the nature and essence of the place, its earth and air and water and of what I must call the humanities – the house, its period and its builders?

If hornbeams flourish here, so too do roses. In case this general scheme should seem too pompous I would add that, behind this green architecture, lies an acre of rose bushes arranged in a maze of simple symmetrical beds. Dark red climbing roses cover the lower storey of the villa and its dependent buildings, and from May until Christmas great vases of long-stemmed roses in many colours make the inside of this pleasant house a bower of colour and scent. Incidentally, the varieties in each rose-bed are marked by glazed faience labels copied from those of Battersea enamel which used to be hung round the necks of decanters.

Here is a garden where all is controlled. Its proportions on the flat as well as in volume were carefully studied and related. Hedges, water, gravel, grass and trees are all disciplined and limited so that each plays its predetermined part in a whole. Here there is a plan and an idea; growth and time have their inevitable place which is allowed for but always controlled.

To be able to play with water in the grand manner is an increasingly rare privilege, although in fact, in our day, bulldozers, scrapers, diggers and dumpers make the construction of lakes and canals easy, rapid and relatively cheap. The handling of water in a more modest and intimate way may well make more onerous demands on labour and time.

Russell Page, *The Education of a Gardener*

The Garden

It is a gesture against the wild,
The ungovernable sea of grass;
A place to remember love in,
To be lonely for a while;
To forget the voices of children
Calling from a locked room;
To substitute for the care
Of one querulous human
Hundreds of dumb needs.

It is the old kingdom of man.
Answering to their names,
Out of the soil the buds come,
The silent detonations
Of power wielded without sin.

R. S. Thomas

The Night Dances

A smile fell in the grass.
Irretrievable!

And how will your night dances
Lose themselves. In mathematics?

Such pure leaps and spirals –
Surely they travel

The world forever, I shall not entirely
Sit emptied of beauties, the gift

Of your small breath, the drenched grass
Smell of your sleeps, lilies, lilies.

Their flesh bears no relation.
Cold folds of ego, the calla,

And the tiger, embellishing itself –
Spots, and a spread of hot petals.

The comets
Have such a space to cross,

Such coldness, forgetfulness.
So your gestures flake off –

Warm and human, then the pink light
Bleeding and peeling

Through the black amnesias of heaven.
Why am I given

These lamps, these planets
Falling like blessings, like flakes

Six-sided, white
On my eyes, my lips, my hair

Touching and melting.
Nowhere.

Sylvia Plath

The Peregrine Strikes

25 March

I found sixteen peregrine kills: three black-headed gulls, a redshank, and
a wigeon, on the shingle; five lapwings, two wigeon, a rook, a jackdaw,
and a shelduck, on the marsh. The shelduck lay at the end of a long trail
of feathers torn out by the ripping impact of the stoop. A black-headed
gull had been plucked and eaten on the smooth green lawn of a summer
bungalow. It lay at the exact centre, reclining in a mass of white feathers,
like a dead flower among spilt petals.

J. A. Baker, *The Peregrine*

An Herbaceous Border

Having had an herbaceous border thrust upon us we proceeded to act as
though we had been born with one. We took it for granted that it was a
simple and easy way of having a large bed of perennial plants – or 'subjects', as the pros call them – which would be no trouble or expense once
they were in; they would flower away happily all summer. In real life,
however, we found that perennials are endless hard work and when they
finally break out into a riot of colour they do so during the only two
weeks of the year when all our friends are away, and even our sub-friends
don't seem to drop in with the hope of a free drink. Sometimes at the
height of our herbaceous season we have even been away ourselves.

For the other fifty weeks of the year the herbaceous border can be a
pretty depressing sight. It is a complete myth, spread around by deeply
vested horticultural interests, that you can just put things in and leave
them. Either everything outgrows its strength so fast that it falls flat on
its face, or it grows so slowly that it will be another year before it's big
enough to be noticed at all.

There is a remedy for the first of these misfortunes – namely, the
planting of stakes in the ground to support the plants; but somehow – in
one's maiden season at any rate – one doesn't remember about this in
time. The reason is obviously psychological: the beginner is too preoccu-

pied with trying to get live things to grow to think of planting anything inanimate. I once planted a three-foot stick of willow to mark where a row of beans had been sown; by the time the beans were up the willow marker had rooted and burst into leaf. When I remarked on this to the farmer next door he pointed to the three 50-ft willow trees behind his barn. Those trees, he said, had originally been tethering posts for horses when the place was a stud farm.

Which explains, I think, all that business in the last act of *Tannhäuser* when, as the errant hero dies on the way back from Rome, his pilgrim's staff bursts into leaf to show that his sins are forgiven, or something. This was no miracle or sign from heaven. The staff was made of willow, and any piece of willow leant on long enough for a Wagner tenor to finish singing has plenty of time to take root and come into full leaf.

In any normal environment no doubt the clumps of hollyhocks and lilies, peonies and larkspur, irises and sweet rocket would carry their height with ease and have no need of stakes in our herbaceous border. But our garden is not set in a normal environment. Though the South Downs are only a mile to the south and south-west of us, and there are houses a hundred yards to the west of us, we are more battered and bruised by gales than any other house in the village. It is as though a private tunnel brought the wind direct from Channel to consumer, whirling its way through the Ouse valley, up the hill, over the top, along the Downs, and around the corner before unleashing its full concentrated force on our garden.

We were told by our smug friends who live in shady hollows and wood-encircled manor houses that what we needed was a wind-break. This had occurred to us, too, and we had in fact already given the question some thought during our first planning of the garden. What we hadn't bargained for, however, was the strength and persistence of the wind that needed to be broken. By the time we first encountered the gales, which settled down to a state of equinoctial fury from which they have never emerged, we realised that we had left things too late. Everything we thought of that might serve as a decorative, as well as an efficient, wind-break was either too slow-growing or had unfortunate habits.

The truth is that a wind-break in this country cannot be planted from scratch; it must be inherited, or included in the price of the house you buy, and must have been growing for at least a generation or more. It is no use breaking your heart over the cypresses that protect and conceal your friends' garden in Italy and have grown to thirty feet in less than ten years; in England it takes thirty years. But perhaps you might expect that, because, after all, cypress is a very foreign tree; it doesn't really like it here and has to be bribed and pampered to grow as high as our hedge is now. On the other hand, was there ever anything so apparently unwilling to grow, or more determined to live for centuries, than the typical native yew of England? And holly is another slow-coach, as temperamental and independent as they come, infuriatingly casual about deciding whether to bear berries or not, and dangerously aggressive towards humans.

Poplar would have done, even though one of our gardening ency-clopaedias described it a little discouragingly as 'suitable for forming screens in town and suburban gardens'. But it seems that poplars have the most alarming habit of looking for water without caring at all where they find it. If we had planted them where we wanted them – that is, about thirty yards from the house – expert opinion assured us that it wouldn't have been long before the roots of the trees had reached the drains and mains outside the kitchen, strangling them like boa constric-tors, and cracking the lot.

Whether things would really have been as bad as all that we didn't know, but it seemed a considerable risk to take to try to find out. True, poplars are deciduous but they grow an efficient wind-breaking, filtering network of small branches that helps during the winter; and during the summer, their rustling leaves can make them the most musical-sounding of all trees.

The object of having a wind-break was naturally to shelter as much of the garden in general as was possible, and to provide a quieter life in par-ticular for the plants in the herbaceous border five yards to leeward. The herbaceous border proved to be something of a problem-child right from the start, and for it to have to fight the gales as well as the pests and diseases and hazard to which it was prone, was a burden we feel we could have been spared in our opening season. By the time we had come round to tying herbaceous plants firmly to stakes there was so little left of the plants that the bed began to look like a stockade – but a stockade powerless to ward off the first of the many, many armies of slugs which embarked, without formal declaration, on what has proved to be the opening campaign of another Hundred Year War.

Until we managed to divert some of their attention by growing vegetables specially for them the slugs liked nothing better than the tender shoots of our larkspurs and peonies. If the price of freedom is said to be eternal vigilance obviously the price is not high enough for slugs. In the herbaceous border we surrounded the plants with rough cindery ashes, since we understood slugs hate that sort of thing. Perhaps they do; but within a day or two of laying this barricade the rains came, the ashes were washed into the earth, and the slugs had only to walk round the cinders to be home and dry. After years of this sort of thing we have decided that unless every slug in the garden is given individual attention the only way to deal with this endless problem is to persuade the great chemical concerns to give up manufacturing one useless slug poison after another and concentrate instead on making something so palatable that the slugs will never want to eat anything else. At a rough guess I would say this slug food should contain plenty of Vitamin C, celery salt, carbohydrate in the form of powdered King Edward potatoes, and be coloured green. The colour is very important. Slugs will strip a row of green lettuces overnight, but will not go near any of the red ones, whether we grow them from Italian or English seed.

During our early experience of cultivating the herbaceous border we did in fact malign the slugs in one respect; we blamed them for eating whatever parts of Sweet William and Canterbury Bells are vital to the plants if they are to flower. What we hadn't realised was that Sweet Williams and Canterbury Bells are biennials and don't flower until the year after you've planted them.

With the impossibility of finding trees that would be of any practical use in coping efficiently with our Prevailing Peculiar, the Force Eight-to-Ten S.W. wind, we considered the idea of a solid clinker-built wooden fence as protection. This was pronounced to be madness by our friends. Didn't we know that, owing to some freak aerodynamic law or other, wind came over the top of a solid fence with twice the force it would have had if it had been unobstructed? As we did not want to get too closely involved with aerodynamics – after all, we were trying to lay out a garden, not an airfield – we abandoned all thought of a fence and decided to follow the advice we were given – namely, if trees were not practicable, to plant shrubs through which the wind would filter without causing structural damage.

And that, roughly, is how we came to have a shrub border.

Spike Hughes, *The Art of Coarse Gardening or The Care and Feeding of Slugs*

Composting and Mulching

It has often been pointed out that the gardener burns his inheritance on the garden bonfire. So convenient a method of destroying rubbish is hard to resist; but except for the roots of perennial weeds, for wood and for old cabbage stalks (which are virtually wood), all vegetable refuse should go to the making of composted manure. For those of us living near an assured supply of farmyard or deep-litter chicken manure, the fag of composting may not always be worth the labour. But most gardeners live in or near towns, and for them the compost heap, if there is room for one, is sacred indeed.

In order to decompose, all vegetable matter needs supplies of nitrogen. This encourages a build-up in the population of the micro-organisms responsible for decomposition. The other necessary ingredients are air and water. Lime also helps by preventing conditions in the heap from becoming too acid.

To make a compost heap, then, you start with a six-inch-deep layer of refuse, covering an area of up to 12ft square. If the refuse contains long stems such as old herbaceous plant stalks, they should be chopped up into shorter lengths, or else they will not pack down enough; the heap will be too well aired and will not heat. On the other hand, refuse like green lawn mowings packs down too well. These should be kept as loose as possible by mixing with coarser rubbish. If mowings pack down too tightly, the absence of air has the effect of not allowing them to heat properly, and you end up with silage instead of compost.

You thoroughly wet this layer and then add a proprietary accelerator (containing nitrogen and lime) before going on to the next. The stack can be added to until 4 or 5 ft high. After six weeks, it should be turned so as to get the outside into the centre and also so as to admit more air, for it will have subsided and compacted considerably. Properly made in this way, the heap will be ready for use in six months. An alternative to the addition of a proprietary 'compost-maker' between layers of refuse is to add sulphate of ammonia and garden lime (which is ground-up chalk – calcium carbonate) in alternate layers. They must be kept separate in this way, because together they react with one another with a consequent loss of nitrogen.

Most of our own compost is made from hay. If you have rough grass planted up with bulbs, you will probably not want to cut it before the end of June. A rotary cutter chews up the grass into just the right length and consistency for composting. As the grass may be rather sere, it should be raked up and whisked away to the heap as quickly as possible. It will need considerable watering, not only at the time of stacking but at intervals of every ten days or so.

We subsequently cut our rough grass again in August and in October, so as to keep the turf from becoming coarse and tussocky. These later cuts can also be composted, but, as they are fairly free of weed seeds, we largely use them as direct surface mulches. All our lawn mowings are also used for this purpose; and you can mulch with bulky manure or with ready-made compost, with leafmould, peat, straw and so on. When the mulch is of undecayed material such as straw or grass cuttings, you should again remember that it will take nitrogen from the soil in the process of decomposition. If put among growing plants, you should at the same time add a nitrogenous fertiliser such as sulphate of ammonia at an ounce to the square yard.

It is important never to mulch on dry ground, as this will prevent rain from penetrating. But if you can apply your mulch to wet ground, then the moisture is retained in the soil and the effects of drought are much reduced. Mulches also have the effect of building up the population of the soil fauna, including earthworms and micro-organisms, and this is a healthy reaction. If applied thickly enough, they suppress weeds.

We have two permanently mulched areas in our garden. First, the blackcurrants: these are under straw, a few extra bales being scattered over the area every winter. The bushes' tendency to root near the surface is accentuated by mulching, and it is therefore very important not to discontinue the treatment, otherwise the currants' surface-feeding roots would be terribly susceptible to drought. The berries, of course, are absolutely mud-free, and no weeding or digging is called for.

Second, there is the rose garden. This used to be a very badly drained area, but a vast earthworm population has made the heavy soil beautifully crumbly and full of channels. Also, the permanent mulch has here practically eliminated blackspot – much to my surprise. Our rose beds are surrounded by paving. In the process of turning the mulch over, blackbirds are constantly flinging it out on to the paths, and a daily sweep-up is necessary in summer. This would be an insupportable nuisance with mown grass verges. A box-hedge edging might be one solution. No system is perfect: one has to balance the advantages with the drawbacks.

Christopher Lloyd, *The Well-Tempered Garden*

March

One of the best possible ways to learn about gardens is to visit as many as possible. June and July are the climax of every garden-visiting year but the more you visit, the less you are inclined to leave your own garden and sacrifice one precious day in the weekend to somebody else's. One's own Bourbon roses are more special than their superiors at Sissinghurst: Hidcote's lacecap hydrangeas have nothing on the bushes you have chosen and planted yourself. Rather than miss the results of your own selections, you are reduced to garden-visiting in the lesser seasons.

It was in just such a mood that I made a visit to Hampton Court in March. I had come more to inspect the remains of Cardinal Wolsey's 280 guest-bedrooms, his arched kitchens and great court than to take in the details of the surrounding gardens. But even that worldly intriguing Cardinal had time for his garden amidst the cares of state: wheelbarrows, watering cans, 'pots for the 'erbs and twine to fix the arbours' all feature among the earliest accounts for his grand buildings. Visiting the palace gardens, very much later than the intimate style of Wolsey's own day, I was amazed out of season by a towering specimen tree.

In the winter sunlight, against the twirled and twisted Tudor chimneys, a gigantic Magnolia grandiflora had spread itself to the full. It must have been all of 20 feet tall and every inch as wide. Now March is hardly the accepted season for magnolias, largely because we concentrate our eyes and attention on flowers. It is an understandable prejudice, but with a little training and a little more attention it is easy to start noticing where before one had only been seeing and thus to pick out details of form, outline and reflection which the dedicated searcher for flowers would normally hurry past. To my way of thinking there is more beauty in a bush of ripe redcurrants than in the most floriferous cactus dahlia.

In winter, Magnolia grandiflora comes more into the class of a redcurrant. It has no flowers, only leaves. But the leaves are quite magnificent; they are as stiff and as long as a rhododendron's but without the ribbing or the deadening dankness of its well-known green. When Magnolia grandiflora is struck by the sun, it lives two different lives. On the leaf's upper surface, the light dances, reflected by shining green while the under surface gleams with ginger-brown, absorbing the light in its layer of natural fur. For if you turn over this magnolia's leaves, you will find them lined with pale suede, the colour of a country colonel's racecourse shoes. That alone makes it too good to miss in the garden.

Besides being evergreen, this king of all trees is also a magnolia. Among shrubs which flower, magnolias have no equals. Grandiflora is a late but long flowerer. In a warm summer, it begins to show signs of opening in July and does not finish until late October. The buds are like long white candles, hidden amongst the thick green leaves. Though you often have to search to find them, the more they unfold, the more unmistakable they become. The flowers grow huge, as much as a foot wide, with petals like very smooth white wax held together by a central cluster of stamens. They look too exotic to be true; even so, their final glory is untold. Grandiflora's leaves may be fascinating, its flowers incomparable among whites, but it is for their scent that they are enjoyed most of all. On a late summer's evening, they overpower you with spices and lemons and an ingredient of their own, like the smell of a stone-pillared church, so cold that it makes you shiver even in August. I cannot describe the strength of the resulting mixture; I can only urge you to try it, if you have the room, for yourselves. Often the flowers hold a nest of beetles who have come for the pollen; they have enjoyed this, say scientists, since the world's early days, for beetles and magnolias made friends before the bee existed. Beetles always know where to go for the best.

In America, its home, this magnolia is free-flowering and free-growing but in England it is so shy that it needs the shelter of a good south wall. In the south, with other shrubs around it, it will form into a rounded tree in an open position, but with young plants costing over £3 each, I do not suggest you risk it in this way.

If you have a wall with a chimney behind it, that is the perfect place: the chimney's warmth can bring a young plant through a cold winter. But it will never hasten grandiflora into flower. For that happy event, you must often wait ten years, allowing it to spread and thicken while you enjoy it as evergreen cover. You can sometimes encourage it by careful 'barking' in the spring, by stripping off a ring of bark near the trunk and leaving a piece in the front untouched, so your scraping does not prove fatal; try to cut a circle, stopping before you make the ends meet. This restricts the flow of sap and encourages flowers, not leaves, above. If you do not fancy the risk, plant the Exmouth variety instead, which is shorter, quicker to flower and freer when it does so. Like all magnolias, it is best planted in April, enjoying an annual top-dressing of leaf-mould, protection in its first winter and plenty of water in dry weather.

'Call no flower happy until it's dead.' Even in the garden reputations rise and fall. Yesterday's favourite is tomorrow's abomination; bedding nowadays is out and the ferns of our forefathers are no longer visited upon us children. Tastes, of necessity, change and change is often cruel. To none has fashion been crueller than to *Bellis perennis*, the common English daisy.

The daisy's disgrace is complete. Her reward is a fortnightly dose of poison, her death a growth industry for chemicals and machines. Like all tragic heroines she has been brought to ruin by her own qualities. Imprudently, she began to grow too easily in grass. Obtrusively, she flowered from February to October. The Furies gathered, the shears snipped but the daisy refused to surrender. Where cutting and poisoning had failed, only hormones could humble and reform. Bellis must grow till she burst, victim of her own pride. Daisytox was born to kill her. There are, however, two sides to a tragic story. For centuries, the daisy was admired, prized for the very qualities we now revile. Lovers would appeal to her wisdom, children would turn her into chains and poets would praise the artlessness of her charms. She was even believed to exude a juice which would stunt the growth of dogs.

A dossier of daisy lovers still reads impressively, a list of sensibilities which are not to be despised. At its head stands Chaucer, Bellis's best friend, who called her the 'Emperice and flour of floures alle'. He would lie in the field to watch her open in the morning: he would return to see her close again at night, a peculiarity which earned her popular name: daisy is a corruption of day's eye. In the *Legend of Fair Women*, his Queen Alceste is turned into a daisy and retains as many virtues as the florets in a daisy flower. The compliment is not to be despised, as the yellow centre of the daisy is a mass of these tight-packed florets, and what we would loosely call the white outer-petals are only a fraction of the total. Queen Alceste is a woman too good to be true.

Chaucer's example was not neglected. Ophelia in her madness, Burns in his coyness, Keats near his grave and Milton in his blindness, all showed favour for the day's eye's beauty. Thomas Hardy's wife adored it; Tennyson addressed it in four separate poems and Shelley considered it the pearled Arcturus of the earth. Wordsworth made two attempts, failing abysmally with one and rising sublimely with the other; 'A little Cyclops with one eye Staring to threaten and defy . . .' That was the secret of the daisy's success. From the tombs of the Egyptians to the floors of medieval monasteries, from the decoration of the Petit Trianon to Lady Beaufort's emblem in the Henry VII chapel in Westminster, *Bellis perennis* flowered its way into many responsive hearts.

But hearts began to harden. 'Oh, daisy, daisy cease thy varied song, a plant may chant too often and too long.' In 1831, Mr Budding's first lawnmower lumbered into attack. Wearied by the poet's praises, we were persuaded that henceforward, our daisies were better numbered. Flowers were stamped out from the largest single area of an English garden and paradoxically, the most boring perennial plant in the gardener's dictionary, bent, creeping or browntop fescue, became the symbol of horticultural excellence. The English took it exclusively to heart, for all must be for the greenest in the greenest of all possible lands. If the daisy's downfall was hastened by her own persistence, part of the blame for her disgrace belongs to the society into which she was born.

Daisies, I suggest, are due for a revival. They need no mowing, manuring, spiking, worming, sanding or liming. They flower for seven months of the year, smelling sweetly and shining whitely, and they wear as well as those fine bowling green grasses which are named Emerald Velvet, as if velvet or emeralds were two materials upon which any sensible gardener would wish to walk.

Of course, a gardener is tied to the soil and to the length of his lawn, living with only an illusion of his freedom. But by coming to terms with the daisy, learning to love what advertisements ask him to abuse, he can cut through the worst of his labours, decking his hours in the grass with daisy-chains. For even the poisoners and grumblers admit, with a grudge, that Bellis perennis will have the last word. All go in the end to push up the daisies, however much they love and spray their lawn.

March is not a particularly easy time for a scented garden. The good smells of winter are going over. The long sprays of mahonia are dropping and rapidly dwindling to their tips. With me, it is too early for Pheasant Eye narcissus, and common daffodils smell fresh but not powerfully. Late snowdrops and scillas do not really smell at all. Hellebores would not allow themselves such meretricious attractions; one is emphatically known as Stinking. Hyacinths, however, spread a heavy sweetness which carries far and is almost too much of a blessing; in death or nearby, they are repulsive. Neither primroses nor violets are at their best. I have never come close enough to a heather to know whether it smells or not. Maliciously, I suspect the worst.

However, spring has a smell of its own, especially on wet nights, and lured into the garden on a wet evening I find myself passing from scent to scent. It might be the papery smell of a cypress or the aggressive pungency of a bruised sprig of rosemary. But they are available all the year round. Another March smell attracts my attention more forcibly. It is not a very common plant, but I would always give it a home.

It belongs to that temperamental family, the daphne. This time it is not our native mezereon so much as a variegated relation which I warmly recommend to patient gardeners. It is *Daphne odora aureomarginata*, a 2-foot-high bush which eventually spreads to about a yard in width.

I first tried the ordinary *odora*, not caring for variegation and not realizing that it is often not very hardy. Two months later, it was killed by frost. Since then, I have grown to like gold-variegated plants, though my dislike of spotted laurel is as fervent as ever. Of them all, this daphne is my favourite.

Its gold is not so strident as that of a variegated elaeagnus nor so valuable as that of the admirable Privet. It runs round the edges of the pale green leaf and keeps the whole bush as interesting as any flower in summer. It is evergreen, of course. But March, undoubtedly, is this daphne's season of glory; the off-white flowers finally open among the tips of the branches, though their buds have been swelling magenta-pink for weeks before. They are small and rather tubular; their outsides retain the bud's bright magenta.

This daphne, as befits an *odora*, is the sweetest-smelling of its family. It smells supremely of spring but it is not a quick customer to please. It must be in a sheltered corner, preferably beneath a south wall, and must have a light soil, well laced with leaf mould. It can be grown prettily in a 6-inch pot. Drainage, as with most daphnes, is important, and when young, it should not be allowed to beg for water. Young plants move most easily. If you can afford to wait for five years or more, do try it in a bed against the warm wall of the house, one of those narrow strips which we all have and which can be so difficult to fill. When you fling open the windows to begin spring cleaning, this daphne will charm you into inactivity.

Robin Lane Fox, *Variations on a Garden*

The Yard Garden

The essence of the garden that is little more than a yard is enclosure, and fairly intimate, detailed paving and planting lend themselves to a small area in town admirably, the end result being a true extension to the home from which it leads. It is what its name suggests, and is not to be confused with the American idea of a yard – which is what we call a garden. Originally it might well have served simply as a concreted service area, the circulation space between the house and coalshed, wash-house and W.C.

In a tight urban situation, gardens are often overlooked and some overhead protection as well as peep-proof boundary walls are needed for privacy – these could both be equally well constructed of timber.

Such a garden is primarily for adults, young or old, with room perhaps for a small sand-pit for children or grandchildren. Because of its sheltered character it is ideal for sunbathing, parking a pram, and lush plant growth. Such areas are usually frost-free as well, and surprisingly tender subjects can be grown there.

Again, being small, grass within such an area is probably impractical, and a hard surface necessary.

Where such a garden is approached from the house by french windows or sliding doors or is overlooked by a lot of glazing a feeling of interpenetration can be encouraged by using the same flooring material inside and out. Whereas such an idea might be expensive if carried out on a large scale, it becomes quite feasible here. Slate, Old York stone, or quarry tiles could all be used – if not for the whole floor at least for a strip inside on which to stand house plants (bringing the garden in) or as small areas outside set within larger areas of a cheaper material (taking the living-room feeling out). Such a courtyard garden often gets very hot, and encourages people to pad out in bare feet so that a slight texture to the surfacing whatever it may be can be rather pleasant. Consider one of the dozens of types of concrete slab, interlocking concrete paving blocks (fairly new on the market), brick perhaps matching the house and garden walls, granite setts or cobbles in small areas, or even areas of brushed *in situ* concrete within a larger pattern of brick or timber . . .

Slight changes of level make an area more interesting, but should not be enough to prohibit wheeled trolleys or children's toys.

Relate the furniture you use in this type of area to the general decoration and style of the whole house and build in the odd bench seat, barbecue or bar if you are the party type. Tubs or pots should again match the interior style; the selection at garden centres is now fairly good. Think too of lighting – not necessarily a vast flood scheme in changing colours, but something subtle to play up the best features, and cast the remainder in shade. Lighting can make the most of your garden, not only at night but throughout the winter as well.

As you are so much on top of the plants in a yard garden, they should be selected to give you maximum value the whole year round, not only in flower performance, but in leaf shape, texture, scent, and overall form grouped both to blend and to contrast. In such a small intimate area, it is as well to stick to a particular colour range of plant material, taking the key from the colours of your interior perhaps, or the colour of your external walls, so that the garden becomes a clear statement – a yellow and white garden, or pink and purple, for instance – contrasted, of course, with grey and green, silver or gold foliages. As a personal preference I would steer clear of conifers and heathers as well. You can then afford to liven up the space with bright splashes of annual colour or bulbs in your tubs and pots.

Again, don't overdo the furnishings. There is a temptation to bring in more and more bits in an effort to prop or jolly up a weak design.

Lastly, this courtyard can be extremely attractive simply treated as a nice place to be – in your own country. One need not succumb to the fashion for simulating a Spanish patio; applied bright colour and ornate furnishings can look extremely tawdry on those grey days when the sun isn't shining.

John Brookes, *Improve Your Lot*

The Mower

The mower stalled, twice; kneeling, I found
A hedgehog jammed up against the blades,
Killed. It had been in the long grass.

I had seen it before, and even fed it, once.
Now I had mauled its unobtrusive world
Unmendably. Burial was no help:

Next morning I got up and it did not.
The first day after a death, the new absence
Is always the same; we should be careful

Of each other, we should be kind
While there is still time.

Philip Larkin

Lighting

The kind of light in which you see a garden makes all the difference to its enjoyment. It seems a pity, though inevitable, that gardens which are opened to the public during the summer months are seen in the flat and unflattering noontide light. Shadows are minimal, the glare is crude, the flowers (roses in particular) are limp. After a few scorching days it is a relief to be capped by cloud again.

And yet, in our northern latitudes, we yearn for sun and the times when we can most enjoy it is on summer mornings and evenings; in other seasons, at any time of day. The shadows will be long enough and the contrast of shadows is a great help, even though they are the photographer's bane.

So you should always place certain plants where you know that the sun's slanting rays will flatter them. Particularly is this true of autumn and winter sunlight, whose quality is yellow. Place your variegated elaeagnus bush so that it is sunlit then. It will look bright as a glade of daffodils.

Dark backgrounds to side-lit plants look good, as when the late afternoon sun reaches a northwest-facing border that's backed by trees or a building. On a visit to the Savill Gardens (near Windsor) in late May, I caught their planting of ornamental rhubarb (they call it *Rheum australe* but I think it was a good strain of the variable *R. palmatum*) at the right moment. Its plumes of white flowers were highlighted by a dark background of trees in shadow. The jagged, blackish purple leaves are held obliquely for weeks after they unfold, so that the sun, particularly early and late, catches their under-surfaces which are dusky plum red. What a plant. But it's as well to have other plants that will grow up in front of it in later summer, to mask its latter days. The stately 6ft *Nicotiana sylvestris* would be my choice.

Back lighting is even more dramatic. We have an 8ft wall behind a north-facing border, but by early May the sun's declination allows it to illuminate much of the border's contents from behind while the actual wall face appears blacker than ever by contrast. It makes a setting for *Philadelphus coronarius* 'Aureus', the golden-leaved form of the common mock orange, whose translucent young leaves the sun illuminates like bits of glass in a medieval church window.

Purple foliage like that of the darkest sumachs (*Cotinus*) can seem almost glum with the sun behind you, but see it the other way and it is transfigured into ruby jewels.

A German photographer visited me recently and showed me enlarged colour prints of some of his work. He had only recently taken to photographing plants and I was particularly intrigued by one picture of *Acer palmatum* 'Dissectum Purpureum' taken against the light. This cut-leaved Japanese maple normally makes a very low, hummocky specimen with the tips of its branches trailing on the ground. I asked him whether he had had to crawl inside the bush in order to get his back-lighted picture, and he had done precisely that! But there are plenty of purple-leaved *Acer palmatums* that grow into decent-sized trees and allow you to admire a curtain of back-lit foliage.

The greater the size of a leaf, the greater the scope for lighting effects, especially when the leaf has an interesting shape and casts shadows on itself. *Melianthus major* has a big glaucous, pinnate leaf. The deep marginal serrations are replicated in shadow on the smooth leaf surfaces and this is particularly noticeable early and late in the day.

The largest leaf we can grow on a hardy plant is that of *Gunnera manicata* from the Brazilian highlands. Young leaves point upwards and are readily transfused by sunlight. And since this is a waterside plant, you will often see the golden lines of sun-reflected ripples moving across a gunnera leaf's lower surface.

Flowers respond to lighting in many different ways. Sometimes it drains them of colour; at others they seem to have their own inner source of light, so intensely do they glow. This is oftenest true of red and orange flowers. Towards sunset and sometimes even more so afterwards, they burn with a volcanic glow, only to turn quite black as night falls.

Some of the best flower lighting effects come from within an arbour. It is wonderful to be within a flowering laburnum tunnel when all the sun's light is transmitted through the blossom above and around. You are bathed in this light and in the flowers' sweet scent, which is scarcely noticed from a tree in the open.

Christopher Lloyd, *The Well-Chosen Garden*

Writing in Prison

Years ago I was a gardener.
I grew the flowers of my childhood,
lavender and wayside lilies
and my first love the cornflower.

The wind on the summer wheat.
The blue glaze in the vanished woods.
In the space of my yard I glimpsed again
all the lost places of my life.

I was remaking them. Here in a space
smaller still I make them again.

Ken Smith

Blue

Blue is the colour for distance. Think of mountains far away, or of Claude Lorrain's paintings which have warm brown foregrounds fading to silvery blue, so that you feel you can step into them for miles. A painting is much smaller than a garden: if it is possible to trick people into believing that a canvas six feet by four can lead them into infinite space, then you can use a similar magic to make your garden look as though it goes on for ever. Gertrude Jekyll, who specialized in outsize herbaceous borders, always put blues at the far end. As you walked down their length it must have seemed as though the ribbons of flowers would unroll for ever. A similar illusion is to be found in bluebell woods, where the trees almost seem to be afloat. Could it be this feeling of perpetual motion which lends enchantment to the view?

If it is the property of some blues to lengthen the view and make you stand and dream, others, the clearer hues, have a more immediate effect. Like yellows, the blues come in two cadences, happy and sad: they do not all create the same mood. Positive blue, or blue which is sharpened by white, lifts the spirits as a summer sky or a sight of the azure sea might do. Think of forget-me-nots, or blue-and-white china, or a bright blue dress. The expression 'feeling blue' would probably not call any such agreeable sights into mind. The melancholy blues are the ones which do not tend to provoke an immediate reaction of pleasure. These are the minor key shades, the twilight lavenders and misty Michaelmas daisies which leave you feeling calm and thoughtful rather than ebullient. While bright blues might be said to induce feelings more appropriate to major key harmonies, the sad blues give to a garden the depth and overall moodiness that you would expect from a minor movement in music.

If I have laboured this point it is to demonstrate that there are as many shades of meaning in a colour as there are tones within its range. And when all that has been said, light, which dissolves and changes everything, will work its magic on blues as it does on all colours, so that in shade even the bright blues will dim and behave as though they are moody ones. Towards the end of the day the blue of forget-me-nots will fade, so that what appeared as a cheerful slice of sky under the midday sun can give an illusion of depth and distance late in the afternoon. And if you stick to a hazy palette, that too will change with the light, for in the sun the colour will be richer and will echo the languorous pace of a hot day, while in shade it will be greyer and cooler. Think of cornflowers in bright sunshine and then think of lavender. The first image produces a sharper effect, like the colours people wear by the sea. The second is heavier, almost like a violet sky before a thunderstorm. Then think of both plants in shade, where the lavender becomes greyer and less sensual and the cornflowers, so unaffected and cheerful in the sunshine, are transformed into something mysterious and cool.

In order to stage a mirage effect you might, then, choose to use clear blues in the shade, or the soft grey and hazy purple ones to lead the eye on in sun – remembering perhaps that while clear blues remain stimulating in shade, on grey days the lavender-blues can look very doleful indeed. To intensify any blue, avoid too many dark green leaves and choose glaucous or silver ones instead. With misty shades this might tend to give you a fit of the blues under sullen skies, so you might like to lean more heavily on silver than on blue-green leaves, or even add a dash of white to lighten it all. But then you would be sacrificing your illusion to distance.

Van Gogh said, 'There is no blue without yellow and orange, and when you paint blue, paint yellow and orange as well.' It is true that if not placed near a contrasting colour blue seems almost negative, like the absence of colour, which is perhaps why it is so good at creating a mirage effect. But if, like van Gogh, you want to appreciate the blueness of blue then you need to follow his advice and use yellow and orange to define the colour. One of the best illustrations of this can be seen in the painter John Hubbard's garden, where orange marigolds and blue felicia edge a narrow path. Non-colourists might not, however, want to take their experiment that far, for flowers somehow cease to be flowers when they are used in such broad brush strokes. Gertrude Jekyll, whose early training as an artist encouraged her to explore the use of colour in the garden, wrote that 'any experienced colourist knows that blue will be more telling – more purely blue – by the juxtaposition of rightly placed complementary colour'. In a scheme for a blue garden she used citron and canary-yellow lupins with snapdragons, as well as white lilies and tree lupins, to set off what she called 'pure blues'. No purple blues, like the bluest of the campanulas and the perennial lupins, were to be included, for 'they would be inadmissible', she ruled. It may be that an exception to Monet and Jekyll's rule should be made for meconopsis, the Himalayan blue poppy. In some forms, such as *Meconopsis x sheldonii*, the blue is so intense and luminous that it can stand alone. Indeed it is a difficult colour to combine with others in the same range, and there is something to be said for enjoying this meconopsis in a woodland setting unaccompanied by other flowers, which only dilute or vulgarise its impact. Hydrangeas grown on acid soil present similar problems, for their piercing blue tends to look synthetic against plants which flower in quieter tones.

Innocent blues belong most of all to spring, when the limpid light suits their clarity and the pallor of fresh leaves provides enough yellow to balance the blue. 'Blue and green should ne'er be seen' goes the old saying, but provided the green veers towards yellow rather than blue, it is easy to dispel this prejudice. The pale green bottlebrushes or *Euphorbia characias* work better with the bright blue of scillas, for example, than would the dark leaves of evergreens like yew or box.

In any composition of green and blue the balance is a difficult one. The two colours share the same primary base, which tends to deaden the blue when they are used together. Lightening the green until it becomes almost yellow will bring the blue back to life again. Putting a pale blue flower against a dark green hedge would produce a different effect. Here the balance is more a question of value than of hue, as the colours of the plants do not compete with one another at all. Pale blue against the dark green produces what appears to be no more than a contrast of light and dark, whereas with euphorbia and the scillas what you notice first is not the definition of light and shade but the different colours of the plants.

In high summer, when leaves are darker, blue and green are hard to manage in the same bed. They look dull together because their range of tones is too similar. Introducing white or pale yellow flowers can help, or where you want more permanent light relief, silver or variegated leaves may be the answer. In summer, without the addition of some yellow or orange, a predominantly blue border will have a deadening effect unless green leaves are sharpened to lime, white or silver. The negative properties of blue can work in the gardener's favour, on the other hand, when used to temper hot colour schemes. For blue is the most cool and restful of all colours, adding a sense of space and calm to any composition.

Mary Keen, *Colour Your Garden*

Autumn

I am thankful we have four distinct seasons, then we can appreciate the different moods of each. The choice of trees and shrubs for autumn colour will depend on the soil. If it is acid, fothergilla, enkianthus and most eucryphias flourish and colour well and trees like *Nyssa sylvatica*, *Stewartia serratta* and *S. sinensis* will turn brilliant colours.

In the lime (alkaline) soil at Barnsley we have planted several sorbus, mountain ash, and these make beautiful displays with their berries and autumn colour. Sorbus have white, pink, yellow and red berries and in autumn you will discover which berries are first to ripen, for the birds will naturally go to these. With us the white and pink-tinged berries of *Sorbus hupehensis* stay on well after the leaves have fallen and so do the fruits on the crabs *Malus toringoides* and *M. transitoria*.

We have been working hard on planting herbaceous flowers which will keep blooming well into October. These are the Compositae heleniums, helianthus and heliopsis as well as the annual sunflowers. Many of the salvias do not come into flower until autumn and the varied lobelias are the same. Sometimes I wish that autumn would last longer.

GREAT DIXTER

Every year autumn is different. Sometimes it comes on us in a tremendous rush, and an early frost catches us unawares before all our tender plants have been given their winter protection. One day I may walk round my garden at Barnsley thinking how perfect the lobelias, salvias and dahlias all look, then overnight the scene changes dramatically: a hard frost has blackened the dahlias, and the lobelias and salvias have lost their pristine charm.

Fortunately, frost does not often occur in the Cotswolds as early as September, so our borders go on looking well structured and colourful for several more weeks. One year we had a frost on 28 September, but it did not hit us again until 9 and 10 November. According to my garden diary, the first hard frost came on 17 November another year; in 1992 the first ground frost was on 15 October, and in 1995 our first, very mild, frost was on 28 October. So, you see, you cannot rely on the diary for frost dates – you must study the sky, the clouds and the feel of the temperature, as well as the moon, and become your own weatherman. It is often the clouds which give the weather prophet the most useful clues.

In September and October, as through the rest of the year, every detail must be cared for. Dying flowers, if allowed to remain on the plant, will produce seeds to provide a feast for garden birds and migrants, or to be collected and sown for a future display – or maybe they will self-sow. My loyalties are divided. Nature is very generous with her gifts and we must reciprocate.

Hopefully by September the watering cans and hosepipes will be less in demand as the need for watering tubs and pots reduces, but another daily routine will soon be on us: leaf-fall starts gently in September, rising to a crescendo in October and November; by December all our deciduous trees should be bare, allowing the evergreens to come into their own and give the winter garden its own structure.

Last September I thought our borders at Barnsley were doing well in spite of the drought and the fawn lawns. We had penstemons, monardas, lobelias, phlox, lots of violas and everlasting sweet peas, sunflowers and rudbeckias, among others. Then, early in the month, I went to Christopher Lloyd's garden at Great Dixter. As I walked round his borders with him, my pride-bubble burst. I like to think our borders are planted in layers so there is a succession of plants in bloom through most of the year: the Dixter borders looked much like ours, but were definitely more interesting, and Christo had the edge on us with his clever use of unusual annuals and biennials. These, if dead-headed, give a longer display than most perennials, but they take more time, thought and work. Christo had generous clumps of *Tithonia rotundifolia*, 'Torch', *Ageratum* 'Blue Horizon', *Zinnia linarifolia* 'Orange Star' and white cosmos, which he had grown specially to follow on after the lupins.

Christo says 'Spring happens', but we must plan and work for a good display in summer and through autumn. For example the lupins (treated as biennials), which flowered with such effect in early summer are dug up and replaced with penstemons, verbenas, or with his summer-flowering annuals. All this is very labour-intensive, especially when there is a ready back-up supply of plants lined up waiting to fill the spaces and revitalize the borders. Christo advises that before you move any plants you give them a good soaking, replant them and then re-soak them in their new home.

That was the first lesson I learnt on my September day at Dixter: Nick Burton, my new head gardener, must study the seed catalogues to increase our repertoire of annuals. It is simple to sow pans of seeds early in the year, but time-consuming to prick them out and pot them on. Remember there is no need to prick out more seedlings than you will need in your own garden – you can always give the remaining young seedlings in their pan to a gardening friend.

A cheering thought for keen gardeners is that Christo uses cold frames (no artificial heat) to bring on these plants.

This master gardener always has an ace up his sleeve, and his new planting in the old rose garden will I'm sure influence many English country gardeners (the trend of the late 1990s?): now in its third season, it has been transformed into a tropical delight. Christo and Fergus have created this startling paradise in a space enclosed by old yew hedges on three sides, and by a red-roofed barn on the other side. In winter the beds are flat, almost empty, then by the end of May planting begins afresh.

The structure of paths and hedges designed by Sir Edwin Lutyens remains from the rose garden era, but the 'new' concept of planting harks back to the nineteenth century, to William Robinson and Shirley Hibberd. This reinforces my belief that there is little new in the tradition of our English country gardens. We have used the same recurring themes for centuries, but now a much wider variety of plants – some imported, some 'improved' – is available to us.

To quote from Shirley Hibberd's *Rustic Adornments for Homes of Taste*, published in 1872:

> A great number of plants of most noble proportions, many of them gaily coloured, and when lacking colour making ample amends by the splendour of their leafage, may be made perfectly at home in our gardens during the summer ... Perhaps the first place in this glorious company should be assigned to the Cannas ... These are just as easy to grow as dahlias ... The Yuccas, Agave, Bamboos, the *Papyrus antiquorum*, afford fine masses for suitable positions.

We probably associate William Robinson with his strong influence, at the end of the nineteenth century, on the change from the bedding-out of high Victorian times to more natural gardens, herbaceous borders, wild-flower meadows and woodland planting. We overlook the fact that as a young gardener in the 1860s he spent time in Paris as correspondent of *The Times*; in his exhilarating book *The Parks, Promenades and Gardens of Paris* he devotes a long chapter to 'Subtropical Plants for the Flower Garden'. His explanation of 'subtropical' is

> The introduction of a rich and varied vegetation, chiefly distinguished by beauty of form ... The system had its origin in Paris, (then) Mr Gibson, the able and energetic superintendent of Battersea Park ... boldly tried the system, and with what a result all know who have seen his charming 'subtropical garden' in Battersea Park.

William Robinson goes on to recommend agaves, aralias, ferns, cannas, echeveria, nicotiana, solanums. A study of his chapter is well worth while.

I do not know if Christo has been influenced by these two writers, but it illustrates the natural recurrence of fashion – an interesting thought, and also applicable to clothes, architecture and interior design. Recently I have been reading Vivian Russell's book about Monet's colour thoughts and his garden at Giverny. We could all follow his example, using some of his ideas to enliven our gardens through the whole year.

To return to Great Dixter, where exciting exotics pervade: cannas, some with especially handsome and well-veined leaves, are treated in groups, not as the 'dot plants' of urban park beds. Castor-oil plants have grown 1.8 metres (6ft) tall from seed in a season. There are carefully chosen dahlias – the most elegant-flowered varieties combined with good foliage. Kniphofias sparkle between the banana plants, Japanese musa, and the huge leaves of *Paulownia tomentosa*, and the tree of heaven, *Ailanthus altissima*, both of which are stooled back every spring to create this surprising leaf effect. I was excited by the *Nicotiana glauca* – a wonderful grey foliage with a not-so-insignificant yellow flower.

It was the early autumn light showing up this eclectic collection of plants which gripped my attention – in autumn, as in spring, all leaves have such a diversity of veining. I was spellbound, and so were the bees, butterflies and hover flies homing in on the verbenas, especially *V. bonariensis*, the 'see-through' plant. I felt that I was in an unfamiliar forest – the top storey of paulownia and ailanthus, the understorey of bananas and cannas, the ground cover of kniphofia and cosmos. This was an experience not to be missed, especially walking through with its creator, who murmured, 'I feel there may be tigers and parrots round the next corner – I hope they're more friendly than the roses were.'

Christo experienced roses as tyrants, dictators – demanding attention, only sticks in water – so decided to uproot them. His new garden reaches a crescendo of exuberance, of flowers as well as foliage, all through the late summer months. When nature is kind, this display carries on into October, and sometimes into November. We must always make the most of late summer and autumn days. Christo does so, and his garden is still full of colour – backed up by many different greens.

Rosemary Verey, *The English Country Garden*

Cowpies for Termites

A termite is one of those remarkably social insects whose ability to cooperate with one another is typically viewed with either admiration or fear, depending on whether one is an academic entomologist or a homeowner. Despite the fact that I belong to both camps, my predominant emotion falls heavily on the admiration side of the equation, especially because I believe that the little termites in the front yard belong to the native species *Gnathamitermes perplexus*, which is said to favor dead grasses, dried twigs and stems, and fallen cholla cactus bits, in which case they will probably leave the lumber in our house alone. Or so I hope.

Confident enough of our termites' harmless nature, I have encouraged them to stay around by serving up a number of large, dried cowpats, the crème de la crème of termite chow, as far as *Gnathamitermes* are concerned. Fortunately for them, if not for the rest of us, cow dung is a feature of almost every corner of the Sonoran Desert of Arizona (and Mexico), due to the affection that Arizonan (and Mexican) ranchers have for cows, huge numbers of which feed on private and public lands throughout the West.

In fact, my initial motivation for dropping cowpies onto the front yard had nothing to do with charity toward termites. Instead, I wanted a front yard with a true desert feel, and since cattle and their by-products are universal in the Sonoran Desert, I knew I had to import a few cowpies to attach the seal of authenticity to my creation. When I go out walking in the Superstitions or Mazatzals, I keep my eye open for just the right cowpats to bring home. A highly rated one must be dry and odorless but not so old as to be falling apart. It must be attractively circular rather than asymmetric, and big, at least a foot in diameter and preferably closer to eighteen inches. Given the dominance of cows in the desert, I rarely have to hunt far for these treasures, which go into my daypack for later positioning by a paloverde or fairy duster in my yard.

My wife tells me that several neighbors have taken her aside to speak of the cowpies in our front yard. They claim to be unconcerned about their effect on local real estate values but rather wonder if I had a completely normal childhood. The local termites do not ask such hard questions. During fall and spring, when they forage on or near the surface, the termites immediately colonize my offerings by tunnelling into the cellulose pie. There in total darkness, they excavate bits of food to carry down into their subterranean home for nestmates. When I carefully pick up my cowpat, I can usually find several pale white workers clinging on the underside of the pat, their work on behalf of the colony interrupted for a moment. According to the termitologist William L. Nutting, a typical colony of *Gnathamitermes perplexus* consists of about 10, 000 individuals, so that I am seeing only the top of the tip of the iceberg when I count the few worker termites clinging to the cowpie.

Where my front-yard *Gnathamitermes* came from in the first place mystifies me, but perhaps they are the progeny of colonies that occupied nearby back alleys or possibly even a neighbor's house. In any event, my colony or colonies almost certainly formed on a late summer day when there was a nuptial flight on Loyola Drive.

John Alcock, *In A Desert Garden, Love & Death Among the Insects*

Amnesty in the Garden

A brim of light leaks out across the sea
to lift the bevel in the wave, the water's lens,
and everything moves again:
the pleated land renewed in its bloom
of gold, the broom and yellow gorse.
Gulls hang their hinges of light
over the loosened water, calling,
calling me down from the hill's height
and through the high stones that remain,
what marks we made on them long effaced.

The forest creaks like a door.
Where children will come this morning
to make handsels for the May Queen
– gathering flowers of the forest
to draw the harvest of the sea –
a rabbit scutters in the leaf-litter,

squirrels shrug up trees, and a pheasant
clatters away like a mechanical toy.
Steeped again in the blent green,
A boy enters the walled garden.

A wind. The lilac and laburnum trees
seethe and churn, then settle. Above him,
the buds are swollen and opening;
below, red shoots spirl to the morning sun.
The roots swarm. In the walled garden
form is imposed on this fugitive green,
this rinsing light: to enclose is to make sacred,
to frame life's chaos for a slow repair,
to make an art of healing, of release,
an amnesty against despair.

Robin Robertson

The 'Natural' Approach

In any wild landscape, nature establishes natural plant communities
which depend on the climate and aspect: heat and cold, soil, sun and
shade, rain and moisture, altitude and latitude. In the best gardens, man-
made communities of garden plants – many coming from different lands
but with similar needs – live and thrive together in natural harmonies.
When you first start to garden you see the plants only as tools to be used
for composing pictures. Colours, shapes, forms and habits of plants are
combined together to produce certain aesthetically pleasing results. In
arranging the plants to make a beautiful garden the gardener needs to be
an artist; but he also needs to know his plants and the individual plants'
requirements in order to get them to grow well. Plants will only give a
sustainable 'performance' if they are given the sort of growing conditions
they enjoy. In appreciating garden planting it is worthwhile looking
beyond the purely pictorial effects and thinking about whether the plant
associations will work in the long term, with plants from similar habitats
growing together in harmony. It is far more jarring to the eye and mind
to see a garden where the wrong plants have been placed beside one

another, plants which, in nature, have completely different requirements, than it is to feel that the wrong sorts of colour scheme have been used – a very subjective and unimportant judgement. The experienced gardener finds that plants have other characteristics besides their obvious and rather superficial colours and shapes. These may be nothing to do with their botanical characteristics. They have certain identifiable traits which can help identify their garden requirements, and give a hint as to the sort of habitats they will have come from. Just by looking at a plant, it is often possible to make a good guess as to what sort of conditions it will enjoy. Grey-leaved plants generally come from countries with hot summers and will need a well-drained garden soil; lush thick-stemmed plants with large leaves come from wet regions, and they need moisture. A plant's appearance, or physiognomy, will reveal whether it thrives in dry stony ground and will endure hot sun, or comes from swampy marshy meadows and will need plenty of moisture, especially in its growing period in spring. Large soft exotic-shaped leaves which allow rain to run off will come from tropical regions and be too tender for most garden situations above a certain latitude or altitude.

More and more gardeners today want to garden in a natural way. They do not necessarily want to make gardening dull by growing only indigenous plants, but they want to make garden tasks less onerous, less labour-intensive, by growing plants together which will not require endless sorting out, dividing, and replanting. They also want to prevent pollution by using artificial fertilisers and pesticides as little as possible.

Planting in natural ways – that is 'planting to please plants' – can be done in different ways. Leaving out true native plant gardening – for which there may often be sound ecological arguments – the most obvious is to select only plants which are native to your region or come from regions which are almost identical in aspect. An example would be gardening in California with natives and Mediterranean-type plants. This should mean literally gardening with nature and, apart from design and aesthetic considerations, entails minimum preparation and amendment of the site, although there may well be frequent and quite skilful 'editing'. William Robinson recommended this sort of planting in his wild garden. The second natural approach involves using plants from all parts of the world and trying to re-create for each plant the garden conditions as similar as possible to those of their own habitat, and growing plants with similar needs together, so that they look comfortable and 'right' in association. Beth Chatto has been the great teacher in this context. Obviously this approach, while still 'natural', is less ecologically and environmentally orientated and more labour-intensive, but it does mean that the possible range of plants you can grow is extended. Soil can be amended, microclimatic pockets created and any other horticultural skills employed to 'improve' the site in a permanent way so that the exotic plants from other regions will form their own artificial plant communities. The important point is that plants are given conditions to please them, and will reward you by thriving. This 'right association' theme can and should be extended to include emphasising growing plants which not only look right together but look right in their landscape. In a country garden on chalk downs or alkaline clay (such as my own new garden in Dorset) it would seem folly to try to make a rhododendron garden. And it would be unsuitable. John Brookes has reminded us how important it is to look at your own countryside and try to match seasonal colours to the landscape, fitting your garden into its surroundings. As a designer I want to consider all these things. First, to discover the nature of the landscape in which the garden you are about to work on is set, and then try to make an appropriate garden. Then in choosing the actual plants I need to know as much as possible about the terrain and climate of the original habitat of any exotics, and decide how they will mix with plants native to the region. In some circumstances, for conservation reasons or in order to keep an unspoiled landscape 'pure', it may be good to use only natives – especially where (as in North America) so much damage has been done by the spread of escaped aliens; originally introduced to gardens or planted to prevent erosion, these are now known as ecological bandits and prevent recreation of vanished landscape features such as the Midwest prairies.

Penelope Hobhouse, *Natural Planting*

The Tree

The next door cat likes to stretch out
his formidable length on my fresh
black earth, paws fore and aft

like a gunboat, then roll back
into a sort of coma, letting the world
go hang, even when raising

the ton weight of his head, watching
his own fur sit up in the wind.
I am doing what that flinty old

rationalist with the warm heart said
I should and digging my garden, which
has a bright green froth of weeds on top

and a sunk armada of broken glass
and china underneath. I sometimes wonder
if I have broken into a tomb. It's

been abandoned for years. I had to
tunnel my way in through head-high
nettles and brambles, that pale green

weed with the white trumpet flowers
which likes to sprint up anything remotely
vertical and sing to itself softly in the sun.

There's a stag-headed lime tree
up above me, eighty or a hundred
feet of it, half dead and half alive,

its topmost limbs splayed out
Grünewald style, in need of care
and attention; the rest swathed less

thickly than they might be in the
proper *gestalt*. I have adopted

a certain interest in its progress,

seating myself on a flat bit of warm
rock to look up at it when not
wrestling with the flesh of a whole root –

this sometimes takes precedence over
the nine o'clock news – or turning up
little worms still fresh behind the ears.

I go on rushing at it, into the dark,
sifting appearances through feet and hands
and then letting my two pioneer

strawberry plants have it with the
watering can, the curlew's wheep wheep,
that wanton afterglow of the longest day.

William Scammell

Jamaica Kincaid suggests that even a perfect garden does not satisfy for ever: something more is desired. This dissatisfaction is one of our greatest virtues, without which our creative culture would never have existed. To imagine an ideal and to work to bring it about is an ambition never so benignly expressed as when applied to gardens.

Strong personalities with vision have always been behind great (and terrible) gardens. Three very different types are represented here. The Alnwick Garden has been one of the success stories of the new century. Designed specifically for public access, it stands in the tradition of Vauxhall (ref. A Walk with Sir Roger), although its recreational opportunities are different. The concerns for 'Health and Safety', the education agenda, and the mass appeal, make it very much a garden for our times. Little Sparta should no longer be surprising after Shenstone's Leasowes, but I find it curious that the world is still interested in such an elitist and didactic garden. My heart is with the Garden of Cosmic Speculation, where Charles Jencks has taken inspiration from acknowledged sources and found new physical forms of expression, and fresh meanings to suit our modern cosmology. It is a garden which demands a level of concentration and mental effort which has been unfashionable for centuries, and yet remains essentially inclusive and accessible.

It is good to recognize that garden conventions can be subverted or broken, and new space colonised. Roof Gardens may have been around since Babylon, but this might just be their age, as land use, particularly in our cities, is reconsidered. Likewise, all strength to the arms of those who beau-

tify waste-grounds under cover of dark: a gentle and profound criticism of our negligent stewardship.

There is a peculiar melancholy running through 'Saturday in the Cloister'; a recognition that the love is too fragile to survive beyond the sacred space; a sanctuary where the oak will outlive us and our works, given time. A recognition too, that these sanctuaries continue to be vital. 'Avian Intention' and 'Bees' both acknowledge that other species than Homo sapiens need gardens, linking nicely with the ecological aspiration of reclaiming the 'dead space' of roofs, and roundabouts. It would be great if we were learning, at last, to garden for others and not just ourselves, as Marion Cran advised.

The Garden I Have in Mind

I know gardeners well (or at least I think I do, for I am a gardener, too, but I experience gardening as an act of utter futility). I know their fickleness, I know their weakness for wanting in their own gardens the thing they have never seen before, or never possessed before, or saw in a garden (their friends'), something which they do not have and would like to have (though what they really like and envy – and especially that, envy – is the entire garden they are seeing, but as a disguise they focus on just one thing: the Mexican poppies, the giant butter burr, the extremely plump blooms of white, purple, black, pink, green, or the hellebores emerging from the cold, damp, and brown earth).

I would not be surprised if every gardener I asked had something definite that he or she liked or envied. Gardeners always have something they like intensely and in particular, right at the moment you engage them in the reality of the borders they cultivate, the space in the garden they occupy; at any moment, they like in particular this, or they like in particular that, nothing in front of them (that is, in the borders they cultivate, the space in the garden they occupy) is repulsive and fills them with hatred, or this thing would not be in front of them. They only love, and they only love in the moment; when the moment has passed, they love the memory of the moment, they love the memory of that particular plant or that particular bloom, but the plant of the bloom itself they have moved on from, they have left it behind for something else, something new, especially something from far away, and from so far away, a place where they will never live (occupy, cultivate; the Himalayas, just for an example).

Of all the benefits that have come from having endured childhood (for it is something to which we must submit, no matter how beautiful we find it, no matter how enjoyable it has been), certainly among them will be the garden and the desire to be involved with gardening. A gardener's grandmother will have grown such and such a rose, and the smell of that rose at dusk (for flowers always seem to be most fragrant at the end of the day, as if that, smelling, was the last thing to do before going to sleep), when the gardener was a child and walking in grandmother's footsteps as she went about her business in the garden – the memory of that smell of the rose combined with the memory of that smell of the grandmother's skirt will forever inform and influence the life of the gardener, inside or outside the garden itself. And so in a conversation with such a person (a gardener), a sentence, a thought that goes something like this – 'You know, when I was such and such an age, I went to the market for a reason that is no longer of any particular interest to me, but it was there I saw for the first time something that I have never and can never forget' – floats out into the clean air, and the person from whom these words or this thought emanates is standing in front of you all bare and trembly, full of feeling, full of memory. Memory is a gardener's real palette; memory as it summons up the past, memory as it shapes the present, memory as it dictates the future.

I have never been able to grow *Meconopsis betonicifolia* with success (it sits there, a green rosette of leaves looking at me, with no bloom. I look back at myself, without a pleasing countenance), but the picture of it that I have in my mind, a picture made up of memory (I saw it some time ago), a picture made up of 'to come' (the future, which is the opposite of remembering), is so intense that whatever happens between me and this plant will never satisfy the picture I have of it (the past remembered, the past to come). I first saw it (*Meconopsis betonicifolia*) in Wayne Winterrowd's garden (a garden he shares with that other garden eminence Joe Eck), and I shall never see this plant (in flower or not, in the wild or cultivated) again without thinking of him (of them, really – he and Joe Eck) and saying to myself, It shall never look quite like this (the way I saw it in their garden), for in their garden it was itself and beyond comparison (whatever that amounts to right now, whatever that might ultimately turn out to be), and I will always want it to look that way, growing comfortably in the mountains of Vermont, so far away from the place to which it is endemic, so far away from the place in which it was natural, unnoticed, and so going about its own peculiar ways of perpetuating itself (perennial, biannual, monocarpic, or not).

I first came to the garden with practicality in mind, a real beginning that would lead to a real end: where to get this, how to grow that. Where to get this was always nearby, a nursery was never too far away; how to grow that led me to acquire volume upon volume, books all with the same advice (likes shade, does not tolerate lime, needs staking), but in the end I came to know how to grow things I like to grow through looking – at other people's gardens. I imagine they acquired knowledge of such things in much the same way – looking and looking at somebody else's garden.

But we who covet our neighbor's garden must finally return to our own, with all its ups and downs, its disappointments, its rewards. We come to it with a blindness, plus a jumble of feelings that mere language (as far as I can see) seems inadequate to express, to define an attachment that is so ordinary: a plant loved especially for something endemic to it (it cannot help its situation: it loves the wet, it loves the dry, it reminds the person seeing it of a wave or a waterfall or some event that contains so personal an experience as when my mother would not allow me to do something I particularly wanted to do and in my misery I noticed that the frangipani tree was in bloom).

I shall never have the garden I have in my mind, but that for me is the joy of it; certain things can never be realized and so all the more reason to attempt them. A garden, no matter how good it is, must never completely satisfy. The world as we know it, after all, began in a very good garden, a completely satisfying garden – Paradise – but after a while the owner and the occupants wanted more.

Jamaica Kincaid, *My Garden (Book)*

Saturday in the Cloister

Beneath the broken tracery of the monastery window,
I loved you.
Shutting out the world for those few, short hours:
sacred moments of suspended time
in which our fingers entwined
and our hearts knew nothing but peace.
My soul, at rest, in your eyes
shook free this body of cares and drifted
on the melody of the blackbird's air
through the branches of the oak, sturdy and enduring,
into a sky of forming cloud
bringing rain by evening.

Gil Morro

Hatred, Passion and Tolerance

I think it was being sent away to boarding school that started my critical reactions, pushing me to hate school dormitory sparseness, discipline, fir and silver birch trees as well as the dreaded rhododendron. I have a pair of tubs with 'Pink Pearl' rhododendrons in them, in an unimportant place, in order to remind me of how much I loathed going back to my prep school, Barfield. At a tender age a hatred was formed that has never been tempered.

I am afraid that, as I have grown older, my original hates have multiplied: turquoise swimming pools, rotating summer houses, sitting room-type conservatories, cement rabbits, irregularly shaped plastic ponds, paths and pools shaped like intestines, plant labels everywhere, hoses left out, crazy paving, wood stained a revolting orange, mini lanterns in wrought iron, orange or green floodlighting, asphalt paths, inexpensive wrought iron gates, and 'decorative' wells. White plastic garden chairs, grey gravel, bird baths, concrete balustrading, hanging baskets, and small fountains are all abominable.

367

In the plant world I have a loathing for flowerbeds, rockeries, aster, aubrieta, almost all marigolds, tapestry hedges, arboretums, mixed avenues, orange lilies, forsythia, valerian, scarlet geraniums and salvias, aubergine-coloured shrubs, fuchsia, lupins, Michaelmas daisy, red hot poker, lavetera, impatiens, snapdragons, begonia, Leylandii hedges, pampas grass, dahlias, gladioli, and the year-round commercial chrysanthemums.

I could happily do away with any variegated or bicoloured plants, shrubs and trees; it's their indecisiveness that I detest – they have been encouraged not to make up their minds. Really good herbaceous planting can be superb, as at Buckingham Palace or New College, Oxford, but on any less high plane, herbaceous borders are a nightmare and extremely labour intensive.

All this, however, is balanced by my ever-growing list of passionate likes.

I love *Rosa viridiflora*, 'American Pillar' rose, 'Mrs. Cholmondeley', 'Madame Boiselot', 'Madame Isaac Periere', 'Constance Spry', and 'Lord Louis' (after my late father-in-law), indeed all roses except miniature ones and the County series. I long all year for the joy of June when my Secret Garden explodes into a heady scented paradise of roses, which sadly lasts only too short a time.

I love architectural gardens, clipped trees, long grass, wild flowers, yellow gravel, ground cover between roses, hollyhocks, pink and aubergine herbaceous poppies, tree and herbaceous peonies and sweet peas that really smell, which I like on wigwams of cane.

In the early part of the year I love snowdrops, aconites, bluebells (in woods only), *Hippeastrum amaryllis*, except for 'Picotee' and one or two others, fritillaries and crocus. I like all the narcissi family and hyacinths, which always remind me of Louis XV arriving for lunch at the Grand Trianon with the parterres all yellow with jonquils; when he emerged after lunch they were all pink with hyacinths!

Tulips are a lovely herald of the glories of colour to come and I delight each winter in ordering them. I especially like the smell, not a scent but a smell, of tulips; my favourite is Rembrandt.

I adore rhubarb (more delicate when growing than it can ever be for lunch on Sunday), cabbages, onions, lettuces and all vegetables growing, especially artichokes, daisies on a lawn, hostas galore, honeysuckle, clematis, all forms of Russian vine, *Vitis coignetiae*, gunnera, crambe, paulownia, catalpas, *Heracleum giganteum*, espaliered fruit trees, yew (but not golden), hornbeam, beech, privet (not variegated or golden), lonicera, laurel, smooth-edged holly, copper beech (but never in the landscape or in a park), sunflowers, *Salvia turkestanica*, delphiniums in pots, allium, feverfew, rodgersia, inulas, bergenias, choisya, lavender, rosemary, autumn crocus and cyclamen.

I love ginger plants but they need heat. My darling Winnie (Countess of Portarlington), who never had a cut flower in any of her houses, had six of them, massed in a huge Korean dish. Zinnias, which I thought the world of as a child, I still like, but only the bright ones, and cut not growing. Plumbago is a great favourite and there it is in my greenhouse with daturas, jasmine and two geraniums growing up the wall.

Humea elegans is also lovely but it's not an easily available seed. I also love campanulas, ceanothus, phlox and orchids. Lilac and philadelphus, hellebores, gypsophila, camellias, hydrangeas, dianthus and *Phytolacca americana* all have important places in my garden.

I was determined that my list of hates should be shorter than my list of favourites because enthusiasm is far more important in gardening than negativeness, than complaining about one's soil and poor results. I have often had to remind myself that you cannot grow everything. Be adventurous, try many things and then spurn or discard; rule out certain plants if they don't work well with you. Stop being cross about your failures and concentrate on what grows well with you.

David Hicks, *My Kind of Garden*

Little Sparta

*Certain gardens are described as retreats
when they are really attacks.*

Ian Hamilton Finlay

The paradox – the unexpected challenge to assumptions and the revelation of depth in the apparently simple – will be a recurring feature of the garden.

Deep in the Wild Garden, where the path leads on to the upper ponds, stand two imposing gate piers crowned by what seem, at a casual glance, to be classical urns or finials, but are hand grenades of the British Second World War design, often nicknamed 'pineapples' because of their shape. They stand monumentally made from stone, their firing rings draping over their shoulders as ivy might over the expected finials; a characteristic conundrum whose elements are humour, beauty and threat.

A very different little wicket gate is set into the fence surrounding the Stonypath Allotment. Its simple inscription KAILYARD repeats the name given to the late-nineteenth-century group of Scottish writers such as J. M. Barrie and S. R. Crockett who treated the lives and concerns of Scots people in a sentimental way often unjustly scorned by critics. Kail, sometimes spelled kale, a particularly hardy kind of cabbage, was at one time a staple of the Scottish diet and its usurpation in contemporary life by more glamorously exotic foods is not likely to have done the Scots much good.

In an upland garden such as this it is appropriate to find stiles connecting the wilder hillsides with the tamer garden, and there are two connecting the upper pond garden with the moorland. A philosophical one has a triple inscription in the manner of Friedrich Hegel, whose idealism held reason to be the heart of reality. The proposition reads THESIS *fence* ANTITHESIS *gate*, then, as the farther side is reached, SYNTHESIS *stile*.

The adapted dictionary definition, a device Finlay uses frequently, underlines the poetic and literary nature of his work. The apparent precision and conciseness of a definition is brought to bear in ways which reveal unexpected aspects of the objects they describe and often dissolve the accepted meaning of terms, or interpretation of their reference in the 'real' world. The second stile carries such a definition of its physical and its ideal nature:

STILE *n. an escalation of the footpath*

Water is almost omnipresent in the garden, with ponds, lochan and streams plentifully fed by the rain falling on the hillside. An imposing aqueduct brings a trickle of water to splash down and continue as a stream just beside a tablet inscribed with lines from Homer's *Iliad*, Book

IV, in Greek and Alexander Pope's English translation:

> Worked into sudden rage by wintry showrs
> Down the steep hill the roaring torrent pours
> The mountain shepherd hears the distant noise

The stream flows on through the Middle Pond beneath an arch of stone inscribed WAVE. The word *wave*, the tide of the stream, is made to contain the Latin *ave*, the formal word of greeting. Thus an attitude of reverence is suggested to the human observer as the stream greets in homage the spirit of the pool as it passes through.

The sounds of the rush, splash and trickle of the streams and fountains are as much part of the garden as the sheen and flicker of the rills and ponds. Bridges and stepping stones lead the way from bank to bank. Spanning the stream between the Wild Garden and Lochan Eck, as the gaze travels towards the receding moors, there is a bridge of pink concrete, a single word cut into its side – CLAUDI – the signature of Claude Lorrain. So the vista of classical ruin, rippling water, sussurating grasses and rustling trees beyond the bridge is transfigured into a landscape as he might have painted it, a reinvention of nature after art, with an element of grandeur added by the huge stands of rhubarb ('the poor man's gunnera', Ian Hamilton Finlay) growing beside the bridge.

Jessie Sheeler, Little Sparta, The Garden of Ian Hamilton Finlay

The Snail and the Poetics of Going Slow

By November 1990, Hugh Hastings and his bulldozers and diggers had widened the stream and dug out a pond, twelve feet down in parts, deep enough for swimming. Here, like the discarded stumps, was another opportunity. What should we do with the leftover soil, a gift from the hole in the ground? Maggie thought of spreading it over the fields, where cows and sheep might benefit from the nutrients, but I thought if there was going to be a free pile of earth, let it be a sculptural object, experiment with it.

Hastings's earth-movers got to work digging out mud and sculpting the land extremely fast. To keep up, I produced one plasticine model after another and walked out to the building site with an updated drawing every day. Because it is hard to shape sand and gravel precisely, one redesigns in response to what has happened and tries to reshape blobs into desirable figures. Using drawings, models, and, in the field, sawdust and stakes with flags and string, one shapes the earth like an action painter, yelling at men in bulldozers, 'More to the left,' directing dumpers with soil like a traffic cop, 'Over there.' they may be able to understand the grand design but they are often too close to the action to see the pattern emerge. I have often found design and its realization to happen this way: you have to continuously remodel an idea, in many media, and then make adjustments as you go along. The rewards are great: something new may emerge, something better than you could have imagined or designed on paper.

Because the digging of the swimming hole was moving so fast and changes would be expensive, Maggie concentrated on shaping the water while I designed the Snail Mound. I had to give it this common name in order to communicate an unambiguous shape to Hastings's men, and to distinguish it from other shapes on which I would soon be working. The 'Snail' drawings and models showed a double-curved ascent, two paths that only meet at the top and that lie at an angle.

In my mind were several different ideas. I thought of the most important shape behind life, the double helix of DNA. This has two spirals of ascent and they reminded me in turn of a utopian design of 1919 that had a diminishing spiral: Tatlin's tower. A wonderful quality of this is the way it illustrates the dance of history's dialectic; it often proceeds in a counter rhythm, as two steps forward and one step back, a progress in fits and starts, an ascent that has a descent built into it. Another idea in the back of my mind was the 16th-century spiral stairway at Chambord which the French king, François I, had designed so that if he saw an unwelcome guest coming up one way, he could escape down the other. I would not understand the beauty of this until much later, when the mound was used in a way I had not foreseen: during a memorial service it separated those going up with flowers from those coming down empty handed.

Another precedent was the oldest pyramidal form in history, the stepped ziggurat of the Egyptians and its later incarnation, the Renaissance mound. And a final motive was the function of the whole thing, a focus toward which one could move, an axis for the various views and a place to survey the entire garden. Too many ideas behind the design? Not at all: never design with one reference or function in mind, never – that would be a waste of money and a one-liner. It would destroy the mystery and surprise of the garden; it would make consumption too quick and easy. Renaissance garden designers, following ideas developed in the seminal Villa Medici at Fiesole, noted the importance of slow perception. A landscape garden should not be a place through which one races on the way to somewhere else, but rather a place of imaginative exploration. 'Go slow' is a warning sign with multiple meanings: tease out the hidden signs, discover new ones. 'Festina lente' was even advised in the Renaissance garden – 'Make haste slowly' – a wonderful oxymoron that I was later to use in a garden design. Does it mean 'Make haste in order to prepare so that you can later go slow in the garden,' or 'Just hurry up and calm down'? A goal of symbolic design is to provoke viewers into discovering latent and even unintended meanings, a provocation that will only work if they assume there is something there to find.

In this way design and discovery amplify each other. As I was thinking about the spiral Snail, for instance, I happened to be reading about the pavement maze at Chartres Cathedral. This has the captivating idea behind it of presenting the pilgrimage route to Jerusalem as a type of counter-intuitive play: in order to get to the Holy City at the center of the labyrinth the pilgrim has to face away from his goal. Once there, in order to leave, he has to face back toward it. How suitably perverse for the pilgrimage of life. I decided to remint the idea. When climbing the DNA/Snail/Ziggurat you have to go down in order to go up; and when going down, by contrast, you are forced to go up. The ascent of life has descent built into it – not easy and counter to expectation. Go slow. The idea is to surprise, perplex, entice, confound, madden, amuse, as you discover these contradictions of life.

To relate the mound to the water we designed the tail of the snail in the shape of a French curve and brought it over the deep part of the pond; then Maggie had it lined with wood edging so that it would keep its shape. The tail allows one to descend almost into the middle of the pond, to be surrounded by water and to see different shapes from various angles. In fact, one of the virtues of a spiral mound is that it dramatizes discovery: unexpected vistas and shapes suddenly come into view. Another unsuspected bonus is that a mound looks very different in changing seasons: in the snow, for instance, its shapes are simplified and it can glow like a polished cylinder.

The mound building was so quick and satisfying that Maggie said, 'Let's excavate another bit and expand the pond and create a causeway.' From her researches in the East she knew that a thin causeway cutting across a lake is one of the most dramatic elements found in a Chinese garden. She imagined this as covered with a line of trees, something we never carried through, but she did make a move that had not occurred to me (though apparently Alistair had also thought of it). One day, struggling as usual to get the earth and water into a satisfactory relationship, I found Maggie atop the snail waving and shouting to the men digging a trench: 'More to the right, Hugh, more to the right.' In effect, she was pushing the emergence of the water a few feet out of sight, behind some trees, to obscure its source. Not seeing where the burn comes from gives it a mystery and leads the eye and imagination further back. The source was so mysterious that some people thought that, in order to make the ponds, we had actually diverted the River Nith – an economic not to say legal impossibility. But Maggie's concern for introducing a hidden source was absolutely right. It has given the ponds and landforms an enigmatic atmosphere that is quite uncanny, hard to figure out.

Another truth emerged on reflection, and when I went on to build other landforms in Edinburgh and elsewhere. The exact shape of the curves and their fine-tuning is key for creating what gives these mounds their strength – the sharp edges and defined shadows. It is the morning or evening sun, a raking light, that makes them come alive with subtle differences in tone. In certain lights bright carpets of green seem to hover above dark looming volumes. One has to sculpt continuous, gentle undulations – 'sweet curves' as the Scots say – not wobbly profiles. Such refinements are essential for the success of landforms, and their realization was due largely to the skill of the gardeners working at Portrack. Neil Brown, Doug McCormick, and Alistair created these sharp continuous curves by constantly surveying their work on the turf from different positions. Since large curves create strange perspectival distortions – and can look good from one position and bad from another – one has to review progress as one goes along, and this Alistair would do from many positions, near and far, above and below. While Hugh Hastings did the rough, large-scale earth moving according to constantly revised designs, the next stage of turfing and shaping needed just as much continuous modification. After working on six landforms, Alistair has sharpened his own skills and eye for the well-turned shadow.

THE SNAIL

Two Paths – a double helix – rise up the Snail Mound on one side and fall gently on the other so the ascent goes up and down. Various ideas were behind this: DNA, the double staircase at Chambord that allows two people to pass without meeting, a ziggurat, the contrary movement of the giant floor-paving maze at Chartres, Tatlin's monument to the Third International – multiple meanings that have to be decoded, slowly. Maggie had dug out an old marsh, creating a series of connected, curving ponds, and a leftover pile of earth. We moved the pile with diggers and bulldozers and we could see that this equipment naturally created blob-curves that were like the shape-grammar of rooms I had been designing. The scale, equipment, and material – sand and gravel – make a broad-brush approach inevitable: it is hard to get earth to within five feet of the place you want it and have it stay there and accept grass. The constant rains of western Scotland smear out all but the largest gesture, making design extremely primitive. Nevertheless, the basic ideas of twists, folds, and waves of energy are in the mounds.

Charles Jencks, The Garden of Cosmic Speculation

The Poison Garden at Alnwick

The Poison Garden is one of the gardens designed by Wirtz International and is one element of the original Garden master plan created in 1997. Due to the poisonous nature of this garden, some of the plants have been hard to source due to their rarity and in some cases licences are needed to possess them. Indeed, in November of 2004 The Alnwick Garden Trust was successful in obtaining Home Office approval to grow 'cannabis' and 'coca' (cocaine).

The new £400, 000 themed garden will have over 50 toxic, dangerous and scarce plants to help demonstrate how plants have poisoned and killed through the ages.

Many of the plants themselves are very beautiful even though they are deadly. The garden will have a dangerous feel to it – the beds are laid in the shape of flickering flames.

The most toxic plants will be incarcerated in caged beds allowing visitors to inspect these plants only through barred cloches. Many people are not aware of how dangerous some plants are, the ecological reasons for plant toxicity and the natural healing powers of some plant chemicals.

80% of the global population relies mainly on natural plant medicine

World Health Organisation

Some of the Plants in the Poison Garden

Vitex agnus castus – common name: Monks Pepper or The Chaste Tree. This is a shrub which has been in cultivation since 1570. It originates from the Mediterranean and from Central Asia. Its seeds used to be sprinkled on Monks' food to suppress the libido.

Salix alba 'Liempde' – common name: White Willow. The sap was used for pain relief and to lower fever. The wood is used for artificial limbs (arms and legs) and polo balls.

Laburnam anagyroides – all parts of the plant are poisonous: roots, bark, wood, leaves, flowers, pods and seeds. If digested symptoms are sleepiness and vomiting.

Arbutus unedo – common name: Killarney Strawberry Tree. Unedo means 'One I eat' and has strawberry-like fruit. In 1694 Pechey's 'Complete Herbal' states that it is an excellent antidote against the plague and poisons.

Aconitum ferox – common name: Monks Hood. Native to the Himalayas. Carried by Indians to poison wells to slow down invading armies. The plant is also used for poison arrows, spears, and darts.

Mandragora officinarum – common name: Mandrake. This plant if eaten excites voluptuous emotions. The fruit tempted Adam and Eve. 'Give me a drink – Mandragora, that I may sleep out this great gap of time' (Shakespeare – *Antony & Cleopatra*).

Citigate Dewe Rogerson Ltd

Plot Twists

As misnomers go, the Green Revolution, which began in the Sixties, is a clanger. It ushered in industrialised agriculture with 'improved' high-yield crops, more responsive to petrochemical fertilisers. And it led to monocultures, irrigation, today's billion-pound global agrichemical industry, poisoned rivers, drained aquifers, loss of biodiversity and, according to the WHO, 220, 000 deaths a year due to pesticide poisoning.

All of which suggests that it wasn't really all that green. To find revolutionary activity that is truly 'green', you have to look very hard, and sometimes by torchlight. That's when the guerrilla gardeners, anarchic horticulturalists committed to giving misused or disused land a purpose, come out to play, or rather plant. These are the stealth tillers committed to turning railway sidings, neglected council flowerbeds, and the corners of car parks into impromptu vegetable patches and flowerbeds.

Ordinarily, I would be suspicious of people prone to sneaking around at night armed with gardening implements. But I like the idea of these gardeners who leave floral tags (graffiti using poppies or pansies as opposed to spray cans) and indulge in acts of random tree planting. They may sound like people who just can't control themselves once they get a trowel in their hands, but there's a much deeper agenda to guerrilla gardening, which addresses issues of food security, disappearing green space and access to fresh local food.

Often this means stealth vegetable plots. I know of at least one person who has happily cultivated a flourishing vegetable plot on the sidings of a railway for the past nine years. For those who prefer legitimised horticultural activity, there's always an allotment. Growing your own is a supreme ethical activity.

Research shows that apart from acquiring gardening skills (something of a given), participants also greatly increase their cooking skills and improve their diets. And it's a way to avoid 'food miles', or contributing to climate-change emissions accrued by supermarket produce – a 2003 *Guardian* investigation found the cumulative distance travelled by 20 items in a basket of fresh food, including peas and lettuce, to be 100, 043 miles – or half the distance to the moon.

Lucy Siegle, *Observer*, Sunday 26 June 2005

Living Roofs

If you can see any roofs from your house or office, the chances are that they are fairly lifeless and unappealing – perhaps made of bitumen or asphalt. But roofs don't have to be dull and dead. With effort and imagination, we could change these sterile surfaces into green oases. These would not only provide a haven for wildlife but also transform the view from upstairs windows!

Living roofs are not just good for wildlife: they make a positive contribution to the environment in a number of other ways.

§ They help to cool the room below in hot weather. Conversely, in winter a living roof can provide insulation.

§ Living roofs act as sponges, retaining water before allowing it to evaporate into the atmosphere. In heavy rainfall, this can reduce the likelihood of local floods and this is one of the main reasons living roofs are now a legal requirement in Germany.

§ They protect a roof's waterproofing from the effects of ultra-violet light and the weather, especially frost. This means that the roof is less likely to leak.

Flat roofs lend themselves most readily to being 'greened'. It is also possible to green other types such as pitched, barrel and domed roofs. In these cases, however, restraints are needed to ensure that the growing medium does not slide off. Roofs with very steep slopes are clearly not suitable!

Garages

§ Garages with tiles or corrugated roofing may not be able to have a full living roof. The structure may need to be assessed. However, encouraging moss on the roof will provide habitats for invertebrates and feeding areas for birds such as blackbirds.

§ Garages with flat asphalt roofs should be able to support a lightweight living roof such as a sedum blanket or, if a concrete deck has been used, a deeper substrate-based, extensive living roof that can be used to grow wildflowers.

Sheds

§ As sheds are generally very lightweight structures, even putting a sedum blanket may be inadvisable without some structural strengthening. However, it is easy to encourage moss to grow on sheds.

§ It is often reasonably easy to provide added structural support to a commercial shed, so allowing a heavier, wildflower-rich living roof to be installed.

EXTENSIONS, OUTHOUSES AND BALCONIES

§ It should be possible to install living roofs on small extensions, outhouses and balconies. Again, whether a sedum mat system or a heavier substrate-based system is used will depend on the structure below.

MOSSES AND LICHENS

The lightest living roofs – and the simplest to create – are those supporting mosses and lichens.

Mosses are a group of small green plants that do not flower or fruit but produce spores. They require such small amounts of nutrients that many species are able to live in inhospitable places, clinging to walls and stone and tiles waiting for rain.

The 'moss forest' provides cover for thousands of microscopic animals, such as water bears (*Tardigrades*), and a habitat for other invertebrates which, in turn, are food for birds. Moss on buildings is often – and unfairly – associated with neglect, but it can bring many of the benefits of a living roof, such as shielding the roof from ultra-violet light, absorbing water and cooling.

Lichens are composite, symbiotic organisms made up of fungi (which dominate) and algae or cyanobacteria. Food manufactured by the vegetative element of the organism through photosynthesis is enjoyed by the host fungus. As a result, lichens are able to survive extremes of temperature and drought and can colonise surfaces too sterile for most other organisms (including metal, glass and plastic).

Look closely and you will see that these anciently-evolved plants adorn even the most urban environment. Walls often support the grey cushions of the moss *Grimmia pulvinata* or the conspicuous yellow seta (stalk-like structures) of wall screw-moss *Tortula muralis*. Where there is enough moisture, carpet-forming mosses like rough-stalked feather-moss *Brachythecium rutabulum* may be found. That yellow crust you can see on many tile roofs is *Xanthoria* lichen.

Although it is possible to encourage or cultivate lichens and mosses, patience is required because these are relatively slow-growing organisms. Some lichens, for example, may grow less than a millimetre a year!

There is a centuries-old tradition of growing moss gardens in Japan. Self-established moss carpets can be encouraged on a layer of sandy soil 20mm deep or less and, if kept damp, moss communities will establish themselves here through airborne spores. If you can find moss which has been stripped from a building (by those who do not appreciate it!) you can replant these sods on your own roof. Even if planted sods fail, they will encourage the colonisation of other, better-suited mosses.

It is worth noting that various species of moss will flourish on the sedum-type living roofs discussed below.

Sedum Roofs

Sedums are the most widely-used plants for living roofs as they have many of the advantages in terms of hardiness and drought tolerance. Being succulents, they actively store water in their tissues and have a number of ways of reducing their need for water in dry weather.

Under conditions of severe stress many sedums change colour from green through to red, purple and brown. Although they are very tough, you must remember that sedums growing on very thin substrates, or on simple moisture mats, may die back and become patchy during periods of extreme dryness.

Commonly-used species on living roofs include white stonecrop *Sedum album*, *S. hispanicum* and *S. reflexum*. These species are not native, however, so for preference use biting stonecrop *Sedum acre*, a relatively common native of rock outcrops and old walls. All sedums are evergreen and most low-growing species flower for a relatively short period in midsummer. White stonecrop and biting stonecrop have some of the most spectacular flowering displays and are very attractive to bees, butterflies and other insects.

Wildflower Roofs

The conditions on a living roof (free-draining substrates with low fertility) are ideal for the creation of highly diverse and species-rich grassland plant communities. More often than not, these dry grassland 'roof meadows' are more successful than those that people try to grow in their gardens.

Rooftop meadows have a number of advantages:

§ A diversity of flowering plant species will result in a longer overall flowering season, thereby extending the period during which the roof flora acts as a nectar source for insects. Late-flowering species are particularly useful in this respect.

§ If the meadow is left uncut throughout the autumn and winter, the standing seed-heads will provide food sources for seed-eating birds, and the dried-out stems and stalks will provide over-wintering shelter for a range of invertebrates.

§ Living roofs can support local or regional plant communities and vegetation types that might be endangered in the wild.

MAINTENANCE

Most people want a living roof that is low on maintenance. As with all other types of garden and landscape, the amount of work needed will depend on the intended outcome! If a perfect, manicured green space is what's required then the area will need a lot of attention. However, extensive living roofs need relatively little maintenance. Semi-extensive areas will need more attention to keep them looking good and to maintain their diversity of species.

SEDUM ROOFS

If a pristine green carpet of sedums is the goal, then this will mean a fair amount of weeding to control invading plants. This may have to be done two or three times a year. However, a less intensive regime will result in the development of a more mixed vegetation, as grasses and other plants invade. If a sedum living roof is left largely unmanaged it is likely to gradually develop into a more mixed community, with a greater proportion of grasses in the vegetation. However, some maintenance – even if you only intervene once a year – should be done to remove invading woody plants (such as birch tree seedlings) that have the potential to disrupt, or even puncture, the waterproof lining of the roof.

WILDFLOWER ROOFS

For extensive living roof types it should be possible to develop a wildflower meadow with little or no intervention. Low fertility substrates will give rise to short vegetation that will not need cutting back each year. Where growth is more productive or tall – as on a semi-extensive living roof – it will be necessary to cut back and remove growth every year. This will prevent the died-back remains of the previous season's growth, accumulating on the surface of the roof. Unlike conventional meadows, which are normally cut in summer, it's recommended that roof meadows are cut back in late winter. Leaving the dried and dead vegetation in place not only provides over-winter shelter for invertebrates and food for seed-eating birds, but also a degree of protection to the plants beneath it during severe weather. It can also look attractive.

Bugs and Living Roofs

Common, widespread and highly mobile invertebrates will easily colonise living roofs. Examples found so far include many ladybird species as well as various shieldbugs, hoverflies, bees and grasshoppers. But since these species occur anyway in our well-tended and nutrient-rich gardens, living roofs offer them little extra. However, the owner of a good, dry grassland roof can hope to attract some of the more unusual and scarce insects that are linked with similar habitats in the wild.

A good living roof will also attract ground-dwelling insects such as predatory ground beetles and root- or seed-eating invertebrates. These particularly favour loose, dry soil, into which they can burrow among the plant roots, or areas under rocks and stones. Such soil also suits a wide range of soil-nesting solitary bees and wasps. Unusual visitors you might see include the bombardier beetle *Brachinus crepitans*, the Adonis ladybird *Hippodamia variegata*, mining bees and sand wasps, such as the sand-tailed digger wasp *Cerceris arenaria* and the ornate-tailed digger wasp *C. rybyensis*.

A living roof is a great place to encourage those butterfly and moth species not normally found in rich, lush gardens. Being both low in nutrients and well-drained, such roofs allow food plants for a number of important butterfly and moth species to flourish. Horseshoe vetch, kidney vetch and bird's-foot-trefoil, for example – all with beautiful yellow flowers – are important food plants for butterflies such as the dingy skipper and the common blue.

Birds

Even a small living roof can provide a good feeding area for common species such as blackbird, song thrush, robin and wren. Dry grassland roofs, with plenty of good seed plants will attract seed-eating birds such as goldfinch, linnet, greenfinch and chaffinch. If the roof is in Birmingham or London it may even attract a black redstart, a bird rare in Britain but one well known for using living roofs on the Continent.

English Nature, *Living Roofs*

Avian Intention

The male bower bird [is] an accomplished avian architect that has long fascinated scientists with its remarkably complex courting behaviour. Instead of using just showy plumes or a romantic melody to attract a mate, the pigeon-sized bower bird constructs an elaborate structure – a bower – on the forest floor from twigs, leaves, and moss. It then decorates the bower with colourful baubles, from feathers and pebbles to berries and shells.

The bowers aren't nests for raising kids; they are bachelor pads designed to attract and seduce one or more mates. When a female arrives to inspect the bower, the male struts and sings. He hopes to convince her to enter the bower, where mating takes place. The female then flies off to build a nest close by, leaving the male to try and convince another female to join in a romantic tryst. Bower birds 'exhibit pretty extreme display behaviours,' says Gerald Borgia, a University of Maryland, College Park, biologist who has been studying the birds for nearly two decades. As a result, he says, they are of special interest to scientists seeking to understand how such complex traits evolve and function. His research team, for instance, is using trip-wired surveillance video cameras and robotic birds to probe the hidden world of the bower bird. Overall, there are 17 kinds of bower birds in Australia and on the neighbouring island of New Guinea. Some are known as catbirds, while others are called 'gardeners' or 'stagemakers'.

Each builds its own shape of bower and prefers a different decorating scheme. A few, for instance, surround their bowers with carefully planted lawns of moss. Others have been known to steal shiny coins, spoons, bits of aluminium foil – even a glass eye – in an effort to create the perfect romantic mood. Some, like the iridescent blue Satin bower bird, even 'paint' the walls of their structures with chewed berries or charcoal.

For the male Satin, which builds a U-shaped bower from parallel walls of twigs, the favoured colour is blue. To decorate its 'avenue', as scientists call it, he collects blue feathers, berries, shells, and flowers. While some of these decorations are found in the forest, others are stolen from the bowers of other males; young males, in particular, are prone to this petty thievery. However obtained, the precious knickknacks are then scattered around the bower. The male then waits, passing time by constantly fine-tuning his structure and rearranging the decorations.

For many males, the effort will be mostly futile. A younger male, for instance, may be able to seduce only a single one of his dozens of visitors – or none at all. Indeed, many males get not even a single glance: in a recent study, 75 percent of female birds visited only one bower before mating. In contrast, older males often have potential mates constantly stopping by for a peek. These more experienced suitors may mate with dozens of different females in a single breeding season.

'An Odd Bird', *Nature, www.pbs.org/wnet/nature/bowerbird*

Bees

It is a garden of dead bees. And it's a mystery why. They line the ground, like ideas, some destroyed, some still intact. Then, one day it isn't a mystery any more. You're downstairs making tea. It's early, sunny again, warm, the end of summer. You haven't been outside yet today. You haven't looked in the bathroom mirror and thought about him or what's been lost from you and where it can be. From the window in the kitchen you can see outside and there in the corner of the shrubbery next to the wooden bench is a disruption of bright colour. You look properly, give it your attention. You think you must be mistaken at first. But you're not. It's a fox. It's true red, rust red, blaze red. It's big, though appears juvenile, with over-sized ears; and it seems, more than anything else, oddly placed here, in the city, in this tiny plot. It's sitting upright, arch-jawed, snouty, and is scanning the scenery with eerie yellow eyes. You don't know if it can see you moving in the kitchen. You keep still and silent in case noise travels through the window glazing and out into the garden, disturbing the creature, though there is always the perpetual sound of the city to do that, the screech of trains, the acceleration of cars and the ordinary commotion of humans. Your housemate told you there were foxes in London, lots of them, urban scavengers responsible for tearing bin liners and scenting up lintels, but you didn't believe it, not really, not until now. You'll tell her she was right, when she gets home. You'll tell her everything. You feel oddly thrilled by this sighting, enlivened. The foxes you've seen up north seemed small, pale orange and discreet, sloping along roadsides at night, or cowering from the hounds, diminutive on the moors. This one is unapologetic, bold, and striking, as if it owns this city allotment. It's captivating, fiery, like it's been stoked up from the surroundings to a high temperature. You watch it in your garden, a keen covetous thing, its fur a furnace amid the undergrowth. And as you watch it, your heart starts up in earnest, raw, heated, a strong beat pushing the blood around. The fox tracks the resinous flight of an insect in the air nearby, eyes sparking like lit fuses. It opens its jaws then snaps them shut, un-stung and accurate, and shakes its head in a red fury.

Sarah Hall, *Bees*

COPYRIGHT ACKNOWLEDGEMENTS

The editor and publisher are grateful for permission to include the following
copyright material in this volume.

ANNA AKHMATOVA: 'I Will Leave Your White House' from *The Complete Poems of
Anna Akhmatova*, translated by Judith Hemschemeyer (Canongate Books, 1990).
Reprinted by permission of the publisher. JOHN ALCOCK: from *In A Desert Garden*
(W. W. Norton & Company, 1997), © 1997 by John Alcock. Reprinted by permission
of the publisher. THE ALNWICK GARDEN: *The Poison Garden at The Alnwick
Garden* from *Media Fact File* (2005). Reprinted by permission of Citigate Dewe
Rogerson on behalf of The Alnwick Garden Trust. HANS CHRISTIAN ANDERSEN:
The Elf of the Rose from *Forty Two Stories*, translated by M. R. James (Faber &
Faber, 1971). Reprinted by permission of the publisher. E. A. BOWLES: from *My
Garden in Summer* (T. C. & E. C. Jack, London 1914; reprinted Timber Press Inc,
Oregon 1998), copyright Brigadier A. H. Parker Bowles OBE. JOHN BROOKES: from
Improve Your Lot (William Heinemann, 1977), copyright © 1977 by John Brookes.
Reprinted by permission of Felicity Bryan and the author. FRANCESCO COLONNA:
from *Hypnerotomachia Poliphili: The Strife of Love in a Dream*, translated by
Joscelyn Godwin, © 1999 Joscelyn Godwin. Reprinted by kind permission of Thames
& Hudson Ltd., London. COLUMELLA: from *On Agriculture: Volume III, LCL 408*,
translated by E. S. Forster and Edward H. Heffner, Cambridge, Mass.: Harvard
University Press, copyright © 1955 by the President and Fellows of Harvard College.
The Loeb Classical Library ® is a registered trademark of the President and Fellows
of Harvard College. Reprinted by permission of the publishers and the Trustees of
the Loeb Classical Library. SYLVIA CROWE: from *Garden Design* (Garden Art Press,
2003). Reprinted by permission of Packard Publishing. E. E. CUMMINGS: 'this is the
garden:colours come and go' from *Complete Poems 1904–1962*, edited by George J.
Firmage, copyright © 1991 by the Trustees for the E. E. Cummings Trust and
George James Firmage. Reprinted by permission of W. W. Norton & Company.

BIBLIOGRAPHY

Addison, Joseph, *Spectator*, No.383, Tuesday 20 May 1712, ed. Henry Morley; pub. Routledge, London, 1896

Akhmatova, Anna, *Love Poems*, trans. Judith Hemschemeyer, Everyman's Library, London, 1993

Alcock, John, *In a Desert Garden, Love and Death Among the Insects*, W.W. Norton, New York, 1997

Andersen, Hans Christian, *The Elf of the Rose* (1839) in *Forty Two Stories*, trans. M. R. James, Faber and Faber, London, 1953

Anon. 14th century AD, *Secular Lyrics of the XIVth and XVth Centuries*, ed. Rossell Hope Robbins, Oxford University Press, 1952, ed. Philip Robinson, 2006

Anon. *The Squire of Low Degree*, *c*.1450, from *Middle English Verse Romances*, ed. Donald B. Sands, pub. Holt, Rinehart and Winston, New York, 1966

Austen, Jane, *Mansfield Park* (1814), Penguin Books, London, 1979

Austin, Alfred, *The Garden That I Love*, Macmillan, London, 1907

Bacon, Francis, 'Of Gardens' (1625), *The Essays*, Penguin Books, London, 1986; *www.authorama.com*

Baker, J. A., *The Peregrine*, Penguin Books, London, 1967

Basho, Matsuo, *Haiku* (*c*.1670), trans. Lucien Stryk, Penguin Classics 60s S, 1995

Blake, William, from *Songs of Experience*, 1794, in *Romanticism: An Anthology*, ed. Duncan Wu, Blackwell Publishing, Oxford, 1994

Blomfield, Reginald, *The Formal Garden in England* (1892), Waterstone & Co. Ltd, London, 1985

Bowles, E. A., *My Garden in Summer* (1914), Timber Press, Inc., Portland, Oregon, 1998

Boys, Sir Charles Vernon, *Weeds, Weeds, Weeds*, Wightman and Co., London, 1937

Brontë, Charlotte, *Jane Eyre* (1847), Penguin Books, London, 1996

Brookes, John, *Improve Your Lot*, William Heinemann, London, 1977

Browne, Sir Thomas, *The Garden of Cyrus* (1658), *Religio Medici, Hydriotaphia and*

The Garden of Cyrus, ed. R. H. A. Robbins, Oxford University Press, 1972

Browning, Robert, 'Adam, Lilith, and Eve' (1883) in *Robert Browning: The Poems Vol.2*, ed. John Pettigrew and Thomas J. Collins, Penguin Books, London, 1981

Burke, Edmund, *A Philosophical Enquiry into the Origin of Our Ideas of the Sublime and Beautiful*, Section XIV, 1756 (2nd edition. 1798)

Burnett, Frances Hodgson, *The Secret Garden* (1911), Puffin Books, London, 1994

Campion, Thomas, from *The Albatross Book of Living Verse*, Collins, London, 1950

Čapek, Karel, *The Gardener's Year* (1929) trans. Geoffrey Newsome, The Garden Book Club, 14th impression, 1951; Continuum International Publishing Group, London and New York, 2005

Carroll, Lewis, *Through the Looking-Glass* (1871), Collins, London, 1944

Cather, Willa, *My Ántonia* (1918), Virago Press, London, 1993

Cato, Marcus Porcius, 234–149 BC, *On Agriculture*, William Heinemann, London. 1934

Chambers, Sir William, *A Dissertation on Oriental Gardening*, 1772

Chaucer, Geoffrey, *The Romance of the Rose* (*c.*1360), in *The Riverside Chaucer*, Oxford University Press, 1988

Folk Songs of Chhattisgarh, Verrier Elwin, Oxford University Press, 1946 ('Three Songs about the Bee')

Citigate Dewe Rogerson Ltd, Media Fact File: 'The Alnwick Garden', London, 2005

Cobbett, William, *The English Gardener* (1829) Oxford University Press, 1980

Colonna, Francesco, Hypnerotomachia Poliphili (*c.*1467), trans. Joscelyn Godwin, Thames & Hudson, London, 1999

Columella, Lucius Junius Moderatus, *De Re Rustica*, (*c.*AD 65), trans. E. S. Forster, Edward H. Heffner, William Heinemann, London, 1955

Cortés, Hernán, *Letters from Mexico*, Second Letter 1520,.trans. Anthony Pagden, Yale University Press, New Haven, Conn., 2001

Cowley, Abraham, Preface to *The Garden* (1669), ed. A. F. Sieveking, Chatto & Windus, London, 1908

Cran, Marion, *Garden Talks*, Methuen & Co. Ltd, London, 1925

Crowe, Sylvia, *Garden Design* (1958), Garden Art Press, 2003

Cummings, E. E. from *Tulips and Chimneys* (1923), Faber and Faber, London

D'Argenville, Antoine-Joseph Dezallier, *The Theory and Practice of Gardening* (1709; illustrated by Alexandre-Jean-Baptiste Le Blond), trans. John James, 1712

de la Vega, Garcilaso (1530) from John Carey (ed.) *The Faber Book of Reportage*, Faber and Faber, London, 1989

Díaz del Castillo, Bernal, *The Conquest of New Spain* (1559), trans. J. M. Cohen, Penguin Books, London, 1969

Diodorus of Sicily, Bk. II, ch.9 (*c.*30 BC), trans. C. H. Oldfather, William Heinemann, London, 1933

Dodsley, R. *A Description of the Leasowes*, 1784, Bell's second edition, Vol. I, Edinburgh, 1784

Don, George, *A General History of the Dichlamydeous Plants*, Vol. I, Longman and Co., London, 1831

Donne, John, 'Twicknam Garden' (1608), *Songs and Sonnets*, 1635

Du Maurier, Daphne, *Rebecca* (1938) Victor Gollancz (Orion Publishing), London, 1992

Eliot, T. S., 'Ash Wednesday' (1930) in *Collected Poems 1909-1962*, Faber and Faber, London, 1974

Emerson, Ralph Waldo, *The Conduct of Life*: 'Wealth', 1860

English Nature, *Living Roofs*, 2006

Evelyn, John, Letter, from *Sir William Temple upon the Gardens of Epicurus, With Other XVIIth Century Garden Essays*, ed. A. F. Sieveking, Chatto and Windus, London, 1908

Farrer, Reginald, *The Rock Garden*, T. Nelson & Sons Ltd, London, 1912

Fish, Margery, *We Made A Garden*, W. H. and L. Collingridge Ltd, London, 1956

Fitzgerald, F. Scott, *Tender is the Night* (1934), Penguin Books, London, 1997

Flaubert, Gustave, *Madame Bovary* (1857), Penguin Books, London, 1992

Folk songs, *see Garden of Bright Waters, The*

Fortunatus, Venantius, (*c*.AD 540–600) trans. Helen Waddell (1889–1965), in *Love Poems*, ed. Peter Washington, Everyman's Library, London, 1992

Garden of Bright Waters, The: One Hundred and Twenty Asiatic Love Poems, ed. and trans. Edward Powys Mathers, Basil Blackwell, Oxford, 1920: Afghan songs (Ballade of Nurshali, Ghazal of Mira), Song of Annam, Song of Daghestan, Ebn Maatuk

Genesis 2:7–3:10, Revised Standard Version

Gesta Romanorum (anon. *c*.1250), in *Mediæval Tales*, Routledge, London, 1884

Gilpin, William, *Observations, Relative Chiefly to Picturesque Beauty, Made in the Year 1772, On Several Parts of England; Particularly the Mountains, and Lakes of Cumberland and Westmoreland*, 3rd edition, London, 1792

Gilpin, William S., *Practical Hints upon Landscape Gardening*, T. Cadell, London, 1832

Grigson, Geoffrey, *Gardenage* or *The Plants of Ninhursaga*, Routledge and Kegan Paul, London, 1952

Hall, Sarah, *Bees*, Maia Press, London, 2006

Hardy, Thomas, *Jude the Obscure* (1895), Macmillan, London, 1971

Herbert, George, *The Flower* (1633), in *The Metaphysical Poets*, ed. Helen Gardner, Penguin Books, London, 1973

Hibberd, Shirley, *The Amateur's Kitchen Garden, Frame-Ground and Forcing Pit: A handy guide to the formation and management of the kitchen garden and the cultivation of useful vegetables and fruits*, Collingridge, London, 1893

Hicks, David, *My Kind of Garden*, Garden Art Press, Woodbridge, 1999, 2004

Hill, Thomas, *The Gardener's Labyrinth* (1577), Oxford University Press, 1987

Hobhouse, Penelope, *Natural Planting*, Pavilion Books, London, 1997

Hole, S. Reynolds, *Our Gardens*, J. M. Dent & Co., London, 1899

Homer, *Odyssey*, 8th century BC, trans. Walter Shewring, Oxford University Press, 1980

Howard, Ebenezer, *Garden Cities of To-Morrow* (3rd edition of *To-morrow: a Peaceful Path to Real Reform*), Swan Sonnenschein & Co. Ltd, 1902

Hughes, Spike, *The Art of Coarse Gardening or The Care and Feeding of Slugs*, Hutchinson, London, 1968

Hughes, Ted, 'Thrushes' (*c.*1960), from *Selected Poems 1957-1981*, Faber and Faber, London, 1982

Hyams, Edward, *The Speaking Garden*, Longmans, Green and Co., London, 1957

Isaiah, The Book of Isaiah 1:24-1:31, Revised Standard Version

Jefferson, Thomas, *Thomas Jefferson's Garden Book 1766-1824*, The American Philosophical Society, Philadelphia, 1944

Jekyll, Gertrude, *Home and Garden*, Longmans, Green, and Co., London, 1900

Jellicoe, G. A., *Studies in Landscape Design*, Oxford University Press, 1960

Jencks, Charles, *The Garden of Cosmic Speculation*, Frances Lincoln Publishers Ltd, London, 2003

John, Humphrey, *The Skeptical Gardener*, Harrap, London, 1940

Justice, Donald, from *The Summer Anniversaries*, Wesleyan University Press, Middleton, Conn., 1960

Kavanagh, Patrick (*c.*1939) in *The Faber Book of Contemporary Irish Poetry*, Faber and Faber, London, 1986

Keats, John, 'Ode on Melancholy' (*c.* May 1819) in *Romanticism: An Anthology*, ed. Duncan Wu, Blackwell Publishing, Oxford, 1994

Keen, Mary, *Colour Your Garden*, Conran Octopus Ltd., London, 1991

Kincaid, Jamaica, *My Garden (Book)*, Farrar, Straus & Giroux, New York, 1999

King, Henry, 'A Contemplation upon Flowers' (1657), in *The Metaphysical Poets*, ed. Helen Gardner, Penguin Books, London, 1973

Kingdon Ward, Frank, *The Romance of Gardening*, Jonathan Cape Ltd, London, 1935

Kipling, Rudyard, 'Gethsemane' (*c.*1918), in *A Choice of Kipling's Verse* ed. T. S. Eliot, Faber and Faber, London, 1950

Knight, Richard Payne, *An Analytical Inquiry into the Principles of Taste*, 2nd edition, T. Payne and J. White, London, 1805

Koran, (AD 610) trans. N. J. Dawood, Penguin Books, London, 2003

Laertius, Diogenes, *Lives of Eminent Philosophers*, (*c.*3rd century AD), trans. R. D. Hicks

Lampedusa, Giuseppe Tomasi di, *The Leopard* (1958), Harvill, London, 1996 William Heinemann, London, 1925

Lane Fox, Robin, *Variations on a Garden*, Macmillan, London, 1974

Langley, Batty, *New Principles of Gardening*, A. Bettesworth and J. Batley, London, 1728

Larkin, Philip, 'The Mower', first pub. in *Humberside*, Autumn 1979

Lawrence, D. H., *Women in Love* (1916), Wordsworth Editions, Ware, Herts, 1992

Lawson, William, *A New Orchard and Garden* (1618), facsimile edition, The Cresset Press, London, 1927

Le Corbusier, *Towards a New Architecture*, trans. Frederick Etchells, John Rodker (Ovid Press), London, 1927

Li Ch'ing-chao (Li Qingzhao), *Complete Poems*, trans. Kenneth Rexroth, New Directions, New York, 1979

Liger, Louis, *The Retir'd Gardener* (1706), trans. George London and Henry Wise, 2nd edition, J. Tonson, 1717

Li Ho (Li He), *The Poems of Li Ho*, trans. J. D. Frodsham, Oxford University Press, 1970

Li Po (Li Bai, 701–762), trans. Ezra Pound, in *Love Poems*, Everyman's Library, London, 1993

Lloyd, Christopher, *The Well-Tempered Garden*, Collins, London, 1970

– *The Well-Chosen Garden*, Elm Tree Books, London, 1984

Loudon, J. C., *An Encyclopaedia of Gardening*, Longman, Hurst, Rees, Orme, and Brown, London, 1822

Louis XIV, King of France (attrib.), *Manière de montrer les jardins de Versailles* (*c*.1694), trans. Christopher Thacker, *Garden History*, vol.1 (Sep. 1972), from www.jstor.org

Lutyens, Edwin, *The Letters of Edwin Lutyens to his Wife, Lady Emily*, ed. Clayre Percy and Jane Ridley, Collins, London, 1985

Maatuk, Ebn, 17th century, from *The Garden of Bright Waters*, Basil Blackwell, Oxford, 1920

Marvell, Andrew, 'The Garden' (1649?) in *The Metaphysical Poets*, ed. Helen Gardner, Penguin Books, London, 1973

Mason, George, *An Essay on Design in Gardening*, London, 1768

Maupassant de, Guy, 'The Matter with André' (*c*.1886), *Selected Short Stories*, trans. Roger Colet, Penguin Books, London, 1971

Middleton, C. H., *Digging for Victory*, Allen & Unwin, London, 1942

Milne, A. A., *When We Were Very Young* (1924), Methuen & Co Ltd, London, 1969

Milton, John, *Paradise Lost*, Bk. 4 (1667), ed. Alastair Fowler, Longman, London, 1971

More, Thomas, *Utopia* (1516), ed. P. Turner, Penguin Books, London, 1969

Morro, Gil ©, 1999

Nature, 'An Odd Bird', *www.pbs.org/wnet/nature/bowerbird*, 2006

Neckam, Alexander, *De Naturis Rerum* (*c*.1190), Bk.2 Ch.66, trans. J. F. N. Robinson & P. G. Robinson (ed.) 2006

Nicolson, Harold, *Diaries 1930–1964*, ed. Stanley Olson, Penguin Books, London, 1984

Page, Russell, *The Education of a Gardener*, Collins, London, 1962

Parker, Eric, *The Gardener's Week-End Book*, with Eleanour Sinclair Rohde, Seeley
    Service & Co. Ltd, London, 1939, 1947

Parkinson, John, *Paradisi In Sole*, Humfrey Lownes and Robert Young, London,
    1629

Pearl (*c.* 1370), ed. Clifford Peterson; trans. Casey Finch, University of California
    Press, Berkeley, Calif., 1993

Pepys, Samuel, *Diary* (1666), Collins, London, 1970

Phillpotts, Eden, *My Garden*,. Offices of *Country Life*, London, 1906

Plath, Sylvia, *Ariel*, Faber and Faber Ltd, London, 1965

Pliny, *Natural History*, Bk XIX, ch.19 & 20, trans. John Bostock and H. T. Riley,
    Henry G. Bohn, London, 1893, 1936.

Po Chü-I (Bai Juyi, 772–846) from *170 Chinese Poems*, trans. Arthur Waley,
    Constable & Co, London, 1962

Polo, Marco (1254-1324), *Travels in the Land of Kubilai Khan*, trans. Ronald Latham,
    Penguin Books, London, 1958

Pope, Alexander, 'On Gardens' (1713), from *Alexander Pope* ed. Pat Rogers, Oxford
    University Press, *1993*

Price, Sir Uvedale, *An Essay on the Picturesque* (1794), from 2nd edition, 1796

Reid, John, *The Scots Gard'ner, together with The Gard'ners Kalender* (1683), T. N.
    Foulis, 1907

Repton, Humphry, *Observations on the Theory and Practice of Landscape
    Gardening*, J. Taylor, London, 1803

Reynolds, Sir Joshua, *Discourses Delivered to the Students of the Royal Academy*
    (1778), Seeley & Co. Ltd, London, 1905

Rilke, Rainer Maria, 'Garden-Night' and 'Counterweight' (1924), from *Poems 1906-
    26*, trans. J. B. Leishman, The Hogarth Press, London, 1976

Rivers, Thomas, *The Orchard House* (1851), 3rd edition, Longman, Brown, Green,
    and Longmans, 1854

Robertson, Robin, *A Painted Field*, Picador, London, 1997

Robinson, William, *The Wild Garden*, John Murray, London, 1870

Rohde, Eleanour Sinclair, *The Gardener's Week-End Book*, with Eric Parker, Seeley
    Service, London, 1939, 1947

Rossetti, Christina, 'A Daughter of Eve' (1865), from *Goblin Market, The Prince's
    Progress, and Other Poems*, Macmillan, London, 1875

Rumi, Jalal ad-Din Muhammad Din ar-; (1207–1273) from *The Essential Rumi:
    Selected Poems* trans. Coleman Banks, John Moyne and A. J. Arberry, Penguin
    Books, London, 2004

Sackville-West, Vita, *In Your Garden* (1950), Frances Lincoln Publishers, London,
    2004

Sa'di (or Saadi, Muslih-ud-Din Mushrif-ibn-Abdullah (1184–1283/1291?), *The Book
    of Love* or *Bôstân* (*c.*1280), trans. Sir Edward Arnold, Kegan Paul, Trench,
    Trübner, & Co. Ltd, London, 1893

Scammell, William, 'The Tree', from *All Set to Fall off the Edge of the World*, Flambard Press, Hexham, Northumberland, 1998

Shakespeare, William, *The Tragedy of King Richard the Second* (1597), III, iv, in *The Complete Works*, Oxford University Press

Sheeler, Jessie, *Little Sparta, The Garden of Ian Hamilton Finlay*, Frances Lincoln Publishers, London, 2003

Shelley, Percy Bysshe, 'The Sensitive Plant' (1820), in *The Complete Poetical Works*, E. Moxon, son & Co., London, 1878

Shikibu, Izumi, 'Come Quickly' (*c.*1000), in *Love Poems*, Everyman's Library, London, 1993

Sei Shonagon, The Pillow Book of (*c.*994) trans. Ivan Morris, Penguin Books, London, 1971

Siegle, Lucy, Plot Twists, *Observer*, Sunday 26 June 2005, *www.guardian.co.uk*

Sitwell, Sir George, *On the Making of Gardens* (1909), 3rd edition. Duckworth, London, 1951

Smith, Ken, from *The Heart, the Border,* Bloodaxe Books, London, 1990

Solomon, *The Song of Solomon* 4:12–5:2, Revised Standard Version

Spenser, Edmund, 'Garden of Adonis', *The Faerie Queene, Book 3, canto VI,* (*c.*1590), T. C. & E. C. Jack, 1907

Stevenson, Robert Louis, *A Child's Garden of Verses*, Longmans, Green, and Co., London, 1895

Stewart, King James I of Scotland, *The Kingis Quair* (*c.*1420), Oxford University Press, 1971

Strauss, Richard, 'September', *Four Last Songs* (*c.*1948), from EMI Classics CD

Switzer, Stephen, *Ichnographica Rustica*, 1718

Tamura, Tsuyoshi, *Art of the Landscape Garden in Japan*, Kokusai Bunka Shinkokai, Tokyo, 1935

Temple, Sir William, *Upon the Gardens of Epicurus* (1685), Pallas Athene Publishers, London, 2004

Tennyson, Alfred, Lord, from *Poems, Chiefly Lyrical* (1830), in *Romanticism: An Anthology*, ed. Duncan Wu, Blackwell Publishing, Oxford, 1994

Thomas, Dylan, 'Incarnate Devil' (1935), in *Poems* (Everyman Poetry), Everyman Ltd, 1997

Thomas, Edward, 'Digging' (1915) from *Poems* ed. William Cooke (Everyman Poetry), Phoenix Press (Orion), London, 1997

Thomas, Graham Stuart, *Colour in the Winter Garden* (1957, revised 1967), Phoenix Press (Orion), London, 1998

Thomas, R. S., *The Bread of Truth*, Hart-Davis, London, 1963

Varro, Marcus Terentius, *On Agriculture* (36 BC), trans, William Davis Hooper and Harrison Boyd Ash, William Heinemann (Loeb classical library) London, 1934

Verey, Rosemary, *The English Country Garden*, BBC Books, London, 1996

Vilmorin-Andrieux, MM., *The Vegetable Garden* (1885), ed. William Robinson,

John Murray, London, 1920

Virgil (Publius Vergilius Maro, 70–19 BC) *Georgics* Book 4, *The Eclogues The Georgics*, trans. C. Day-Lewis, Oxford University Press, 1999

Walpole, Horace, *On Modern Gardening* (1770), Pallas Athene Publishers, London, 2004

Watts, Isaac, 'The Church the Garden of Christ', Hymn 74, *Hymns and Spiritual Songs*, 1707; www.poemhunter.com

White, Gilbert, *The Natural History & Antiquities of Selborne*, 1788, from Macmillan and Co., London, 1911

Whitman, Walt, from 'Autumn Rivulets' (*c*.1870), collected in *Complete Poems and Prose*, Ferguson Bros., Philadelphia, 1888

Wordsworth, William 1807, from *The Poems of William Wordsworth*, ed. Nowell Charles Smith, Methuen and Co., London, 1908

Worlidge, J., *The Mystery of Husbandry Discovered*, London ('Printed for Tho. Dring, at the Harrow at the corner of Chancery-lane in Fleetstreet, 1687'), 1697

Yeats, W. B., 'The Rose Tree' (1921), from *Collected Poems of W. B. Yeats*, Macmillan, London and New York, 1989

Yoch, Florence, 'The Little Garden of Gaiety' from *Garden and Home Builder 47* (May 1928), in James J. Yoch, *Landscaping the American Dream: The Gardens and Film Sets of Florence Yoch: 1890-1972*, Sagapress, New York, 1989

Young, Arthur, *Arthur Young's Travels in France* (1790), from J. M. Thompson, *English Witnesses of the French Revolution* (1938) in John Carey (ed.) *The Faber Book of Reportage*, Faber and Faber, London, 1989

INDEX